# I CHING

# (BOOK OF CHANGES)

# Translated by JAMES LEGGE

I Ching, or, Book of Changes
By Anonymous
Translated with Annotations by James Legge

Print ISBN 13: 978-1-4209-7467-6
eBook ISBN 13: 978-1-4209-7634-2

Cover Image: a detail of "A Way of Telling the Future", engraved by Mlle. Formentin, 1824-27 (litho), after Henri Grevedon (1776-1860) / Private Collection / The Stapleton Collection / Bridgeman Images.

Please visit *www.digireads.com*

# CONTENTS

## SECTION II.

# PLATE I.

THE HEXAGRAMS, in the order in which they appear in the Yî, and were arranged by king Wăn.

| 8 | 7 | 6 | 5 | 4 | 3 | 2 | 1 |
|---|---|---|---|---|---|---|---|
| pî | sze | sung | hsü | măng | kun | khwăn | khien |

| 16 | 15 | 14 | 13 | 12 | 11 | 10 | 9 |
|---|---|---|---|---|---|---|---|
| yü | khien | tâ yû | thung zăn | phî | thâi | lî | hsiâo khû |

| 24 | 23 | 22 | 21 | 20 | 19 | 18 | 17 |
|---|---|---|---|---|---|---|---|
| fû | po | pî | shih ho | kwăn | lin | kû | sui |

| 32 | 31 | 30 | 29 | 28 | 27 | 26 | 25 |
|---|---|---|---|---|---|---|---|
| hăng | hsien | lî | khan | tâ kwo | î | tâ khû | wû wang |

| 40 | 39 | 38 | 37 | 36 | 35 | 34 | 33 |
|---|---|---|---|---|---|---|---|
| kieh | kien | khwei | kiâ zăn | ming î | zin | tâ kwang | thun |

| 48 | 47 | 46 | 45 | 44 | 43 | 42 | 41 |
|---|---|---|---|---|---|---|---|
| zing | khwăn | shăng | zhui | kâu | kwâi | yî | sun |

| 56 | 55 | 54 | 53 | 52 | 51 | 50 | 49 |
|---|---|---|---|---|---|---|---|
| lü | făng | kwei mei | kien | kăn | kăn | ting | ko |

| 64 | 63 | 62 | 61 | 60 | 59 | 58 | 57 |
|---|---|---|---|---|---|---|---|
| wei zî | kî zî | hsiâo kwo | kung fû | kieh | hwăn | tui | sun |

# PLATE II.

## Fig. 1.

The Hexagrams, exhibited circularly and in a square, according to the natural process of development from the whole and divided lines, and the order of arrangement ascribed to Fŭ-hsí.

# PLATE II.

## FIG. 2.

The Trigrams distinguished as Yin and Yang.

### LATER ARRANGEMENT OF KING WĂN.

| yang | | yin | |
|---|---|---|---|
| ☰ khien | ☷ khwăn | | |
| ☶ kăn | ☴ sun | | |
| ☵ khan | ☲ lî | | |
| ☳ kăn | ☱ tui | | |

### EARLY ARRANGEMENT OF FŬ-HSÎ.

| yang | | yin | |
|---|---|---|---|
| ☷ kăn | ☴ sun | | |
| ☲ lî | ☵ khan | | |
| ☱ tui | ☶ kăn | | |
| ☰ khien | ☷ khwăn | | |

# PLATE III.

## FIG. 1.

Illustrating the tenth paragraph of Appendix V.

| tui youngest daughter | khwăn mother | lî second daughter | sun eldest daughter | kăn youngest son | khien father | khăn second son | kăn eldest son |
|---|---|---|---|---|---|---|---|
| upper line of khwăn | second line of khwăn | first line of khwăn | upper line of khien | second line of khien | first line of khien |

# PLATE III.

## FIG. 2.

ORDER OF THE TRIGRAMS, with the cardinal and other points to which they are severally referred.

| ACCORDING TO KING WĂN. | ACCORDING TO FŬ-HSĬ. |
|---|---|

## PREFACE.

I wrote out a translation of the Yî King, embracing both the Text and the Appendixes, in 1854 and 1855; and have to acknowledge that when the manuscript was completed, I knew very little about the scope and method of the book. I laid the volumes containing the result of my labour aside, and hoped, believed indeed, that the light would by and by dawn, and that I should one day get hold of a clue that would guide me to a knowledge of the mysterious classic.

Before that day came, the translation was soaked, in 1870, for more than a month in water of the Red Sea. By dint of careful manipulation it was recovered so as to be still legible; but it was not till 1874 that I began to be able to give to the book the prolonged attention necessary to make it reveal its secrets. Then for the first time I got hold, as I believe, of the clue, and found that my toil of twenty years before was of no service at all.

What had tended more than anything else to hide the nature of the book from my earlier studies was the way in which, with the Text, ordinarily and, as I think, correctly ascribed to king Wăn and his son Tan, there are interspersed, under each hexagram, the portions of the Appendixes I, II, and IV relating to it. The student at first thinks this an advantage. He believes that all the Appendixes were written by Confucius, and combine with the text to form one harmonious work; and he is glad to have the sentiments of 'the three sages' brought together. But I now perceived that the composition of the Text and of the Appendixes, allowing the Confucian authorship of the latter, was separated by about 700 years, and that their subject-matter was often incongruous. My first step towards a right understanding of the Yî was to study the Text by itself and as complete in itself. It was easy to do this because the imperial edition of 1715, with all its critical apparatus, keeps the Text and the Appendixes separate.

The wisdom of the course thus adopted became more apparent by the formation of eight different concordances, one for the Text, and one for each of the Appendixes. They showed that many characters in the Appendixes, and those especially which most readily occur to sinologists as characteristic of the Yî, are not to be found in the Text at all. A fuller acquaintance, moreover, with the tone and style of the Appendixes satisfied me that while we had sufficient evidence that the greater part of them was not from Confucius, we had no evidence that any part was his, unless it might be the paragraphs introduced by the compiler or compilers as sayings of 'the Master.'

Studying the Text in the manner thus described, I soon arrived at the view of the meaning and object of the Yî, which I have described in the second chapter of the Introduction; and I was delighted to find that there was a substantial agreement between my interpretations of the hexagrams and their several lines and those given by the most noted commentators from the Han dynasty down to the present. They have not formulated the scheme so concisely as I have done, and they were fettered by their belief in the Confucian authorship of the Appendixes; but they held the same general opinion, and were similarly controlled by it in construing the Text. Any sinologist who will examine the Yü *K*ih *Z*ăh *K*iang Yî King *K*ieh Î, prepared by one of the departments of the Han Lin college, and published in 1682, and which I have called the 'Daily Lessons,' or 'Lectures,' will see the agreement between my views and those underlying its paraphrase.

After the clue to the meaning of the Yî was discovered, there remained the difficulty of translating. The peculiarity of its style makes it the most difficult of all the Confucian classics to present in an intelligible version. I suppose that there are sinologists who will continue, for a time at least, to maintain that it was intended by its author or authors, whoever they were, merely as a book of divination; and of course the oracles of divination were designedly wrapped up in mysterious phraseology. But notwithstanding the account of the origin of the book and its composition by king Wăn and his son, which I have seen reason to adopt, they, its authors, had to write after the manner of diviners. There is hardly another work in the ancient literature of China that presents the same difficulties to the translator.

When I made my first translation of it in 1854, I endeavoured to be as concise in my English as the original Chinese was. Much of what I wrote was made up, in consequence, of so many English words, with little or no mark of syntactical connexion. I followed in this the example of P. Regis and his coadjutors (Introduction, page p. 24) in their Latin version. But their version is all but unintelligible, and mine was not less so. How to surmount this difficulty occurred to me after I had found the clue to the interpretation;—in a fact which I had unconsciously acted on in all my translations of other classics) namely, that the written characters of the Chinese are not representations of words, but symbols of ideas, and that the combination of them in composition is not a representation of what the writer would say, but of what he thinks. It is vain therefore for a translator to attempt a literal version. When the symbolic characters have brought his mind en rapport with that of his author, he is free to render the ideas in his own or any other speech in the best manner that he can attain to. This is the rule which Mencius followed in interpreting the old poems of his country:—'We must try with our thoughts to meet the scope of a sentence, and then we shall apprehend it.' In the study of a Chinese classical book there is not so much an interpretation of the characters employed by the writer as a participation of his thoughts;—there is the seeing of mind to mind. The canon hence derived for a translator is not one of license. It will be his object to express the meaning of the original as exactly and concisely as possible. But it will be necessary for him to introduce a word or two now and then to indicate what the mind of the writer supplied for itself. What I have done in this way will generally be seen enclosed in parentheses, though I queried whether I might not dispense with them, as there is nothing in the English version which was not, I believe, present in the writer's thought. I hope, however, that I have been able in this way to make the translation intelligible to readers. If, after all, they shall conclude that in what is said on the hexagrams there is often 'much ado about nothing,' it is not the translator who should be deemed accountable for that, but his original.

I had intended to append to the volume translations of certain chapters from Kû Hsî and other writers of the Sung dynasty; but this purpose could not be carried into effect for want of space. It was found necessary to accompany the version with a running commentary, illustrating the way in which the teachings of king Wăn and his son are supposed to be drawn from the figures and their several lines; and my difficulty was to keep the single Yî within the limits of one volume. Those intended translations therefore are reserved for another opportunity; and indeed, the Sung philosophy did not grow out of the Yî proper, but from the Appendixes to it, and especially from the third of them. It is more Tâoistic than Confucian.

When I first took the Yî in hand, there existed no translation of it in any western language but that of P. Regis and his coadjutors, which I have mentioned above and in various places of the Introduction. The authors were all sinologists of great attainments; and their view of the Text as relating to the transactions between the founders of the Kâu dynasty and the last sovereign of the Shang or Yin, and capable of being illustrated historically, though too narrow, was an approximation to the truth. The late M. Mohl, who had edited the work in 1834, said to me once, 'I like it; for I come to it out of a sea of mist, and find solid ground.' No sufficient distinction was made in it, however, between the Text and the Appendixes; and in discussing the third and following Appendixes the translators were haunted by the name and shade of Confucius. To the excessive literalness of the version I have referred above.

In 1876 the Rev. Canon McClatchie, M.A., published a version at Shanghai with the title, 'A Translation of the Confucian Yî King, or the "Classic of Changes," with Notes and Appendix.' This embraces both the Text and the Appendixes, the first, second, and fourth of the latter being interspersed along with the Text, as in the ordinary school editions of the classic. So far as I can judge from his language, he does not appear to be aware that the first and second Appendixes were not the work of king Wăn and the duke of Kâu, but of a subsequent writer—he would say of Confucius—explaining their explanations of the entire hexagrams and their several lines. His own special object was 'to open the mysteries of the Yî by applying to it the key of Comparative Mythology.' Such a key was not necessary; and the author, by the application of it, has found sundry things to which I have occasionally referred in my notes. They are not pleasant to look at or dwell upon; and happily it has never entered into the minds of Chinese scholars to conceive of them. I have followed Canon McClatchie's translation from paragraph to paragraph and from sentence to sentence, but found nothing which I could employ with advantage in my own.

Long after my translation had been completed, and that of the Text indeed was printed, I received from Shanghai the third volume of P. Angelo Zottoli's 'Cursus Litteraturae Sinicae,' which had appeared in 1880. About 100 pages of it are occupied with the Yî. The Latin version is a great improvement on that in the work of Regis; but P. Zottoli translates only the Text of the first two hexagrams, with the portions of the first, second, and fourth Appendixes relating to them; and other six hexagrams with the explanations of king Wăn's Thwan and of the Great Symbolism. Of the remaining fifty-six hexagrams only the briefest summary is given; and then follow the Appendixes III, V, VI, and VII at length. The author has done his work well. His general view of the Yî is stated in the following sentences:—'Ex Fû-hsî figuris, Wăn regis definitionibus, Kâu ducis symbolis, et Confucii commentariis, Liber conficitur, qui a mutationibus, quas duo elementa in hexagrammatum compositione inducunt, Yî (Mutator) vel Yî King (Mutationum Liber) appellatur. Quid igitur tandem famosus iste Yî King? Paucis accipe: ex linearum qualitate continua vel intercisa; earumque situ, imo, medio, vel supremo; mutuaque ipsarum relatione, occursu, dissidio, convenientia; ex ipso scilicet trigrammatum corpore seu forma, tum ex trigrammatum symbolo seu imagine, tum ex trigrammatum proprietate seu virtute, tum etiam aliquando ex unius ad alterum hexagramma varietate, eruitur aliqua imago, deducitur aliqua sententia, quoddam veluti oraculum continens, quod sorte etiam consulere possis ad documentum obtinendum, moderandae vitae solvendove dubio consentaneum. Ita liber juxta Confucii explicationem in scholis tradi solitam. Nil igitur sublime aut mysteriosum, nil foedum aut vile hic quaeras; argutulum potius lusum ibi video ad instructiones morales politicasque eliciendas, ut ad satietatem usque in Sinicis passim classicis, obvias, planas, naturales; tantum, cum liber iste, ut integrum legenti textum facile patebit, ad sortilegii usum deductus fuerit, per ipsum jam summum homo obtinebit vitae beneficium, arcanam cum spiritibus communicationem secretamque futurorum eventuum cognitionem; theurgus igitur visus est iste liber, totus lux, totus spiritus, hominisque vitae accommodatissimus; indeque laudes a

Confucio ei tributas, prorsus exaggeratas, in hujus libri praesertim appendice videre erit, si vere tamen, ut communis fert opinio, ipse sit hujus appendicis auctor.'

There has been a report for two or three years of a new translation of the Yî, or at least of a part of it, as being in preparation by M. Terrien de Lacouperie, and Professor R. K. Douglas of the British Museum and King's College, London. I have alluded on pages 24, 24 of the Introduction to some inaccurate statements about native commentaries on the Yî and translations of it by foreigners, made in connexion with this contemplated version. But I did not know what the projected undertaking really was, till I read a letter from M. Terrien in the 'Athenæum' of the 21st January of this year. He there says that the joint translation 'deals only with the oldest part of the book, the short lists of characters which follow each of the sixty-four headings, and leaves entirely aside the explanations and commentaries attributed to Wen Wang, *K*âu Kung, Confucius, and others, from 1200 B. C. downwards, which are commonly embodied as an integral part of the classic;' adding, 'The proportion of the primitive text to these additions is about one-sixth of the whole.' But if we take away these explanations and commentaries attributed to king Wăn, the duke of *K*âu, and Confucius, we take away the whole Yî. There remain only the linear figures attributed to Fû-hsî, without any lists of characters, long or short, without a single written character of any kind whatever. The projectors have been misled somehow about the contents of the Yî; and unless they can overthrow all the traditions and beliefs about them, whether Chinese or foreign, their undertaking is more hopeless than the task laid on the children of Israel by Pharaoh, that they should make bricks without straw.

I do not express myself thus in any spirit of hostility. If, by discoveries in Accadian or any other long-buried and forgotten language, M. Terrien de Lacouperie can throw new light on the written characters of China or on its speech, no one will rejoice more than myself; but his ignorance of how the contents of the classic are made up does not give much prospect of success in his promised translation.

In the preface to the third volume of these 'Sacred Books of the East,' containing the Shû King, Shih King, and Hsiâo King, I have spoken of the Chinese terms Tî and Shang Tî, and shown how I felt it necessary to continue to render them by our word God, as I had done in all my translations of the Chinese classics since 1861. My doing so gave offence to some of the missionaries in China and others; and in June, 1880, twenty-three gentlemen addressed a letter to Professor F. Max Müller, complaining that, in such a work edited by him, he should allow me to give my own private interpretation of the name or names in question instead of translating them or transferring them. Professor

Müller published the letter which he had received, with his reply to it, in the 'Times' newspaper of Dec. 30, 1880. Since then the matter has rested, and I introduce it again here in this preface, because, though we do not meet with the name in the Yî so frequently as in the Shû and Shih, I have, as before, wherever it does occur, translated it by God. Those who object to that term say that Shang Tî might be rendered by 'Supreme Ruler' or 'Supreme Emperor,' or by 'Ruler (or Emperor) on high;' but when I examined the question, more than thirty years ago, with all possible interest and all the resources at my command, I came to the conclusions that Tî, on its first employment by the Chinese fathers, was intended to express the same concept which our fathers expressed by God, and that such has been its highest and proper application ever since. There would be little if any difference in the meaning conveyed to readers by 'Supreme Ruler' and 'God;' but when I render Tî by God and Shang Tî by the Supreme God, or, for the sake of brevity, simply by God, I am translating, and not giving a private interpretation of my own. I do it not in the interests of controversy, but as the simple expression of what to me is truth; and I am glad to know that a great majority of the Protestant missionaries in China use Tî and Shang Tî as the nearest analogue for God.

It would be tedious to mention the many critical editions and commentaries that I have used in preparing the translation. I have not had the help of able native scholars, which saved time and was otherwise valuable when I was working in the East on other classics. The want of this, however, has been more than compensated in some respects by my copy of the 'Daily Lectures on the Yî,' the full title of which is given on page 13. The friend who purchased it for me five years ago in Canton was obliged to content himself with a second-hand copy; but I found that the previous owner had been a ripe scholar who freely used his pencil in pursuing his studies. It was possible, from his punctuation, interlineations, and many marginal notes, to follow the exercises of his mind, patiently pursuing his search for the meaning of the most difficult passages. I am under great obligations to him; and also to the *K*âu Yî *K*eh *K*ung, the great imperial edition of the present dynasty, first published in 1715. I have generally spoken of its authors as the Khang-hsî editors. Their numerous discussions of the meaning, and ingenious decisions, go far to raise the interpretation of the Yî to a science.

J. L.

OXFORD,
16th March, 1882.

# THE YÎ KING

## OR

## BOOK OF CHANGES.

## INTRODUCTION.

### CHAPTER I. THE YÎ KING FROM THE TWELFTH CENTURY B.C. TO THE COMMENCEMENT OF THE CHRISTIAN ERA.

*There was a Yî in the time of Confucius.* 1. Confucius is reported to have said on one occasion, 'If some years were added to my life, I would give fifty to the study of the Yî, and might then escape falling into great errors.'[1] The utterance is referred by the best critics to the closing period of Confucius' life, when he had returned from his long and painful wanderings among the States, and was settled again. In his native Lû. By this time he was nearly seventy, and it seems strange, if he spoke seriously, that he should have thought it possible for his life to be prolonged other fifty years. So far as that specification is concerned, a corruption of the text is generally admitted. My reason for adducing the passage has simply been to prove from it the existence of a Yî King in the time of Confucius. In the history of him by Sze-mâ *Kh*ien it is stated that, in the closing years of his life, he became fond of the Yî, and wrote various appendixes to it, that he read his copy of it so much that the leathern thongs (by which the tablets containing it were bound together) were thrice worn out, and that he said, 'Give me several years (more), and I should be master of the Yî.'[2] The ancient books on which Confucius had delighted to discourse with his disciples were those of History, Poetry, and Rites and Ceremonies;[3] but ere he passed away from among them, his attention was much occupied also by the Yî as a monument of antiquity, which in the prime of his days he had too much neglected.

*The Yî is now made up of the Text which Confucius saw and the Appendixes ascribed to him.* 2. *Kh*ien says that Confucius wrote various appendixes to the Yî, specifying all but two of the treatises, which go by the name of the 'Ten Appendixes,' and are, with hardly a dissentient voice, attributed to the sage. They are published along with the older Text, which is based on still older lineal figures, and are received by

---

[1] Confucian Analects, VII, xvi.
[2] The Historical Records; Life of Confucius, p. 12.
[3] Analects, VII, xvii.

most Chinese readers, as well as by foreign Chinese scholars, as an integral portion of the Yî King. The two portions should, however, be carefully distinguished. I will speak of them as the Text and the Appendixes.

*The Yî escaped the fires of Ʒhin.* 3. The Yî happily escaped the fires of Ʒhin, which proved so disastrous to most of the ancient literature of China in B. C. 213. In the memorial which the premier Lî Sze addressed to his sovereign, advising that the old books should be consigned to the flames, an exception was made of those which treated of 'medicine, divination, and husbandry.'[4] The Yî was held to be a book of divination, and so was preserved.

In the catalogue of works in the imperial library, prepared by Liû Hin about the beginning of our era, there is an enumeration of those on the Yî and its Appendixes,—the books of thirteen different authors or schools, comprehended in 294 portions of larger or smaller dimensions 2:3.[5] I need not follow the history and study of the Yî into the line of the centuries since the time of Liû Hin. The imperial Khang-hsî edition of it, which appeared in 1715, contains quotations from the commentaries of 218 scholars, covering, more or less closely, the time from the second century B. C. to our seventeenth century. I may venture to say that those 218 are hardly a tenth of the men who have tried to interpret the remarkable book, and solve the many problems to which it gives rise.

*The Yî before Confucius, and when it was made.* 4. It may be assumed then that the Yî King, properly so called, existed before Confucius, and has come down to us as correctly as any other of the. ancient books of China; and it might also be said, as correctly as any of the old monuments of Hebrew, Sanskrit, Greek, or Latin literature. The question arises of how far before Confucius we can trace its existence. of course an inquiry into this point will not include the portions or appendixes attributed to the sage himself. Attention will be called to them by and by, when I shall consider how far we are entitled, or whether we are at all entitled, to ascribe them to him. I do not doubt, however, that they belong to what may be called the Confucian period, and were produced some time after his death, probably between B.C. 450 and 350. By whomsoever they were written, they may be legitimately employed in illustration of what were the prevailing views in that age on various points connected with the Yî. Indeed, but for the guidance and hints derived from them as to the meaning of the text, and the relation between its statements and the linear figures, there would be great difficulty in making out any consistent interpretation of it.

---

[4] Legge's Chinese Classics, I, prolegomena, pp. 6-9.
[5] Books of the Earlier Han; History of Literature, pp. 1, 2.

*The Yî mentioned in the Official Book of Kâu.* (i) The earliest mention of the classic is found in the Official Book of the *K*âu dynasty, where it is said that, among the duties of 'the Grand Diviner,' 'he had charge of the rules for the three Yî (systems of Changes), called the Lien-shan, the Kweî-ʒhang, and the Yî of *K*âu; that in each of them the regular (or primary) lineal figures were 8, which were multiplied, in each, till the), amounted to 64.' The date of the Official Book has not been exactly ascertained. The above passage can hardly be reconciled with the opinion of the majority of Chinese critics that it was the work of the duke of *K*âu, the consolidator and legislator of the dynasty so called; but I think there must have been the groundwork of it at a very early date. When that was composed or compiled, there was existing, among the archives of the kingdom, under the charge of a high officer, 'the Yî of *K*âu,'—what constitutes the Text of the present Yî; the Text, that is, as distinguished from the Appendixes. There were two other Yî, known as the Lien-shan and the Kwei-ʒhang. It would be a waste of time to try to discover the meaning of these designations. They are found in this and another passage of the Official Book; and nowhere else. Not a single trace of what they denoted remains, while we possess 'the Yî of *K*âu' complete.[6]

*The Yî mentioned in the ʒo Khwan.* (ii) In the Supplement of ʒo *Kh*iû-ming to 'the Spring and Autumn,' there is abundant evidence that divination by the Yî was frequent, throughout the states of China, before the time of Confucius. There are at least eight narratives of such a practice, between the years B.C. 672 and 564, before he was born; and five times during his life-time the divining stalks and the book were had recourse to on occasions with which he had nothing to do. In all these cases the text of the Yî, as we have it now, is freely quoted. The 'Spring and Autumn' commences in B.C. 722. If it extended back

---

[6] See the *K*âu Kwan (or Lî), Book XXIV, parr. 3, 4, and 27. Biot (Le Tcheou Lî, vol. ii, pp. 70, 71) translates the former two paragraphs thus: 'Il (Le Grand Augure) est préposé aux trois methodes pour les changements (des lignes divinatoires). La première est appelée Liaison des montagnes (Lien-shan); la seconde, Retour et Conservation (Kwei-ʒhang); la troisième, Changements des *K*âu. Pour toutes il y a huit lignes symboliques sacrées, et soixante-quatre combinaisons de ces lignes.'

Some tell us that by Lien-shan was intended Fû-hsî, and by Kwei-ʒhang Hwang Tî; others, that the former was the Yî of the Hsiâ dynasty, and the latter that of Shang or Yin. A third set will have it that Lien-shan was a designation of Shăn Năng, between Fû-hsî and Hwang Tî. I should say myself, as many Chinese critics do say, that Lien-shan was an arrangement of the lineal symbols in which the first figure was the present 52nd hexagram, Kăn ☶ ☶ consisting of the trigram representing mountains doubled; and that Kwei-ʒhang was an arrangement where the first figure was the present 2nd hexagram, Khwăn ☷ ☷ consisting of the trigram representing the earth doubled,— with reference to the disappearance and safe keeping of plants in the bosom of the earth in winter. All this, however, is only conjecture.

to the rise of the *K*âu dynasty, we should, no doubt, find accounts of divination by the Yî interspersed over the long intervening period. For centuries before Confucius appeared on the stage of his country, the Yî was well known among the various feudal states, which then constituted the Middle Kingdom.[7]

(iii) We may now look into one of the Appendixes for its testimony to the age and authorship of the Text. The third Appendix is the longest, and the most important.[8] In the 49th paragraph of the second Section of it it is said:—

'Was it not in the middle period of antiquity that the Yî began to flourish? Was not he who made it (or were not they who made it) familiar with anxiety and calamity?'

The highest antiquity commences, according to Chinese writers, with Fû-hsî, B.C. 3322; and the lowest with Confucius in the middle of the sixth century B.C. Between these is the period of middle antiquity, extending a comparatively short time, from the rise of the *K*âu dynasty, towards the close of the twelfth century B.C., to the Confucian era. According to this paragraph it was in this period that our Yî was made.

The 69th paragraph is still more definite in its testimony:—

'Was it not in the last age of the Yin (dynasty), when the virtue of *K*âu had reached its highest point, and during the troubles between king Wăn and (the tyrant) *K*âu, that (the study of) the Yî began to flourish? On this account the explanations (in the book) express (a feeling of) anxious apprehension, (and teach) how peril may be turned into security, and easy carelessness is sure to meet with overthrow.'

The dynasty of Yin was superseded by that of *K*âu in B. C. 1122. The founder of *K*âu was he whom we call king Wăn, though he himself never occupied the throne. The troubles between him and the last sovereign of Yin reached their height in B. C. 1143, when the tyrant threw him into prison in a place called Yû-lî, identified as having been in the present district of Thang-yin, department of *K*ang-teh, province of Ho-nan. Wăn was not kept long in confinement. His friends succeeded in appeasing the jealousy of his enemy, and securing his

---

[7] See in the *K*o *K*hwan, under the 22nd year of duke *K*wang (B.C. 672); the 1st year of Min (1661); and in his 2nd year (660); twice in the 15th year of Hsî (645); his 25th year (635); the 12th year of Hsüan, (597); the 16th year of *K*hăng (575); the 9th year of Hsiang (564); his 25th year (548); the 5th year of *K*hâo (537); his 7th year (535); his 12th year (530); and the 9th year of Âi (486).

[8] That is, the third as it appears farther on in this volume in two Sections. With the Chinese critics it forms the fifth and sixth Appendixes, or, 'Wings,' as they are termed.

liberation in the following year. It follows that the Yî, so far as we owe it to king Wăn, was made in the year B.C. 1143 or 1142, or perhaps that it was begun in the former year and finished in the latter.[9]

But the part which is thus ascribed to king Wăn is only a small portion of the Yî. A larger share is attributed to his son Tan, known as the duke of *K*âu, and in it we have allusions to king Wû, who succeeded his father Wăn, and was really the first sovereign of the dynasty of *K*âu.[10] There are passages, moreover, which must be understood of events in the early years of the next reign. But the duke of *K*âu died in the year B. C. 1105, the 11th of king *K*hăng. A few years then before that time, in the last decade of the twelfth century B. C., the Yî King, as it has come down to us, was complete.[11]

*The Yî is not the most ancient of the Chinese books.* 5. We have thus traced the text of the Yî to its authors, the famous king Wăn in the year 1143 B. C., and his equally famous son, the duke of *K*âu, in between thirty and forty years later. It can thus boast of a great antiquity; but a general opinion has prevailed that it belonged to a period still more distant. Only two translations of it have been made by European scholars. The first was executed by Regis and other Roman Catholic missionaries in the beginning of last century, though it was given to the public only in 1834 by the late Jules Mohl, with a title commencing 'Y-King, antiquissimus Sinarum liber.'[12] The language of

---

[9] Sze-mâ *K*hien (History of the *K*âu Dynasty, p. 3) relates that, 'when he was confined in Yû-lî, Wăn increased the 8 trigrams to 64 hexagrams.'

[10] E.g., hexagrams XVII, 1. 6; XLVI, 1. 4. Tan's authorship of the symbolism is recognised in the 3o *K*hwan, B. C. 540.

[11] P. Regis (vol. ii, P. 379) says: 'Vel nihil vel parum errabit qui dicet opus Yî King fuisse perfectum anno quinto *K*hăng Wang, seu anno 1109 aut non ultra annum 1108, ante aerae Christianae initium; quod satis in rebus non omnino certis.' But the fifth year of king *K*hăng was B. C. 1111.

[12] It has been suggested that 'Antiquissimus Sinarum liber' may mean only 'A very ancient book of the Chinese,' but the first sentence of the Preface to the work commences:—'Inter onmes constat librorum Sinicorum, quos classicos vocant, primum et antiquissimum esse Y-King.'

At the end of M. De Guignes' edition of P. Gaubil's translation of the Shû, there is a notice of the Yî King sent in 1738 to the Cardinals of the Congregation de Propaganda Fide by M. Claude Visdelou, Bishop of Claudiopolis. M. De Guignes says himself, 'L' Y-King est le premier des Livres Canoniques des Chinois.' But P. Visdelou writes more guardedly and correctly:—'Pour son ancienneté, s'il en faut croire les Annales des Chinois, il a été commencé quarante-six siècles avant celui-ci. Si cela est vrai, comme toute la nation l'avoue unanimement, ou peut à juste titre l'appeler le plus ancien des livres.' But he adds, 'Ce n'étoit pas proprement un livre, ni quelque chose d'approchant; c'étoit une énigme très obscure, et plus difficile cent fois à expliquer que celle du sphinx.'

P. Couplet expresses himself much to the same effect in the prolegomena (p. xviii) to the work called 'Confucius Sinarum Philosophus,' published at Paris in 1687 by himself and three other fathers of the Society of Jesus (Intorcetta, Herdritch, and Rougemont). Both they and P. Visdelou give an example of a portion of the text and its the other European translator of it, the Rev. Canon McClatchie of Shanghâi, whose work appeared in 1876, is still more decided. The first sentence of his Introduction contains two very serious misstatements, but I have at present to do only with the former of them;—that 'the Yî King is regarded by the Chinese with peculiar veneration, . . . . as being the most ancient of their classical writings.' The Shû is the oldest of the Chinese classics, and contains documents more, than a thousand years earlier than king Wăn. Several pieces of the Shih King are also older than anything in the Yî; to which there can thus he assigned only the third place in point of age among the monuments of Chinese literature. Existing, however, about 3000 years ago, it cannot be called modern. Unless it be the books of the Pentateuch, Joshua, and judges, an equal antiquity cannot be claimed for any portion of our Sacred Scriptures.

*The Text much older than the Appendixes.* It will be well to observe here also how much older the Text is than the Appendixes. Supposing them to be the work of Confucius, though it will appear by and by that this assumption can be received as only partially correct, if indeed it be received at all, the sage could not have entered on their composition earlier than B.C. 483, 660 years later than the portion of the text that came from king Wăn, and nearly 630 later than what we owe to the duke of *K*âu. But during that long period of between six and seven centuries changes may have arisen in the views taken by thinking men of the method and manner of the Yî; and I cannot accept the Text and the Appendixes as forming one work in any proper sense of the term. Nothing has prevented the full understanding of both, so far as parts of the latter can be understood, so much as the blending of them together, which originated with Pî *K*ih of the first Han dynasty. The common editions of the book have five of the Appendixes (as they are ordinarily reckoned) broken up and printed side by side with the Text; and the confusion thence arising has made it difficult, through the intermixture of incongruous ideas, for foreign students to lay hold of the meaning.

*Labours of native scholars on the Yî.* 6. Native scholars have of course been well aware of the difference in time between the appearance of the Text and the Appendixes; and in the Khang-hsî edition of them the two are printed separately. Only now and then, however, has any critic ventured to doubt that the two parts formed one homogeneous whole, or that all the appendixes were from the style or pencil of Confucius. Hundreds of them have brought a wonderful and consistent meaning out of the Text; but to find in it or in the Appendixes what is unreasonable, or any inconsistency between them, would be to impeach the infallibility of Confucius, and stamp on

---

interpretation, having singularly selected the same hexagram,—the 15th, on Humility.

themselves the brand of heterodoxy.

*An imperfect description of their labours.* At the same time it is an unfair description of what they have accomplished to say, as has been done lately, that since the fires of 3hin, 'the foremost scholars of each generation have edited the Text (meaning both the Text and the Appendixes), and heaped commentary after commentary upon it; and one and all have arrived at the somewhat lame conclusion that its full significance is past finding out.'[13] A multitude of the native commentaries are of the highest value, and have left little to be done for the elucidation of the Text; and if they say that a passage in an Appendix is 'unfathomable' or 'incalculable,' it is because their authors shrink from allowing, even to themselves, that the ancient sages intermeddled, and intermeddled unwisely, with things too high for them.

*Erroneous account of the labours of European Chinese scholars.* When the same writer who thus speaks of native scholars goes on to say that 'in the same way a host of European Chinese scholars have made translations of the Yî, and have, if possible, made confusion worse confounded,' he only shows how imperfectly he had made himself acquainted with the subject. 'The host of European Chinese scholars who have made translations of the Yî' amount to two,—the same two mentioned by me above on p. 22. The translation of Regis and his coadjutors[14] is indeed capable of improvement; but their work as a whole, and especially the prolegomena, dissertations, and notes, supply a mass of correct and valuable information. They had nearly succeeded in unravelling the confusion, and solving the enigma of the Yî.

## CHAPTER II. THE SUBJECT-MATTER OF THE TEXT. THE LINEAL FIGURES AND THE EXPLANATION OF THEM.

1. Having described the Yî King as consisting of a text in explanation of certain lineal figures, and of appendixes to it, and having traced the composition of the former to its authors in the twelfth century B. C., and that of the latter to between six and seven centuries later at least, I proceed to give an account of what we find in the Text,

---

[13] See a communication on certain new views about the Yî in the 'Times' of April 20, 1880; reprinted in Trübner's American, European, and Oriental Literary Record, New Series, vol. i, pp. 125-127.

[14] Regis' coadjutors in the work were the Fathers Joseph de Mailla, who turned the Chinese into Latin word for word, and compared the result with the Man*k*âu version of the Yî; and Peter du Tartre, whose principal business was to supply the historical illustrations. Regis himself revised all their work and enlarged it, adding his own dissertations and notes. See Prospectus Operis, immediately after M. Mohl's Preface.

and how it is deduced from the figures.

*The Yî consists of essays based on lineal figures.* The subject-matter of the Text may be briefly represented as consisting of sixty-four short essays, enigmatically and symbolically expressed, on important themes, mostly of a moral, social, and political character, and based on the same number of lineal figures, each made up of six lines, some of which are whole and the others divided.

The first two and the last two may serve for the present as a specimen of those figures: ☰☰, ☷☷, and ☳☶, ☶☳.[15] The Text says nothing about their origin and formation. There they are. King Wăn takes them up, one after another, in the order that suits himself, determined, evidently, by the contrast in the lines of each successive pair of hexagrams, and gives their significance, as a whole, with some indication, perhaps, of the action to be taken in the circumstances which he supposes them to symbolise, and whether that action will be lucky or unlucky. Then the duke of *Kâu*, beginning with the first or bottom line, expresses, by means of a symbolical or emblematical illustration, the significance of each line, with a similar indication of the good or bad fortune of action taken in connexion with it. The king's interpretation of the whole hexagram will be found to be in harmony with the combined significance of the six lines as interpreted by his son.

Both of them, no doubt, were familiar with the practice of divination which had prevailed in China for more than a thousand years, and would copy closely its methods and style. They were not divining themselves, but their words became oracles to subsequent ages, when men divined by the hexagrams, and sought by means of what was said under them to ascertain how it would be with them in the future, and learn whether they should persevere in or withdraw from the courses they were intending to pursue.

*The origin of the lineal figures.* 2. I will give an instance of the lessons which the lineal figures are made to teach, but before I do so, it will be necessary to relate what is said of their origin, and of the rules observed in studying and interpreting them. For information on these points we must have recourse to the Appendixes; and in reply to the question by whom and in what way the figures were formed, the third, of which we made use in the last chapter, supplies us with three different answers.

i) The 11th paragraph of Section ii says:—

---

[15] See Plate I at the end of the Introduction.

'Anciently, when the rule of all under heaven was in the hands of Pâo-hsî, looking up, he contemplated the brilliant forms exhibited in the sky; and looking down, he surveyed the patterns shown on the earth. He marked the ornamental appearances on birds and beasts, and the (different) suitabilities of the soil. Near at hand, in his own person, he found things for consideration, and the same at a distance, in things in general. On this he devised the eight lineal figures of three lines each, to exhibit fully the spirit-like and intelligent operations (in nature), and to classify the qualities of the myriads of things.'

Pâo-hsî is another name for Fû-hsî, the most ancient personage who is mentioned with any definiteness in Chinese history, while much that is fabulous is current about him. His place in chronology begins in B.C. 3322, 5203 years ago. He appears in this paragraph as the deviser of the eight kwâ or trigrams. The processes by which he was led to form them, and the purposes which he intended them to serve, are described, but in vague and general terms that do not satisfy our curiosity. The eight figures, however, were ☰, ☱, ☲, ☳, ☴, ☵, ☶, and ☷; called *kh*ien, tui, lî, *k*ǎn, sun, khân, kǎn, and khwǎn; and representing heaven or the sky; water, especially a collection of water as in a marsh or lake; fire, the sun, lightning; thunder; wind and wood; water, especially as in rain, the clouds, springs, streams in defiles, and the moon; a hill or mountain; and the earth. To each of these figures is assigned a certain attribute or quality which should be suggested by the natural object it symbolises; but on those attributes we need not enter at present.

(ii) The 70th and 71st paragraphs of Section i give another account of the origin of the trigrams:—

'In (the system of) the Yî there is the Great Extreme, which produced the two Î (Elementary Forms). These two Forms produced the four Hsiang (Emblematic Symbols); which again produced the eight Kwâ (or Trigrams). The eight Kwâ served to determine the good and evil (issues of events), and from this determination there ensued the (prosecution of the) great business of life.'

The two elementary Forms, the four emblematic Symbols, and the eight Trigrams can all be exhibited with what may be deemed certainty. A whole line (——) and a divided (— —) were the two Î. These two lines placed over themselves, and each of them over the other, formed the four Hsiang: ⚌; ⚎; ⚍; ⚏. The same two lines placed successively over these Hsiang, formed the eight Kwâ, exhibited above.

Who will undertake to say what is meant by 'the Great Extreme' which produced the two elementary Forms? Nowhere else does the name occur in the old Confucian literature. I have no doubt myself that it found its way into this Appendix in the fifth (?or fourth) century B.C. from a Tâoist source. *Kû Hsî*, in his 'Lessons on the Yî for the Young,' gives for it the figure of a circle,—thus, ◯; observing that he does so from the philosopher *Kâu* (A.D. 1017-1073),[16] and cautioning his readers against thinking that such a representation came from Fû-hsî himself. To me the circular symbol appears very unsuccessful. 'The Great Extreme,' it is said, 'divided and produced two lines,—a whole line and a divided line.' But I do not understand how this could be. Suppose it possible for the circle to unroll itself;—we shall have one long line, ——————. If this divide itself, we have two whole lines; and another division of one of them is necessary to give us the whole and the divided lines of the lineal figures. The attempt to fashion the Great Extreme as a circle must be pronounced a failure.

But when we start from the two lines as bases, the formation of all the diagrams by a repetition of the process indicated above is easy. The addition to each of the trigrams of each of the two fundamental lines produces 16 figures of four lines; dealt with in the same way, these produce 32 figures of five lines; and a similar operation with these produces the 64 hexagrams, each of which forms the subject of an essay in the text of the Yî. The lines increase in an arithmetical progression whose common difference is 1, and the figures in a geometrical progression whose common ratio is 2. This is all the mystery in the formation of the lineal figures; this, I believe, was the process by which they were first formed; and it is hardly necessary to imagine them to have come from a sage like Fû-hsî. The endowments of an ordinary man were sufficient for such a work. It was possible even to shorten the operation by proceeding at once from the trigrams to the hexagrams, according to what we find in Section i, paragraph 2:—

'A strong and a weak line were manipulated together (till there were the 8 trigrams), and those 8 trigrams were added each to itself and to all the others (till the 64 hexagrams were formed).'

*Who first multiplied the figures to 64?* It is a moot question who first multiplied the figures from the trigrams universally ascribed to Fû-hsî to the 64 hexagrams of the Yî The more common view is that it was

---

[16] *Kâu-ʒze*, called *Kâu* Tun-î and *Kâu* Mâu-shuh, and, still more commonly, from the rivulet near which was his favourite residence, *Kâu* Lien-*khî*. Mayers (Chinese Reader's Manual, p. 23) says:—'He held various offices of state, and was for many years at the head of a galaxy of scholars who sought for instruction in matters of philosophy and research:—second only to *Kû* Hsî in literary repute.'

king Wăn; but *Kû* Hsî, when he was questioned on the subject, rather inclined to hold that Fû-hsî had multiplied them himself, but declined to say whether he thought that their names were as old as the figures themselves, or only dated from the twelfth century B.C.[17] I will not venture to controvert his opinion about the multiplication of the figures, but I must think that the names, as we have them now, were from king Wăn.

*Why the figures were not continued after 64.* No Chinese writer has tried to explain why the framers stopped with the 64 hexagrams, instead of going on to 128 figures of 7 lines, 256 of 8, 512 of 9, and so on indefinitely. No reason can be given for it, but the cumbrousness of the result, and the impossibility of dealing, after the manner of king Wăn, with such a mass of figures.

(iii) The 73rd paragraph of Section i, with but one paragraph between it and the two others which we have been considering, gives what may be considered a third account of the origin of the lineal figures:—

'Heaven produced the spirit-like things (the tortoise and the divining plant), and the sages took advantage of them. (The operations of) heaven and earth are marked by so many changes and transformations, and the sages imitated them (by means of the Yî). Heaven hangs out its (brilliant) figures, from which are seen good fortune and bad, and the sages made their emblematic interpretations accordingly. The Ho gave forth the scheme or map, and the Lo gave forth the writing, of (both of) which the sages took advantage.'

The words with which we have at present to do are 'The Ho (that is, the Yellow River) gave forth the Map.' This map, according to tradition and popular belief, contained a scheme which served as a model to Fû-hsî in making his 8 trigrams. Apart from this passage in the Yî King, we know that Confucius believed in such a map, or spoke at least as if he did.[18] In the 'Record of Rites' it is said that 'the map was borne by a horse;'[19] and the thing, whatever it was, is mentioned in the Shû as still preserved at court, among other curiosities, in B.C. 1079.[20] The story of it, as now current, is this, that 'a dragon-horse' issued from the Yellow River, bearing on its back an arrangement of marks, from which Fû-hsî got the idea of the trigrams.

All this is so evidently fabulous that it seems a waste of time to

---

[17] *Kû*-ʒze *Kh*wan shû, or Digest of Works of *Kû*-ʒze, chap. 26 (the first chapter on the Yî), art. 16.
[18] Analects IX, viii.
[19] Lî *Kî* VIII, iv, 16.
[20] Shû V, xxii, 19.

enter into any details about it. My reason for doing so is a wish to take advantage of the map in giving such a statement of the rules observed in interpreting the figures as is necessary in this Introduction.

*The form of the River Map.* The map that was preserved, it has been seen, in the eleventh century B.C., afterwards perished, and though there was much speculation about its form from the time that the restoration of the ancient classics was undertaken in the Han dynasty, the first delineation of it given to the public was in the reign of Hui Ʒung of the Sung dynasty (A. D. 1101-1125).[21] The most approved scheme of it is the following:—

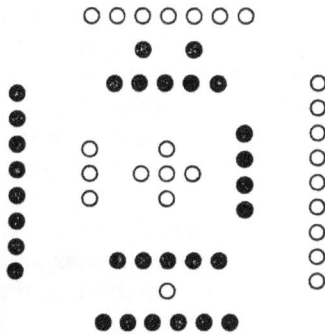

It will be observed that the markings in this scheme are small circles, pretty nearly equally divided into dark and light. All of them whose numbers are odd are light circles, 1, 3, 5, 7, 9; and all of them whose numbers are even are dark,—2, 4, 6, 8, 10. This is given as the origin of what is said in paragraphs 49 and 50 of Section i about the numbers of heaven and earth. The difference in the colour of the circles occasioned the distinction of them and of what they signify into Yin and Yang, the dark and the bright, the moon-like and the sun-like; for the sun is called the Great Brightness (Thâi Yang), and the moon the Great Obscurity (Thâi Yin). I shall have more to say in the next chapter on the application of these names. Fû-hsî in making the trigrams, and king Wăn, if it was he who first multiplied them to the 64 hexagrams, found it convenient to use lines instead of the circles:—the whole line (———) for the bright circle (O), and the divided line (— —) for the dark (●). The first, the third, and the fifth lines in a hexagram, if they are 'correct' as it is called, should all be whole, and the second, fourth, and sixth lines should all be divided. Yang lines are strong (or hard), and Yin lines are weak (or soft). The former indicate vigour and

---

[21] See Mayers' Chinese Reader's Manual, pp. 56, 57.

authority; the latter, feebleness and submission. It is the part of the former to command; of the latter to obey.

The lines, moreover, in the two trigrams that make up the hexagrams, and characterise the subjects which they represent, are related to one another by their position, and have their significance modified accordingly. The first line and the fourth, the second and the fifth, the third and the sixth are all correlates; and to make the correlation perfect the two members of it should be lines of different qualities, one whole and the other divided. And, finally, the middle lines of the trigrams, the second and fifth, that is, of the hexagrams, have a peculiar value and force. If we have a whole line ⟨——⟩ in the fifth place, and a divided line ⟨— —⟩ in the second, or vice versâ, the correlation is complete. Let the subject of the fifth be the sovereign or a commander-in-chief, according to the name and meaning of the hexagram, then the subject of the second will be an able minister or a skilful officer, and the result of their mutual action will be most beneficial and successful. It is specially important to have a clear idea of the name of the hexagram, and of the subject or state which it is intended to denote. The significance of all the lines comes thus to be of various application, and will differ in different hexagrams.

I have thus endeavoured to indicate how the lineal figures were formed, and the principal rules laid down for the interpretation of them. The details are wearying, but my position is like that of one who is called on to explain an important monument of architecture, very bizarre in its conception and execution. A plainer, simpler structure might have answered the purpose better, but the architect had his reasons for the plan and style which he adopted. If the result of his labours be worth expounding, we must not grudge the study necessary to detect his processes of thought, nor the effort and time required to bring the minds of others into sympathy with his.

My own opinion, as I have intimated, is, that the second, account of the origin of the trigrams and hexagrams is the true one. However the idea of the whole and divided lines arose in the mind of the first framer, we must start from them; and then, manipulating them in the manner described, we arrive, very easily, at all the lineal figures, and might proceed to multiply them to billions. We cannot tell who devised the third account of their formation from the map or scheme on the dragon-horse of the, Yellow River.[22] Its object, no doubt, was to impart a supernatural character to the trigrams and produce a religious veneration for them. It may be doubted whether the scheme as it is now fashioned be the correct one,—such as it was in the *K*âu dynasty. The

---

[22] Certainly it was not Confucius. See on the authorship of the Appendixes, and especially of Appendix III, in the next chapter.

paragraph where it is mentioned, goes on to say—'The Lo produced the writing.' This writing was a scheme of the same character as the Ho map, but on the back of a tortoise, which emerged from the river Lo, and showed it to the Great Yü, when he was engaged in his celebrated work of draining off the waters of the flood, as related in the Shû. To the hero sage it suggested 'the Great Plan,' an interesting but mystical document of the same classic, 'a Treatise,' according to Gaubil, 'of Physics, Astrology, Divination, Morals, Politics, and Religion,' the great model for the government of the kingdom. The accepted representation of this writing is the following:—

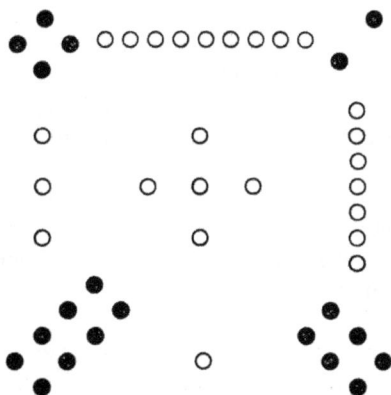

But substituting numbers for the number of marks, we have

| 4 | 9 | 2 |
|---|---|---|
| 3 | 5 | 7 |
| 8 | 1 | 6 |

This is nothing but the arithmetical puzzle, in which the numbers from 1 to 9 are arranged so as to make 15 in whatever way we add them.[23] If we had the original form of 'the River Map,' we should probably find it a numerical trifle, not more difficult, not more supernatural, than this magic square.

3. Let us return to the Yî of *K*âu, which, as I have said above on p. 25, contains, under each of the 64 hexagrams, a brief essay of a moral, social, or political character, symbolically expressed.

---

[23] For this dissection, which may also be called reductio ad absurdum, of the Lo writing, I was indebted first to P. Regis. See his Y-King I, p. 60. But *K*û Hsî also has got it in the Appendix to his 'Lessons on the Yî for the Young.'

*State of the country in time of king Wăn.* To understand it, it will be necessary to keep in mind the circumstances in which king Wăn addressed himself to the study of the lineal figures. The kingdom, under the sovereigns of the Yin or Shang dynasty, was utterly disorganised and demoralised. A brother of the reigning king thus described its condition:—

'The house of Yin can no longer exercise rule over the land. The great deeds of our founder were displayed in a former age, but through mad addiction to drink we have destroyed the effects of his virtue. The people, small and great, are given to highway robberies, villainies, and treachery. The nobles and officers imitate one another in violating the laws. There is no certainty that criminals will be apprehended. The lesser people rise up and commit violent outrages on one another. The dynasty of Yin is sinking in ruin; its condition is like that of one crossing a large stream, who can find neither ford nor bank.'[24]

*The character of the monarch.* This miserable state of the nation was due very much to the character and tyranny of the monarch. When the son of Wăn took the field against him, he thus denounced him in 'a Solemn Declaration' addressed to all the states:—

'Shâu, the king of Shang, treats all virtue with contemptuous slight, and abandons himself to wild idleness and irreverence. He has cut himself off from Heaven, and brought enmity between himself and the people. He cut through the leg-bones of those who were wading in a (winter-)morning he cut out the heart of the good man.[25] His power has been shown in killing and murdering. His honours and confidence are given to the villainous and bad. He has driven from him his instructors and guardians. He has thrown to the winds the statutes and penal laws. He neglects the sacrifices to Heaven and Earth. He has discontinued the offerings in the ancestral temple. He makes (cruel) contrivances of wonderful device and extraordinary ingenuity to please his wife.[26]— God will no longer bear with him, but with a curse is sending down his

---

[24] The Shû IV, xi, 1, 2.

[25] These were well-known instances of Shâu's wanton cruelty. Observing some people one winter's day wading through a stream, he ordered their legs to be cut through at the shank-bone, that he might see the marrow which could so endure the cold. 'The good man' was a relative of his own, called Pî-kan. Having enraged Shâu by the sternness of his rebukes, the tyrant ordered his heart to be cut out, that he might see the structure of a sage's heart.

[26] We do not know what these contrivances were. But to please his wife, the infamous Tâ-*kî*, Shâu had made 'the Heater' and, 'the Roaster,' two instruments of torture. The latter was a copper pillar laid above a pit of burning charcoal, and made slippery; culprits were forced to walk along it.

ruin.'[27]

*The lords of Kâu; and especially king Wăn.* Such was the condition of the nation, such the character of the sovereign. Meanwhile in the west of the kingdom, in a part of what is now the province of Shen-hsî, lay the principality of *K*âu, the lords of which had long been distinguished for their ability, and virtue. Its present chief, now known to us as king Wăn, was *Kh*ang, who had succeeded to his father in B. C. 1185. He was not only lord of *K*âu, but had come to be a sort of viceroy over a great part of the kingdom. Equally distinguished in peace and war, a model of all that was good and attractive, he conducted himself with remarkable wisdom and self-restraint. Princes and people would have rejoiced to follow him to attack the tyrant, but he shrank from exposing himself to the charge of being disloyal. At last the jealous suspicion of Shâu was aroused. Wăn, as has been already stated, was thrown into prison in B. C. 1143, and the order for his death might arrive at any moment. Then it was that he occupied himself with the lineal figures.

The use of those figures—of the trigrams at least—had long been practised for the purposes of divination. The employment of the divining stalks is indicated in 'the Counsels of the Great Yü,' one of the earliest Books of the Shû,[28] and a whole section in 'the Great Plan,' also a Book of the Shû, and referred to the times of the Hsiâ dynasty, describes how 'doubts were to be examined' by means of the tortoise-shell and the stalks.[29] Wăn could not but be familiar with divination as an institution of his country.[30] Possibly it occurred to him that nothing was more likely to lull the suspicions of his dangerous enemy than the study of the figures; and if his keepers took notice of what he was doing, they would smile at his lines, and the sentences which he appended to them.

*King Wăn in prison, occupied with the lineal figures.* I like to think of the lord of *K*âu, when incarcerated in Yû-lî, with the 64 figures arranged before him. Each hexagram assumed a mystic meaning, and glowed with a deep significance. He made it tell him of the qualities of various objects of nature, or of the principles of human society, or of the condition, actual and possible, of the kingdom. He named the figures, each by a term descriptive of the idea with which he had connected it in his mind, and then he proceeded to set that idea forth, now with a note of exhortation, now with a note of warning. It was an

---

[27] The Shû V, i, Sect. iii, 2, 3.

[28] Shû II, ii, 18.

[29] Shû V, iv, 20-31.

[30] In the Book of Poetry we have Wăn's grandfather (Than-fû, III, i, ode 3, 3) divining, and his son (king Wû, III, i, ode 10. 7) doing the same.

attempt to restrict the follies of divination within the bounds of reason. The last but one of the Appendixes bears the name of 'Sequence of the Diagrams.' I shall have to speak of it more at length in the next chapter. I only remark at present that it deals, feebly indeed, with the names of the hexagrams in harmony with what I have said about them, and tries to account for the order in which they follow one another. It does all this, not critically as if it needed to be established, but in the way of expository statement, relating that about which there was no doubt in the mind of the author.

*Work of the duke of Kâu on the separate lines.* But all the work of prince *Kh*ang or king Wăn in the Yî thus amounts to no more than 64 short paragraphs. We do not know what led his son Tan to enter into his work and complete it as he did. Tan was a patriot, a hero, a legislator, and a philosopher. Perhaps he took the lineal figures in hand as a tribute of filial duty. What had been done for the whole hexagram he would do for each line, and make it clear that all the six lines 'bent one way their precious influence,' and blended their rays in the globe of light which his father had made each figure give forth. But his method strikes us as singular. Each line seemed to become living, and suggested some phenomenon in nature or some case of human experience, from which the wisdom or folly, the luckiness or unluckiness, indicated by it could be inferred. It cannot be said that the duke carried out his plan in a way likely to interest any one but a hsien shăng who is a votary of divination, and admires the style of its oracles. According to our notions, a framer of emblems should be a good deal of a poet, but those of the Yî only make us think of a dryasdust. Out of more than 350, the greater number are only grotesque. We do not recover from the feeling of disappointment till we remember that both father and son had to write 'according to the trick,' after the manner of diviners, as if this lineal augury had been their profession.

*The seventh hexagram.* 4. At length I come to illustrate what I have said on the subject-matter of the Yî by an example. It shall be the treatment of the seventh hexagram ⚎, which king Wăn named Sze, meaning Hosts. The character is also explained as meaning 'multitudes;' and in fact, in a feudal kingdom, the multitudes of the people were all liable to become its army, when occasion required, and the 'host' and the 'population' might be interchangeable terms. As Froude expresses it in the introductory chapter to his History of England, 'Every man was regimented somewhere.'

The hexagram Sze is composed of the two trigrams Khan ☵ and Khwăn ☷, exhibiting waters collected on the earth; and in other symbolisms besides that of the Yî, waters indicate assembled multitudes of men. The waters on which the mystical Babylon sits in the Apocalypse are explained as 'peoples and multitudes and nations and tongues.' I do not positively affirm that it was by this interpretation of the trigrams that king Wăn saw in ☰☷ the feudal hosts of his country collected, for neither from him nor his son do we learn, by their direct affirmation, that they had any acquaintance with, the trigrams of Fû-hsî. The name which he gave the figure shows, however, that he saw in it the feudal hosts in the field. How shall their expedition be conducted that it may come to a successful issue?

Looking again at the figure, we see that it is made up of five divided lines, and of one undivided. The undivided line occupies the central place in the lower trigram,—the most important place, next to the fifth, in the whole hexagram. It will represent, in the language of the commentators, 'the lord of the whole figure;' and the parties represented by the other lines may be expected to be of one mind with him or obedient to him. He must be the leader of the hosts. If he were on high, in the fifth place, he would be the sovereign of the kingdom. This is what king Wăn says:—

'Sze indicates how (in the case which it supposes), with firmness and correctness, and (a leader of) age and experience, there will be good fortune and no error.'

This is a good auspice. Let us see how the duke of *K*âu expands it. He says:—

'The first line, divided, shows the host going forth according to the rules (for such a movement). If those (rules) be not good, there will be evil.'

We are not told what the rules for a military expedition were. Some commentators understand them of the reasons justifying the movement,—that it should be to repress and punish disorder and rebellion. Others, with more likelihood, take them to be the discipline or rules laid down to be observed by the troops. The line is divided, a weak line in a strong place, 'not correct:' this justifies the caution given in the duke's second sentence.

The Text goes on:—

'The second line, undivided, shows (the leader) in the midst of the hosts. There will be good fortune and no error. The king has thrice conveyed to him his charge.'

This does not need any amplification. The duke saw in the strong line the symbol of the leader, who enjoyed the full confidence of his sovereign, and whose authority admitted of no opposition.

On the third line it is said:—

'The third line, divided, shows how the hosts may possibly have many commanders:—(in such a case) there will be evil.'

The third place is odd, and should be occupied by a strong line, instead of which we have a weak line in it. But it is at the top of the lower trigram, and its subject should be in office or activity. There is suggested the idea that its subject has vaulted over the second line, and wishes to share in the command and honour of him who has been appointed sole commander-in-chief. The lesson in the previous line is made of none effect. We have a divided authority in the expedition. The result can only be evil.

On the fourth line the duke wrote:—

'The fourth line, divided, shows the hosts in retreat: there is no error.'

The line is also weak, and victory cannot be expected but in the fourth place a weak line is in its correct position, and its subject will do what is right in his circumstances. He will retreat, and a retreat is for him the part of wisdom. When safely affected, where advance would be disastrous, a retreat is as glorious as victory.

Under the fifth line we read:—

'The fifth line, divided, shows birds in the fields which it is advantageous to seize (and destroy). There will be no error. If the oldest son lead the host, and younger men be (also) in command, however firm and correct he may be, there will be evil.'

We have an intimation in this passage that only defensive war, or war waged by the rightful authority to put down rebellion and lawlessness, is right. The 'birds in the fields' are emblematic of plunderers and invaders, whom it will be well to destroy. The fifth line symbolises the chief authority, but here he is weak or humble, and has given all power and authority to execute judgment into the hands of the commander-in-chief, who is the oldest son; and in the subject of line 3 we have an example of the younger men who would cause evil if allowed to share his power.

Finally, on the sixth line the duke wrote:—

'The topmost line, divided, shows the great ruler delivering his charges (to the men who have distinguished themselves), appointing some to be rulers of states, and others to be chiefs of clans. But small men should not be employed (in such positions).'

The action of the hexagram has been gone through. The expedition has been conducted to a successful end. The enemy has been subdued. His territories are at the disposal of the conqueror. The commander-in-chief has done his part well. His sovereign, 'the great ruler,' comes upon the scene, and rewards the officers who have been conspicuous by their bravery and skill, conferring on them rank and lands. But he is warned to have respect in doing so to their moral character. Small men, of ordinary or less than ordinary character, may be rewarded with riches and certain honours; but land and the welfare of its population should not be given into the hands of any who are not equal to the responsibility of such a trust.

The above is a specimen of what I have called the essays that make up the Yî of *K*âu. So would king Wăn and his son have had all military expeditions conducted in their country 3000 years ago. It seems to me that the principles which they lay down might find a suitable application in the modern warfare of our civilised and Christian Europe. The inculcation of such lessons cannot have been without good effect in China during the long course of its history.

Sze is a fair specimen of its class. From the other 63 hexagrams lessons are deduced, for the most part equally good and striking. But why, it may be asked, why should they be conveyed to us by such an array of lineal figures, and in such a farrago of emblematic representations? It is not for the foreigner to insist on such a question. The Chinese have not valued them the less because of the antiquated dress in which their lessons are arrayed. Hundreds of their commentators have evolved and developed their meaning with a minuteness of detail and felicity of illustration that leave nothing to be desired. It is for foreign students of Chinese to gird up their loins for the mastery of the book instead of talking about it as mysterious and all but inexplicable.

Granting, however, that the subject-matter of the Yî is what has been described, very valuable for its practical wisdom, but not drawn up from an abysmal deep of philosophical speculation, it may still be urged, 'But in all this we find nothing to justify the name of the book as Yî King, the "Classic of Changes." Is there not something more, higher or deeper, in the Appendixes that have been ascribed to Confucius, whose authority is certainly not inferior to that of king Wăn, or the duke of *K*âu?' To reply fully to this question will require another chapter.

## CHAPTER III. THE APPENDIXES.

*Subjects of the chapter*. 1. Two things have to be considered in this chapter:—the authorship of the Appendixes, and their contents. The Text is ascribed, without dissentient voice, to king Wăn, the founder of the *K*âu dynasty, and his son Tan, better known as the duke of *K*âu; and I have, in the preceding chapters, given reasons for accepting that view. As regards the portion ascribed to king Wăn, the evidence of the third of the Appendixes and the statement of Sze-mâ *Kh*ien are as positive as could be desired; and as regards that ascribed to his son, there is no ground for calling in question the received tradition. The Appendixes have all been ascribed to Confucius, though not with entirely the same unanimity. Perhaps I have rather intimated my own opinion that this view cannot be sustained. I have pointed out that, even if it be true, between six and seven centuries elapsed after the Text of the classic appeared before the Appendixes were written; and I have said that, considering this fact, I cannot regard its two parts as a homogeneous whole, or as constituting one book in the ordinary acceptation of that name. Before entering on the question of the authorship, a very brief statement of the nature and number of the Appendixes will be advantageous.

*Number and Nature of the Appendixes*. 2. They are reckoned to be ten, and called the Shih Yî or 'Ten Wings.' They are in reality not so many; but the Text is divided into two sections, called the Upper and Lower, or, as we should say, the first and second, and then the commentary on each section is made to form a separate Appendix. I have found it more convenient in the translation which follows to adopt a somewhat different arrangement.

My first Appendix, in two sections, embraces the first and second 'wings,' consisting of remarks on the paragraphs by king Wăn in the two parts of the Text.

My second Appendix, in two sections, embraces the third and fourth 'wings,' consisting of remarks on the symbolism of the duke of *K*âu in his explanation of the individual lines of the hexagrams.

My third Appendix, in two sections, embraces the fifth and sixth 'wings,' which bear the name in Chinese of 'Appended Sentences,' and constitute what is called by many 'the Great Treatise.' Each wing has been divided into twelve chapters of very different length, and I have followed this arrangement in my sections. This is the most important Appendix. It has less of the nature of commentary than the previous four wings. While explaining much of what is found in the Text, it diverges to the origin of the trigrams, the methods pursued in the practice of divination, the rise of many arts in the progress of civilisation, and other subjects.

My fourth Appendix, also in two sections, forms the seventh 'wing.' It is confined to an amplification of the expositions of the first and second hexagrams by king Wăn and his son, purporting to show how they may be interpreted of man's nature and doings.

My fifth Appendix is the eighth 'wing,' called 'Discourses on the Trigrams.' It treats of the different arrangement of these in respect of the seasons of the year and the cardinal points by Fû-hsî and king Wăn. It contains also one paragraph, which might seem to justify the view that there is a mythology in the Yî.

My sixth Appendix, in two sections, is the ninth 'wing,'—'a Treatise on the Sequence of the Hexagrams,' intended to trace the connexion of meaning between them in the order in which they follow one another in the Text of king Wăn.

My seventh Appendix is the tenth 'wing,' an exhibition of the meaning of the 64 hexagrams, not taken in succession, but promiscuously and at random, as they approximate to or are opposed to one another in meaning.

*The authorship of the Appendixes.* 3. Such are the Appendixes of the Yî King. We have to enquire next who wrote them, and especially whether it be possible to accept the dictum that they were all written by Confucius. If they have come down to us, bearing unmistakeably the stamp of the mind and pencil of the great sage, we cannot but receive them with deference, not to say with reverence. If, on the contrary, it shall appear that with great part of them he had nothing to do, and that it is not certain that any part of them is from him, we shall feel entirely at liberty to exercise our own judgment on their contents, and weigh them in the balances of our reason.

*There is no superscription of Confucius on any of the Appendixes.* None of the Appendixes, it is to be observed, bear the superscription of Confucius. There is not a single sentence in any one of them ascribing it to him. I gave in the first chapter, on p. 18, the earliest testimony that these treatises were produced by him. It is that of Sze-mâ *Kh*ien, whose 'Historical Records' must have appeared about the year 100 before our era. He ascribes all the Appendixes, except the last two of them, which he does not mention at all, expressly to Confucius; and this, no doubt, was the common belief in the fourth century after the sage's death.

*The third and fourth Appendixes evidently not from Confucius.* But when we look for ourselves into the third and fourth Appendixes—the fifth, sixth, and seventh 'wings'—both of which are specified by *Kh*ien, we find it impossible to receive his statement about them. What is remarkable in both parts of the third is, the frequent occurrence of the formula, 'The Master said,' familiar to all readers of the Confucian Analects. Of course, the sentence following that formula, or the paragraph covered by it, was, in the judgment of the writer, in the language of Confucius; but what shall we say of the portions preceding and following? If he were the author of them, he would not thus be distinguishing himself from himself. The formula occurs in the third Appendix at least twenty-three times. Where we first meet with it, *Kû Hsî* has a note to the effect that 'the Appendixes having been all made by Confucius, he ought not to be himself introducing the formula, "The Master said;" and that it may be presumed, wherever it occurs, that it is a subsequent addition to the Master's text.' One instance will show the futility of this attempt to solve the difficulty. The tenth chapter of Section i commences with the 59th paragraph:—

'In the Yî there are four things characteristic of the way of the sages. We should set the highest value on its explanations, to guide us in speaking; on its changes, for the initiation of our movements; on its emblematic figures, for definite action, as in the construction of implements; and on its prognostications, for our practice of divination.'

This is followed by seven paragraphs expanding its statements, and we come to the last one of the chapter which says,—'The Master said, "Such is the import of the statement that there are four things in the Yî, characteristic of the way of the sages."' I cannot understand how it could be more fully conveyed to us that the compiler or compilers of this Appendix were distinct from the Master whose words they quoted, as it suited them, to confirm or illustrate their views.

In the fourth Appendix, again, we find a similar occurrence of the formula of quotation. It is much shorter than the third, and the phrase, 'The Master said,' does not come before us so frequently; but in the thirty-six paragraphs that compose the first section we meet with it six times.

Moreover, the first three paragraphs of this Appendix are older than its compilation, which could not have taken place till after the death of Confucius, seeing it professes to quote his words. They are taken in fact from a narrative of the 3o *K*wan, as having been spoken by a marchioness-dowager of Lû fourteen years before Confucius was born. To account for this is a difficult task for the orthodox critics among the Chinese literati. *Kû Hsî* attempts to perform it in this way:— that anciently there was the explanation given in these paragraphs of the four adjectives employed by king Wăn to give the significance of the first hexagram; that it was employed by Mû *K*iang of Lû; and that Confucius also availed himself of it, while the chronicler used, as be does below, the phraseology of 'The Master said,' to distinguish the real words of the sage from such ancient sayings. But who was 'the chronicler?' No one can tell. The legitimate conclusion from *Kû*'s criticism is, that so much of the Appendix as is preceded by 'The Master said' is from Confucius,—so much and no more. I am thus obliged to come to the conclusion that Confucius had nothing to do with the composition of these two Appendixes, and that they were not put together till after his death. I have no pleasure in differing from the all but unanimous opinion of Chinese critics and commentators. What is called 'the destructive criticism' has no attractions for me; but when an opinion depends on the argument adduced to support it, and that argument turns out to be of no weight, you can no longer set your seal to this, that the opinion is true. This is the position in which an examination of the internal evidence as to the authorship of the third and fourth Appendixes has placed me. Confucius could not be their author. This conclusion weakens the confidence which we have been accustomed to place in the view that 'the ten wings' were to be ascribed to him unhesitatingly. The view has broken down in the case of three of them;—possibly there is no sound reason for holding the Confucian origin of the other seven.

*Bearing of the conclusion as to the third and fourth on the other Appendixes.* I cannot henceforth maintain that origin save with bated breath. This, however, can be said for the first two Appendixes in my arrangement, that there is no evidence against their being Confucian like the fatal formula, 'The Master said.' So it is with a good part of my fifth Appendix; but the concluding paragraphs of it, as well as the seventh Appendix, and the sixth also in a less degree, seem too trivial to be the production of the great man. As a translator of every sentence both in the Text and the Appendixes, I confess my sympathy with P. Regis, when he condenses the fifth Appendix into small space, holding that the 8th and following paragraphs are not worthy to be translated. 'They contain,' he says, 'nothing but the mere enumeration of things, some of which may be called Yang, and others Yin, without any other cause for so thinking being given. Such a method of procedure would be unbecoming any philosopher, and it cannot be denied to be unworthy of Confucius, the chief of philosophers.'[31]

I could not characterise Confucius as 'the chief of philosophers,' though he was a great moral philosopher, and has been since he went out and in among his disciples, the best teacher of the Chinese nation. But from the first time my attention was directed to the Yî, I regretted that he had stooped to write the parts of the Appendixes now under remark. It is a relief not to be obliged to receive them as his. Even the better treatises have no other claim to that character besides the voice of tradition, first heard nearly 400 years after his death.

4. I return to the Appendixes, and will endeavour to give a brief, but sufficient, account of their contents.

*The first Appendix.* The first bears in Chinese the name of Thwan *Kwan,* 'Treatise on the Thwan,' thwan being the name given to the

---

[31] Regis' Y-King, vol. ii, p 576.

paragraphs in which Wăn expresses his sense of the significance of the hexagrams. He does not tell us why he attaches to each hexagram such and such a meaning, nor why he predicates good fortune or bad fortune in connexion with it, for he speaks oracularly, after the manner of a diviner. It is the object of the writer of this Appendix to show the processes of king Wăn's thoughts in these operations, how he looked at the component trigrams with their symbolic intimations, their attributes and qualities, and their linear composition, till he could not think otherwise of the figures than he did. All these considerations are sometimes taken into account, and sometimes even one of them is deemed sufficient. In this way some technical characters appear which are not found in the Text. The lines, for instance, and even whole trigrams are distinguished as kang and zâu, hard or strong' and 'weak or soft.' The phrase Kwei-shăn, 'spirits,' or 'spiritual beings,' occurs, but has not its physical signification of 'the contracting and expanding energies or operations of nature.' The names Yin and Yang, mentioned above on p. 29, do not present themselves.

I delineated, on p. 26, the eight trigrams of Fû-hsî, and gave their names., with the natural objects they are said to represent, but did. not mention the attributes, the virtues, ascribed to them. Let me submit here a table of them, with those qualities, and the points of the compass to which they are referred. I must do this because king Wăn made a change in the geographical arrangement of them, to which reference is made perhaps in his text and certainly in this treatise. He also is said to have formed an entirely different theory as to the things represented by the trigrams, which it will be well to give now, though it belongs properly to the fifth Appendix.

FÛ-HSÎ'S TRIGRAMS.

| 1 | 2 | 3 | 4 | 5 | 6 | 7 | 8 |
|---|---|---|---|---|---|---|---|
| *khien* | tui | lî | *kăn* | sun | khân | kăn | khwăn |
| Heaven, the sky. | Water, collected as in a marsh or lake. | Fire, as in lightning; the sun. | Thunder. | The wind ; wood. | Water, as in rain, clouds, springs, streams, and defiles. The moon. | Hills, or mountains. | The earth. |
| S. | S. E. | E. | N. E. | S.W. | W. | N.W. | N. |
| Untiring strength; power. | Pleasure; complacent satisfaction. | Brightness ; elegance. | Moving, exciting power. | Flexibility ; penetration. | Peril; difficulty. | Resting ; the act of arresting. | Capaciousness ; submission. |

The natural objects and phenomena thus represented are found up and down in the Appendixes. It is impossible to believe that the several objects were assigned to the several figures on any principles of science, for there is no indication of science in the matter: it is difficult even to suppose that they were assigned on any comprehensive scheme of thought. Why are tui and khân used to represent water in different conditions, while khân, moreover, represents the moon? How is sun set apart to represent things so different as wind and wood? At a very early time the Chinese spoke of 'the five elements,' meaning water, fire, wood, metal, and earth; but the trigrams were not made to indicate them, and it is the general opinion that there is no reference to them in the Yî.[32]

Again, the attributes assigned to the trigrams are learned mainly from this Appendix and the fifth. We do not readily get familiar with them, nor easily accept them all. It is impossible for us to tell whether they were a part of the jargon of divination before king Wăn, or had grown up between his time and that of the author of the Appendixes.

King Wăn altered the arrangement of the trigrams so that not one of them should stand at the same point of the compass as in the ancient plan. He made them also representative of certain relations among themselves, as if they composed a family of parents and children. It will be sufficient at present to give a table of his scheme.

KING WĂN'S TRIGRAMS.

| 1 | 2 | 3 | 4 | 5 | 6 | 7 | 8 |
|---|---|---|---|---|---|---|---|
| lî | sun | kăn | kăn | khân | khien | tui | khwăn |
| Second daughter. | Oldest daughter. | Oldest son. | Youngest son. | Second son. | Father. | Youngest daughter. | Mother. |
| S. | S.E. | E. | N.E. | N. | N.W. | W. | S.W. |

There is thus before us the apparatus with which the writer of the Appendix accomplishes his task. Let me select one of the shortest instances of his work. The fourteenth hexagram is ☰, called Tâ Yû, and meaning 'Possessing in great abundance.' King Wăn saw in it the symbol of a government prosperous and realising all its proper objects; but all that he wrote on it was 'Tâ Yû (indicates) great progress and success.' Unfolding that view of its significance, the Appendix

---

[32] See *K*âo Yî's Hâi Yü ʒhung Khâo, Book I, art. 3 (1790).

says:—

'In Tâ Yû the weak (line) has the place of honour, is grandly central, and (the strong lines) above and below respond to it. Hence comes its name of "Possession of what is great." The attributes (of its constituent trigrams, *kh*ien and lî) are strength and vigour, elegance and brightness. (The ruling line in it) responds to (the ruling line in the symbol of) heaven, and its actings are (consequently all) at the proper times. Thus it is that it is said to indicate great progress and success.'

In a similar way the paragraphs on all the other 63 hexagrams are gone through; and, for the most part, with success. The conviction grows upon the student that the writer has on the whole apprehended the mind of king Wăn.

*The name Kwei-shăn.* I stated, on p. 42, that the name kwei-shăn occurs in this Appendix. It has not yet, however, received the semi-physical, semi-metaphysical signification which the comparatively modern scholars of the Sung dynasty give to it. There are two passages where it is found;—the second paragraph on *Kh*ien, the fifteenth hexagram, and the third on Făng, the fifty-fifth. By consulting them the reader will be able to form an opinion for himself. The term kwei denotes specially the human spirit disembodied, and shăn is used for spirits whose seat is in heaven. I do not see my way to translate them, when used binomially together, otherwise than by spiritual beings or spiritual agents.

*K*û Hsî once had the following question suggested by the second of these passages put to him:—'Kwei-shăn is a name for the traces of making and transformation; but when it is said that (the interaction of) heaven and earth is now vigorous and abundant, and now dull and void, growing and diminishing according to the seasons, that constitutes the traces of making and transformation; why should the writer further speak of the Kwei-shăn?' He replied, 'When he uses the style of "heaven and earth," he is speaking of the result generally; but in ascribing it to the Kwei-shăn, he is representing the traces of their effective interaction, as if there were men (that is, some personal agency) bringing it about.'[33] This solution merely explains the language away. When we come to the fifth Appendix, we shall understand better the views of the period when these treatises were produced.

---

[33] See the 'Collected Comments' on hexagram 55 in the Khang-hsî edition of the Yî (App. I). 'The traces of making and transformation' mean the ever changing phenomena of growth and decay. Our phrase 'Vestiges of Creation' might be used to translate the Chinese characters. See the remarks of the late Dr. Medhurst on the hexagrams 15 and 55 in his 'Dissertation on the Theology of the Chinese,' pp. 107-112. In hexagram 15, Canon McClatchie for kwei-shăn gives gods and demons;' in hexagram 55, the Demon-gods.'

The single character shăn is used in explaining the thwan on Kwân, the twentieth hexagram, where we read:—

'In Kwân we see the spirit-like way of heaven, through which the four seasons proceed without error. The sages, in accordance with (this) spirit-like way, laid down their instructions, and all under heaven yield submission to them.'

The author of the Appendix delights to dwell on the changing phenomena taking place between heaven and earth, and which he attributes to their interaction; and he was penetrated evidently with a sense of the harmony between the natural and spiritual worlds. It is this sense, indeed, which vivifies both the thwan and the explanation of them.

The second Appendix. 5. We proceed to the second Appendix, which professes to do for the duke of *K*âu's symbolical exposition of the several lines what the Thwan *K*wan does for the entire figures. The work here, however, is accomplished with less trouble and more briefly. The whole bears the name of Hsiang *K*wan, 'Treatise on the Symbols' or 'Treatise on the Symbolism (of the Yî).' If there were reason to think that it came in any way from Confucius, I should fancy that I saw him sitting with a select class of his disciples around him. They read the duke's Text column after column, and the master drops now a word or two, and now a sentence or two, that illuminate the meaning. The disciples take notes on their tablets, or store his remarks in their memories, and by and by they write them out with the whole of the, Text or only so much of it as is necessary. Whoever was the original lecturer, the Appendix, I think, must have grown up in this way.

It would not be necessary to speak of it at greater length, if it were not that the six paragraphs on the symbols of the duke of *K*âu are always preceded by one which is called 'the Great Symbolism,' and treats of the trigrams composing the hexagram, how they go together to form the six-lined figure, and how their blended meaning appears in the institutions and proceedings of the great men and kings of former days, and of the superior men of all time. The paragraph is for the most part, but by no means always, in harmony with the explanation of the hexagram by king Wăn, and a place in the Thwan *K*wan would be more appropriate to it. I suppose that, because it always begins with the mention of the two symbolical trigrams, it is made, for the sake of the symmetry, to form a part of the treatise on the Symbolism of the Yî.

*The Great Symbolism.* I will give a few examples of the paragraphs of the Great Symbolism. The first hexagram ▤ is formed by a repetition of the trigram *Kh*ien ▤ representing heaven, and it is said on it:—'Heaven in its motion (gives) the idea of strength. The superior man, in accordance with this, nerves himself to ceaseless activity.'

The second hexagram ䷁ is formed by a repetition of the trigram Khwǎn ☷ ☷ representing the earth, and it is said on it:—'The capacious receptivity of the earth is what is denoted by Khwǎn. The superior man, in accordance with this, with his large virtue, supports men and things.'

The forty-fourth hexagram, called *Kâu* ䷫, is formed by the trigrams Sun ☴, representing wind, and *Kh*ien ☰ representing heaven or the sky, and it is said on it:—'(The symbol of) wind, beneath that of the sky, forms *Kâu*. In accordance with this, the sovereign distributes his charges, and promulgates his announcements throughout the four quarters (of the kingdom).'

The fifty-ninth hexagram, called Hwân ䷺ is formed by the trigrams *Kh*ân ☵, representing water, and Sun ☴, representing wind, and it is said on it:—(The symbol of) water and (that of wind) above it form Hwân. The ancient kings, in accordance with this, presented offerings to God, and established the ancestral temple.' The union of the two trigrams suggested to king Wǎn the idea of dissipation in the alienation of men from the Supreme Power, and of the minds of parents from their children; a condition which the wisdom of the ancient kings saw could best be met by the influences of religion.

One more example. The twenty-sixth hexagram, called Tâ *Khû* ䷙, is formed of the trigrams *Kh*ien, representing heaven or the sky, and Kân ☶, representing a mountain, and it is said on it:—'(The symbol of) heaven in the midst of a mountain forms Tâ *Khû*. The superior man, in accordance with this, stores largely in his memory the words of former men and their conduct, to subserve the accumulation of his virtue.' We are ready to exclaim and ask, 'Heaven, the sky, in the midst of a mountain! Can there be such a thing?' and *Kû* Hsî will tell us in reply, 'No, there cannot be such a thing in reality; but you can conceive it for the purpose of the symbolism.'

From this and the other examples adduced from the Great Symbolism, it is clear that, so far as its testimony bears on the subject, the trigrams of Fû-hsî did not receive their form and meaning with a deep intention that they should serve as the basis of a philosophical scheme concerning the constitution of heaven and earth and all that is in them. In this Appendix they are used popularly, just as one

'Finds tongues in trees, books in the running brooks,
Sermons in stones, and good in everything.'

The writer moralises from them in an edifying manner. There is ingenuity, and sometimes instruction also, in what he says, but there is no mystery. Chinese scholars and gentlemen, however, who have got some little acquaintance with western science, are fond of saying that all the truths of electricity, heat, light, and other branches of European physics, are in the eight trigrams. When asked how then they and their countrymen have been and are ignorant of those truths, they say that they have to learn them first from western books, and then, looking into the Yî, they see that they were all known to Confucius more than 2000, years ago. The vain assumption thus manifested is childish; and until the Chinese drop their hallucination about the Yî as containing all things that have ever been dreamt of in all philosophies, it will prove a stumbling-block to them, and keep them from entering on the true path of science.

*The third Appendix.* 6. We go on to the third Appendix in two sections, being the fifth and sixth 'wings,' and forming what is called 'The Great Treatise.' It will appear singular to the reader, as it has always done to myself, that neither in the Text, nor in the first two Appendixes, does the character called Yî, which gives its name to the classic, once appear. It is the symbol of 'change,' and is formed from the character for 'the sun' placed over that for 'the moon.'[34] As the sun gives place to the moon, and the moon to the sun, so is change always proceeding in the phenomena of nature and the experiences of society. We meet with the character nearly fifty times in this Appendix;—applied most commonly to the Text of our classic, so that Yî King or Yî Shû is 'the Classic or Book of Changes.' It is also applied often to the changes in the lines of the figures, made by the manipulations of divination, apart from any sentence or oracle concerning them delivered by king Wăn or his son. There is therefore the system of the Yî as well as the book of the Yî. The definition of the name which is given in one paragraph will suit them both:—'Production and reproduction is what is called (the process of) change.'[35] In nature there is no vacuum. When anything is displaced, what displaces it takes the empty room. And in the lineal figures, the strong and the weak lines push each other out.

*Harmony between the lines ever changing and the changes in external phenomena.* Now the remarkable thing asserted is, that the changes in the lines of the figures and the changes of external phenomena show a wonderful harmony and concurrence. We read:—

---

[34] 易 = 日, the sun, placed over 勿, a form of the old 𝔻 (=月), the moon.
[35] III, i, 29 (chap. 5. 6).

'The Yî was made on a principle of accordance with heaven and earth, and shows us therefore, without rent or confusion, the course (of things) in heaven and earth.'[36]

'There is a similarity between the sage and heaven and earth; and hence there is no contrariety in him to them. His knowledge embraces all things, and his course is intended to be helpful to all under the sky; and therefore he falls into no error. He acts according to the exigency of circumstances, without being carried away by their current; he rejoices in Heaven, and knows its ordinations; and hence he has no anxieties. He rests in his own (present) position, and cherishes the spirit of generous benevolence; and hence he can love (without reserve).'[37]

'(Through the Yî) he embraces, as in a mould or enclosure, the transformations of heaven and earth without any error; by an ever-varying adaptation he completes (the nature of) all things without exception; he penetrates to a knowledge of the course of day and night (and all other correlated phenomena). It is thus that his operation is spirit-like, unconditioned by place, while the changes (which he produces) are not restricted to any form.'

One more quotation:—

'The sage was able to survey all the complex phenomena under the sky. He then considered in his mind how they could be figured, and (by means of the diagrams) represented their material forms and their character.'[38]

All that is thus predicated of the sage, or ancient sages, though the writer probably had Fû-hsî in his mind, is more than sufficiently extravagant, and reminds us of the language in 'the Doctrine of the Mean,' that 'the sage, able to assist the transforming and nourishing powers of heaven and earth, may with heaven and earth form a ternion.'[39]

*Divination.* I quoted largely, in the second chapter, from this Appendix the accounts which it gives of the formation of the lineal figures. There is no occasion to return to that subject. Let us suppose the figures formed. They seem to have the significance, when looked at from certain points of view, which have been determined for us by king Wăn and the duke of *K*âu. But this does not amount to divination. How can the lines be made to serve this purpose? The Appendix professes to

---

[36] III, i, 20 (chap. 4. 1).

[37] III, i, 22.

[38] III, i, 38 (chap. 8. 1).

[39] Doctrine of the Mean, chap. xxii.

tell us.

*Ancient divination.* Before touching on the method which it describes, let me observe that divination was practised in China from a very early time. I will not say 5,200 years ago, in the days of Fû-hsî, for I cannot repress doubts of his historical personality; but as soon as we tread the borders of something like credible history, we find it existing. In the Shû King, in a document that purports to be of the twenty-third century B. C.,[40] divination by means of the tortoise-shell is mentioned; and somewhat later we find that method continuing, and also divination by the lineal figures, manipulated by means of the stalks of a plant,[41] the Ptarmica Sibirica,[42] which is still cultivated on and about the grave of Confucius, where I have myself seen it growing.

*Object of the divination.* The object of the divination, it should be acknowledged, was not to discover future events absolutely, as if they could be known beforehand,[43] but to ascertain whether certain schemes, and conditions of events contemplated by the consulter, would turn out luckily or unluckily. But for the actual practice the stalks of the plant were necessary; and I am almost afraid to write that this Appendix teaches that they were produced by Heaven of such a nature as to be fit for the purpose. 'Heaven,' it says, in the 73rd paragraph of Section i, quoted above on p. 28, 'Heaven produced the spirit-like things.' The things were the tortoise and the plant, and in paragraph 68, the same quality of being shǎn, or 'spirit-like,' is ascribed to them. Occasionally, in the field of Chinese literature, we meet with doubts as to the efficacy of divination, and the folly of expecting any revelation of the character of the future from an old tortoise-shell and a handful of withered

---

[40] The Shû II, ii, 18.

[41] The Shû V, iv, 20, 31.

[42] See Williams' Syllabic Dictionary on the character 蓍.

[43] Canon McClatchie (first paragraph of his Introduction) says:—'The Yî is regarded by the Chinese with peculiar veneration . . . . as containing a mine of knowledge, which, if it were possible to fathom it thoroughly, would, in their estimation, enable the fortunate possessor to foretell all future events.' This misstatement does not surprise me so much as that Morrison, generally accurate on such points, should say (Dictionary, Part II, i, p. 1020, on the character 易 ):—

'Of the odd and even numbers, the kwâ or lines of Fû-hsî are the visible signs; and it being assumed that these signs answer to the things signified, and from a knowledge of all the various combinations of numbers, a knowledge of all possible occurrences in nature may be previously known.' The whole article from which I take this sentence is inaccurately written. The language of the Appendix on the knowledge of the future given by the use of the Yî is often incautious, and a cursory reader may be misled; to a careful student, however, the meaning is plain. The second passage of the Shû, referred to above, treats of 'the Examination of Doubts,' and concludes thus:—'When the tortoise-shell and the stalks are both opposed to the views of men, there will be good fortune in stillness, and active operations will be unlucky.'

twigs;[44] but when this Appendix was made, the writer had not attained to so much common sense. The stalks were to him 'spirit-like,' possessed of a subtle and invisible virtue that fitted them for use in divining.

*Formation of the lineal figures by the divining stalks.* Given the stalks with such virtue, the process of manipulating them so as to form the lineal figures is described (Section i, chap. 9, parr. 49-58), but it will take the student much time and thought to master the various operations. Forty-nine stalks were employed, which were thrice manipulated for each line, so that it took eighteen manipulations to form a hexagram. The lines were determined by means of the numbers derived from the River Map or scheme. Odd numbers gave strong or undivided lines, and even numbers gave the weak or divided. An important part was played in combining the lines, and forming the hexagrams by the four emblematic symbols, to which the numbers 9, 8, 7, 6 were appropriated.[45] The figures having been formed, recourse was had for their interpretation to the thwan of king Wăn, and the emblematic sentences of the duke of *K*âu. This was all the part which numbers played in the divination by the Yî, helping the operator to make up his lineal figure. An analogy has often been asserted between the numbers of the Yî and the numbers of Pythagoras; and certainly we might make ten, and more than ten, antinomies from these Appendixes in startling agreement with the ten principia of the Pythagoreans. But if Aristotle was correct in holding that Pythagoras regarded numbers as entities, and maintained that Number was the Beginning (Principle, ἀρχή) of things, the cause of their material existence, and of their modifications and different states, then the doctrine of the philosopher

---

[44] A remarkable instance is given by Lîu *K*î (of the Ming dynasty, in the fifteenth century) in a story about Shâo Phing, who had been marquis of Tung-ling in the time of Ȝhin, but was degraded tinder Han. Having gone once to Sze-mâ Ki-*k*û, one of the most skilful diviners of the country, and wishing to know whether there would be a brighter future for him, Sze-mâ said, 'Ah! is it the way of Heaven to love any (partially)? Heaven loves only the virtuous. What intelligence is possessed by spirits? They are intelligent (only) by their connexion with men. The divining stalks are so much withered grass; the tortoise-shell is a withered bone. They are but things, and man is more intelligent than things. Why not listen to yourself instead of seeking (to learn) from things?' The whole piece is in many of the collections of Kû Wăn, or Elegant Writing.

[45] These numbers are commonly derived from the River Scheme, in the outer sides of which are the corresponding marks:— ●●●●●●, opposite to ●●; ○○○○○○○,opposite to ○; ●●●●●●●● opposite to ●●●●; and ○○○○○○○○○, opposite to ○○○. Hence the number 6 is assigned to ☷, 7 to ☶, 8 to ☵, and 9 to ☰. Hence also, in connexion with the formation of the figures by manipulation of the stalks, 9 becomes the number symbolical of the undivided line, as representing *Kh*ien ☰ and 6 of the divided line, as representing Khwăn ☷ ☷ But the late delineation of the map, as given on p. 19, renders all this uncertain, so far as the scheme is concerned. The numbers of the hsiang, however, may have been fixed, must have been fixed indeed, at an early period.

of Samos was different from that of the Yî,[46] in which numbers come in only as aids in divining to form the hexagrams. Of course all divination is vain, nor is the method of the Yî less absurd than any other. The Chinese themselves have given it up in all circles above those of the professional quacks, and yet their scholars continue to maintain the unfathomable science and wisdom of these appended treatises!

*The names Yin and Yang.* It is in this Appendix that we first meet with the names yin and yang,[47] of which I have spoken briefly on p. 29. Up to this point, instead of them, the names for the two elementary forms of the lines have been kang and zâu, which I have translated by 'strong and weak,' and which also occur here ten times. The following attempt to explain these different names appears in the fifth Appendix, paragraph 4:—

'Anciently when the sages made the Yî, it was with the design that its figures should be in conformity with the principles underlying the natures (of men and things), and the ordinances appointed (for them by Heaven). With this view they exhibited in them the way of heaven, calling (the lines) yin and yang; the way of earth, calling them the strong (or hard) and the weak (or soft); and the way of man, under the names of benevolence and righteousness. Each (trigram) embraced those three Powers, and being repeated, its full form consisted of six lines.'

However difficult it may be to make what is said here intelligible, it confirms what I have affirmed of the significance of the names yin and yang, as meaning bright and dark, derived from the properties of the sun and moon. We may use for these adjectives a variety of others, such as active and inactive, masculine and feminine, hot and cold, more or less analogous to them; but there arise the important questions,—Do we find yang and yin not merely used to indicate the quality of what they are applied to, but at the same time with substantival force, denoting what has the quality which the name denotes? Had the doctrine of a primary matter of an ethereal nature, now expanding and showing itself full of activity and power as yang, now contracting and becoming weak and inactive as yin:—had this doctrine become matter of speculation when this Appendix was written? The Chinese critics and commentators for the most part assume that it had. P. Regis, Dr. Medhurst, and other foreign Chinese scholars repeat their statements without question. I have sought in vain for proof of what is asserted. It

---

[46] See the account of Pythagoras and his philosophy in Lewes' History of Philosophy, pp. 18-38 (1871).

[47] See Section i, 24, 32, 35; Section ii, 28, 29, 30, 35.

took more than a thousand years after the closing of the Yî to fashion in the Confucian school the doctrine of a primary matter. We do not find it fully developed till the era of the Sung dynasty, and in our eleventh and twelfth centuries.[48] To find it in the Yî is the logical, or rather illogical, error of putting 'the last first.' Neither creation nor cosmogony was before the mind of the author whose work I am analysing. His theme is the Yî,—the ever-changing phenomena of nature and experience. There is nothing but this in the 'Great Treatise' to task our powers;—nothing deeper or more abstruse.

*The name Kwei-shăn.* As in the first Appendix, so in this, the name kwei-shăn occurs twice; in paragraphs 21 and 50 of Section i. In the former instance, each part of the name has its significance. Kwei denotes the animal soul or nature, and Shăn, the intellectual soul, the union of which constitutes the living rational man. I have translated them, it will be seen, by 'the anima and the animus.' Canon McClatchie gives for them 'demons and gods;' and Dr. Medhurst said on the passage, 'The kwei-shăns are evidently the expanding and contracting principles of human life The kwei-shăns are brought about by the dissolution of the human frame, and consist of the expanding and ascending shăn, which rambles about in space, and of the contracted and shrivelled kwei, which reverts to earth and nonentity.'[49]

This is pretty much the same view as my own, though I would not here use the phraseology of 'expanding and contracting.' Canon McClatchie is consistent with himself, and renders the characters by 'demons and gods.'

In the latter passage it is more difficult to determine the exact meaning. The writer says, that 'by the odd numbers assigned to heaven and the even numbers assigned to earth, the changes and

---

[48] As a specimen of what the ablest Sung scholars teach, I may give the remarks (from the I Collected Comments') of Kû Kăn (of the same century as Kû Hsî, rather earlier) on the 4th paragraph of Appendix V:—In the Yî there is the Great Extreme. When we speak of the yin and yang, we mean the air (or ether) collected in the Great Void. When we speak of the Hard and Soft, we mean that ether collected, and formed into substance. Benevolence and righteousness have their origin in the great void, are seen in the ether substantiated, and move under the influence of conscious intelligence. Looking at the one origin of all things we speak of their nature; looking at the endowments given to them, we speak of the ordinations appointed (for them). Looking at them as (divided into) heaven, earth, and men, we speak of their principle. The three are one and the same. The sages wishing that (their figures) should be in conformity with the principles underlying the natures (of men and things) and the ordinances appointed (for them), called them (now) yin and yang, (now) the hard and the soft, (now) benevolence and righteousness, in order thereby to exhibit the ways of heaven, earth, and men; it is a view of them as related together. The trigrams of the Yî contain the three Powers; and when they are doubled into hexagrams, there the three Powers unite and are one. But there are the changes and movements of their (several) ways, and therefore there are separate places for the yin and yang, and reciprocal uses of the hard and the soft.'

[49] Dissertation on the Theology of the Chinese, pp. 111, 112.

transformations are effected, and the spirit-like agencies kept in movement;' meaning that by means of the numbers the spirit-like lines might be formed on a scale sufficient to give a picture of all the changing phenomena, taking place, as if by a spiritual agency, in nature. Medhurst contents himself on it with giving the explanation of *Kû Hsî*, that 'the kwei-shăns refer to the contractions and expandings, the recedings and approachings of the productive and completing powers of the even and odd numbers.'[50] Canon McClatchie does not follow his translation of the former passage and give here 'demons and gods,' but we have 'the Demon-god (i.e. Shang Tî).'[51] I shall refer to this version when considering the fifth Appendix.

*Shan alone.* The single character shăn occurs more than twenty times;—used now as a substantive, now as an adjective, and again as a verb. I must refer the reader to the translation and notes for its various significance, subjoining in a note a list of the places where it occurs.[52]

Much more might be said on the third Appendix, for the writer touches on many other topics, antiquarian and speculative, but a review of them would help us little in the study of the leading subject of the Yî. In passing on to the next treatise, I would only further say that the style of this and the author's manner of presenting his thoughts often remind the reader of 'the Doctrine of the Mean.' I am surprised that 'the Great Treatise' has never been ascribed to the author of that Doctrine, Ʒze-sze, the grandson of Confucius, whose death must have taken place between B. C. 400 and 450.

*The fourth Appendix.* 7. The fourth Appendix, the seventh wing' of the Yî, need not detain us long. As I stated on p. 39, it is confined to an exposition of the Text on the first and second hexagrams, being an attempt to show that what is there affirmed of heaven and earth may also be applied to man, and that there is an essential agreement between the qualities ascribed to them, and the benevolence, righteousness, propriety, and wisdom, which are the four constituents of his moral and intellectual nature.

It is said by some of the critics that Confucius would have treated all the other hexagrams in a similar way, if his life had been prolonged, but we found special grounds for denying that Confucius had anything to do with the composition of this Appendix; and, moreover, I cannot think of any other figure that would have afforded to the author the same opportunity of discoursing about man. The style and method are after the manner of 'the Doctrine of the Mean' quite as much as those of 'the Great Treatise.' Several paragraphs, moreover, suggest to us the

---

[50] Theology of the Chinese, p. 122.
[51] Translation of the Yî King, p. 312.
[52] Section i, 23, 32, 51, 58, 62, 64, 67, 68, 69, 73, 76, 81; Section ii, 11, 15, 33, 34, 41, 45.

magniloquence of Mencius. It is said, for instance, by 3ze-sze, of the sage, that 'he is the equal or correlate of Heaven,'[53] and in this Appendix we have the sentiment expanded into the following:—

'The great man is he who is in harmony in his attributes with heaven and earth; in his brightness with the sun and moon; in his orderly procedure with the four seasons; and in his relation to what is fortunate and what is calamitous with the spiritual agents. He may precede Heaven, and Heaven will not act in opposition to him; he may follow Heaven, but will act only as Heaven at the time would do. If Heaven will not act in opposition to him, how much less will man! how much less will the spiritual agents!'[54]

One other passage may receive our consideration:—

'The family that accumulates goodness is sure to have superabundant happiness, and the family that accumulates evil is sure to have superabundant misery.'[55]

The language makes us think of the retribution of good and evil as taking place in the family, and not in the individual; the judgment is long deferred, but it is inflicted at last, lighting, however, not on the head or heads that most deserved it. Confucianism never falters in its affirmation of the difference between good and evil, and that each shall have its appropriate recompense; but it has little to say of the where and when and how that recompense will be given. The old classics are silent on the subject of any other retribution besides what takes place in time. About the era of Confucius the view took definite shape that, if the issues of good and evil, virtue and vice, did not take effect in the experience of the individual, they would certainly do so in that of his posterity. This is the prevailing doctrine among the Chinese at the present day; and one of the earliest expressions, perhaps the earliest expression, of it was in the sentence under our notice that has been copied from this Appendix into almost every moral treatise that circulates in China. A wholesome and an important truth it is, that 'the sins of parents are visited on their children;' but do the parents themselves escape the curse? It is to be regretted that this short treatise, the only 'wing' of the Yî professing to set forth its teachings concerning man as man, does not attempt any definite reply to this question. I leave it, merely observing that it has always struck me as the

[53] *Kung-yung* xxxi, 4.
[54] Section i, 34. This is the only paragraph where kwei-shăn occurs.
[55] Section ii, 5.

result of an after-thought, and a wish to give to man, as the last of 'the Three Powers,' a suitable place in connexion with the Yî. The doctrine of 'the Three Powers' is as much out of place in Confucianism as that of 'the Great Extreme.' The treatise contains several paragraphs interesting in themselves, but it adds nothing to our understanding of the Text, or even of the object of the appended treatises, when we try to look at them as a whole.

*The fifth Appendix.* 8. It is very different with the fifth of the Appendixes, which is made up of 'Remarks on the Trigrams.' It is shorter than the fourth, consisting of only 22 paragraphs, in some of which the author rises to a height of thought reached nowhere else in these treatises, while several of the others are so silly and trivial, that it is difficult, not to say impossible, to believe that they are the production of the same man. We find in it the earlier and later arrangement of the trigrams,—the former, that of Fû-hsî, and the latter, that of king Wăn; their names and attributes; the work of God in nature, described as a progress through the trigrams; and finally a distinctive, but by no means exhaustive, list of the natural objects, symbolised by them.

First paragraph. It commences with the enigmatic declaration that 'Anciently, when the sages made the Yî,' (that is, the lineal figures, and the system of divination by them),'in order to give mysterious assistance .to the spiritual Intelligences, they produced (the rules for the use of) the divining plant.' Perhaps this means no more than that the lineal figures were made to 'hold the mirror up to nature,' so that men by the study of them would understand more of the unseen and spiritual operations, to which the phenomena around them were owing, than they could otherwise do.

The author goes on to speak of the Fû-hsî trigrams, and passes from them to those of king Wăn in paragraph 8. That and the following two are very remarkable; but before saying anything of them, I will go on to the 14th, which is the only passage that affords any ground for saying that there is a mythology in the Yî. It says:—

*Mythology of the Yî.* 'Khien is (the symbol of) heaven, and hence is styled father. Khwăn is (the symbol of) earth, and hence is styled mother. Kăn (shows) the first application (of khwăn to khien), resulting in getting (the first of) its male (or undivided lines), and hence we call it the oldest son. Sun (shows) a first application (of khien to khwăn), resulting in getting (the first of) its female (or divided lines), and hence we call it the oldest daughter. Khăn (shows) a second application (of khwăn to khien), and Lî a second (of khien to khwăn), resulting in the second son and second daughter. In Kăn and Tui we have a third application (of khwăn to khien and of khien to khwăn), resulting in the youngest son and youngest daughter.'

From this language has come the fable of a marriage between
*Kh*ien and Khwăn, from which resulted the six other trigrams,
considered as their three sons and three daughters; and it is not to be
wondered at, if some men of active and ill-regulated imaginations
should see Noah and his wife in those two primary trigrams, and in the
others their three sons and the three sons' wives. Have we not in both
cases an ogdoad? But I have looked in the paragraph in vain for the
notion of a marriage-union between heaven and earth.

It does not treat of the genesis of the other six trigrams by the
union of the two, but is a rude attempt to explain their forms when they
were once existing.[56] According to the idea of changes, *Kh*ien and
Khwăn are continually varying their forms by their interaction. As here
represented, the other trigrams are not 'produced'[57] by a marriage-
union, but from the application, literally the seeking, of one of them of
Khwăn as much as of *Kh*ien—addressed to the other.[58]

This way of speaking of the trigrams, moreover, as father and
mother, sons and daughters, is not so old as Fû-hsî; nor have we any
real proof that it originated with king Wăn. It is not of 'the highest
antiquity.' It arose some time in 'middle antiquity,' and was known in
the era of the Appendixes; but it had not prevailed then, nor has it
prevailed since, to discredit and supersede the older nomenclature. We
are startled when we come on it in the place which it occupies. And
there it stands alone. It is not entitled to more attention than the two
paragraphs that precede it, or the eight that follow it, none of which
were thought by P. Regis worthy to be translated. I have just said that it
stands 'alone.' Its existence, however, seems to me to be supposed in
the fourth chapter, paragraphs 28-30, of the third Appendix, Section ii;
but there only the trigrams of 'the six children' are mentioned, and
nothing is said of 'the parents.' *K*ăn, khân, and kăn are referred to as
being yang, and sun, lî, and tui as being yin. What is said about them is
trifling and fanciful.

*Operation of God in nature throughout the year.* Leaving the
question of the mythology of the Yî, of which I am myself unable to

---

[56] This view seems to be in accordance with that of Wû *Kh*ăng (of the Yüan
dynasty), as given in the 'Collected Comments' of the Khang-hsî edition. The editors
express their approval of it in preference to the interpretation of *K*û Hsî, who understood
the whole to refer to the formation of the lineal figures, the 'application' being 'the
manipulation of the stalks to find the proper line.'

[57] But the Chinese term Shăng 生, often rendered 'produced,' must not be pressed,
so as to determine the method of production, or the way in which one thing comes from
another.

[58] The significance of the mythological paragraph is altogether lost in Canon
McClatchie's version:—'*Kh*ien is Heaven, and hence he is called Father; Khwăn is Earth,
and hence she is called Mother; *K*ăn is the first male, and hence he is called the eldest
son,' &c. &c.

discover a trace, I now call attention to paragraphs 8-10, where the author speaks of the work of God in nature in all the year as a progress through the trigrams, and as being effected by His Spirit. The description assumes the peculiar arrangement of the trigrams, ascribed to king Wăn, and which I have exhibited above, on page 43.[59] Father Regis adopts the general view of Chinese critics that Wăn purposely altered the earlier and established arrangement, as a symbol of the disorganisation and disorder into which the kingdom had fallen.[60] But it is hard to say why a man did something more than 3000 years ago, when he has not himself said anything about it. So far as we can judge from this Appendix, the author thought that king Wăn altered the existing order and position of the trigrams with regard to the cardinal points, simply for the occasion,—that he might set forth vividly his ideas about the springing, growth, and maturity in the vegetable kingdom from the labours of spring to the cessation from toil in winter. The marvel is that in doing this he brings God upon the scene, and makes Him in the various processes of nature the 'all and in all.'

The 8th paragraph says:—

'God comes forth in *K*ăn (to his producing work); He brings (His processes) into full and equal action in Sun; they are manifested to one another in Lî; the greatest service is done for Him in Khwăn; He rejoices in Tui; He struggles in *Kh*ien; He is comforted and enters into rest in Khân; and he completes (the work of) the year in Kăn.'

God is here named Tî, for which P. Regis gives the Latin 'Supremus Imperator,' and Canon McClatchie, after him, 'the Supreme Emperor.' I contend that 'God' is really the correct translation in English of Tî; but to render it here by 'Emperor' would not affect the meaning of the paragraph. *K*û Hsî says that 'by Tî is intended the Lord and Governor of heaven;' and Khung Ying-tâ, about five centuries earlier than *K*û, quotes Wang Pî, who died A.D. 249, to the effect that 'Tî is the lord who produces (all) things, the author of prosperity and

---

[59] The reader will understand the difference in the two arrangements better by a reference to the circular representations of them on Plate III.

[60] E. g. 1, 23, 24:—'Observant etiam philosophi (lib. 15 Sinicae philosophiae Sing-11) principem. Wăn-wang antiquum octo symbolorum, unde aliae figurae omnes pendent, ordinem invertisse; quo ipsa imperii suis temporibus subversio graphice exprimi poterat, mutatis e naturali loco, quem genesis dederat, iis quatuor figuris, quae rerum naturalium pugnis ac dissociationibus, quas posterior labentis anni pars afferre solet, velut in antecessum, repraesentandis idoneae videbantur; v. g. si symbolum ☲ Lî, ignis, supponatur loco symboli ☵ Khân, aquae, utriusque elementi inordinatio principi visa est non minus apta ad significandas ruinas et clades reipublicae male ordinatae, quam naturales ab hieme aut imminente aut saeviente rerum generatarum corruptiones.' See also pp. 67, 68.

increase.'

I must refer the reader to the translation in the body of the volume for the 9th paragraph, which is too long to be introduced here. As the 8th speaks directly of God, the 9th, we are told, 'speaks of all things following Him, from spring to winter, from the east to the north, in His progress throughout the year.' In words strikingly like those of the apostle Paul, when writing his Epistle to the Romans, Wan *Kh*ung-ʒung (of the Khang-hsî period) and his son, in their admirable work called, 'A New Digest of Collected Explanations of the Yî King,' say:—'God (Himself) cannot be seen; we see Him in the things (which He produces).' The first time I read these paragraphs with some understanding, I thought of Thomson's Hymn on the Seasons, and I have thought of it in connexion with them a hundred times since. Our English poet wrote:—

> 'These, as they change, Almighty Father, these
> Are but the varied God. The rolling year
> Is full of Thee. Forth in the pleasing spring
> Thy beauty walks, Thy tenderness and love.
> Then comes Thy glory in the summer months,
> With light and heat refulgent. Then Thy sun
> Shoots full perfection through the swelling year.
> Thy bounty shines in autumn unconfined,
> And spreads a common feast for all that lives.
> In winter awful Thou!'

Prudish readers have found fault with some of Thomson's expressions, as if they savoured of pantheism. The language of the Chinese writer is not open to the same captious objection. Without poetic ornament, or swelling phrase of any kind, he gives emphatic testimony to God as renewing the face of the earth in spring, and not resting till He has crowned the year with His goodness.

*Concluding paragraphs.* And there is in the passage another thing equally wonderful. The 10th paragraph commences:—'When we speak of Spirit, we mean the subtle presence (and operation of God) with all things;' and the writer goes on to illustrate this sentiment from the action and influences symbolized by the six 'children,' or minor trigrams,—water and fire, thunder and wind, mountains and collections of water. *K*û Hsî says, that there is that in the paragraph which he does not understand. Some Chinese scholars, however, have not been far from descrying the light that is in it. Let Liang Yin, of our fourteenth century, be adduced as an example of them. He says:—'The spirit here simply means God. God is the personality (literally, the body or substantiality) of the Spirit; the Spirit is God in operation. He who is lord over and rules all things is God; the subtle presence and operation of God with all things is by His Spirit.' The language is in fine accord with the definition of shăn or spirit, given in the 3rd Appendix, Section i, 32.

I wish that the Treatise on the Trigrams had ended with the 10th paragraph. The writer had gradually risen to a noble elevation of thought from which he plunges into a slough of nonsensical remarks which it would be difficult elsewhere to parallel. I have referred on p. 41 to the judgment of P. Regis about them. He could not receive them as from Confucius, and did not take the trouble to translate them, and transfer them to his own pages, My plan required me to translate everything published in China as a part of the Yî King; but I have given my reasons for doubting whether any portion of these Appendixes be really from Confucius. There is nothing that could better justify the supercilious disregard with which the classical literature of China is frequently treated than to insist on the concluding portion of this treatise as being from the pencil of its greatest sage. I have dwelt at some length on the 14th paragraph, because of its mythological semblance; but among the eight paragraphs that follow it, it would be difficult to award the palm for silliness. They are descriptive of the eight trigrams, and each one enumerates a dozen or more objects of which its subject is symbolical. The writer must have been fond of and familiar with horses. *Kh*ien, the symbol properly of heaven, suggests to him the idea of a good horse; an old horse; a lean horse; and a piebald. *K*ăn, the symbol of thunder, suggests the idea of a good neigher; of the horse with white hind-legs; of the prancing horse; and of one with a white star in his forehead. Khân, the symbol of water, suggests the idea of the horse with an elegant spine; of one with a high spirit; of one with a drooping head; and of one with a shambling step. The reader will think he has had enough of these symbolisings of the trigrams. I cannot believe that the earlier portions and this concluding portion of the treatise were by the same author. If there were any evidence that paragraphs 8 to 10 were by Confucius, I should say that they were worthy, even more than worthy, of him; what follows is mere drivel. Horace's picture faintly pourtrays the inconsistency between the parts:—

'Desinit in piscem mulier formosa superne.'

In reviewing the second of these Appendixes, I was led to speak of the original significance of the trigrams, in opposition to the views of some Chinese who pretend that they can find in them the physical truths discovered by the researches of western science. May I not say now, after viewing the phase of them presented in these paragraphs, that they were devised simply as aids to divination, and partook of the unreasonableness and uncertainty belonging to that?

*The sixth Appendix.* 9. The sixth Appendix is the Treatise on the Sequence of the Hexagrams, to which allusion has been made more than once. It is not necessary to dwell on it at length. King Wăn, it has been seen, gave a name to each hexagram, expressive of the idea—some moral, social, or political truth—which he wished to set forth by means of it; and this name enters very closely into its interpretation. The author of this treatise endeavours to explain the meaning of the name, and also the sequence of the figures, or how it is that the idea of the one leads on to that of the next. Yet the reader must not expect to find in the 64 a chain 'of linked sweetness long drawn out.' The connexion between any two is generally sufficiently close; but on the whole the essays, which I have said they form, resemble 'a heap of orient pearls at random strung.' The changeableness of human affairs is a topic never long absent from the writer's mind. He is firmly persuaded that 'the fashion of the world passeth away.' Union is sure to give place to separation, and by and by that separation will issue in re-union.

There is nothing in the treatise to suggest anything about its authorship; and as the reader will see from the notes, we are perplexed occasionally by meanings given to the names that differ from the meanings in the Text.

*The seventh Appendix.* 10. The last and least Appendix is the seventh, called 3â Kwâ *K*wan, or 'Treatise on the Lineal Figures taken promiscuously,'—not with regard to any sequence, but as they approximate, or are opposed, to one another in meaning. It is in rhyme, moreover, and this, as much as the meaning, determined, no doubt, the grouping of the hexagrams. The student will learn nothing of value from it; it is more a 'jeu d'esprit' than anything else.

# THE YÎ KING.

## THE TEXT.

### SECTION I.

#### I.[i] THE *KH*IEN HEXAGRAM.

Explanation of the entire figure by king Wăn.

*Kh*ien (represents) what is great and originating, penetrating, advantageous, correct and firm.

Explanation of the separate lines by the duke of *K*âu.

1. In the first (or lowest) line, undivided, (we see its subject as) the dragon lying hid (in the deep). It is not the time for active doing.

2. In the second line, undivided, (we see its subject as) the dragon appearing in the field. It will be advantageous to meet with the great man.

3. In the third line, undivided, (we see its subject as) the superior man active and vigilant all the day, and in the evening still careful and apprehensive. (The position is) dangerous, but there will be no mistake.

4. In the fourth line, undivided, (we see its subject as the dragon looking) as if he were leaping up, but still in the deep. There will be no mistake.

5. In the fifth line, undivided, (we see its subject as) the dragon on the wing in the sky. It will be advantageous to meet with the great man.

6. In the sixth (or topmost) line, undivided, (we see its subject as) the dragon exceeding the proper limits. There will be occasion for repentance.

7. (The lines of this hexagram are all strong and undivided, as appears from) the use of the number line. If the host of dragons (thus) appearing were to divest themselves of their heads, there would be good fortune.

## II.[ii] THE KHWĂN HEXAGRAM.

Khwăn (represents) what is great and originating, penetrating, advantageous, correct and having the firmness of a mare. When the superior man (here intended) has to make any movement, if he take the initiative, he will go astray; if he follow, he will find his (proper) lord. The advantageousness will be seen in his getting friends in the south-west, and losing friends in the north-east. If he rest in correctness and firmness, there will be good fortune.

1. In the first line, divided, (we see its subject) treading on hoarfrost. The strong ice will come (by and by).
2. The second line, divided, (shows the attribute of) being straight, square, and great. (Its operation), without repeated efforts, will be in every respect advantageous.
3. The third line, divided, (shows its subject) keeping his excellence under restraint, but firmly maintaining it. If he should have occasion to engage in the king's service, though he will not claim the success (for himself), he will bring affairs to a good issue.
4. The fourth line, divided, (shows the symbol of) a sack tied up. There will be no ground for blame or for praise.
5. The fifth line, divided, (shows) the yellow lower garment. There will be great good fortune.
6. The sixth line, divided (shows) dragons fighting in the wild. Their blood is purple and yellow.
7. (The lines of this hexagram are all weak and divided, as appears from) the use of the number six. If those (who are thus represented) be perpetually correct and firm, advantage will arise.

## III.[iii] THE *K*UN HEXAGRAM.

*K*un (indicates that in the case which it presupposes) there will be great progress and success, and the advantage will come from being correct and firm. (But) any movement in advance should not be (lightly) undertaken. There will be advantage in appointing feudal princes.

1. The first line, undivided, shows the difficulty (its subject has) in advancing. It will be advantageous for him to abide correct and firm; advantageous (also) to be made a feudal ruler.

2. The second line, divided, shows (its subject) distressed and obliged to return; (even) the horses of her chariot (also) seem to be retreating. (But) not by a spoiler (is she assailed), but by one who seeks her to be his wife. The young lady maintains her firm correctness, and declines a union. After ten years she will be united, and have children.

3. The third line, divided, shows one following the deer without (the guidance of) the forester, and only finding himself in the midst of the forest. The superior man, acquainted with the secret risks, thinks it better to give up the chase. If he went forward, he would regret it.

4. The fourth line, divided, shows (its subject as a lady), the horses of whose chariot appear in retreat. She seeks, however, (the help of) him who seeks her to be his wife. Advance will be fortunate; all will turn out advantageously.

5. The fifth line, undivided, shows the difficulties in the way of (its subject's) dispensing the rich favours that might be expected from him. With firmness and correctness there will be good fortune in small things; (even) with them in great things there will be evil.

6. The topmost line, divided, shows (its subject) with the horses of his chariot obliged to retreat, and weeping tears of blood in streams.

## IV.[iv] THE MĂNG HEXAGRAM.

Măng (indicates that in the case which it presupposes) there will be progress and success. I do not (go and) seek the youthful and inexperienced, but he comes and seeks me. When he shows (the sincerity that marks) the first recourse to divination, I instruct him. If he apply a second and third time, that is troublesome; and I do not instruct the troublesome. There will be advantage in being firm and correct.

1. The first line, divided, (has respect to) the dispelling of ignorance. It will be advantageous to use punishment (for that purpose), and to remove the shackles (from the mind). But going on in that way (of punishment) will give occasion for regret.

2. The second line, undivided, (shows its subject) exercising forbearance with the ignorant, in which there will be good fortune; and admitting (even the goodness of women, which will also be fortunate. (He may be described also as) a son able to (sustain the burden of) his family.

3. The third line, divided, (seems to say) that one should not marry

a woman whose emblem it might be, for that, when she sees a man of wealth, she will not keep her person from him, and in no wise will advantage come from her.

4. The fourth line, divided, (shows its subject as if) bound in chains of ignorance. There will be occasion for regret.

5. The fifth line, divided, shows its subject as a simple lad without experience. There will be good fortune.

6. In the topmost line, undivided, we see one smiting the ignorant (youth). But no advantage will come from doing him an injury. Advantage would come from warding off injury from him.

## V.ᵛ THE HSÜ HEXAGRAM.

Hsü intimates that, with the sincerity which is declared in it, there will be brilliant success. With firmness there will be good fortune; and it will be advantageous to cross the great stream.

1. The first line, undivided, shows its subject waiting in the distant border. It will be well for him constantly to maintain (the purpose thus shown), in which case there will be no error.

2. The second line, undivided, shows its subject waiting on the sand (of the mountain stream). He will (suffer) the small (injury of) being spoken (against), but in the end there will be good fortune.

3. The third line, undivided, shows its subject in the mud (close by the stream). He thereby invites the approach of injury.

4. The fourth line, divided, shows its subject waiting in (the place of) blood. But he will get out of the cavern.

5. The fifth line, undivided, shows its subject waiting amidst the appliances of a feast. Through his firmness and correctness there will be good fortune.

6. The topmost line, divided, shows its subject entered into the cavern. (But) there are three guests coming, without being urged, (to his help). If he receive them respectfully, there will be good fortune in the end.

## VI.[vi] THE SUNG HEXAGRAM.

Sung intimates how, though there is sincerity in one's contention, he will yet meet with opposition and obstruction; but if he cherish an apprehensive caution, there will be good fortune, while, if he must prosecute the contention to the (bitter) end, there will be evil. It will be advantageous to see the great man; it will not be advantageous to cross the great stream.

1. The first line, divided, shows its subject not perpetuating the matter about which (the contention is). He will suffer the small (injury) of being spoken against, but the end will be fortunate.
2. The second line, undivided, shows its subject unequal to the contention. If he retire and keep concealed (where) the inhabitants of his city are (only) three hundred families, he will fall into no mistake.
3. The third line, divided, shows its subject keeping in the old place assigned for his support, and firmly correct. Perilous as the position is, there will be good fortune in the end. Should he perchance engage in the king's business, he will not (claim the merit of) achievement.
4. The fourth line, undivided, shows its subject unequal to the contention. He returns to (the study of Heaven's) ordinances, changes (his wish to contend), and rests in being firm and correct. There will be good fortune.
5. The fifth line, undivided, shows its subject contending;—and with great good fortune.
6. The topmost line, undivided, shows how its subject may have the leathern belt conferred on him (by the sovereign), and thrice it shall be taken from him in a morning.

## VII.[vii] THE SZE HEXAGRAM.

Sze indicates how, in the case which it supposes, with firmness and correctness, and (a leader of) age and experience, there will be good fortune and no error.

1. The first line, divided, shows the host going forth according to the rules (for such a movement). If these be not good, there will be evil.

2. The second line, undivided, shows (the leader) in the midst of the host. There will be good fortune and no error. The king has thrice conveyed to him the orders (of his favour).

3. The third line, divided, shows how the host may, possibly, have many inefficient leaders. There will be evil.

4. The fourth line, divided, shows the host in retreat. There is no error.

5. The fifth line, divided, shows birds in the fields, which it will be advantageous to seize (and destroy). In that case there will be no error. If the oldest son leads the host, and younger men (idly occupy offices assigned to them), however firm and correct he may be, there will be evil.

6. The topmost line, divided, shows the great ruler delivering his charges, (appointing some) to be rulers of states, and others to undertake the headship of clans; but small men should not be employed (in such positions).

## VIII.[viii] THE PÎ HEXAGRAM.

Pî indicates that (under the conditions which it supposes) there is good fortune. But let (the principal party intended in it) re-examine himself, (as if) by divination, whether his virtue be great, unintermitting, and firm. If it be so, there will be no error. Those who have not rest will then come to him; and with those who are (too) late in coming it will be ill.

1. The first line, divided, shows its subject seeking by his sincerity to win the attachment of his object. There will be no error. Let (the breast) be full of sincerity as an earthenware vessel is of its contents, and it will in the end bring other advantages.

2. In the second line, divided, we see the movement towards union and attachment proceeding from the inward (mind). With firm correctness there will be good fortune.

In the third line, divided, we see its subject seeking for union with such as ought not to be associated with.

4. In the fourth line, divided, we see its subject seeking for union with the one beyond himself. With firm correctness there will be good fortune.

5. The fifth line, undivided, affords the most illustrious instance of seeking union and attachment. (We seem to see in it) the king urging his pursuit of the game (only) in three directions, and allowing the escape of all the animals before him, while the people of his towns do not warn one another (to prevent it). There will be good fortune.

6. In the topmost line, divided, we see one seeking union and attachment without having taken the first step (to such an end). There will be evil.

## IX.[ix] THE HSIÂO *KHÛ* HEXAGRAM.

Hsiâo *Khû* indicates that (under its conditions) there will be progress and success. (We see) dense clouds, but no rain coming from our borders in the west.

1. The first line, undivided, shows its subject returning and pursuing his own course. What mistake should he fall into? There will be good fortune.

2. The second line, undivided, shows its subject, by the attraction (of the former line), returning (to the proper course). There will be good fortune.

3. The third line, undivided, suggests the idea of a carriage, the strap beneath which has been removed, or of a husband and wife looking on each other with averted eyes.

4. The fourth line, divided, shows its subject possessed of sincerity. The danger of bloodshed is thereby averted, and his (ground for) apprehension dismissed. There will be no mistake.

5. The fifth line, undivided, shows its subject possessed of sincerity, and drawing others to unite with him. Rich in resources, he employs his neighbours (in the same cause with himself).

6. The topmost line, undivided, shows how the rain has fallen, and the (onward progress) is stayed;—(so) must we value the full accumulation of the virtue (represented by the upper trigram). But a wife (exercising restraint), however firm and correct she may be, is in a position of peril, (and like) the moon approaching to the full. If the superior man prosecute his measures (in such circumstances), there will be evil.

## X.[x] THE LÎ HEXAGRAM.

(Lî suggests the idea of) one treading on the tail of a tiger, which does not bite him. There will be progress and success.

1. The first line, undivided, shows its subject treading his accustomed path. If he go forward, there will be no error.
2. The second line, undivided, shows its subject treading the path that is level and easy;—a quiet and solitary man, to whom, if he be firm and correct, there will be good fortune.
3. The third line, divided, shows a one-eyed man (who thinks he) can see; a lame man (who thinks he) can walk well; one who treads on the tail of a tiger and is bitten. (All this indicates) ill fortune. We have a (mere) bravo acting the part of a great ruler.
4. The fourth line, undivided, shows its subject treading on the tail of a tiger. He becomes full of apprehensive caution, and in the end there will be good fortune.
5. The fifth line, undivided, shows the resolute tread of its subject. Though he be firm and correct, there will be peril.
6. The sixth line, undivided, tells us to look at (the whole course) that is trodden, and examine the presage which that gives. If it be complete and without failure, there will be great good fortune.

## XI.[xi] THE THÂI HEXAGRAM.

In Thâi (we see) the little gone and the great come. (It indicates that) there will be good fortune, with progress and success.

1. The first line, undivided, suggests the idea of grass pulled up, and bringing with it other stalks with whose roots it is connected. Advance (on the part of its subject) will be fortunate.
2. The second line, undivided, shows one who can bear with the uncultivated, will cross the Ho without a boat, does not forget the distant, and has no (selfish) friendships. Thus does he prove himself acting in accordance with the course of the due Mean.
3. The third line, undivided, shows that, while there is no state of peace that is not liable to be disturbed, and no departure (of evil men)

so that they shall not return, yet when one is firm and correct, as he realises the distresses that may arise, he will commit no error. There is no occasion for sadness at the certainty (of such recurring changes); and in this mood the happiness (of the present) may be (long) enjoyed.

4. The fourth line, divided, shows its subject fluttering (down);—not relying on his own rich resources, but calling in his neighbours. (They all come) not as having received warning, but in the sincerity (of their hearts).

5. The fifth six, divided, reminds us of (king) Tî-yî's (rule about the) marriage of his younger sister. By such a course there is happiness and there will be great good fortune.

6. The sixth six, divided, shows us the city wall returned into the moat. It is not the time to use the army. (The subject of the line) may, indeed, announce his orders to the people of his own city; but however correct and firm he may be, he will have cause for regret.

## XII.xii THE PHÎ HEXAGRAM.

In Phî there is the want of good understanding between the (different classes of) men, and its indication is unfavourable to the firm and correct course of the superior man. We see in it the great gone and the little come.

1. The first line, divided, suggests the idea of grass pulled up, and bringing with it other stalks with whose roots it is connected. With firm correctness (on the part of its subject), there will be good fortune and progress.

2. The second line, divided, shows its subject patient and obedient. To the small man (comporting himself so) there will be good fortune. If the great man (comport himself) as the distress and obstruction require, he will have success.

The third line, divided, shows its subject ashamed of the purpose folded (in his breast).

4. The fourth line, undivided, shows its subject acting in accordance with the ordination (of Heaven), and committing no error. His companions will come and share in his happiness.

5. In the fifth line, undivided, we see him who brings the distress and obstruction to a close,—the great man and fortunate. (But let him say), 'We may perish! We may perish!' (so shall the state of things become firm, as if) bound to a clump of bushy mulberry trees.

6. The sixth line, undivided, shows the overthrow (and removal of)

the condition of distress and obstruction. Before this there was that condition. Hereafter there will be joy.

## XIII.[xiii] THE THUNG ZĂN HEXAGRAM.

Thung Zăn (or 'Union of men') appears here (as we find it) in the (remote districts of the) country, indicating progress and success. It will be advantageous to cross the great stream. It will be advantageous to maintain the firm correctness of the superior man.

1. The first line, undivided, (shows the representative of) the union of men just issuing from his gate. There will be no error.
2. The second line, divided, (shows the representative of) the union of men in relation with his kindred. There will be occasion for regret.
3. The third line, undivided, (shows its subject) with his arms hidden in the thick grass, and at the top of a high mound. (But) for three years he makes no demonstration.
4. The fourth line, undivided, (shows its subject) mounted on the city wall; but he does not proceed to make the attack (he contemplates). There will be good fortune.
5. In the fifth line, undivided, (the representative of) the union of men first wails and cries out, and then laughs. His great host conquers, and he (and the subject of the second line) meet together.
6. The topmost line, undivided, (shows the representative of) the union of men in the suburbs. There will be no occasion for repentance.

## XIV.[xiv] THE TÂ YÛ HEXAGRAM.

Tâ Yû indicates that, (under the circumstances which it implies), there will be great progress and success.

1. In the first line, undivided, there is no approach to what is injurious, and there is no error. Let there be a realisation of the difficulty (and danger of the position), and there will be no error (to the end).
2. In the second line, undivided, we have a large waggon with its load. In whatever direction advance is made, there will be no error.
3. The third line, undivided, shows us a feudal prince presenting

his offerings to the Son of Heaven. A small man would be unequal (to such a duty).

4. The fourth line, undivided, shows its subject keeping his great resources under restraint. There will be no error.

5. The fifth line, divided, shows the sincerity of its subject reciprocated by that of all the others (represented in the hexagram). Let him display a proper majesty, and there will be good fortune.

6. The topmost line, undivided, shows its subject with help accorded to him from Heaven. There will be good fortune, advantage in every respect.

## XV.[xv] THE *KH*IEN HEXAGRAM.

*Kh*ien indicates progress and success. The superior man, (being humble as it implies), will have a (good) issue (to his undertakings).

1. The first line, divided, shows us the superior man who adds humility to humility. (Even) the great stream may be crossed with this, and there will be good fortune.

2. The second line, divided, shows us humility that has made itself recognised. With firm correctness there will be good fortune.

3. The third line, undivided, shows the superior man of (acknowledged) merit. He will maintain his success to the end, and have good fortune.

4. The fourth line, divided, shows one, whose action would be in every way advantageous, stirring up (the more) his humility.

5. The fifth line, divided, shows one who, without being rich, is able to employ his neighbours. He may advantageously use the force of arms. All his movements will be advantageous.

6. The sixth line, divided, shows us humility that has made itself recognised. The subject of it will with advantage put his hosts in motion; but (he will only) punish his own towns and state.

## XVI.[xvi] THE YÜ HEXAGRAM.

Yü indicates that, (in the state which it implies), feudal princes may be set up, and the hosts put in motion, with advantage.

1. The first line, divided, shows its subject proclaiming his pleasure and satisfaction. There will be evil.

2. The second line, divided, shows one who is firm as a rock. (He sees a thing) without waiting till it has come to pass; with his firm correctness there will be good fortune.

3. The third line, divided, shows one looking up (for favours), while he indulges the feeling of pleasure and satisfaction. If he would understand!—If he be late in doing so, there will indeed be occasion for repentance.

4. The fourth line, undivided, shows him from whom the harmony and satisfaction come. Great is the success which he obtains. Let him not allow suspicions to enter his mind, and thus friends will gather around him.

5. The fifth six, divided, shows one with a chronic complaint, but who lives on without dying.

6. The topmost six, divided, shows its subject with darkened mind devoted to the pleasure and satisfaction (of the time); but if he change his course even when (it may be considered as) completed, there will be no error.

## XVII.[xvii] THE SUI HEXAGRAM.

Sui indicates that (under its conditions) there will be great progress and success. But it will be advantageous to be firm and correct. There will (then) be no error.

1. The first line, undivided, shows us one changing the object of his pursuit; but if he be firm and correct, there will he good fortune. Going beyond (his own) gate to find associates, he will achieve merit.

2. The second line, divided, shows us one who cleaves to the little boy, and lets go the man of age and experience.

3. The third line, divided, shows us one who cleaves to the man of age and experience, and lets go the little boy. Such following will get what it seeks; but it will be advantageous to adhere to what is firm and correct.

4. The fourth line, undivided, shows us one followed and obtaining (adherents). Though he be firm and correct, there will be evil. If he be sincere (however) in his course, and make that evident, into what error will he fall?

5. The fifth line, undivided, shows us (the ruler) sincere in

(fostering all) that is excellent. There will be good fortune.

6. The topmost line, divided, shows us (that sincerity) firmly held and clung to, yea, and bound fast. (We see) the king with it presenting his offerings on the western mountain.

## XVIII.[xviii] THE KÛ HEXAGRAM.

Kû indicates great progress and success (to him who deals properly with the condition represented by it). There will be advantage in (efforts like that of) crossing the great stream. (He should weigh well, however, the events of) three days before the turning point, and those (to be done) three days after it.

1. The first line, divided, shows (a son) dealing with the troubles caused by his father. If he be an (able) son, the father will escape the blame of having erred. The position is perilous, but there will be good fortune in the end.

2. The second line, undivided, shows (a son) dealing with the troubles caused by his mother. He should not (carry) his firm correctness (to the utmost).

3. The third line, undivided, shows (a son) dealing with the troubles caused by his father. There may be some small occasion for repentance, but there will not be any great error.

4. The fourth line, divided, shows (a son) viewing indulgently the troubles caused by his father. If he go forward, he will find cause to regret it.

5. The fifth line, divided, shows (a son) dealing with the troubles caused by his father. He obtains the praise of using (the fit instrument for his work).

6. The sixth line, undivided, shows us one who does not serve either king or feudal lord, but in a lofty spirit prefers (to attend to) his own affairs.

## XIX.<sup>xix</sup> THE LIN HEXAGRAM.

Lin (indicates that under the conditions supposed in it) there will be great progress and success, while it will be advantageous to be firmly correct. In the eighth month there will be evil.

1. The first line, undivided, shows its subject advancing in company (with the subject of the second line). Through his firm correctness there will be good fortune.
2. The second line, undivided, shows its subject advancing in company (with the subject of the first line). There will be good fortune; (advancing) will be in every way advantageous.
3. The third line, divided, shows one well pleased (indeed) to advance, (but whose action) will be in no way advantageous. If he become anxious about it (however), there will be no error.
4. The fourth line, divided, shows one advancing in the highest mode. There will be no error.
5. The fifth line, divided, shows the advance of wisdom, such as befits the great ruler. There will be good fortune.
6. The sixth line, divided, shows the advance of honesty and generosity. There will be good fortune, and no error.

## XX.<sup>xx</sup> THE KWÂN HEXAGRAM.

Kwân shows (how he whom it represents should be like) the worshipper who has washed his hands, but not (yet) presented his offerings;—with sincerity and an appearance of dignity (commanding reverent regard).

1. The first line, divided, shows the looking of a lad;—not blamable in men of inferior rank, but matter for regret in superior men.
2. The second line, divided, shows one peeping out from a door. It would be advantageous if it were (merely) the firm correctness of a female.
3. The third line, divided, shows one looking at (the course of) his own life, to advance or recede (accordingly).

4. The fourth line, divided, shows one contemplating the glory of the kingdom. It will be advantageous for him, being such as he is, (to seek) to be a guest of the king.

5. The fifth line, undivided, shows its subject contemplating his own life (-course). A superior man, he will (thus) fall into no error.

6. The sixth line, undivided, shows its subject contemplating his character to see if it be indeed that of a superior man. He will not fall into error.

## XXI.[xxi] THE SHIH HO HEXAGRAM.

Shih Ho indicates successful progress (in the condition of things which it supposes). It will be advantageous to use legal constraints.

1. The first line, undivided, shows one with his feet in the stocks and deprived of his toes. There will be no error.

2. The second line, divided, shows one biting through the soft flesh, and (going on to) bite off the nose. There will be no error.

3. The third line, divided, shows one gnawing dried flesh, and meeting with what is disagreeable. There will be occasion for some small regret, but no (great) error.

4. The fourth line, undivided, shows one gnawing the flesh dried on the bone, and getting the pledges of money and arrows. It will be advantageous to him to realise the difficulty of his task and be firm,—in which case there will be good fortune.

5. The fifth line, divided, shows one gnawing at dried flesh, and finding the yellow gold. Let him be firm and correct, realising the peril (of his position). There will be no error.

6. The sixth line, undivided, shows one wearing the cangue, and deprived of his ears. There will be evil.

## XXII.[xxii] THE PÎ HEXAGRAM.

Pî indicates that there should be free course (in what it denotes). There will be little advantage (however) if it be allowed to advance (and take the lead).

1. The first line, undivided, shows one adorning (the way of) his feet. He can discard a carriage and walk on foot.

2. The second line, divided, shows one adorning his beard.

3. The third line, undivided, shows its subject with the appearance of being adorned and bedewed (with rich favours). But let him ever maintain his firm correctness, and there will be good fortune.

4. The fourth line, divided, shows one looking as if adorned, but only in white. As if (mounted on) a white horse, and furnished with wings, (he seeks union with the subject of the first line), while (the intervening third pursues), not as a robber, but intent on a matrimonial alliance.

5. The fifth line, divided, shows its subject adorned by (the occupants of) the heights and gardens. He bears his roll of silk, small and slight. He may appear stingy; but there will be good fortune in the end.

6. The sixth line, undivided, shows one with white as his (only) ornament. There will be no error.

## XXIII.[xxiii] THE PO HEXAGRAM.

Po indicates that (in the state which it symbolises) it will not be advantageous to make a movement in any direction whatever.

1. The first line, divided, shows one overturning the couch by injuring its legs. (The injury will go on to) the destruction of (all) firm correctness, and there will be evil.

2. The second line, divided, shows one overthrowing the couch by injuring its frame. (The injury will go on to) the destruction of (all) firm correctness, and there will be evil.

3. The third line, divided, shows its subject among the overthrowers; but there will be no error.

4. The fourth line, divided, shows its subject having overthrown the couch, and (going to injure) the skin (of him who lies on it). There will be evil.

5. The fifth line, divided, shows (its subject leading on the others like) a string of fishes, and (obtaining for them) the favour that lights on the inmates of the palace. There will be advantage in every way.

6. The topmost line, undivided, shows its subject (as) a great fruit which has not been eaten. The superior man finds (the people again) as a chariot carrying him. The small men (by their course) overthrow their own dwellings.

## XXIV.[xxiv] THE FÛ HEXAGRAM.

Fû indicates that there will be free course and progress (in what it denotes). (The subject of it) finds no one to distress him in his exits and entrances; friends come to him, and no error is committed. He will return and repeat his (proper) course. In seven days comes his return. There will be advantage in whatever direction movement is made.

1. The first line, undivided, shows its subject returning (from an error) of no great extent, which would not proceed to anything requiring repentance. There will be great good fortune.
2. The second line, divided, shows the admirable return (of its subject). There will be good fortune.
3. The third line, divided, shows one who has made repeated returns. The position is perilous, but there will be no error.
4. The fourth line, divided, shows its subject moving right in the centre (among those represented by the other divided lines), and yet returning alone (to his proper path).
5. The fifth line, divided, shows the noble return of its subject. There will be no ground for repentance.
6. The topmost line, divided, shows its subject all astray on the subject of returning. There will be evil. There will be calamities and errors. If with his views he put the hosts in motion, the end will be a great defeat, whose issues will extend to the ruler of the state. Even in ten years he will not be able to repair the disaster.

## XXV.[xxv] THE WÛ WANG HEXAGRAM.

Wû Wang indicates great progress and success, while there will be advantage in being firm and correct. If (its subject and his action) be not correct, he will fall into errors, and it will not be advantageous for him to move in any direction.

1. The first line, undivided, shows its subject free from all insincerity. His advance will be accompanied with good fortune.
2. The second line, divided, shows one who reaps without having ploughed (that he might reap), and gathers the produce of his third

year's fields without having cultivated them the first year for that end. To such a one there will be advantage in whatever direction he may move.

3. The third line, divided, shows calamity happening to one who is free from insincerity;—as in the case of an ox that has been tied up. A passer by finds it (and carries it off), while the people in the neighbourhood have the calamity (of being accused and. apprehended).

4. The fourth line, undivided, shows (a case) in which, if its subject can remain firm and correct, there will be no error.

5. The fifth line, undivided, shows one who is free from insincerity, and yet has fallen ill. Let him not use medicine, and he will have occasion for joy (in his recovery).

6. The topmost line, undivided, shows its subject free from insincerity, yet sure to fall into error, if he take action. (His action) will not be advantageous in any way.

## XXVI.[xxvi] THE TÂ *KHÛ* HEXAGRAM.

Under the conditions of Tâ *Khû* it will be advantageous to be firm and correct. (If its subject do not seek to) enjoy his revenues in his own family (without taking service at court), there will be good fortune. It will be advantageous for him to cross the great stream.

1. The first line, undivided, shows its subject in a position of peril. It will be advantageous for him to stop his advance.

2. The second line, undivided, shows a carriage with the strap under it removed.

3. The third line, undivided, shows its subject urging his way with good horses. It will be advantageous for him to realise the difficulty (of his course), and to be firm and correct, exercising himself daily in his charioteering and methods of defence; then there will be advantage in whatever direction he may advance.

4. The fourth six, divided, shows the young bull, (and yet) having the piece of wood over his horns. There will be great good fortune.

5. The fifth six, divided, shows the teeth of a castrated hog. There will be good fortune.

6. The sixth line, undivided, shows its subject (as) in command of the firmament of heaven. There will be progress.

## XXVII.[xxvii] THE I HEXAGRAM.

Î indicates that with firm correctness there will be good fortune (in what is denoted by it). We must look at what we are seeking to nourish, and by the exercise of our thoughts seek for the proper aliment.

1. The first line, undivided, (seems to be thus addressed), 'You leave your efficacious tortoise, and look at me till your lower jaw hangs down.' There will be evil.

2. The second line, divided, shows one looking downwards for nourishment, which is contrary to what is proper; or seeking it from the height (above), advance towards which will lead to evil.

3. The third line, divided, shows one acting contrary to the method of nourishing. However firm he may be, there will be evil. For ten years let him not take any action, (for) it will not be in any way advantageous.

4. The fourth line, divided, shows one looking downwards for (the power to) nourish. There will be good fortune. Looking with a tiger's downward unwavering glare, and with his desire that impels him to spring after spring, he will fall into no error.

5. The fifth line, divided, shows one acting contrary to what is regular and proper; but if he abide in firmness, there will be good fortune. He should not, (however, try to) cross the great stream.

6. The sixth line, undivided, shows him from whom comes the nourishing. His position is perilous, but there will be good fortune. It will be advantageous to cross the great stream.

## XXVIII.[xxviii] THE TÂ KWO HEXAGRAM.

Tâ Kwo suggests to us a beam that is weak. There will be advantage in moving (under its conditions) in any direction whatever; there will be success.

1. The first line, divided, shows one placing mats of the white mâo grass under things set on the ground. There will be no error.

2. The second line, undivided, shows a decayed willow producing

shoots, or an old husband in possession of his young wife. There will be advantage in every way.

3. The third line, undivided, shows a beam that is weak. There will be evil.

4. The fourth line, undivided, shows a beam curving upwards. There will be good fortune. If (the subject of it) looks for other (help but that of line one), there will be cause for regret.

5. The fifth line, undivided, shows a decayed willow producing flowers, or an old wife in possession of her young husband. There will be occasion neither for blame nor for praise.

6. The topmost line, divided, shows its subject with extraordinary (boldness) wading through a stream, till the water hides the crown of his head. There will be evil, but no ground for blame.

## XXIX.[xxix] THE KHAN HEXAGRAM.

Khan, here repeated, shows the possession of sincerity, through which the mind is. penetrating. Action (in accordance with this) will be of high value.

1. The first line, divided, shows its subject in the double defile, and (yet) entering a cavern within it. There will be evil.

2. The second line, undivided, shows its subject in all the peril of the defile. He will, however, get a little (of the deliverance) that he seeks.

3. The third line, divided, shows its subject, whether he comes or goes ( = descends or ascends), confronted by a defile. All is peril to him and unrest. (His endeavours) will lead him into the cavern of the pit. There should be no action (in such a case).

4. The fourth line, divided, shows its subject (at a feast), with (simply) a bottle of spirits, and a subsidiary basket of rice, while (the cups and bowls) are (only) of earthenware. He introduces his important lessons (as his ruler's) intelligence admits. There will in the end be no error.

5. The fifth line, undivided, shows the water of the defile not yet full, (so that it might flow away); but order will (soon) be brought about. There will be no error.

6. The topmost line, divided, shows its subject bound with cords of three strands or two strands, and placed in the thicket of thorns. But in three years he does not learn the course for him to pursue. There will be evil.

## XXX.<sup>xxx</sup> THE LÎ HEXAGRAM.

Lî indicates that, (in regard to what it denotes), it will be advantageous to be firm and correct, and that thus there will be free course and success. Let (its subject) also nourish (a docility like that of) the cow, and there will be good fortune.

1. The first line, undivided, shows one ready to move with confused steps. But he treads at the same time reverently, and there will be no mistake.

2. The second line, divided, shows its subject in his place in yellow. There will be great good fortune.

3. The third line, undivided, shows its subject in a position like that of the declining sun. Instead of playing on his instrument of earthenware, and singing to it, he utters the groans of an old man of eighty. There will be evil.

4. The fourth line, undivided, shows the manner of its subject's coming. How abrupt it is, as with fire, with death, to be rejected (by all)!

5. The fifth line, divided, shows its subject as one with tears flowing in torrents, and groaning in sorrow. There will be good fortune.

6. The topmost line, undivided, shows the king employing its subject in his punitive expeditions. Achieving admirable (merit), he breaks (only) the chiefs (of the rebels). Where his prisoners were not their associates, he does not punish. There will be no error.

## SECTION II.

## XXXI.<sup>xxxi</sup> THE HSIEN HEXAGRAM.

Hsien indicates that, (on the fulfilment of the conditions implied in it), there will be free course and success. Its advantageousness will depend on the being firm and correct, (as) in marrying a young lady. There will be good fortune.

1. The first six, divided, shows one moving his great toes.

2. The second line, divided, shows one moving the calves of his leg. There will be evil. If he abide (quiet in his place), there will be good fortune.

3. The third line, undivided, shows one moving his thighs, and keeping close hold of those whom he follows. Going forward (in this way) will cause regret.

4. The fourth line, undivided, shows that firm correctness whi.ch will lead to good fortune, and prevent all occasion for repentance. If its subject be unsettled in his movements, (only) his friends will follow his purpose.

5. The fifth line, undivided, shows one moving the flesh along the spine above the heart. There will be no occasion for repentance.

6. The sixth six, divided, shows one moving his jaws and tongue.

## XXXII.[xxxii] THE HĂNG HEXAGRAM.

Hăng indicates successful progress and no error (in what it denotes). But the advantage will come from being firm and correct; and movement in any direction whatever will be advantageous.

1. The first line, divided, shows its subject deeply (desirous) of long continuance. Even with firm correctness there will be evil; there will be no advantage in any way.

2. The second line, undivided, shows all occasion for repentance disappearing.

3. The third line, undivided, shows one who does not continuously maintain his virtue. There are those who will impute this to him as a disgrace. However firm he may be, there will be ground for regret.

4. The fourth line, undivided, shows a field where there is no game.

5. The fifth line, divided, shows its subject continuously maintaining the virtue indicated by it. In a wife this will be fortunate; in a husband, evil.

6. The topmost line, divided, shows its subject exciting himself to long continuance. There will be evil.

## XXXIII.<sup>xxxiii</sup> THE THUN HEXAGRAM.

Thun indicates successful progress (in its circumstances). To a small extent it will (still) be advantageous to be firm and correct.

1. The first line, divided, shows a retiring tail. The position is perilous. No movement in any direction should be made.
2. The second line, divided, shows its subject holding (his purpose) fast as if by a (thong made from the) hide of a yellow ox, which cannot be broken.
3. The third line, undivided, shows one retiring but bound,—to his distress and peril. (If he were to deal with his binders as in) nourishing a servant or concubine, it would be fortunate for him.
4. The fourth line, undivided, shows its subject retiring notwithstanding his likings. In a superior man this will lead to good fortune; a small man cannot attain to this.
5. The fifth line, undivided, shows its subject retiring in an admirable way. With firm correctness there will be good fortune.
6. The sixth line, undivided, shows its subject retiring in a noble way. It will be advantageous in every respect.

## XXXIV.<sup>xxxiv</sup> THE TÂ *K*WANG HEXAGRAM.

Tâ *K*wang indicates that (under the conditions which it symbolises) it will be advantageous to be firm and correct.

1. The first line, undivided, shows its subject manifesting his strength in his toes. But advance will lead to evil,—most certainly.
2. The second line, undivided, shows that with firm correctness there will be good fortune.
3. The third line, undivided, shows, in the case of a small man, one using all his strength; and in the case of a superior man, one whose rule is not to do so. Even with firm correctness the position would be perilous. (The exercise of strength in it might be compared to the case of) a ram butting against a fence, and getting his horns entangled.
4. The fourth line, undivided, shows (a case in which) firm

correctness leads to good fortune, and occasion for repentance disappears. (We see) the fence opened without the horns being entangled. The strength is like that in the wheel-spokes of a large waggon.

5. The fifth line, divided, shows one who loses his ram(-like strength) in the ease of his position. (But) there will be no occasion for repentance.

6. The sixth line, divided, shows (one who may be compared to) the ram butting against the fence, and unable either to retreat, or to advance as he would fain do. There will not be advantage in any respect; but if he realise the difficulty (of his position), there will be good fortune.

## XXXV.<sup>xxxv</sup> THE 3IN HEXAGRAM.

In 3in we see a prince who secures the tranquillity (of the people) presented on that account with numerous horses (by the king), and three times in a day received at interviews.

1. The first line, divided, shows one wishing to advance, and (at the same time) kept back. Let him be firm and correct, and there will be good fortune. If trust be not reposed in him, let him maintain a large and generous mind, and there will be no error.

2. The second line, divided, shows its subject with the appearance of advancing, and yet of being sorrowful. If he be firm and correct, there will be good fortune. He will receive this great blessing from his grandmother.

3. The third line, divided, shows its subject trusted by all (around him). All occasion for repentance will disappear.

4. The fourth line, undivided, shows its subject with the appearance of advancing, but like a marmot. However firm and correct he may be, the position is one of peril.

5. The fifth line, divided, shows how all occasion for repentance disappears (from its subject). (But) let him not concern himself about whether he shall fail or succeed. To advance will be fortunate, and in every way advantageous.

6. The topmost line, undivided, shows one advancing his horns. But he only uses them to punish the (rebellious people of his own) city. The position is perilous, but there will be good fortune. (Yet) however firm and correct he may be, there will be occasion for regret.

## XXXVI.<sup>xxxvi</sup> THE MING Î HEXAGRAM.

Ming Î indicates that (in the circumstances which it denotes) it will be advantageous to realise the difficulty (of the position), and maintain firm correctness.

1. The first line, undivided, shows its subject, (in the condition indicated by) Ming Î, flying, but with drooping wings. When the superior man (is revolving) his going away, he may be for three days without eating. Wherever he goes, the people there may speak (derisively of him).

2. The second line, divided, shows its subject, (in the condition indicated by) Ming Î, wounded in the left thigh. He saves himself by the strength of a (swift) horse; and is fortunate.

3. The third line, undivided, shows its subject, (in the condition indicated by) Ming Î, hunting in the south, and taking the great chief (of the darkness). He should not be eager to make (all) correct (at once).

4. The fourth six, divided, shows its subject (just) entered into the left side of the belly (of the dark land). (But) he is able to carry out the mind appropriate (in the condition indicated by) Ming Î, quitting the gate and courtyard (of the lord of darkness).

5. The fifth six, divided, shows how the count of Kî fulfilled the condition indicated by Ming Î. It will be advantageous to be firm and correct.

6. The sixth six, divided, shows the case where there is no light, but (only) obscurity. (Its subject) had at first ascended to (the top of) the sky; his future shall be to go into the earth.

## XXXVII.<sup>xxxvii</sup> THE *KIÂ ZĂN* HEXAGRAM.

For (the realisation of what is taught in) *Kiâ Zăn*, (or for the regulation of the family), what is most advantageous is that the wife be firm and correct.

1. The first line, undivided, shows its subject establishing restrictive regulations in his household Occasion for repentance will disappear.

2. The second line, divided, shows its subject taking nothing on herself, but in her central place attending to the preparation of the food. Through her firm correctness there will be good fortune.

3. The third line, undivided, shows its subject (treating) the members of the household with stern severity. There will be occasion for repentance, there will be peril, (but) there will (also) be good fortune. If the wife and children were to be smirking and chattering, in the end there would be occasion for regret.

4. The fourth line, divided, shows its subject enriching the family. There will be great good fortune.

5. The fifth line, undivided, shows the influence of the king extending to his family. There need be no anxiety; there will be good fortune.

6. The topmost line, undivided, shows its subject possessed of sincerity and arrayed in majesty. In the end there will be good fortune.

XXXVIII.<sup>xxxviii</sup> THE *KH*WEI HEXAGRAM.

Khwei indicates that, (notwithstanding the condition of things which it denotes), in small matters there will (still) be good success.

1. The first line, undivided, shows that (to its subject) occasion for repentance will disappear. He has lost his horses, but let him not seek for them;—they will return of themselves. Should he meet with bad men, he will not err (in communicating with them).

2. The second line, undivided, shows its subject happening to meet with his lord in a bye-passage. There will be no error.

3. In the third line, divided, we see one whose carriage is dragged back, while the oxen in it are pushed back, and he is himself subjected to the shaving of his head and the cutting off of his nose. There is no good beginning, but there will be a good end.

4. The fourth line, undivided, shows its subject solitary amidst the (prevailing) disunion. (But) he meets with the good man (represented by the first line), and they blend their sincere desires together. The position is one of peril, but there will be no mistake.

5. The fifth line, divided, shows that (to its subject) occasion for repentance will disappear. With his relative (and minister he unites

closely and readily) as if he were biting through a piece of skin. When he goes forward (with this help), what error can there be?

6. The topmost line, undivided, shows its subject solitary amidst the (prevailing) disunion. (In the subject of the third line, he seems to) see a pig bearing on its back a load of mud, (or fancies) there is a carriage full of ghosts. He first bends his bow against him, and afterwards unbends it, (for he discovers) that he is not an assailant to injure, but a near relative. Going forward, he shall meet with (genial) rain, and there will be good fortune.

## XXXIX.<sup>xxxix</sup> THE *K*IEN HEXAGRAM.

In (the state indicated by) *K*ien advantage will be found in the south-west, and the contrary in the north-east. It will be advantageous (also) to meet with the great man. (In these circumstances), with firmness and correctness, there will be good fortune.

1. From the first line, divided, we learn that advance (on the part of its subject) will lead to (greater) difficulties, while remaining stationary will afford ground for praise.

2. The second line, divided, shows the minister of the king struggling with difficulty on difficulty, and not with a view to his own advantage.

3. The third line, undivided, shows its subject advancing, (but only) to (greater) difficulties. He remains stationary, and returns (to his former associates).

4. The fourth line, divided, shows its subject advancing, (but only) to (greater) difficulties. He remains stationary, and unites (with the subject of the line above).

5. The fifth line, undivided, shows its subject struggling with the greatest difficulties, while friends are coming to help him.

6. The topmost line, divided, shows its subject going forward, (only to increase) the difficulties, while his remaining stationary will be (productive of) great (merit). There will be good fortune, and it will be advantageous to meet with the great man.

## XL.[xl] THE *K*IEH HEXAGRAM.

In (the state indicated by) *K*ieh advantage will be found in the south-west. If no (further) operations be called for, there will be good fortune in coming back (to the old conditions). If some operations be called for, there will be good fortune in the early conducting of them.

1. The first line, divided, shows that its subject will commit no error.

2. The second line, undivided, shows its subject catch, in hunting, three foxes, and obtain the yellow (= golden) arrows. With firm correctness there will be good fortune.

3. The third line, divided, shows a porter with his burden, (yet) riding in a carriage. He will (only) tempt robbers to attack him. However firm and correct he may (try to) be, there will be cause for regret.

4. (To the subject of) the fourth line, undivided, (it is said), 'Remove your toes. Friends will (then) come, between you and whom there will be mutual confidence.'

5. The fifth line, divided, shows (its subject), the superior man (= the ruler), executing his function of removing (whatever is injurious to the idea of the hexagram), in which case there will he good fortune, and confidence in him will be shown even by the small men.

6. In the sixth line, divided, we see a feudal prince (with his bow) shooting at a falcon on the top of a high wall, and hitting it. (The effect of his action) will be in every way advantageous.

## XLI.[xli] THE SUN HEXAGRAM.

In (what is denoted by) Sun, if there be sincerity (in him who employs it), there will be great good fortune:—freedom from error; firmness and correctness that can be maintained; and advantage in every movement that shall be made. In what shall this (sincerity in the exercise of Sun) be employed? (Even) in sacrifice two baskets of grain, (though there be nothing else), may be presented.

1. The first line, undivided, shows its subject suspending his own affairs, and hurrying away (to help the subject of the fourth line). He will commit no error, but let him consider how far he should contribute of what is his (for the other).

2. The second line, undivided, shows that it will be advantageous for its subject to maintain a firm correctness, and that action on his part will be evil. He can give increase (to his correlate) without taking from himself

3. The third line, divided, shows how of three men walking together, the number is diminished by one; and how one, walking, finds his friend.

4. The fourth line, divided, shows its subject diminishing the ailment under which he labours by making (the subject of the first line) hasten (to his help), and make him glad. There will be no error.

5. The fifth line, divided, shows parties adding to (the stores of) its subject ten pairs of tortoise shells, and accepting no refusal. There will be great good fortune.

6. The topmost line, undivided, shows its subject giving increase to others without taking from himself. There will be no error. With firm correctness there will be good fortune. There will be advantage in every movement that shall be made. He will find ministers more than can be counted by their clans.

## XLII.[xlii] THE YÎ HEXAGRAM.

Yî indicates that (in the state which it denotes) there will be advantage in every movement which shall be undertaken, that it will be advantageous (even) to cross the great stream.

1. The first line, undivided, shows that it will be advantageous for its subject in his position to make a great movement. If it be greatly fortunate, no blame will be imputed to him.

2. The second line, divided, shows parties adding to the stores of its subject ten pairs of tortoise shells whose oracles cannot be opposed. Let him persevere in being firm and correct, and there will be good fortune. Let the king, (having the virtues thus distinguished), employ them in presenting his offerings to God, and there will be good fortune.

3. The third line, divided, shows increase given to its subject by means of what is evil, so that he shall (be led to good), and be without blame. Let him be sincere and pursue the path of the Mean, (so shall he

secure the recognition of the ruler, like) an officer who announces himself to his prince by the symbol of his rank.

4. The fourth line, divided, shows its subject pursuing the due course. His advice to his prince is followed. He can with advantage be relied on in such a movement as that of removing the capital.

5. The fifth line, undivided, shows its subject with sincere heart seeking to benefit (all below). There need be no question about it; the result will be great good fortune. (All below) will with sincere heart acknowledge his goodness.

6. In the sixth line, undivided, we see one to whose increase none will contribute, while many will seek to assail him. He observes no regular rule in the ordering of his heart. There will be evil.

## XLIII.[xliii] THE KWÂI HEXAGRAM.

Kwâi requires (in him who would fulfil its meaning) the exhibition (of the culprit's guilt) in the royal court, and a sincere and earnest appeal (for sympathy and support), with a consciousness of the peril (involved in cutting off the criminal). He should (also) make announcement in his own city, and show that it will not be well to have recourse at once to arms. (In this way) there will be advantage in whatever he shall go forward to.

1. The first line, undivided, shows its subject in (the pride of) strength advancing with his toes. He goes forward, but will not succeed. There will be ground for blame.

2. The second line, undivided, shows its subject full of apprehension and appealing (for sympathy and help). Late at night hostile measures may be (taken against him), but he need not be anxious about them.

3. The third line, undivided, shows its subject (about to advance) with strong (and determined) looks. There will be evil. (But) the superior man, bent on cutting off (the criminal), will walk alone and encounter the rain, (till he be hated by his proper associates) as if he were contaminated (by the others). (In the end) there will be no blame against him.

4. The fourth line, undivided, shows one from whose buttocks the skin has been stripped, and who walks slowly and with difficulty. (If he could act) like a sheep led (after its companions), occasion for repentance would disappear. But though he hear these words, he will not believe them.

5. The fifth line, undivided, shows (the small men like) a bed of purslain, which ought to be uprooted with the utmost determination. (The subject of the line having such determination), his action, in harmony with his central position, will lead to no error or blame.

6. The sixth line, divided, shows its subject without any (helpers) on whom to call. His end will be evil.

## XLIV.[xliv] THE *KÂU* HEXAGRAM.

*K*âu shows a female who is bold and strong. It will not be good to marry (such) a female.

1. The first line, divided, shows how its subject should be kept (like a carriage) tied and fastened to a metal drag, in which case with firm correctness there will be good fortune. (But) if he move in any direction, evil will appear. He will be (like) a lean pig, which is sure to keep jumping about.

2. The second line, undivided, shows its subject with a wallet of fish. There will be no error. But it will not be well to let (the subject of the first line) go forward to the guests.

3. The third line, undivided, shows one from whose buttocks the skin has been stripped so that he walks with difficulty. The position is perilous, but there will be no great error.

4. The fourth line, undivided, shows its subject with his wallet, but no fish in it. This will give rise to evil.

5. The fifth line, undivided, (shows its subject as) a medlar tree overspreading the gourd (beneath it). If he keep his brilliant qualities concealed, (a good issue) will descend (as) from Heaven.

6. The sixth line, undivided, shows its subject receiving others on his horns. There will be occasion for regret, but there will be no error.

## XLV.[xlv] THE 3HUI HEXAGRAM.

In (the state denoted by) 3hui, the king will repair to his ancestral temple. It will be advantageous (also) to meet with the great man; and then there will be progress and success, though the advantage must come through firm correctness. The use of great victims will conduce to good fortune; and in whatever direction movement is made, it will be advantageous.

1. The first line, divided, shows its subject with a sincere desire (for union), but unable to carry it out, so that disorder is brought into the sphere of his union. If he cry out (for help to his proper correlate), all at once (his tears) will give place to smiles. He need not mind (the temporary difficulty); as he goes forward, there will be no error.

2. The second line, divided, shows its subject led forward (by his correlate). There will be good fortune, and freedom from error. There is entire sincerity, and in that case (even the small offerings of) the vernal sacrifice are acceptable.

3. The third line, divided, shows its subject striving after union and seeming to sigh, yet nowhere finding any advantage. If he go forward, he will not err, though there may be some small cause for regret.

4. The fourth line, undivided, shows its subject in such a state that, if he be greatly fortunate, he will receive no blame.

5. The fifth line, undivided, shows the union (of all) under its subject in the place of dignity. There will be no error. If any do not have confidence in him, let him see to it that (his virtue) be great, long-continued, and firmly correct, and all occasion for repentance will disappear.

6. The topmost line, divided, shows its subject sighing and weeping; but there will be no error.

## XLVI.[xlvi] THE SHĂNG HEXAGRAM.

Shăng indicates that (under its conditions) there will be great progress and success. Seeking by (the qualities implied in it) to meet with the great man, its subject need have no anxiety. Advance to the south will be fortunate.

1. The first line, divided, shows its subject advancing upwards with the welcome (of those above him). There will be great good fortune.

2. The second line, undivided, shows its subject with that sincerity which will make even the (small) offerings of the vernal sacrifice acceptable. There will be no error.

3. The third line, undivided, shows its subject ascending upwards (as into) an empty city.

4. The fourth line, divided, shows its subject employed by the king to present his offerings on mount *Khî*. There will be good fortune; there will be no mistake.

5. The fifth six, divided, shows its subject firmly correct, and therefore enjoying good fortune. He ascends the stairs (with all due ceremony).

6. The sixth six, divided, shows its subject advancing upwards blindly. Advantage will be found in a ceaseless maintenance of firm correctness.

## XLVII.<sup>xlvii</sup> THE KHWĂN HEXAGRAM.

In (the condition denoted by) Khwăn there may (yet be) progress and success. For the firm and correct, the (really) great man, there will be good fortune. He will fall into no error. If he make speeches, his words cannot be made good.

1. The first line, divided, shows its subject with bare buttocks straitened under the stump of a tree. He enters a dark valley, and for three years has no prospect (of deliverance).

2. The second line, undivided, shows its subject straitened amidst his wine and viands. There come to him anon the red knee-covers (of the ruler). It will be well for him (to maintain his sincerity as) in sacrificing. Active operations (on his part) will lead to evil, but he will be free from blame.

3. The third line, divided, shows its subject straitened before a (frowning) rock. He lays hold of thorns. He enters his palace, and does not see his wife. There will be evil.

4. The fourth line, undivided shows its subject proceeding very slowly (to help the subject of the first line), who is straitened by the carriage adorned with metal in front of him. There will be occasion for regret, but the end will be good.

5. The fifth line, undivided, shows its subject with his nose and feet cut off. He is straitened by (his ministers in their) scarlet aprons. He is leisurely in his movements, however, and is satisfied. It will be well for him to be (as sincere) as in sacrificing (to spiritual beings).

6. The sixth line, divided, shows its subject straitened, as if bound with creepers; or n a high and dangerous position, and saying (to himself), 'If I move, I shall repent it.' If he do repent of former errors, there will be good fortune in his going forward.

## XLVIII.<sup>xlviii</sup> THE ȜING HEXAGRAM.

(Looking at) Ȝing, (we think of) how (the site of) a town may be changed, while (the fashion of) its wells undergoes no change. (The water of a well) never disappears and never receives (any great) increase, and those who come and those who go can draw and enjoy the benefit. If (the drawing) have nearly been accomplished, but, before the rope has quite reached the water, the bucket is broken, this is evil.

1. The first line, divided, shows a well so muddy that men will not drink of it; or an old well to which neither birds (nor other creatures) resort.

2. The second line, undivided, shows a well from which by a hole the water escapes and flows away to the shrimps (and such small creatures among the grass), or one the water of which leaks away from a broken basket.

3. The third line, undivided, shows a well, which has been cleared out, but is not used. Our hearts are sorry for this, for the water might be drawn out and used. If the king were (only) intelligent, both he and we might receive the benefit of it.

4. The fourth line, divided, shows a well, the lining of which is well laid. There will be no error.

5. The fifth line, undivided, shows a clear, limpid well, (the waters from) whose cold spring are (freely) drunk.

6. The topmost line, divided, shows (the water from) the well brought to the top, which is not allowed to be covered. This suggests the idea of sincerity. There will be great good fortune.

## XLIX.<sup>xlix</sup> THE KO HEXAGRAM.

(What takes place as indicated by) Ko is believed in only after it has been accomplished. There will be great progress and success. Advantage will come from being firm and correct. (In that case) occasion for repentance will disappear.

1. The first line, undivided, shows its subject (as if he were) bound with the skin of a yellow ox.

2. The second line, divided, shows its subject making his changes after some time has passed. Action taken will be fortunate. There will be no error.

3. The third line, undivided, shows that action taken by its subject will be evil. Though he be firm and correct, his position is perilous. If the change (he contemplates) have been three times fully discussed, he will be believed in.

4. The fourth line, undivided, shows occasion for repentance disappearing (from its subject). Let him be believed in; and though he change (existing) ordinances, there will be good fortune.

5. The fifth line, undivided, shows the great man (producing his changes) as the tiger (does when he) changes (his stripes). Before he divines (and proceeds to action), faith has been reposed in him.

6. The sixth line, divided, shows the superior man producing his changes as the leopard (does when he) changes (his spots), while small men change their faces (and show their obedience). To go forward (now) would lead to evil, but there will be good fortune in abiding firm and correct.

## L.[1] THE TING HEXAGRAM.

Ting gives the intimation of great progress and success.

1. The first line, divided, shows the caldron overthrown and its feet turned up. (But) there will be advantage in its getting rid of what was bad in it. (Or it shows us) the concubine (whose position is improved) by means of her son. There will be no error.

2. The second line, undivided, shows the caldron with the things (to be cooked) in it. (If its subject can say), 'My enemy dislikes me, but he cannot approach me,' there will be good fortune.

3. The third line, undivided, shows the caldron with (the places of) its ears changed. The progress (of its subject) is (thus) stopped. The fat flesh of the pheasant (which is in the caldron) will not be eaten. But the (genial) rain will come, and the grounds for repentance will disappear. There will be good fortune in the end.

4. The fourth line, undivided, shows the caldron with its feet broken; and its contents, designed for the ruler's use, overturned and spilt. Its Subject will be made to blush for shame. There will be evil.

5. The fifth six, divided, shows the caldron with yellow ears and rings of metal in them. There will be advantage through being firm and correct.

6. The sixth line, undivided, shows the caldron with rings of jade. There will be great good fortune, and all action taken will be in every way advantageous.

## LI.[li] THE *KĂN* HEXAGRAM.

*K*ăn gives the intimation of ease and development. When (the time of) movement (which it indicates) comes, (the subject of the hexagram) will be found looking out with apprehension, and yet smiling and talking cheerfully. When the movement (like a crash of thunder) terrifies all within a hundred lî, he will be (like the sincere worshipper) who is not (startled into) letting go his ladle and (cup of) sacrificial spirits.

1. The first line, undivided, shows its subject, when the movement approaches, looking out and around with apprehension, and afterwards smiling and talking cheerfully. There will be good fortune.

2. The second line, divided, shows its subject, when the movement approaches, in a position of peril. He judges it better to let go the articles (in his possession), and to ascend a very lofty height. There is no occasion for him to pursue after (the things he has let go); in seven days he will find them.

3. The third six, divided, shows its subject distraught amid the startling movements going on. If those movements excite him to (right) action, there will be no mistake.

4. The fourth line, undivided, shows its subject, amid the startling movements, supinely sinking (deeper) in the mud.

5. The fifth line, divided, shows its subject going and coming amidst the startling movements (of the time), and always in peril; but perhaps he will not incur loss, and find business (which he can accomplish).

6. The topmost line, divided, shows its subject, amidst the startling movements (of the time), in breathless dismay and looking round him with trembling apprehension. If he take action, there will be evil. If, while the startling movements have not reached his own person and his neighbourhood, (he were to take precautions), there would be no error, though his relatives might (still) speak against him.

## LII.<sup>lii</sup> THE KĂN HEXAGRAM.

When one's resting is like that of the back, and he loses all consciousness of self; when he walks in his courtyard, and does not see any (of the persons) in it,—there will be no error.

1. The first line, divided, shows its subject keeping his toes at rest. There will be no error; but it will be advantageous for him to be persistently firm and correct.
2. The second line, divided, shows its subject keeping the calves of his legs at rest. He cannot help (the subject of the line above) whom he follows, and is dissatisfied in his mind.
3. The third line, undivided, shows its subject keeping his loins at rest, and separating the ribs (from the body below). The situation is perilous, and the heart glows with suppressed excitement.
4. The fourth line, divided, shows its subject keeping his trunk at rest. There will be no error.
S. The fifth line, divided, shows its subject keeping his jawbones at rest, so that his words are (all) orderly. Occasion for repentance will disappear.
6. The sixth line, undivided, shows its subject devotedly maintaining his restfulness. There will be good fortune.

## LIII.<sup>liii</sup> THE *K*IEN HEXAGRAM.

*K*ien suggests to us the marriage of a young lady, and the good fortune (attending it). There will be advantage in being firm and correct.

1. The first line, divided, shows the wild geese gradually approaching the shore. A young officer (in similar circumstances) will be in a position of danger, and be spoken against; but there will be no error.
2. The second line, divided, shows the geese gradually approaching the large rocks, where they eat and drink joyfully and at ease. There will be good fortune.
3. The third line, undivided, shows them gradually advanced to the

dry plains. (It suggests also the idea of) a husband who goes on an expedition from which he does not return, and of a wife who is pregnant, but will not nourish her child. There will be evil. (The case symbolised) might be advantageous in resisting plunderers.

4. The fourth line, divided, shows the geese gradually advanced to the trees. They may light on the flat branches. There will be no error.

5. The fifth line, undivided, shows the geese gradually advanced to the high mound. (It suggests the idea of) a wife who for three years does not become pregnant; but in the end the natural issue cannot be prevented. There will be good fortune.

6. The sixth line, undivided, shows the geese gradually advanced to the large heights (beyond). Their feathers can be used as ornaments. There will be good fortune.

## LIV.[liv] THE KWEI MEI HEXAGRAM.

Kwei Mei indicates that (under the conditions which it denotes) action will be evil, and in no wise advantageous.

1. The first line, undivided, shows the younger sister married off in a position ancillary to the real wife. (It suggests the idea of) a person lame on one leg who yet manages to tramp along. Going forward will be fortunate.

2. The second line, undivided, shows her blind of one eye, and yet able to see. There will be advantage in her maintaining the firm correctness of a solitary widow.

3. The third line, divided, shows the younger sister who was to be married off in a mean position. She returns and accepts an ancillary position.

4. The fourth line, undivided, shows the younger sister who is to be married off protracting the time. She may be late in being married, but the time will come.

5. The fifth line, divided, reminds us of the marrying of the younger sister of (king) Tî-yî, when the sleeves of her the princess were not equal to those of the (still) younger sister who accompanied her in an inferior capacity. (The case suggests the thought of) the moon almost full. There will be good fortune.

6. The sixth line, divided, shows the young lady bearing the basket, but without anything in it, and the gentleman slaughtering the sheep, but without blood flowing from it. There will be no advantage in any way.

## LV.<sup>lv</sup> THE FĂNG HEXAGRAM.

Făng intimates progress and development. When a king has reached the point (which the name denotes) there is no occasion to be anxious (through fear of a change). Let him be as the sun at noon.

1. The first line, undivided, shows its subject meeting with his mate. Though they are both of the same character, there will be no error. Advance will call forth approval.

2. The second line, divided, shows its subject surrounded by screens so large and thick that at midday he can see from them the constellation of the Bushel. If he go (and try to enlighten his ruler who is thus emblemed), he will make himself to be viewed with suspicion and dislike. Let him cherish his feeling of sincere devotion that he may thereby move (his ruler's mind), and there will be good fortune.

3. The third line, undivided, shows its subject with an (additional) screen of a large and thick banner, through which at midday he can see (the small) Mei star. (In the darkness) he breaks his right arm; but there will be no error.

4. The fourth line, undivided, shows its subject in a tent so large and thick that at midday he can see from it the constellation of the Bushel. But he meets with the subject of the (first) line, undivided like himself. There will be good fortune.

5. The fifth line, divided, shows its subject bringing around him the men of brilliant ability. There will be occasion for congratulation and praise. There will be good fortune.

6. The topmost line, divided, shows its subject with his house made large, but only serving as a screen to his household. When he looks at his door, it is still, and there is nobody about it. For three years no one is to be seen. There will be evil.

## LVI.<sup>lvi</sup> THE LÜ HEXAGRAM.

Lü intimates that (in the condition which it denotes) there may be some little attainment and progress. If the stranger or traveller be firm and correct as he ought to be, there will be good fortune.

1. The first line, divided, shows the stranger mean and meanly occupied. It is thus that he brings on himself (further) calamity.

2. The second line, divided, shows the stranger, occupying his lodging-house, carrying with him his means of livelihood, and provided with good and trusty servants.

3. The third line, undivided, shows the stranger, burning his lodging-house, and having lost his servants. However firm and correct he (try to) be, he will be in peril.

4. The fourth line, undivided, shows the traveller in a resting-place, having (also) the means of livelihood and the axe, (but still saying), 'I am not at ease in my mind.'

5. The fifth line, divided, shows its subject shooting a pheasant. He will lose his arrow, but in the end he will obtain praise and a (high) charge.

6. The sixth line, undivided, suggests the idea of a bird burning its nest. The stranger, (thus represented), first laughs and then cries out. He has lost his ox(-like docility) too readily and easily. There will be evil.

## LVII.[lvii] THE SUN HEXAGRAM.

Sun intimates that (under the conditions which it denotes) there will be some little attainment and progress. There will be advantage in movement onward in whatever direction. It will be advantageous (also) to see the great man.

1. The first line, divided, shows its subject (now) advancing, (now) receding. It would be advantageous for him to have the firm correctness of a brave soldier.

2. The second line, undivided, shows the representative of Sun beneath a couch, and employing diviners and exorcists in a way bordering on confusion. There will be good fortune and no error.

3. The third line, undivided, shows its subject penetrating (only) by violent and repeated efforts. There will be occasion for regret.

4. The fourth line, divided, shows all occasion for repentance (in its subject) passed away. He takes game for its threefold use in his hunting.

5. The fifth line, undivided, shows that with firm correctness there will be good fortune (to its subject). All occasion for repentance will disappear, and all his movements will be advantageous. There may have been no (good) beginning, but there will be a (good) end. Three

days before making any changes, (let him give notice of them); and three days after, (let him reconsider them). There will (thus) be good fortune.

6. The sixth line, undivided, shows the representative of penetration beneath a couch, and having lost the axe with which he executed his decisions. However firm and correct he may (try to) be, there will be evil.

## LVIII.<sup>lviii</sup> THE TUI HEXAGRAM.

Tui intimates that (under its conditions) there will be progress and attainment. (But) it will be advantageous to be firm and correct.

1. The first line, undivided, shows the pleasure of (inward) harmony. There will be good fortune.

2. The second line, undivided, shows the pleasure arising from (inward) sincerity. There will be good fortune. Occasion for repentance will disappear.

3. The third line, divided, shows its subject bringing round himself whatever can give pleasure. There will be evil.

4. The fourth line, undivided, shows its subject deliberating about what to seek his pleasure in, and not at rest. He borders on what would be injurious, but there will be cause for joy.

5. The fifth line, undivided, shows its subject trusting in one who would injure him. The situation is perilous.

6. The topmost line, divided, shows the pleasure of its subject in leading and attracting others.

## LIX.<sup>lix</sup> THE HWÂN HEXAGRAM.

Hwân intimates that (under its conditions) there will be progress and success. The king goes to his ancestral temple; and it will be advantageous to cross the great stream. It will be advantageous to be firm and correct.

1. The first line, divided, shows its subject engaged in rescuing (from the impending evil) and having (the assistance of) a strong horse. There will be good fortune.

2. The second line, undivided, shows its subject, amid the dispersion, hurrying to his contrivance (for security). All occasion for repentance will disappear.

3. The third line, divided, shows its subject discarding any regard to his own person. There will be no occasion for repentance.

4. The fourth line, divided, shows its subject scattering the (different) parties (in the state); which leads to great good fortune. From the dispersion (he collects again good men standing out, a crowd) like a mound, which is what ordinary men would not have thought of.

5. The fifth line, undivided, shows its subject amidst the dispersion issuing his great announcements as the perspiration (flows from his body). He scatters abroad (also) the accumulations in the royal granaries. There will be no error.

6. The topmost line, undivided, shows its subject disposing of (what may be called) its bloody wounds, and going and separating himself from its anxious fears. There will be no error.

## LX.<sup>lx</sup> THE *K*IEH HEXAGRAM.

*K*ieh intimates that (under its conditions) there will be progress and attainment. (But) if the regulations (which it prescribes) be severe and difficult, they cannot be permanent.

1. The first line, undivided, shows its subject not quitting the courtyard outside his door. There will be no error.

2. The second line, undivided, shows its subject not quitting the courtyard inside his gate. There will be evil.

3. The third line, divided, shows its subject with no appearance of observing the (proper) regulations, in which case we shall see him lamenting. But there will be no one to blame (but himself).

4. The fourth line, divided, shows its subject quietly and naturally (attentive to all) regulations. There will be progress and success.

5. The fifth line, undivided, shows its subject sweetly and acceptably enacting his regulations. There will be good fortune. The onward progress with them will afford ground for admiration.

6. The topmost line, divided, shows its subject enacting regulations severe and difficult. Even with firmness and correctness there will be evil. But though there will be cause for repentance, it will (by and by) disappear.

## LXI.<sup>lxi</sup> THE *K*UNG FÛ HEXAGRAM.

*K*ung Fû (moves even) pigs and fish, and leads to good fortune. There will be advantage in crossing the great stream. There will be advantage in being firm and correct.

1. The first line, undivided, shows its subject resting (in himself). There will be good fortune. If he sought to any other, he would not find rest.
2. The second line, undivided, shows its subject (like) the crane crying out in her hidden retirement, and her young ones responding to her. (It is as if it were said), 'I have a cup of good spirits,' (and the response were), 'I will partake of it with you.'
3. The third line, divided, shows its subject having met with his mate. Now he beats his drum, and now he leaves off. Now he weeps, and now he sings.
4. The fourth line, divided, shows its subject (like) the moon nearly full, and (like) a horse (in a chariot) whose fellow disappears. There will be no error.
5. The fifth line, undivided, shows its subject perfectly sincere, and linking (others) to him in closest union. There will be no error.
6. The topmost line, undivided, shows its subject in chanticleer (trying to) mount to heaven. Even with firm correctness there will be evil.

## LXII.<sup>lxii</sup> THE HSIÂO KWO HEXAGRAM.

Hsiâo Kwo indicates that (in the circumstances which it implies) there will be progress and attainment. But it will be advantageous to be firm and correct. (What the name denotes) may be done in small affairs, but not in great affairs. (It is like) the notes that come down from a bird on the wing;—to descend is better than to ascend. There will (in this way) be great good fortune.

1. The first line, divided, suggests (the idea of) a bird flying, (and ascending) till the issue is evil.
2. The second line, divided, shows its subject passing by his

grandfather, and meeting with his grandmother; not attempting anything against his ruler, but meeting him as his minister. There will be no error.

3. The third line, undivided, shows its subject taking no extraordinary precautions against danger; and some in consequence finding opportunity to assail and injure him. There will be evil.

4. The fourth line, undivided, shows its subject falling into no error, but meeting (the exigency of his situation), without exceeding (in his natural. course). If he go forward, there will be peril, and he must be cautious. There is no occasion to be using firmness perpetually.

5. The fifth line, divided, (suggests the idea) of dense clouds, but no rain, coming from our borders in the west. It also (shows) the prince shooting his arrow, and taking the bird in a cave.

6. The sixth line, divided, shows its subject not meeting (the exigency of his situation), and exceeding (his proper course). (It suggests the idea of) a bird flying far aloft. There will be evil. The case is what is called one of calamity and self-produced injury.

## LXIII.<sup>lxiii</sup> THE *KÎ* 3Î HEXAGRAM.

*Kî* 3î intimates progress and success in small matters. There will be advantage in being firm and correct. There has been good fortune in the beginning; there may be disorder in the end.

1. The first line, undivided, (shows its subject as a driver) who drags back his wheel, (or as a fox) which has wet his tail. There will be no error.

2. The second line, divided, (shows its subject as) a wife who has lost her (carriage-)screen. There is no occasion to go in pursuit of it. In seven days she will find it.

3. The third line, undivided, (suggests the case of) Kâo 3ung, who attacked the Demon region, but was three years in subduing it. Small men should not be employed (in such enterprises).

4. The fourth line, divided, shows its subject with rags provided against any leak (in his boat), and on his guard all day long.

5. The fifth line, undivided, shows its subject (as) the neighbour in the east who slaughters an ox (for his sacrifice); but this is not equal to the (small) spring sacrifice of the neighbour in the west, whose sincerity receives the blessing.

6. The topmost line, divided, shows its subject with (even) his head immersed. The position is perilous.

## LXIV.[lxiv] THE WEI 3î HEXAGRAM.

Wei 3î intimates progress and success (in the circumstances which it implies). (We see) a young fox that has nearly crossed (the stream), when its tail gets immersed. There will be no advantage in any way.

1. The first line, divided, shows its subject (like a fox) whose tail gets immersed. There will be occasion for regret.

2. The second line, undivided, shows its subject dragging back his (carriage-) wheel. With firmness and correctness there will be good fortune.

3. The third line, divided, shows its subject, with (the state of things) not yet remedied, advancing on; which will lead to evil. But there will be advantage in (trying to) cross the great stream.

4. The fourth line, undivided, shows its subject by firm correctness obtaining good fortune, so that all occasion for repentance disappears. Let him stir himself up, as if he were invading the Demon region, where for three years rewards will come to him (and his troops) from the great kingdom.

5. The fifth line, divided, shows its subject by firm correctness obtaining good fortune, and having no occasion for repentance. (We see in him) the brightness of a superior man, and the possession of sincerity. There will be good fortune.

6. The topmost line, undivided, shows its subject full of confidence and therefore feasting (quietly). There will be no error. (If he) cherish this confidence, till he (is like the fox who) gets his head immersed, it will fail of what is right.

## THE APPENDIXES.

## APPENDIX I.

Treatise on the Thwan[61], or king Wăn's Explanations
of the entire Hexagrams.

## SECTION I.

I.[62] 1. Vast is the 'great and originating (power)' indicated by
*Kh*ien! All things owe to it their beginning:—it contains all the
meaning belonging to (the name) heaven.

2. The clouds move and the rain is distributed; the various things
appear in their developed forms.

3. (The sages) grandly understand (the connexion between) the end
and the beginning, and how (the indications of) the six lines (in the
hexagram) are accomplished, (each) in its season. (Accordingly) they
mount (the carriage) drawn by those six dragons at the proper times,
and drive through the sky.

4. The method of *Kh*ien is to change and transform, so that
everything obtains its correct nature as appointed (by the mind of
Heaven); and (thereafter the conditions of) great harmony are preserved
in union. The result is 'what is advantageous, and correct and firm.

5. (The sage) appears aloft, high above all things, and the myriad
states all enjoy repose.

---

[61] The name Thwan, and the meaning of the character so-called, are sufficiently
established. The Thwan are king Wăn's explanations of the entire hexagrams. It seems
impossible now to ascertain how the character arose, and how it was named Thwan. The
treatise on the Thwan is ascribed to Confucius; and I have considered in the Introduction,
p. 30, whether the tradition to this effect may to any extent be admitted.

[62] I. The hexagram *Kh*ien is made up of six undivided lines, or of the trigram *Kh*ien,
Fû-hsî's symbol for heaven, repeated. The Thwan does not dwell upon this, but starts, in
its exposition, from the word 'heaven,' supposing that the hexagram represented all the
meaning which had ever been intended by that term. In paragraphs 1, 2, 4 the four
attributes in Wăn's Text (2 being occupied with the second, though it is not expressly
named) are illustrated by the phenomena taking place in the physical world.

In paragraphs 3 and 5, the subject is the sage. He is not named indeed; and Khung
Ying-tâ (A. D. 574-648) does not introduce him till paragraph 5, when the meaning
necessitates the presence of a human agent, who rules in the world of men as heaven does
in that of nature. The 'connexion between the end and the beginning,' which he sees, is
that of cause and effect in the operations of nature and the course of human affairs. The
various steps in that course are symbolised by the lines of the hexagram; and the ideal
sage, conducting his ideal government, taking his measures accordingly, is represented as
driving through the sky in a carriage drawn by six dragons. *Kû* Hsî extravagantly says
that 'the sage is Heaven, and Heaven is the sage;' but there is nothing like this in the text.

II.[63] 1. Complete is the 'great and originating (capacity)' indicated by Khwăn! All things owe to it their birth;—it receives obediently the influences of Heaven.

2. Khwăn, in its largeness, supports and contains all things. Its excellent capacity matches the unlimited power (of *Kh*ien). Its comprehension is wide, and its brightness great. The various things obtain (by it) their full development.

3. The mare is a creature of earthly kind. Its (power of) moving on the earth is without limit; it is mild and docile, advantageous and firm:—such is the course of the superior man.

4. 'If he take the initiative, he goes astray:'—he misses, that is, his proper course. 'If he follow,' he is docile, and gets into his regular (course). 'In the south-west he will get friends:'—he will be walking with those of his own class. 'In the north-east he will lose friends:'—but in the end there will be ground for congratulation.

5. 'The good fortune arising from resting in firmness' corresponds to the unlimited capacity of the earth.

III.[64] 1. In Kun we have the strong (*Kh*ien) and the weak (Khwăn)

---

[63] II. As the writer in expounding the Thwan of hexagram 1 starts from the word 'heaven,' so here he does so from the symbolic meaning attached to 'earth.' What I have said on the Text about the difference with which the same attributes are ascribed to *Kh*ien and Khwăn, appears clearly in paragraph 1. It is the difference expressed by the words that I have supplied,—'power' and 'capacity.' *Kh*ien originates; Khwăn produces, or gives birth to what has been originated.

The 'penetrating,' or developing ability of Khwăn, as displayed in the processes of growth, is the subject of paragraph 2. 'The brightness' refers to the beauty that shines forth in the vegetable and animal worlds.

Paragraph 3 treats of the symbol of the 'mare,' to lead the mind to the course of 'the superior man,' the good and faithful minister and servant.

See the note, corresponding to paragraph 4, on the Text. 'Resting in firmness' is the normal course of Khwăn. Where it is pursued, the good effect will be great, great as the unlimited capacity of the earth.

[64] III. *K*un is made up of the trigrams *K*ăn and Khan; but according to the views on king Wăn's arrangement of the trigrams, as set forth especially in Appendix V, chap. 14, the six others come from *Kh*ien and Khwăn, and are said to be their children. On the first application of Khwăn to *Kh*ien, there results *K*ăn, the first line of *Kh*ien taking the place of the last of Khwăn; and on the second application, there results Khan, the middle line of *Kh*ien taking the place of that of Khwăn. McClatchie renders here:—'The Thun (*K*un) diagram represents the hard and the soft (air) beginning to have sexual intercourse, and bringing forth with suffering!' But there is nothing in the Yî, from the beginning to the end, to justify such an interpretation. Nor do I see how, from any account of the genesis by the component trigrams, the idea of the result as signifying a state of difficulty and distress can be readily made out.

In paragraph 2 there is an attempt from the virtues or attributes assigned to the trigrams to make out the result indicated in the Thwan. To move and excite is the quality of *K*ăn; perilousness is the quality of Khan. The power to move is likely to produce great effects; to do this in perilous and difficult circumstances requires firmness and correctness. But neither is this explanation very satisfactory.

The first part of paragraph 3 depicts a condition of trouble and disorder in the commencing their intercourse, and difficulties arising.

2. Movement in the midst of peril gives rise to 'great progress and success, (through) firm correctness.'

3. By the action of the thunder and rain, (which are symbols of Kăn and Khan), all (between heaven and earth) is filled up. But the condition of the time is full of irregularity and obscurity. Feudal princes should be established, but the feeling that rest and peace have been secured should not be indulged (even then).

IV.[65] 1. In Măng we have (the trigram for) a mountain, and below it that of a rugged defile with a stream in it. The conditions of peril and arrest of progress (suggested by these) give (the idea in) Măng.

2. 'Măng indicates that there will be progress and success:'—for there is development at work in it, and its time of action is exactly what is right. 'I do not seek the youthful and inexperienced; he seeks me:'—so does will respond to will. 'When he shows (the sincerity that marks) the first recourse to divination, I instruct him:'—for possessing the qualities of the undivided line and being in the central place, (the subject of the second line thus speaks). 'A second and third application create annoyance, and I do not instruct so as to create annoyance:'—annoyance (he means) to the ignorant.

(The method of dealing with) the young and ignorant is to nourish the correct (nature belonging to them);—this accomplishes the service of the sage.

---

natural world occasioned by the phenomena that are symbols of the significance of Kăn and Khan; but this is symbolical again of the disorder and distress, political and social, characteristic of the time. Good princes throughout the nation would help to remedy that; but the supreme authority should not resign itself to indifference, trusting to them.

[65] IV. The trigram Kăn has for its symbol in the natural world a mountain, which stands up frowningly, and stops or arrests the progress of the traveller. Stoppage, understood sometimes actively, and sometimes passively, is called the virtue or attribute indicated by it. Khan, as I said on p. 31, has water for its symbol, and especially in the form of rain. Here, however, the water appears as a stream in a difficult defile, such as ordinarily appears on an approach to a mountain, and suggesting perilousness as the attribute of a position. From the combination of these symbols and their attributes the writer thinks that he gets the idea of the character (not the entire hexagram) Măng, as symbolical of ignorance and inexperience. See on 'the Great Symbolism' below.

Down to the last sentence of paragraph 2, all that is said is intended to show how it is that the figure indicates progress and success. The whole representation is grounded on the undivided line's being in the central place. It is the symbol of active effort for the teaching of the ignorant in the proper place and time; this being responded to by the divided fifth line, representing the ignorance to be taught as docile, 'will responds to will.' But the subject of line 2 requires sincerity in the applicant for instruction, and feels that he must make his own teaching acceptable, and agreeable. All this serves to bring out the idea of progress and success.

Then finally in the young and ignorant there is 'a correct nature,' a moral state made for goodness. The efficient teacher directing his efforts to bring out and nourish that, the progress and success will be 'great;' the service done will be worthy of 'a sage.'

V.[66] 1. Hsü denotes waiting. (The figure) shows peril in front; but notwithstanding the firmness and strength (indicated by the inner trigram), its subject does not allow himself to be involved (in the dangerous defile);—it is right he should not be straitened or reduced to extremity.

2. When it is said that, 'with the sincerity declared in Hsü, there will be brilliant success, and with firmness there will be good fortune,' this is shown by the position (of the fifth line) in the place assigned by Heaven, and its being the correct position for it, and in the centre. 'It will be advantageous to go through the great stream;'—that is, going forward will be followed by meritorious achievement.

VI.[67] 1. The upper portion of Sung is (the trigram representing) strength, and the lower (that representing) peril. (The coming together of) strength and peril gives (the idea in) Sung.

2. 'Sung intimates how, though there is sincerity in one's contention, he will yet meet with opposition and obstruction; but if he cherish an apprehensive caution, there will be good fortune:'—a strong (line) has come and got the central place (in the lower trigram).

'If he must prosecute the contention to the (bitter) end, there will

---

[66] V. Hsü is composed of *Kh*ien, having the quality of strength, and of Khan, having the quality of perilousness. The strong one might readily dare the peril, but he restrains himself and waits. This is the lesson of the hexagram,—the benefit of action well considered, of plans well matured.

The fifth line, as we have observed more than once already, is the place of honour, that due to the ruler or king. It is here called 'the Heavenly or Heaven-given seat, 'the meaning of which expression is clear from its occurrence in the Shih, III, i, ode 2. 1. Five is an odd number, and the fifth is therefore the 'correct' place for an undivided line; it is also the central place of the trigram, indicating how its occupant is sure to walk in the due mean. See further the notes on the Text, p. 52.

[67] VI. Paragraph 1 here is much to the same effect as the first sentence in the notes on the Thwan of the Text. It is said, 'Strength without peril would not produce contention; peril without strength would not be able to contend.'

2. 'A strong line has come and got the central place:'—this sentence has given rise to a doctrine about the changes of trigrams and hexagrams, which has obscured more than anything else the interpretation of the Yî. Where has the strong second line come from? From a hundred critics we receive the answer,—'From Tun ☰☷.' The reader will see that if the second and third lines of the lower trigram there be made to change places, there results ☰☵ or Sung. The doctrine of changing the figures by the manipulation of the stalks did spring up between the time of Wăn and his son and that of the composition of the Appendixes; but there is no trace of it in the real Text of the Yî; and it renders any scheme for the interpretation of the figures impossible. The editors of the imperial Yî allow this, and on the present passage discard the doctrine entirely, referring to the language of the Thwan on hexagrams 11 and 12 as fatal to it. See the notes there, and the Introduction, pp. 16-19. 'A strong line has come' is to be taken as equivalent simply to a strong line is there.'

What 'the great man sets a value on being the due mean and the correct place,' his decision in any matter of contention is sure to be right.

be evil:'—contention is not a thing to be carried on to extremity.

'It will be advantageous to meet with the great man:'—what he sets a value on is the due mean, and the correct place.

'It will not be advantageous to cross the great stream:'—one (attempting to do so) would find himself in an abyss.

VII.[68] 1. (The name) Sze describes the multitude (of the host). The 'firmness and correctness' (which the hexagram indicates) refer to (moral) correctness (of aim). When (the mover) is able to use the multitude with such correctness, he may attain to the royal sway.

2. There is (the symbol of) strength in the centre (of the trigram below), and it is responded to (by its proper correlate above). The action gives rise to perils, but is in accordance (with the best sentiments of men). (Its mover) may by such action distress all the country, but the people will follow him;—there will be good fortune, and what error should there be?

VIII.[69] 1. 'Pî indicates that there is good fortune:'—(the name) Pî denotes help; (and we see in the figure) inferiors docilely following (their superior).

2. 'Let (the principal party intended in it) reexamine himself, (as if) by divination, whether his virtue be great, unintermitting, and firm;—if it be so, there will be no error:—all this follows from the position of the strong line in the centre (of the upper trigram). 'Those who have not rest will come to him:'—high and low will respond to its subject. 'With those who are (too) late in coming it will be ill:'—(for them) the way (of good fortune here indicated) has been exhausted.

IX.[70] 1. In Hsiâo *Khû* the weak line occupies its (proper) position,

---

[68] VII. That 'multitude' is given here as if it were the meaning of the name Sze arose, probably, from there being but one undivided line in the figure. That is the symbol of the general, all the other lines, divided, suggest the idea of a multitude obedient to his orders. The general's place in the centre of the lower trigram, with the proper correlate in line 5, suggests the idea of firmness and correctness that dominates in the hexagram. But in the last sentence it is the ruler, and not the general of the host, who is the subject. Compare what is said of him with Mencius, I, i, chap. 3; ii, chap. 5, &c.

'Perilousness' is the attribute of Khan, the lower trigram, and 'docility,' or 'accordance with others,' that of Khwăn, the upper. War is like 'poison' to a country, injurious, and threatening ruin to it, and yet the people will endure and encounter it in behalf of the sovereign whom they esteem and love.

[69] VIII. There is some error in the text here,—as all the critics acknowledge. I have adopted the decision of Kû Hsî, which by a very small change makes the whole read consistently, and in harmony with other explanations of the Thwan. 'The inferiors' are the subjects of all the other lines gathering round their superior, represented in the fifth line.

'The way has been exhausted:'—they do not seek to promote and enjoy union till it is too late. The sentiment is the same as that in the lines of Shakespeare about the tide in the affairs of men.

[70] IX. The weak line' is said to occupy 'its proper position,' because it is in the fourth,—an even place. The 'responding' on the part of all the other lines above and

and (the lines) above and below respond to it. Hence comes the name of Hsiâo *Khû* (Small Restraint).

2. (It presents the symbols of) strength and flexibility. Strong lines are in the central places, and the will (of their subjects) will have free course. Thus it indicates that there will be progress and success.

3. 'Dense clouds but no rain' indicate the movement (of the strong lines) still going forward. The 'Commencing at our western border' indicates that the (beneficial) influence has not yet been widely displayed.

X.[71] 1. In Lî we have (the symbol of) weakness treading on (that of) strength.

2. (The lower trigram) indicates pleasure and satisfaction, and responds to (the upper) indicating strength. Hence (it is said), 'He treads on the tail of a tiger, which does not bite him; there will be progress and success.'

3. (The fifth line is) strong, in the centre, and in its correct place. (Its subject) occupies the God-(given) position, and falls into no distress or failure;—(his) action will be brilliant.

---

below is their submitting to be restrained by it; and this arises simply from the meaning which king Wăn chose to attach to the hexagram.

But the restraint can only be small. The attributes of the two parts of the figure do not indicate anything else. The undivided line represents vigour and activity, and such a line is in the middle of each trigram. There cannot but be progress and success.

It is not easy to explain the symbolism of the last paragraph in harmony with the appended explanations. What *Khăng-зze*, Wang Făng, and other scholars say is to this effect:—Dense clouds ought to give rain. That they exist without doing so, shows the restraining influence of the hexagram to be still at work. But the other and active influence is, according to the general idea of the figure, continuing in operation;—there will be rain ere long. And this was taking place in the western regions subject to the House of *Kâu*, which still was only a fief of Shang. It was not for the inferior House to rule the superior. *Kâu* was for a time restrained by Shang. Let their positions be reversed by *Kâu* superseding Shang, and the rain of beneficent government would descend on all the kingdom. This seems to be the meaning of the paragraph. This is the answer to the riddle of it. Confucius, in his treatise on the Thwan, hints at it, but no Chinese critic has the boldness to declare it fully.

[71] X. '(The symbol of) weakness' in paragraph 1, according to Wang Shăn-зze (Yüan dynasty), is line 3, urged by the two strong lines below, and having to encounter the three strong lines above. Hû Ping-wan (also of the Yüan dynasty) says that the whole of the lower trigram, Tui, partaking of the yin nature, is the symbol of weakness, and the whole of *Khien* that of strength. The *Keh-Kung* editors say that, to get the full meaning, we must hold both views.

Paragraph 2 has been sufficiently explained on the Thwan itself.

Paragraph 3 has also been explained; but there remains something to be said on the Chinese text for 'occupies the God-given position,' or, literally, 'treads on the seat of Tî.' Canon McClatchie has—'The imperial throne is now occupied.' I think that 'the seat of Tî' is synonymous with 'the seat of Heaven,' in paragraph 2 of this treatise on hexagram 5. If Confucius, or whoever was the writer, had before him the phrase as it occurs in the Shû, I, 12, the force of Tî will depend on the meaning assigned to it in that part of the Shû. That the fifth line occupies the place of authority is here the only important point.

XI.[72] 'The little come and the great gone in Thâi, and its indication that there will be good fortune with progress and success' show to us heaven and earth in communication with each other, and all things in consequence having free course, and (also) the high and the low, (superiors and inferiors), in communication with one another, and possessed by the same aim. The inner (trigram) is made up of the strong and undivided lines, and the outer of the weak and divided; the inner is (the symbol of) strength, and the outer of docility; the inner (represents) the superior man, and the outer the small man. (Thus) the way of the superior man appears increasing, and that of the small man decreasing.

XII.[73] 'The want of good understanding between the (different classes of) men in Phî, and its indication as unfavourable to the firm and correct course of the superior man; with the intimation that the great are gone and the little come:'—all this springs from the fact that in it heaven and earth are not in communication with each other, and all things in consequence do not have free course; and that the high and the low (superiors and inferiors) are not in communication with one another, and there are no (well-regulated) states under the sky. The inner (trigram) is made up of the weak and divided lines, and the outer of the strong and undivided: the inner is (the symbol of) weakness, and the outer of strength; the inner (represents) the small man, and the outer the superior man. Thus the way of the small man appears increasing, and that of the superior man decreasing.

XIII.[74] 1. In Thung Zǎn the weak (line) has the place (of influence),

---

[72] XI. There is nothing to be said on the explanation of the Thwan here beyond what has been noticed on the different paragraphs of the Text. Canon McClatchie translates:— 'The Thwan means that Heaven and Earth have now conjugal intercourse with each other .... and the upper and lower (classes) unite together.' But in both clauses the Chinese characters are the same. Why did he not go on to say—'the upper and lower classes have conjugal intercourse together;' or rather, why did he not dismiss, the idea of such intercourse from his mind altogether? Why make the Yî appear to be gross, when there is not the shadow of grossness in it? The paragraph here well illustrates how the ruling idea in all the antinomies of the Yî is that of authority and strength on the one side, and of inferiority and weakness on the other.

[73] XII. All the symbolism here springs from the trigram Khwǎn occupying in the figure the inner or lower place, and *Kh*ien the outer or upper. It is for the inner trigram to take the initiative; but how can earth (symbolised by Khwǎn) take the place of heaven (symbolised by *Kh*ien)? As in nature it is heaven that originates and not earth, so in a state the upper classes must take the initiative, and not the lower.

[74] XIII. To understand the various points in this commentary, it is only necessary to refer to the Text of the hexagram. The proper correlate of line 2 is line 5, and I have said therefore that it 'responds to (the corresponding line in) *Kh*ien.' The editors of the Khang-hsî edition, however, would make the correlate to it all the lines of *Kh*ien, as being more agreeable to the idea of union.

I do not think that a second paragraph has been lost. The 'Thung Zǎn says' is merely a careless repetition of the three concluding characters of paragraph 1.

the central place, and responds to (the corresponding line in) *Kh*ien (above); hence comes its name of Thung Zăn (or 'Union of men').

2. Thung Zăn says:—

3. The language, 'Thung Zăn appears here (as we find it) in (the remote districts of) the country, indicating progress and success, and that it will be advantageous to cross the great stream,' is moulded by its containing the strength (symbolled) in *Kh*ien. (Then) we have (the trigram indicating) elegance and intelligence, supported by (that indicating) strength; with the line in the central, and its correct, position, and responding (to the corresponding line above):—(all representing) the correct course of the superior man. It is only the superior man who can comprehend and affect the minds of all under the sky.

XIV.[75] 1. In Tâ Yû the weak (line) has the place of honour, is grandly central, and (the strong lines) above and below respond to it. Hence comes its name of Tâ Yû (Having what is Great).

2. The attributes (of its component trigrams) are strength and vigour with elegance and brightness. (The ruling line in it) responds to (the ruling line in the symbol of) heaven, and (consequently) its action is (all) at the proper times. In this way (it is said to) indicate great progress and success.

XV.[76] 1. *Kh*ien indicates progress and success. It is the way of heaven to send down its beneficial influences below, where they are brilliantly displayed. It is the way of earth, lying low, to send its influences upwards and (there) to act.

2. It is the way of heaven to diminish the full and augment the humble. It is the way of earth to overthrow the full and replenish the humble. Spiritual Beings inflict calamity on the full and bless the humble. It is the way of men to hate the full and love the humble. Humility in a position of honour makes that still more brilliant; and in a low position men will not (seek to) pass beyond it. Thus it is that 'the superior man will have a (good) issue (to his undertakings).'

---

[75] XIV. The position in the fifth place indicates the dignity, and its being central, in the centre of the upper trigram, indicates the virtue, of the lord of the figure.

The strength of the lord, moreover, is directed by intelligence and his actions are always at the proper time, like the seasons of heaven.

[76] XV. The Thwan on this hexagram was so brief, that the writer here deals generally with the subject of humility, showing how it is valued by heaven and earth, by spirits and by men. The descent of the heavenly influences, and the low position of the earth in paragraph 1, are both emblematic of humility. The heavenly influences have their 'display' in the beauty and fertility of the earth.

The way of heaven is seen, e.g. in the daily declining of the sun, and the waning of the moon after it is full; the way of earth in the fall of the year. On the meaning of 'Spiritual Beings (Kwei Shăn),' see the Introduction, pp. 32, 33. It is difficult to say what idea the writer attached to the name. What he says of man's appreciation of humility is striking, and, I believe, correct.

XVI.[77] 1. In Yü we see the strong (line) responded to by all the others, and the will (of him whom it represents) being carried out; and (also) docile obedience employing movement (for its purposes). (From these things comes) Yü (the Condition of harmony and satisfaction).

2. In this condition we have docile obedience employing movement (for its purposes), and therefore it is so as between heaven and earth;—how much more will it be so (among men) in 'the setting up of feudal princes and putting the hosts in motion!'

3. Heaven and earth show that docile obedience in connexion with movement, and hence the sun and moon make no error (in time), and the four seasons do not deviate (from their order). The sages show such docile obedience in connexion with their movements, and hence their punishments and penalties are entirely just, and the people acknowledge it by their submission. Great indeed are the time and significance indicated in Yü!

XVII.[78] 1. In Sui we see the strong (trigram) come and place itself under the weak; we see (in the two) the attributes of movement and pleasure:—this gives (the idea of) Sui.

2. 'There will be great progress and success; and through firm correctness no error:'—all under heaven will be found following at such a time.

3. Great indeed are the time and significance indicated in Sui.

XVIII.[79] 1. In Kû we have the strong (trigram) above, and the weak

---

[77] XVI. What is said in paragraph 1 about the lines has been pointed out in the notes on the Text. 'Obedience' is the attribute of Khwǎn, the lower trigram, which takes the initiative in the action of the figure; and here makes use of the movement, which is the attribute of *K*ǎn, the upper trigram.

I can hardly trace the connexion between the different parts of Paragraph 2. Does it not proceed on the harmony produced by the thunderous explosion between heaven and earth, as declared in Appendix II? Then the analogy between natural phenomena and human and social experiences comes into play.

Paragraph 3 is also tantalising. Why does the writer introduce the subject of punishments and penalties? Are they a consequence of putting the hosts in motion?

[78] XVII. The trigrams *K*ǎn and Tui are distinguished as strong and weak, *K*ǎn representing, on king Wǎn's scheme, 'the eldest son,' and Tui, 'the youngest daughter.' But 'the strong' here may mean the strong line, the lowest in the hexagram. As Wang 3ung-*kw*an (Sung dynasty) says:—'The yang and strong line should not be below a yin and weak line, as we find it here. That is, in Sui the high places himself below the low, and the noble below the mean:'—esteeming others higher than himself, and giving the idea of following. Then *K*ân denotes the production or excitement of motion, and Tui denotes pleasure; and the union of these things suggests the same idea.

[79] XVIII. The symbolism here is the opposite of that in Sui. The upper trigram *K*ǎn is strong, denoting, according to king Wǎn, 'the youngest son;' and the lower, Sun, is weak, denoting 'the eldest daughter.' For the eldest daughter to be below the youngest son is eminently correct, and helps to indicate the auspice of great success. The attribute of Sun is pliancy, and that of *K*ǎn stoppage or arrest. The feeble pliancy confronted by the arresting mountain gives an idea of the evil state implied in Kû.

'Three days before and after the turning-point' is, literally, three days before and one below; we have (below) pliancy, and (above) stopping:—these give the idea of Kû (a Troublous Condition of affairs verging to ruin).

2. 'Kû indicates great progress and success:'—(through the course shown in it), all under heaven, there will be good order. 'There will be advantage in crossing the great stream:'—he who advances will encounter the business to be done. '(He should weigh well, however, the events of) three days before (the turning-point), and those (to be done) three days after it:'—the end (of confusion) is the beginning (of order); such is the procedure of Heaven.

XIX.[80] 1. In Lin (we see) the strong (lines) gradually increasing and advancing.

2. (The lower trigram is the symbol of) being pleased, and (the upper of) being compliant. The strong (line) is in the central position, and is properly responded to.

3. 'There is great progress and success, along with firm correctness:'—this is the way of Heaven.

4. 'In the eighth month there will be evil:'—(the advancing power) will decay after no long time.

XX.[81] 1. The great Manifester occupies an upper place (in the figure), which consists of (the trigrams whose attributes are) docility and flexibility. He is in the central position and his correct place, and thus exhibits (his lessons) to all under heaven.

2. 'Kwan shows its subject like a worshipper who has washed his hands, but not (yet) presented his offerings;—with sincerity and an appearance of dignity (commanding reverent regard):'—(all) beneath look to him and are transformed.

3. When we contemplate the spirit-like way of Heaven, we see how the four seasons proceed without error. The sages, in accordance

---

after *kiâ*,' *kiâ* being the name of the first of the 'earthly stems' among the cyclical characters. Hence it has the meaning of 'beginning,' and here denotes the turning-point, at which disorder gives place to order. According to 'the procedure of Heaven,' history is a narrative of change, one condition of affairs constantly giving place to another and opposite. 'A kingdom that cannot be moved' does not enter into the circle of Chinese ideas.

[80] XIX. See what has been said on the fourth paragraph in p.61 on the Text. The other paragraphs need no explanation beyond what appears in the supplemented translation.

[81] XX. 'The great Manifester' is the ruler, the principal subject of the hexagram, and represented by line 5, near the top of the figure. In that figure the lower trigram. is *Kh*wăn, representing the earth, with the attribute of docility, and the upper is Sun, representing wind, with the attributes of flexibility and penetration. As is the place of line 5, so are the virtues of the ruler.

'The spirit-like way of Heaven' is the invisible and unfathomable agency ever operating by general laws, and with invariable regularity, in what we call nature. Compare with this paragraph, the definition of Shăn or Spirit in Appendix III, i, 32; and the doctrine of the agency of God, taught in Appendix VI, 8, 9.

with (this) spirit-like way, laid down their instructions, and all under heaven yield submission to them.

XXI.[82] 1. The existence of something between the jaws gives rise to the name Shih Ho (Union by means of biting through the intervening article).

2. The Union by means of biting through the intervening article indicates 'the successful progress (denoted by the hexagram).'

The strong and weak (lines) are equally divided (in the figure). Movement is denoted (by the lower trigram), and bright intelligence (by the upper); thunder and lightning uniting in them, and having brilliant manifestation. The weak (fifth) line is in the centre, and acts in its high position. Although it is not in its proper position, this is advantageous for the use of legal constraints.

XXII.[83] 1. (When it is said that) Pî indicates that there should be free course (in what it denotes):—

2. (We see) the weak line coming and ornamenting the strong lines (of the lower trigram), and hence (it is said that ornament) 'should have free course.' On the other hand, the strong line above ornaments the weak ones (of the upper trigram), and hence (it is said) that 'there will be little advantage, if (ornament) be allowed to advance (and take the lead).' (This is illustrated in the) appearances that ornament the sky.

3. Elegance and intelligence (denoted by the lower trigram) regulated by the arrest (denoted by the upper) suggest the observances that adorn human (society).

4. We look at the ornamental figures of the sky, and thereby ascertain the changes of the seasons. We look at the ornamental

---

[82] XXI. The 'equal division of the strong and weak lines' is seen by taking them in pairs, though the order in the first pair is different from that in the two others. This is supposed to indicate the intelligence of the judgments in the action of the hexagram. Kăn, the lower trigram, symbolises movement; Lî, the upper, intelligence. The fifth line's acting in its high position does not intimate the formation of the figure from Yî, the 42nd hexagram, but calls attention to the fact that a weak line is here 'lord of judgment.' This does not seem natural, but the effect is good;—judgment is tempered by leniency.

[83] XXII. The first paragraph is either superfluous or incomplete.

The language of paragraph 2 has naturally been pressed into the service of the doctrine of changing the figures by divining manipulation; see p. 97, on paragraph 2 of the Thwan of hexagram 6. But as the Khang-hsî editors point out, 'the weak line coming and ornamenting the two strong ones' simply indicates how substantiality should have the help of ornament, and 'the strong line above (or ascending) and ornamenting the two weak lines' indicates that ornament should be restrained by substantiality. Ornament has its use, but it must be kept in check.—The closing sentence has no connexion with what precedes. Some characters are wanting, to show how the writer passes on to speak of 'the ornamental figures of the sky.' The whole should then be joined on to paragraph 3. The 'figures of the sky' are all the heavenly bodies in their relative positions and various movements, producing day and night, heat and cold, &c. The observances of society are the ceremonies and performances which regulate and beautify the intercourse of men, and constitute the transforming lessons of sagely wisdom.

observances of society, and understand how the processes of transformation are accomplished all under heaven.

XXIII.[84] 1. Po denotes overthrowing or being overthrown. We see (in the figure) the weak lines (threatening to) change the (last) strong line (into one of themselves).

2. That 'it will not be advantageous to make a movement in any direction whatever' appears from the fact that the small men are (now) growing and increasing. The superior man acts according to (the exigency of the time), and stops all forward movement, looking at the (significance of the) symbolic figures (in the hexagram). He values the processes of decrease and increase, of fulness and decadence, (as seen) in the movements of the heavenly bodies.

XXIV.[85] 1. 'Fû indicates the free course and progress (of what it denotes):'—it is the coming back of what is intended by the undivided line.

2. (Its subject's) actions show movement directed by accordance with natural order. Hence 'he finds no one to distress him in his exits and entrances,' and 'friends come to him, and no error is committed.'

3. 'He will return and repeat his proper course; in seven days comes his return:'—such is the movement of the heavenly (revolution).

4. 'There will be advantage in whatever direction movement is made:—the strong lines are growing and increasing.

5. Do we not see in Fû the mind of heaven and earth?

XXV.[86] In Wû Wang we have the strong (first) line come from the

---

[84] XXIII. 'The symbolic figures in the hexagram' are Khwăn, below, the representative of docility, acting as circumstances require; and Kăn, the representative of a mountain, which arrests the progress of the traveller. The superior man of the topmost line thus interprets them, and acts accordingly. Yet he is not left without hope. Winter is followed by spring; night is succeeded by day; the moon wanes, and then begins to wax again. So will it be in political life. As we read in the Hebrew prophet Isaiah, 'In returning and rest shall ye be saved; in quietness and in confidence shall be your strength.'

[85] XXIV. 'The movement of the heavenly revolution' in paragraph 3 has reference to the regular alternations of darkness and light, and of cold and heat, as seen in the different months of the year. Hâu Hsing-kwo (of the Thang dynasty) refers to the expressions in the Shih, I, xv, ode 1, 'the days of (our) first (month), second (month),' &c., as illustrating the use of day for month, as we have it here; but that is to explain what is obscure by what is more so; though I believe, as stated on the Text, that seven days' is here equivalent to 'seven months.'

'The mind of heaven and earth' is the love of life and of all goodness that rules in the course of nature and providence.

[86] XXV. The advocates of one trigram's changing into another, which ought not to be admitted, we have seen, into the interpretation of the Yî, make Wû Wang to be derived from Sung (No. 6), the second line there being manipulated into the first of this; but this representation is contrary to the words of the text, which make the strong first line come from the outer trigram, i. e. from *Kh*ien. And so it does, as related, not very intelligibly, in Appendix V, 10, *K*ăn, the lower trigram here, being the eldest son,' resulting from the first application of Khwăn to *Kh*ien. The three peculiarities in the structure of the figure

outer (trigram), and become in the inner trigram lord (of the whole figure); we have (the attributes of) motive power and strength; we have the strong line (of the fifth place) in the central position, and responded to (by the weak second):—there will be 'great progress proceeding from correctness; such is the appointment of Heaven.

'If (its subject and his action) be not correct, he will fall into errors, and it will not be advantageous for him to move in any direction:'—whither can he (who thinks he is) free from all insincerity, (and yet is as here described) proceed? Can anything be done (advantageously) by him whom the (will and) appointment of Heaven do not help?

XXVI.[87] 1. In (the trigrams composing) Tâ *Khû* we have (the attributes) of the greatest strength and of substantial solidity, which emit a brilliant light; and indicate a daily renewal of his virtue (by the subject of it).

2. The strong line is in the highest place, and suggests the value set on talents and virtue; there is power (in the upper trigram) to keep the strongest in restraint:—all this shows 'the great correctness' (required in the hexagram).

3. 'The good fortune attached to the subject's not seeking to enjoy his revenues in his own family' shows how talents and virtue are nourished.

4. 'It will be advantageous to cross the great stream:'—(the fifth line, representing the ruler,) is responded to by (the second, the central line of *Khi*en, representing) Heaven.

XXVII.[88] 1. 'Î indicates that with firm correctness there will be good fortune:'—when the nourishing is correct, there will be good fortune. 'We must look at what we are seeking to nourish:'—we must look at those whom we wish to nourish. 'We must by the exercise of

---

afford the auspice of progress and success; and very striking is the brief and emphatic declaration, that such progress is 'the appointment of Heaven.'

[87] XXVI. In paragraph 1, Tâ *Khû* evidently means the 'grand accumulation' of virtue, indicated by the attributes of its component trigrams. 'Substantial solidity' may very well be given as the attribute of mountains.

'The strong line in the highest place' of paragraph 2 is line 6, whose subject is thus above the ruler represented by 5, and has the open firmament for his range in doing his work. This, and his ability to repress the strongest opposition, show how he is supported by all that is correct and right.

In a kingdom where the object of the government is the accumulation of virtue, good and able men will not be left in obscurity.

What will not a high and good purpose, supported by the greatest strength, be able to do?

[88] XXVII. Many of the critics, in illustration of paragraph 1, refer appropriately to Mencius, VI, i, chap. 14.

In illustration of paragraph 2 they refer to the times and court of Yâo and Shun, sage rulers, from whose cherishing and nourishing came Yü to assuage the waters of the deluge, 3î to teach the people agriculture, Hsieh as minister of instruction, Kâo Yâo as minister of crime, and others;—all to do the work of nourishing the people.

our thoughts seek the proper aliment:'—we must look to our own nourishing of ourselves.

2. Heaven and earth nourish all things. The sages nourish men of talents and virtue, by them to reach to the myriads of the people. Great is (the work intended by this) nourishing in its time!

XXVIII.[89] 1. Tâ Kwo shows the great ones (= the undivided lines) in excess.

2. In 'the beam that is weak' we see weakness both in the lowest and the topmost (lines).

3. The strong lines are in excess, but (two of them) are in the central positions. The action (of the hexagram is represented by the symbols of) flexibility and satisfaction. (Hence it is said), 'There will be advantage in moving in any direction whatever; yea, there will be success. '

4. Great indeed is (the work to be done in) this very extraordinary time.

XXIX.[90] 1. Khan repeated shows us one defile succeeding another.

2. This is the nature of water;—it flows on, without accumulating its volume (so as to overflow); it pursues its way through a dangerous defile, without losing its true (nature).

3. That 'the mind is penetrating' is indicated by the strong (line) in the centre. That 'action (in accordance with this) will be of high value' tells us that advance will be followed by achievement.

4. The dangerous (height) of heaven cannot be ascended; the difficult places of the earth are mountains, rivers, hills, and mounds. Kings and princes arrange by means of such strengths, to maintain their territories. Great indeed is the use of (what is here) taught about seasons of peril.

XXX.[91] Lî means being attached to. The sun and moon have their

---

[89] XXVIII. Paragraph 3. In the Great Symbolism 'wood' appears as the natural object symbolised by Sun, and not 'wind,' which we find more commonly. The attribute of 'flexibility,' however, is the quality of Sun, whether used of wind or of wood.

Paragraph 4. Such a time, it is said, was that of Yâo and Shun, of Thang the Successful, and of king Wû. What these heroes did, however, was all called for by the exigency of their times, and not by whim or principle of their own, which they wished to make prominent.

[90] XXIX. On paragraph 2 Liang Yin says:—'Water stops at the proper time, and moves at the proper time. Is not this an emblem of the course of the superior man in dealing with danger?'

On paragraph 4 the Khang-hsî editors say that to exercise one's self in meeting difficulty and peril is the way to establish and strengthen the character, and that the use of such experience is seen in all measures for self-defence, there being no helmet and mail like leal-heartedness and good faith, and no shield and tower like propriety and righteousness.

[91] XXX. 'The double brightness' in paragraph 1 has been much discussed. Some say that it means 'the ruler,' becoming brighter and brighter. Others say that it means

place in the sky. All the grains, grass, and trees have their place on the earth. The double brightness (of the two trigrams) adheres to what is correct, and the result is the transforming and perfecting all under the sky.

2. The weak (second line) occupies the middle and correct position, and gives the indication of 'a free and successful course;' and, moreover, 'nourishing (docility like that of) the cow' will lead to good fortune.

## SECTION II.

XXXI.[92] 1. Hsien is here used in the sense of Kan, meaning (mutually) influencing.

2. The weak (trigram) above, and the strong one below; their two influences moving and responding to each other, and thereby forming a union; the repression (of the one) and the satisfaction (of the other); (with their relative position), where the male is placed below the female:—all these things convey the notion of 'a free and successful course (on the fulfilment of the conditions), while the advantage will depend on being firm and correct, as in marrying a young lady, and there will be good fortune.'

3. Heaven and earth exert their influences, and there ensue the transformation and production of all things. The sages influence the minds of men, and the result is harmony and peace all under the sky. If we look at (the method and issues) of those influences, the true character of heaven and earth and of all things can be seen.

XXXII.[93] 1. Hăng denotes long continuance. The strong (trigram) is above, and the weak one below; (they are the symbols of) thunder

---

both the ruler and his ministers, combining their brightness. The former view seems to me the better. The analogy between the natural objects and a transforming and perfecting rule is far fetched.

The central and correct position' in paragraph 2 can be said only of the second line, and not of the fifth, where an undivided line would be more correct. The 'and moreover' of the translation is 'therefore' in the original; but I cannot make out the force and suitability of that conjunction.

[92] XXXI. Paragraph 2. Tui, the upper trigram, is weak and yin; and Kăn, the lower, is strong and yang; see Appendixes III, ii, 4, and V, 10. Kăn is below Tui; whereas the subject of the lower trigram should always take the initiative in these figures.

[93] XXXII. All the conditions in paragraph 1 must be understood as leading to the indication of progress and success, which is explained in paragraph 2, and illustrated by the analogy of the course of heaven and earth.

'Movement in any direction,' as explained in paragraph 3, indicates the ever-occurring new modes and spheres of activity, to which he who is firm and correct is called.

Paragraph 4, and especially its concluding sentence, are of a meditative and reflective character not uncommon in the treatise on the Thwan.

and wind, which are in mutual communication; (they have the qualities of) docility and motive force; their strong and weak (lines) all respond, each to the other:—these things are all found in Hăng.

2. (When it is said that) 'Hăng indicates successful progress and no error (in what it denotes); but the advantage will come from being firm and correct,' this indicates that there must be long continuance in its way of operation. The way of heaven and earth is to be long continued in their operation without stopping.

3. (When it is said that) 'Movement in any direction whatever will be advantageous,' this implies that when (the moving power) is spent, it will begin again.

4. The sun and moon, realising in themselves (the course of Heaven), can perpetuate their shining. The four seasons, by their changing and transforming, can perpetuate their production (of things). The sages persevere long in their course, and all under the sky are transformed and perfect. When we look at what they continue doing long, the natural tendencies of heaven, earth, and all things can be seen.

XXXIII.[94] 1. 'Thun indicates successful progress:'—that is, in the very retiring which Thun denotes there is such progress. The strong (line) is in the ruling place, (the fifth), and is properly responded to (by the second line). The action takes place according to (the requirement of) the time.

2. 'To a small extent it will (still) be advantageous to be firm and correct:'—(the small men) are gradually encroaching and advancing.

3. Great indeed is the significance of (what is required to be done in) the time that necessitates retiring.

XXXIV.[95] 1. In Tâ Kwang we see that which is great becoming strong. We have the (trigram) denoting strength directing that which denotes movement, and hence (the whole) is expressive of vigour.

2. 'Tâ Kwang indicates that it will be advantageous to be firm and

---

[94] XXXIII. 'The superior man,' it is said, 'advances or withdraws according to the character of the time. The strength and correct position of the fifth line show that he is able to maintain himself; and as it is responded to by the weak second line, no opposition to what is correct in him would come from any others. He might therefore keep his place; but looking at the two weak lines, 1 and 2, he recognises in them the advance and irrepressible progress of small men, and that for a time it is better for him to give way and withdraw from the field. Thus there is successful progress even in his retiring.'

[95] XXXIV. Paragraph 1. 'That which is great' denotes, in the first place, the group of four strong lines which strikes us on looking at the figure, and then the superior man, or the strong men in positions of power, of whom these are the representatives. *Khien* is the trigram of strength, and *Kăn* that of movement.

Paragraph 2. That which is great (should be) correct:—that the 'should be' must be supplied in the translation appears from this, that the paragraph is intended to illustrate the text that 'it will be advantageous to be firm and correct.' The power of man becomes then a reflexion of the great power which we see working in nature, 'impartially,' 'unselfishly.'

correct:'—that which is great (should be) correct. Given correctness and greatness (in their highest degree), and the character and tendencies of heaven and earth can be seen.

XXXV.[96] 1. Ʒin denotes advancing.

2. (In Ʒin we have) the bright (sun) appearing above the earth; (the symbol of) docile submission cleaving to that of the Great brightness; and the weak line advanced and moving above:—all these things give us the idea of 'a prince who secures the tranquillity (of the people), presented on that account with numerous horses (by the king), and three times in a day received at interviews.'

XXXVI.[97] 1. (The symbol of) the Earth and that of Brightness entering into the midst of it give the idea of Ming Î (Brightness wounded or obscured).

2. The inner (trigram) denotes being accomplished and bright; the outer, being pliant and submissive. The case of king Wăn was that of one who with these qualities was yet involved in great difficulties.

3. 'It will be advantageous to realise the difficulty (of the position), and maintain firm correctness:—that is, (the individual concerned) should obscure his brightness. The case of the count of Kî was that of one who, amidst the difficulties of his House, was able (thus) to maintain his aim and mind correct.

XXXVII.[98] I. In Kiâ Ʒăn the wife has her correct place in the inner

---

[96] XXXV. To those who advocate the view that the hexagrams of the Yî have been formed by changes of the lines in manipulating with the divining stalks, the words of paragraph 2, that we have in the figure 'the weak line advanced and moving above,' suggest the derivation of Ʒin from Kwan, whose 4th and 5th lines are made to change places (☷ ☲). But we have seen that that view is inadmissible in the interpretation of the Yî. And a simple explanation of the language at once presents itself. As Hsiang An-shih (Sung dynasty) says, 'Of the three "daughter" trigrams it is only Lî which has its divided line occupying the central place of honour, when it is the upper trigram in a hexagram.'

[97] XXXVI. The sun disappearing, as we say, 'below the earth,' or, as the Chinese writer conceives it, I into the midst of, or within the earth,' sufficiently indicates the obscuration or wounding of brightness,—the repression and resistance of the good and bright.

King Wăn was not of the line of Shang. Though opposed and persecuted by its sovereign, he could pursue his own course, till his line came in the end to supersede the other. It could not be so with the count of Kî, who was a member of the House of Shang. He could do nothing that would help on its downfall.

[98] XXXVII. Paragraph 1 first explains the statement of the Thwan, about the wife, represented by line 2; and then proceeds to the husband, represented by line 5. The two trigrams become representative of the family circle, and the wide world without it. In the reference to heaven and earth it is not supposed that they are really husband and wife; but in their relation and positions they symbolise that social relation and the individuals in it.

Paragraph 2, more closely rendered, would be—'That in Kîa Ʒăn there is an authoritative ruler is a way of naming father and mother.' Does the writer mean to say that while the assertion of authority was indispensable in a family, that authority must (trigram), and the man his correct place in the outer. That man and woman occupy their correct places is the great righteousness shown (in the relation and positions of) heaven and earth.

2. In *K*iâ *Z*ăn we have the idea of an authoritative ruler;—that, namely, represented by the parental authority.

3. Let the father be indeed father, and the son son; let the elder brother be indeed elder brother, and the younger brother younger brother, let the husband be indeed husband, and the wife wife:—then will the family be in its normal state. Bring the family to that state, and all under heaven will be established.

XXXVIII.[99] 1. In Khwei we have (the symbol of) Fire, which, when moved, tends upwards, and that of a Marsh, whose waters, when moved, tend downwards. We have (also the symbols of) two sisters living together, but whose wills do not move in the same direction.

2. (We see how the inner trigram expressive of) harmonious satisfaction is attached to (the outer expressive of) bright intelligence; (we see) the weak line advanced and acting above, and how it occupies the central place, and is responded to by the strong (line below). These indications show that 'in small matters there will (still) be good fortune.'

3. Heaven and earth are separate and apart, but the work which they do is the same. Male and female are separate and apart, but with a common will they seek the same object. There is diversity between the myriad classes of beings, but there is an analogy between their several operations. Great indeed are the phenomena and the results of this condition of disunion and separation.

XXXIX.[100] 1. *K*ien denotes difficulty. There is (the trigram

---

have combined in it both force and gentleness?

[99] XXXVIII. In paragraph 1 we have first an explanation of the meaning of Khwei from the symbolism of Fû-hsî. Then follows an explanation from that ascribed to king Wăn, where Tui represents the youngest daughter and Lî the second. The Khang-hsî editors observe that in many hexagrams we have two daughters dwelling together, but that only in this and 49 is attention called to it. The reason, they say, is that in those two diagrams the sisters are the second and third daughters, while in the others one of them is the eldest, whose place and superiority are fixed, so that between her and either of the others there can be no division or collision.

About what is said, in paragraph 2, on the weak line, as advanced and acting above, see the note on hexagram 35.

The lesson of paragraph 3 is not unity in diversity, but union with diversity.

[100] XXXIX. The upper or front trigram is Khăn, the attribute of which is perilousness; the lower is Kăn, of which the arresting, actively or passively, of movement or advance is the attribute. We can understand how the union of these attributes gives the ideas of difficulty and prudent caution.

The explanations in paragraph 2 of the phraseology of the Thwan are not all easily followed. It is said that the advantageousness of the south-west is due to the central line in 5; but if we are to look for the meaning of south-west in Khwăn, as in the diagram of king Wăn's trigrams, there is no strong central line in it. May Khân, as a yang trigram, be expressive of) perilousness in front. When one, seeing the peril, can arrest his steps (in accordance with the significance of the lower tri. gram), is he not wise?

2. (The language of) *K*ien, that 'advantage will be found in the south-west,' refers to the (strong fifth line) advanced and in the central place. That 'there will be no advantage in the north-east,' intimates that the way (of dealing with the *K*ien state) is exhausted. That 'it will be advantageous to see the great man,' intimates that advance will lead to achievement. That the places (of the different lines after the first) are those appropriate to them indicates firm correctness and good fortune, with which the regions (of the kingdom) are brought to their normal state. Great indeed is the work to be done in the time of *K*ien!

XL.[101] 1. In *K*ieh we have (the trigram expressive of) peril going on to that expressive of movement. By movement there is an escape from the peril:—(this is the meaning of) *K*ieh.

2. 'In (the state indicated by) *K*ieh, advantage will be found in the south-west:'—the movement (thus) intimated will win all. That 'there will be good fortune in coming back (to the old conditions)' shows that such action is that of the due medium. That 'if some operations be necessary, there will be good fortune in the early conducting of them' shows that such operations will be successful.

3. When heaven and earth are freed (from the grasp of winter), we have thunder and rain. When these come, the buds of the plants and trees that produce the various fruits begin to burst. Great indeed are the phenomena in the time intimated by *K*ieh.

XLI.[102] 1. In Sun (we see) the lower (trigram) diminished, and the

---

used for Khwăn?

[101] XL. 1. The meaning of the hexagram is brought out sufficiently well in paragraph 1 by means of the attributes of the constituent trigrams.

2. How it is that the movement indicated in the first condition will, win' all does not immediately appear. The Khang-hsî editors say that 'moving to the south and west' is the same as 'returning back to the old conditions,' and that 'winning all' and acting 'according to the due medium' are descriptive of the effect and method without reference to the symbolism. Another explanation might be devised; but I prefer to leave the matter in doubt.

3. Paragraph 3 shows the analogy of what takes place in nature to the beneficent social and political changes described in the text, as is done very frequently in this Appendix.

[102] XLI. 1. All that we see is two undivided lines in the lower trigram, and then a divided one, and exactly the opposite in the upper. But the whole figure could not but have this form from the process of its formation, whether by the gradual addition of the two primitive lines, or by the imposition of the whole trigrams on one another. To say that the upper lines of *K*hien and Khwăn changed places to express the idea of subjects contributing in taxes to the maintenance of their ruler is absurd; and if that thought were in the mind of king Wăn (which I very much doubt), it would only show how he projected his own idea, formed independently of the figure, into its lines.

On the second sentence, the Khang-hsî editors say:—'When a minister devotes his upper added to. (But) the method (of action) implied in this operates also above (or, mounts upwards (also) and operates).

2. 'If there be sincerity in this method of diminution, there will be great good fortune; freedom from error; firmness and correctness that can be maintained; and advantage in every movement that shall be made. In what shall this (sincerity in the exercise of Sun) be employed? (Even) in sacrifice, two baskets of grain, (though there be nothing else), may be presented:'—for these two baskets there ought to be the fitting time. There is a time when the strong should be diminished, and the weak should be strengthened. Diminution and increase, overflowing and emptiness: —these take place in harmony with the conditions of the time.

XLII.[103] 1. In Yî we see the upper (trigram) diminished, and the

---

life in the service of his lord, or the people undertake their various labours in behalf of their government, these are instances of the ministering of those below to increase those above. But in this way the intercourse of the two becomes close and their aims become the same;—does not the method of action of those below communicate itself to those above?'

In paragraph 2 the subject of contribution, such as the payment of taxes, passes into the background. The Khang-hsî editors say: 'What is meant by diminishing in this hexagram is the regulation of expenditure or contribution according to the time. This would vary in a family according to its poverty or wealth; and in a state according to the abundance or scantiness of its resources. When it is said that there must be sincerity along with a diminution, it means that though such a diminution cannot be helped, yet what is given should be given sincerely. A small sacrifice sincerely offered is accepted. In the language, "There is a time when the strong should be diminished and the weak be strengthened," we are not to find the two baskets in the diminution of the strong. "The strong" is what is essential,—in this case sincerity; "The weak" is what is unimportant,—the amount and manner of the offering. If one supplement the insufficiency of his offering with the abundance of his sincerity, the insignificance of his two baskets will not be despised.'

[103] XLII. 1. The process of the formation of the trigrams here is the reverse of that in the preceding hexagram; and is open to the remarks I have made on that. Of course the people are full of complacency and pleasure in the labours of their ruler for their good.

2. The mention of 'the action of wood' has reference to the upper trigram Sun, which is the symbol both of wind and wood. From wood boats and ships are made, on which the great stream may be crossed. In three hexagrams, this, 59, and 61, of which Sun is a part, we find mention made of crossing the great stream. It is generally said that the lower trigram Kǎn also symbolises wood; but that is obtained by a roundabout process. Kǎn occupies the place of the east in Wan's arrangement of the trigrams; but the east symbolises spring, when the growth of vegetation begins; and therefore Kǎn may symbolise wood! It was stated on p. 32, that the doctrine of 'the five elements' does not appear in the Yî. Khǎng-ʒze takes wood ( 木 mû), 'as a misprint for increase ( 益 yî).'

3. The words 'heaven dispensing and earth producing' are based on the fancied genesis of the figure from Khien and Khwan (☰☰), the first lines in each changing places. It was the author of this Appendix, probably, who first introduced that absurd notion in connexion with the formation of Sun and Yî.

One rhyme runs through and connects these three paragraphs thus:—

lower added to. The satisfaction of the people (in consequence of this) is without limit. What descends from above reaches to all below, so great and brilliant is the course (of its operation).

2. That 'there will be advantage in every movement which shall be undertaken' appears from the central and correct (positions of the second and fifth lines), and the (general) blessing (the dispensing of which they imply).

That 'it will be advantageous (even) to cross the great stream' appears from the action of wood (shown in the figure).

3. Yî is made up of (the trigrams expressive of) movement and docility, (through which) there is daily advancement to an unlimited extent. We have (also) in it heaven dispensing and earth producing, leading to an increase without restriction of place. Everything in the method of this increase proceeds according to the requirements of the time.

XLIII.[104] 1. Kwâi is the symbol of displacing or removing. We see (in the figure) the strong (lines) displacing the weak. (We have in it the attributes of) strength and complacency. There is displacement, but harmony (continues).

2. 'The exhibition (of the criminal's guilt) in the royal courtyard' is suggested by the (one) weak (line) mounted on the five strong lines.

There 'is an earnest and sincere appeal (for sympathy and support), and a consciousness of the peril (involved in the undertaking):'—it is the realisation of this danger, which makes the method (of compassing

---

'Yî spoils the high, gives to the low;
The people feel intense delight.
Down from above to all below,
The blessing goes, so large and bright.
Success will every movement mark,
Central its source, its course aright.
The great stream even may be crossed,
When planks of wood their strength unite.
Yî movement shows and docile feet,
Which progress day by day invite.
Heaven gives; productive earth responds;
Increase crowns every vale and height;
And ceaselessly it hastens on,
Each season's gifts quick to requite.'

---

[104] XLIII. 1. The last clause of paragraph 1 is good in itself, showing that the strong and worthy statesman in removing a bad man from the state is not actuated by arty private feelings. The sentiment, however, as it is expressed, can hardly be said to follow from the symbolism.

Paragraph 2. The same may be said of all the notes appended to the different clauses of this second paragraph. Hû Ping-wăn (Yüan dynasty) says:—'If but a single small man be left, he is sufficient to make the superior man anxious; if but a single inordinate desire be left in the mind, that is sufficient to disturb the harmony of heavenly principles. The eradication in both oases must be complete, before the labour is ended.'

the object) brilliant.

'He should make an announcement in his own city, and show that it will not be well to have recourse at once to arms:'—(if he have recourse to arms), what he prefers will (soon) be exhausted.

'There will be advantage in whatever he shall go forward to:'— when the growth of the strong (lines) has been completed, there will be an end (of the displacement).

XLIV.[105] 1. Kâu has the significance of unexpectedly coming on. (We see in it) the weak (line) coming unexpectedly on the strong ones.

2. 'It will not be good to marry (such) a female:'—one (so symbolised) should not be long associated with.

3. Heaven and earth meeting together (as here represented), all the variety of natural things become fully displayed.

4. When a strong (line) finds itself in the central and correct position, (good government) will greatly prevail all under the sky.

5. Great indeed is the significance of what has to be done at the time indicated by Kâu!

XLV.[106] 1. 3hui indicates (the condition of union, or) being collected. We have in it (the symbol of) docile obedience going on to (what is expressed by that of) satisfaction. There is the strong line in the central place, and rightly responded to. Hence comes the (idea of) union.

2. 'The king will repair to his ancestral temple:'—with the utmost filial piety he presents his offerings (to the spirits of his ancestors).

'It will be advantageous to meet the great man, and there will then

---

[105] XLIV. On paragraph 1 the Khang-hsî editors say:—'"The weak line meets with (or comes unexpectedly on) the strong ones;"—the weak line, that is, plays the principal part. The case is like that of the minister who assumes the power of deciding for himself on all measures, or of a hen's announcing the morning;—is not the name of (shameless) boldness rightly applied to it? Hence nothing more is said about the symbol of the bold female; but attention is called to the second part of the Thwan.'

Paragraph 2 needs no remark. Paragraphs 3, 4, and 5 all speak of the importance of powers and parties meeting together,—in the world of nature, and in the sphere of human affairs. But I do not see how this sentiment is a natural sequel to that in i and 2, nor that it has any connexion with the teaching of the Thwan and Symbolism.

[106] XLV. The lower trigram in 3hui is Khwăn, whose attribute is docile obedience; and the upper is Tui, whose attribute is pleased satisfaction. Then we have the strong line in 5, and its proper correlate in 2. These things may give the idea of union. They might also give the idea of other good things.

The Khang-hsî editors say that though all is done in accordance with the ordinances of Heaven' follows the concluding clauses of the Thwan, yet the sentiment of the words must be extended to the other clauses as well. *Khăng-3ze* says that 'the ordinances of Heaven' are simply the natural and practical outcome of 'heavenly principle;'—in this case what should and may be done according to the conditions and requirements of the time. So do the critics of China try to shirk the idea of personality in 'Heaven.'

With paragraph 3, compare the concluding paragraphs of the Thwan *K*wan on hexagrams 31, 32.

be prosperity and success:'—the union effected by him will be on and through what is correct.

'The, use of great victims will conduce to good fortune; and in whatsoever direction movement is made, it will be advantageous:'—all is done in accordance with the ordinances of Heaven.

3. When we look at the way in which the gatherings (here shown) take place, the natural tendencies (in the outward action) of heaven and earth and of all things can be seen..

XLVI.[107] 1. (We find) the weak (line), as it finds the opportunity, ascending upwards.

2. We have (the attribute) of flexibility and that of obedience; we have the strong line (below) and its proper correlate above:—these things indicate that there will be 'great progress and success.'

3. 'Seeking (by the qualities implied in Shăng) to meet with the great man, its subject need have no anxiety:'—there will be ground for congratulation.

'Advance to the south will be fortunate:'—his aim will be carried out.

XLVII.[108] 1. In Khwăn (we see) the strong (lines) covered and obscured (by the weak).

2. We have in it (the attribute of) perilousness going on to that of satisfaction. Who is it but the superior man that, though straitened, still does not fail in making progress to his proper end?

'For the firm and correct, the (really) great man, there will be good fortune:'—this is shown by the central positions of the strong (lines).

'If he make speeches, his words cannot be made good:'—to be

---

[107] XLVI. The explanation of the first paragraph has given occasion to much difference of opinion. Some will have 'the weak (line)' to be 4; some 5; and some the whole of Khwăn, the upper trigram. The advocates of 4, make it come from hexagram 40, the weak 3 of which ascends to the strong 4, displaces it, and takes its place; but we have seen repeatedly the folly of the doctrine of changing lines and figures. The great symbolism of Appendix II suggests the proper explanation. The lower trigram, Sun, represents here not wind but wood. The first line, weak, is the root of a tree planted beneath the earth. Its gradual growth symbolises the advance upwards of the subject of the hexagram, fostered, that is, by the circumstances of the time.

[108] XLVII. 1. One sees the relative position of the strong and weak lines in the figure; but to deduce from that the idea expressed by Khwăn requires a painful straining of the imagination. That idea was in the mind, and then the lines were interpreted accordingly.

2. 'Perilousness' is the attribute of the lower trigram, and 'satisfaction' that of the upper. The superior man, however straitened, remains master of himself, and pursues the proper end of principle settled in his mind.

Why should the subject of Khwăn make speeches, be fond of arguing or pleading,—as the characters say, if we could translate them literally, 'setting a value on the mouth?' The reply to this is found in the trigram denoting 'satisfaction,' or 'being pleased.' The party in the extremity of Khwăn yet wishes and tries to make men pleased with him.

fond of arguing or pleading is the way to be reduced to extremity.

XLVIII.[109] 1. (We have the symbol of) wood in the water and the raising of the water; which (gives us the idea of) a well. A well supplies nourishment and is not (itself) exhausted.

2. 'The site of a town may be changed, while the fashion of its wells undergoes no change:'—this is indicated by the central position of the strong lines (in the second and fifth places).

'The drawing is nearly accomplished, but the rope has not yet reached the water of the well:'—its service has not yet been accomplished.

'The bucket is broken:'—it is this that occasions evil.

XLIX.[110] 1. In Ko (we see) water and fire extinguishing each other; (we see also) two daughters dwelling together, but with their minds directed to different objects:—(on account of these things) it is called (the hexagram of) Change.

2. 'It is believed in (only) after it has been accomplished:'—when the change has been made, faith is accorded to it.

(We have) cultivated intelligence (as the basis of) pleased satisfaction, (suggesting) 'great progress and success,' coming from what is correct.

When change thus takes place in the proper way, 'occasion for repentance disappears.'

3. Heaven and earth undergo their changes, and the four seasons complete their functions. Thang changed the appointment (of the line of Hsiâ to the throne), and Wû (that of the line of Shang), in accordance with (the will of) Heaven, and in response to (the wishes of) men. Great

---

[109] XLVIII. *Kǎng* Khang-*Khǎng* says:—'Khân, the upper trigram, represents water, and Sun, the lower, wood. This wood denotes the water-wheel or pulley with its bucket, which descends into the mouth of the spring, and brings the water up to the top.' This may be a correct explanation of the figure, though the reading of it from bottom to top seems at first to be strange.

Paragraph 2. That the fashion of the well does not undergo any (great) change is dwelt upon as illustrating the unchangeableness of the great principles of human nature and of government. But that this truth may be learned from the strong and central lines only produces a smile. So do the remarks on the other two sentences of the Thwan.

[110] XLIX. Paragraph 1. Lî, the lower trigram, represents fire, and Tui, the upper, represents water. Water will extinguish fire, and fire again will dry up water. Each, to all appearance, produces a change in the other. Again, according to king Wǎn's scheme of the trigrams, as shown on p. 32, and in Figure 1, Plate III, Lî is the second, and Tui the youngest daughter. Their wills are likely to differ in love and other things; but this symbolism does not so readily suggest the idea of change.

2. The first sentence suggests how the dislike to change on the part of people generally is overcome.

The second suggests how change proceeding from intelligence and giving general satisfaction will be successful.

Paragraph 3 tells us how the greatest natural and the greatest political changes are equally successful and admirable when conducted aright.

indeed is what takes place in a time of change.

L.[111] 1. In Ting we have (symbolically) the figure of a caldron. (We see) the (symbol of) wood entering into that of fire, which suggests the idea of cooking. The sages cooked their offerings in order to present them to God, and made great feasts to nourish their wise and able (ministers).

2. We have the symbol of) flexible obedience, and that (which denotes) ears quick of hearing and eyes clear-sighted. (We have also) the weak (line) advanced and acting above, in the central place, and responded to by the strong (line below). All these things give the idea of 'great progress and success.'

LI.[112] 1. *K*ăn (gives the intimation of) ease and development.

2. 'When the (time of) movement (which it indicates) comes, (its subject) will be found looking out with apprehension:'—that feeling of dread leads to happiness. 'And yet smiling and talking cheerfully:'— the issue (of his dread) is that he adopts (proper) laws (for his course).

'The movement (like a crash of thunder) terrifies all within a hundred lî:'—it startles the distant and frightens the near.

'He will be like the sincere worshipper, who is not startled into letting go his ladle and cup of sacrificial spirits:'—he makes his appearance, and maintains his ancestral temple and the altars of the spirits of the land and grain, as presiding at all sacrifices.

LII.[113] 1. *K*ăn denotes stopping or resting;—resting when it is the

---

[111] L. 1. See the notes on the Text of the Thwan about the figure of a caldron in Ting. Its component trigrams are Sun representing wood, and Lî representing fire; which may very well suggest the idea of cooking. The last sentence of the paragraph is entirely after the style of 'the Great Symbolism.' The Khang-hsî editors say that the distinction between Ʒing and Ting appears here very clearly, the former relating to the nourishment of the people, and the latter to the nourishing men of worth. They add that the reality of the offerings to God is such nourishing. 'God' is here Shang Tî, which Canon McClatchie translates 'the First Emperor,' adding in a note, 'The Chinese Jupiter, the Emperor of gods and men!'

2. The first sentence deduces the sentiment of the Thwan from the attributes or virtues of the trigrams with considerable amplification of the virtue of Lî. The second line of Lî, as being divided, calls forth in other hexagrams the same notice as here. It is the most important line in the figure, and being responded to by the strong 2, gives an indication of the 'great progress and success.'

[112] LI. Paragraph 1. See what is said on the Text.

2. The explanations of the. Thwan here are good; but in no way deduced from the figure.

3. The portion of the text printed in a different type is supposed to have dropt out of the Chinese copies. The explanation of it that follows is based on Wăn's view of *K*ăn as representing the oldest son. See on the Text.

[113] LII.1. The Khang-hsî editors give their opinion that what is said in the first sentence of this paragraph, after the explanation of the name, illustrates the first sentence of the Thwan, and that the other sentence illustrates the: rest of the Thwan. It may be so, but the whole of the Thwan appears in paragraph 2.

2. The hexagram being made up of *K*ăn repeated, lines 1, 2, 3 are of course the

time to rest, and acting when it is the time to act. When one's movements and restings all take place at the proper time for them, his way (of proceeding) is brilliant and intelligent.

2. Resting in one's resting-point is resting in one's proper place. The upper and lower (lines of the hexagram) exactly correspond to each other, but are without any interaction; hence it is said that '(the subject of the hexagram) has no consciousness of self; that when he walks in his courtyard, he does not see (any of) the persons in it; and that there will be no error.'

LIII.[114] 1. The advance indicated by *K*ien is (like) the marrying of a young lady which is attended by good fortune.

2. (The lines) as they advance get into their correct places:—this indicates the achievements of a successful progress.

The advance is made according to correctness:—(the subject of the hexagram) might rectify his country.

3. Among the places (of the hexagram) we see the strong undivided line in the centre.

4. 'In (the attributes of) restfulness and flexible penetration we have (the assurance of) an (onward) movement that is inexhaustible.

LIV.[115] 1. By Kwei Mei (the marrying away of a younger sister)

---

same as 4, 5, and 6. But it will be seen that there is not a proper correlation among them all. I do not see, however, that this furnishes any ground for the entire obliviousness of self, which the Th wan makes out to be in the figure.

[114] LIII. The first sentence of paragraph 2 describes the lines from 2 to 5 all getting into their proper places, as has been pointed out on the Text, and that sentence is symbolical of what is said in the second. 'The rectification of the country' is the reality of 'the successful progress.'

'The strong undivided line' in paragraph 3 is the fifth of the figure.

Out of rest comes movement to go on for an indefinite time, and be succeeded by rest again;—as says paragraph 4.

[115] LIV. 1. Kwei Mei in this Appendix has the meaning simply of marriage, and for Mei we might substitute Nü 'daughter' or 'young lady.' This appears from the writer's going on to point out, as elsewhere, the analogy between the growth of things in nature from the interaction of heaven and earth and the increase of mankind through marriage. He does this with a delicate touch. There is no grossness in the original any more than there is in the translation.

But how are we to reconcile this reference to the action of heaven and earth with the bad auspice of the Thwan? The Khang-hsî editors felt the pressure of this difficulty, and they adduce a similar inconsistency in the account of hexagram 44 in this treatise, adding, 'From this we may say that the interaction of the yin and yang cannot be dispensed with, but that we ought to be careful about it in the beginning in order to prevent mischief in the end. This is the doctrine of the Yî.' This is very well, but it is no solution of the difficulty. The editors could not admit that the author of the Appendix did not understand or did not deal fairly with the Text; for that author, they thought, was Confucius.

2. The same editors say that paragraph 2 implies both that the desire for the marriage originated with the lady, and that she was aware that the gentleman was older than herself.

3. The position of a divided line above an undivided is always represented as an evil omen; it is difficult to understand why. There is less of an appearance of reason about it

the great and righteous relation between heaven and earth (is suggested to us). If heaven and earth were to have no intercommunication, things would not grow and flourish as they do. The marriage of a younger sister is the end (of her maidenhood) and the beginning (of her motherhood).

2. We have (in the hexagram the desire of) pleasure and, on the ground of that, movement following. The marrying away is of a younger sister.

3. 'Any action will be evil:'—the places (of the lines) are not those appropriate to them.

'It will be in no wise advantageous:'—the weak (third and fifth lines) are mounted on strong lines.

LV.[116] 1. Făng has the signification of being great. It is made up of the trigrams (representing) intelligence and movement directed by that intelligence. It is thus that it has that signification.

2. 'The king has reached the condition (denoted by Făng):'—he has still to make it greater.

'There is no occasion to be anxious. Let him be as the sun at noon:'—it is for him to cause his light to shine on all under the sky.

3. When the sun has reached the meridian height, it begins to decline. When the moon has become full, it begins to wane. The (interaction of) heaven and earth is now vigorous and abundant, now dull and scanty, growing and diminishing according to the seasons. How much more must it be so with (the operations of) men! How much more also with the spiritual agency!

LVI.[117] 1. 'Lü indicates that there may be some small attainment and progress:'—the weak (line) occupies the central place in the outer (trigram), and is obedient to the strong (lines on either side of it). (We

---

than in some other things which are said about the lines. The lines are where they cannot but be from the way in which the figures were formed.

[116] LV. The Khang-hsî editors remark that paragraph 1 is not so much explaining the meaning of the name Făng, as; accounting for the hexagram, composed of Lî and Kăn, having such a meaning.

Paragraph 3 seems rather contrary to the lesson of the hexagram. According to it, prosperity cannot be maintained, any more than we can have the other seasons without winter or perpetual day without night; but the object of the essay is to exhort to the maintenance of prosperity. Is it the case that the rise of every commonwealth and cause must be followed by its decay and fall? The mind refuses to admit the changes of the seasons, &c., as a true analogy for all moral and intellectual movements. See an important remark on the concluding sentence in the Introduction, pp. 32, 33.

[117] LVI. What is said in paragraph 1 is intended to explain the Thwan, and not to account for the meaning of the name Lü. It is assumed that Lü means a stranger; and the writer from the position of the fifth line, and from the attributes of the component trigrams, derives the ideas of humility, docility, a quiet restfulness, and intelligence as the characteristics proper to a stranger, and which are likely to lead to his attaining what he desires, and then advancing.

have also the attributes of quiet) resting closely attached to intelligence (in the component trigrams). Hence it is said, 'There may be some small attainment and progress. If the stranger or traveller be firm and correct as he ought to be, there will be good fortune.'

2. Great is the time and great is the right course to be taken as intimated in Lü!

LVII.[118] 1. The double Sun shows how, in accordance with it, (governmental) orders are reiterated.

2. (We see that) the strong (fifth line) has penetrated into the central and correct place, and the will (of its subject) is being carried into effect; (we see also) the weak (first and fourth lines) both obedient to the strong lines (above them). It is hence said, 'There will be some little attainment and progress. There will be advantage in movement onward in whatever direction. It will be advantageous also to see the great man.'

LVIII.[119] 1. Tui has the meaning of pleased satisfaction.

2. (We have) the strong (lines) in the centre, and the weak (lines) on the outer edge (of the two trigrams), (indicating that) in pleasure what is most advantageous is the maintenance of firm correctness. Through this there will be found an accordance with (the will of) heaven, and a correspondence with (the feelings of) men. When (such) pleasure goes before the people, (and leads them on), they forget their toils; when it animates them in encountering difficulties, they forget (the risk of) death. How great is (the power of) this pleased satisfaction, stimulating in such a way the people!

LIX.[120] 1. 'Hwan intimates that there will be progress and

---

[118] LVII. 1. The language of this paragraph has often occurred to me in reading commands and addresses issued by the emperors of China, such as the essays on the precepts in what is called the Sacred Edict, the reiteration employed in many of which is remarkable.

Paragraph 2. The 'obedience of the weak lines to the strong ones' grows, in a way not very perceptible, from the idea of the hexagram, and the quality of the trigram as denoting penetration and flexibility.

[119] LVIII. The feeling of pleasure going before the people and leading them on to endure toil and encounter death must be supposed to be produced in them by the example and lessons of their ruler. La Fad-hsien paraphrases this portion of the text thus:—'When the sage with this precedes them, he can make them endure toil without any wish to decline it, and go with him into difficulty and danger without their having any fear.' I think this was intended to be the teaching of the hexagram, but the positive expression of it is hardly discernible.

[120] LIX. 1. This paragraph has been partially anticipated in the notes on the Thwan. The second line is said to suffer 'no extinction,' because the lower trigram is that of peril. The Khang-hsî editors say that the former part of this paragraph shows how the root of the work of the hexagram is strengthened, and the latter part how the execution of that work is secured.

The conclusion of paragraph 2 is, literally, 'The king indeed is in the middle.' This does not mean, as some say, that the king is in the middle of the temple, but that his mind success:'—(we see) the strong line (in the second place) of the lower trigram, and not suffering any extinction there; and (also) the weak line occupying its place in the outer trigram, and uniting (its action) with that of the line above.

2. 'The king goes to his ancestral temple:'—the king's (mind) is without any deflection.

3. 'It will be advantageous to cross the great stream:'—(the subject of the hexagram) rides in (a vessel of) wood (over water), and will do so with success.

LX.[121] 1. '*K*ieh intimates progress and attainment:'—the strong and weak (lines) are equally divided, and the strong lines occupy the central places.

2. 'If the regulations (which *K*ieh prescribes) be severe and difficult, they cannot be permanent:'—its course (of action) will in that case come to an end.

3. (We have the feeling of) pleasure and satisfaction directing the course amidst peril. (We have) all regulations controlled (by authority) in its proper place. (We have) free action proceeding from the central and correct position.

4. Heaven and earth observe their regular terms, and we have the four seasons complete. (If rulers) frame their measures according to (the due) regulations, the resources (of the state) suffer no injury, and the people receive no hurt.

LXI.[122] 1. In *K*ung Fû we have the (two) weak lines in the

---

or heart is exactly set on the central truth of what is right and good.

The upper trigram Sun represents both wind and wood. To explain the meaning of Hwan, the significance of wind is taken; the writer here seizes on that of wood, as furnishing materials for a boat in which the great stream can be crossed.

[121] LX. Paragraph 1. See what is said on the Text of the Thwan.

'Its course will come to an end' is the opposite of the intimation in *K*ieh of progress and attainment.

In paragraph 3 the writer re-turns to this intimation of the figure:—by the attributes of the trigrams; by the appropriate positions of lines 4 and 5; and boy the central and correct place of 5.

Paragraph 4 illustrates the importance of doing things according to rule by reference to the operations of nature and the enactments and institutions of sage rulers.

[122] LXI. 1. The structure of the lineal figure which is here insisted on has been pointed out in explaining the Thwan. On what is further said as to the attributes of the trigrams and their effect, *Kh*ăng-3ze observes:—'We have in the sincerity shown in the upper trigram superiors condescending to those below them in accordance with their peculiarities, and we have in that of the lower those below delighted to follow their superiors. The combination of these two things leads to the transformation of the country and state.'

Paragraph 2. The two divided lines in the middle of the figure are supposed to give the semblance of an empty boat, and an empty boat, it is said (with doubtful truth), is not liable to be upset. The trigram Sun symbolises both wind and wood.

A good commentary on paragraph 3 is supplied in many passages of 'the Doctrine of the Mean,' e. g. chap. 20. 18:—'Sincerity is the way of Heaven. The attainment of innermost part (of the figure), and strong lines occupying the central places (in the trigrams). (We have the attributes) of pleased satisfaction and flexible penetration. Sincerity (thus symbolled) will transform a country.

2. 'Pigs and fish (are moved), and there will be good fortune:'—sincerity reaches to (and affects even) pigs and fishes.

'There will be advantage in crossing the great stream:'—(we see in the figure) one riding on (the emblem of) wood, which forms an empty boat.

3. In (the exercise of the virtue denoted by) *K*ung Fû, (it is said that) 'there will be advantage in being firm and correct:'—in that virtue indeed we have the response (of man) to Heaven.

LXII.[123] 1. In Hsiâo Kwo (we see) the small (lines) exceeding the others, and (giving the intimation of) progress and attainment.

2. Such 'exceeding, in order to its being advantageous, must be associated with firmness and correctness:'—that is, it must take place (only) according to (the requirements of) the time.

3. The weak (lines) are in the central places, and hence (it is said that what the name denotes) may be done in small affairs, and there will be good fortune.

4. Of the strong (lines one) is not in its proper place, and (the other) is not central, hence it is said that (what the name denotes) 'should not be done in great affairs.'

5. (In the hexagram) we have 'the symbol of a bird on the wing, and of the notes that come down from such a bird, for which it is better to descend than to ascend, thereby leading to great good fortune:'—to ascend is contrary to what is reasonable in the case, while to descend is natural and right.

LXIII.[124] 1. '*K*î 3î intimates progress and success:'—in small

---

sincerity is the way of men.'

[123] LXII. Paragraph 1. That the small lines exceed the others appears at a glance. The intimation of progress and attainment is less clear. Compare the first paragraph of Appendix I to hexagram 33.

'The requirements of the time' in paragraph 2 cannot make right wrong or wrong right; but they may modify the conventional course to be taken in any particular case.

It is easy to explain paragraphs 3 and 4, but what is said in them carries no conviction to the mind.

The sentiment of paragraph 5 is good, apart from the symbolism, which is only perplexing.

[124] LXIII. For paragraphs 1 and 2, see the note on the Text of the Thwan.

It is difficult to see the concatenation in paragraph 3 between the sentiment of the Thwan and the nature of the second line. The Khang-hsî editors compare this hexagram and the next with 11 and 12, observing that the goodness of Thâi (11) is concentrated, as here, in the second line.

The sentiment of paragraph 4 is that which we have often met with,—that things move on with a constant process of change. Disorder succeeds to order, and again order matters, that is, there will be that progress and success.

2. 'There will be advantage in being firm and correct:'—the strong and weak (lines) are correctly arranged, each in its appropriate place.

3. 'There has been good fortune in the beginning:—the weak (second line) is in the centre.

4. 'In the end' there is a cessation (of effort), and 'disorder arises:'—the course (that led to rule and order) is (now) exhausted.

LXIV.[125] 1. 'Wei 3î intimates progress and success (in the circumstances which it implies):'—the weak (fifth) line is in the centre.

2. 'The young fox has nearly crossed the stream:'—but he has not yet escaped from the midst (of the danger and calamity).

'Its tail gets immersed. There will be no advantage in any way:'—there is not at the end a continuance (of the purpose) at the beginning. Although the places (of the different lines) are not those appropriate to them, yet a strong (line) and a weak (line always) respond to each other.

---

to disorder.

[125] LXIV. Paragraph 1. The indication is derived from the fifth line, divided, which is in the ruler's place. It occupies a strong place, has for its correlate the strong 2, and is itself in the centre of the yin trigram Lî.

Paragraph 2. Line 2 represents 'the young fox.' A strong line in the midst of the trigram of peril, its subject will be restless; and responding to the ruler in 5, he will be forward and incautious in taking action. The issue will be evil, and the latter end different from the beginning. What is said in the last sentence shows further how Wei 3î indicates progress.

## APPENDIX II.

Treatise on the Symbolism of the Hexagrams, and of the duke of *K*âu's Explanations of the several Lines[126]

## SECTION I.

I.[127] Heaven, in its motion, (gives the idea of) strength. The superior man, in accordance with this, nerves himself to ceaseless activity.

1. 'The dragon lies hid in the deep;—it is not the time for active doing:'—(this appears from) the strong and undivided line's being in the lowest place.

2. 'The dragon appears in the field:'—the diffusion of virtuous influence has been wide.

3. 'Active and vigilant all the day:'—(this refers to) the treading of the (proper) path over and over again.

4. 'He seems to be leaping up, but is still in the deep:'—if he advance, there will be no error.

5. 'The dragon is on the wing in the sky:'—the great man rouses himself to his work.

6. 'The dragon exceeds the proper limits;—there will be occasion for repentance:'—a state of fulness, that is, should not be indulged in long.

7. 'The same line (undivided) is used' (in all the places of this hexagram), but the attribute of heaven (thereby denoted) should not (always) take the foremost place.

II.[128] The (capacity and sustaining) power of the earth is what is

---

[126] Like the Text under each hexagram, what is said under each in this treatise on its symbolism is divided into two portions. The first is called 'the Great Symbolism,' and is occupied with the trigrammatic composition of the hexagram, to the statement of which is always subjoined an exhibition of the use which should be, or has been, made of the lesson suggested by the meaning of the whole figure in the administration of affairs, or in self-government. If the treatise be rightly ascribed to Confucius, this practical application of the teaching of the symbols is eminently characteristic of his method in inculcating truth and duty; though we often find it difficult to trace the connexion between his premiss and conclusion. This portion of the treatise will be separated by a double space from what follows,—'the Lesser Symbolism,' in the explanations of the several lines.

[127] I. *Kh*ien is formed by redoubling the trigram of the same name. In the case of other hexagrams of similar formation, the repetition of the trigram is pointed out. That is not done here, according to *K*û Hsî, 'because there is but one heaven.' But the motion of heaven is a complete revolution every day, resumed again the next; so moves 'the unwearied sun from day to day,' making it a good symbol of renewed, untiring effort.

[128] II. Khwăn is formed by redoubling the trigram of the same name and having 'the earth for its symbol.' As in the former hexagram, the repetition is emphatic, not otherwise

denoted by Khwǎn. The superior man, in accordance with this, with his large virtue supports (men and) things.

1. 'He is treading on hoarfrost;—the strong ice will come (by and by):'—the cold (air) has begun to take form. Allow it to go on quietly according to its nature, and (the hoarfrost) will come to strong ice.

2. The movement indicated by the second six, (divided),is 'from the straight (line) to the square.' '(Its operation), without repeated effort, in every way advantageous,' shows the brilliant result of the way of earth.

3. 'He keeps his excellence tinder restraint, but firmly maintains it:'—at the proper time he will manifest it. 'He may have occasion to engage in the king's service:—great is the glory of his wisdom.

4. 'A sack tied up;—there will be no error:'—this shows how, through carefulness, no injury will be received.

S. 'The Yellow lower-garment;—there will be great good fortune:'—this follows from that ornamental (colour's) being in the right and central place.

6. 'The dragons fight in the wild:—the (onward) course (indicated by Khwǎn) is pursued to extremity.

7. '(The lines are all weak and divided, as appears from) the use of the number line:—but (those who are thus represented) becoming perpetually correct and firm, there will thereby be a great consummation.

III.[129] (The trigram representing) clouds and (that representing)

affecting the meaning of the hexagram. 'As there is but one heaven,' says *Kû* Hsî, 'so there is but one earth.' The first part of 'the Great Symbolism' appears in Canon McClatchie's version as—'Khwǎn is the generative part of earth.' By 'generative part' he probably means 'the productive or prolific faculty.' If he mean anything else, there comes out a conclusion antagonistic to his own view of the 'mythology' of the Yî. The character Shî, which he translates by 'generative part,' is defined in Dr. Williams' dictionary as 'the virility of males.' Such is the special significance of it. If it were so used here, the earth would be masculine.

It is difficult to say exactly what the writer meant by—'The superior man, in accordance with this, and with his large nature, supports (men and) things.' Lin Hsî-yüan (Ming dynasty) says:—'The superior man, in his single person, sustains the burden of all under the sky. The common people depend on him for their rest and enjoyment. Birds and beasts and creeping things, and the tribes of the vegetable kingdom, depend on him for the fulfilment or their destined being. If he be of a narrow mind and cold virtue, how can he help them? Their hope in him would be in vain.'

'The Smaller Symbolism' is sufficiently dealt with in the notes on the Text.

[129] III. Khan represents water, especially in the form of rain. Here its symbol is a cloud. The whole hexagram seems to place us in the atmosphere of a thunderous sky overhung with thick and gloomy clouds, when we feel oppressed and distressed. This is not a bad emblem of the political state in the mind of the writer. When the thunder has pealed, and the clouds have discharged their burden of rain, the atmosphere is cleared, and there is a feeling of relief. But I fail again to discern clearly the connexion between the symbolism and the lesson about the superior man's administration of affairs.

The subject of the first line of the Smaller Symbolism is represented by the thunder form *K*un. The superior man, in accordance with this, (adjusts his measures of government) as in sorting the threads of the warp and woof.

1. Although 'there is a difficulty in advancing,' the mind (of the subject of the line) is set on doing what is correct. While noble, he humbles himself to the mean, and grandly gains the people.

2. The difficulty (to the subject of) the second six, (divided), arises from, its place over the undivided line below it. 'The union and children after ten years' shows things resuming their regular course.

3. 'One pursues the deer without the (guidance of the) forester:'— (he does so) in (his eagerness to) follow the game. 'The superior man gives up the chase, (knowing that) if he go forward he will regret it:'— he would be reduced to extremity.

4. 'Going forward after such a search (for a helper)' shows intelligence.

5. 'Difficulty is experienced (by the subject of the fifth line) in bestowing his rich favours:'—the extent to which they reach will not yet be conspicuous.

6. 'He weeps tears of blood in streams:'—how can the state (thus emblemed) continue long?

IV.[130] (The trigram representing) a mountain, and beneath it that

---

undivided line, and therefore is firm and correct. He is noble, but his place is below the divided lines, symbols of the weak and mean (see Appendix IV, i, 1).

Line 2. 'Things resume their regular course:'—the subject is now at liberty to seek a union with the subject of line 5, according to the rules of the symbolism. Lines 1 and 4, 2 and 5, 3 and 6, the corresponding lilies of the trigrams, are correlates.

The subject of line 4 naturally recurs to the correlate in line 1. He is the natural helper in the case, and he has the ability.

[130] IV. 'The spring here issuing forth' is different from the defile with a stream in it, in the explanation of the Thwan; different moreover from 'rain,' mentioned also as the phenomenon which is the natural symbol of Khan. The presence of water, however, is common to the three. But the water of the spring, or of the stream, would flow away from the hill, and not be stopped by it; as an emblem therefore of the ignorance and inexperience denoted by Măng it is not suitable. *K*û Hsî says that 'the water of a spring is sure to move on and gradually advance.' This may serve as a symbol of the general process and progress of education, though it gives no account of the symbolism of the hill. It serves also to explain in part the transition of the writer to the subject of the superior man, and his dealing apparently with himself.

Does line 1 set forth the use of punishment as the dernier resort, undesirable, but possibly unavoidable, to bring men in subjection to law?

The force of line 2 comes out fully in the Thwan.

That a woman such as is represented in line 3 should not be taken in marriage is clear enough; but I do not see the bearing of the illustration on the proper lesson in the hexagram.

Line 3 separates 4 from 2, and 5 separates it from 6. Weak in itself, it is farther removed than any other from the two strong lines in the hexagram, and is represented as 'cribbed' in its ignorance.

The fifth is the most honourable place in the figure, and here is occupied by a weak for a spring issuing forth form Măng. The superior man, in accordance with this, strives to be resolute in his conduct and nourishes his virtue.

1. 'It will be advantageous to use punishment:'—the object being to bring under the influence of correcting law.

2. 'A son able to (sustain the burden of) his family:'—as appears from the reciprocation between this strong line and the weak (fifth line).

3. 'A woman (such as is here represented) should not be taken in marriage:'—her conduct is not agreeable to what is right.

4. 'The regret arising from ignorance bound in chains' is due to the special distance of (the subject of this line) from the solidity (shown in lines 2 and 6).

5. 'The good fortune belonging to the simple lad without experience' comes from his docility going on to humility.

6. 'Advantage will come from warding off injury:'—(the subject of this line) above and (the ignorant) below, all do and are done to in accordance with their nature.

V.[131] (The trigram for) clouds ascending over that for the sky forms Hsü. The superior man, in accordance with this, eats and drinks, feasts and enjoys himself (as if there were nothing else to employ him).

1. 'He is waiting in the (distant) border:'—he makes no movement to encounter rashly the difficulties (of the situation). 'It will be advantageous for him constantly to maintain (the purpose thus shown), in which case there will be no error:'—he will not fail to pursue that

---

line. This looks, however, to the occupant of line 2, less honourable than itself, and is marked by the two attributes that are named. Compare what is said on line 2.

A strong line in the topmost place must represent, according to the scheme of the hexagram, one who uses force in the cause of education; but the force is put forth not on the ignorant, but on those who would keep them ignorant, or increase their ignorance. The subject of this line, therefore, acts according to his nature, and the subjects of all the weak lines below are cared for as is best for them.

[131] V. 'The cloud,' it is said, 'that has risen to the top of the sky, has nothing more to do till it is called on, in the harmony of heaven and earth, to discharge its store of rain.' This gives to the writer the idea of waiting; and the superior man is supposed to be taught by this symbolism to enjoy his idle time, while he is waiting for the approach of danger and occasion for action.

'The regular course' of the subject of line 1 seems to be the determination to wait, at a distance from danger, the proper time to act.

The subject of line 2, which is undivided and in the centre, is thereby shown to be possessed of a large and generous forbearance.

The recognition of the circumstances of the time, and hearkening to its requirements, explain, in paragraph 4, 'the retreat from the cavern,' which is not here repeated from the Text. The line being weak and divided, its subject knows his own incompetency, and takes this prudent step.

*Kû* says that he does not understand what is said under line 6,—that the occupant and the place are not suited to each other, for the yin line being in the sixth, an even place, seems to be where it ought to be. We are only surprised that cases of inconsistency in these explanations are not more numerous.

regular course.

2. 'He is waiting on the sand:'—he occupies his position in the centre with a generous forbearance. Though 'he suffer the small injury of being spoken (against),' he will bring things to a good issue.

3. 'He is waiting in the mud:'—calamity is (close at hand, and as it were) in the outer (trigram). 'He himself invites the approach of injury:'—if he be reverent and careful, he will not be worsted.

4. 'He is waiting in (the place of) blood:'—he accommodates himself (to the circumstances of the time), and hearkens to (its requirements).

5. 'The appliances of a feast, and the good fortune through being firm and correct,' are indicated by (the position in) the central and correct place.

6. 'Guests come unurged (to give their help), and if (the subject of the line) receive them respectfully, there will be good fortune in the end:'—though the occupant and the place are not suited to each other, there has been no great failure (in what has been done).

VI.[132] (The trigram representing) heaven and (that representing) water, moving away from each other, form Sung. The superior man, in accordance with this, in the transaction of affairs takes good counsel about his first steps.

1. 'He does not perpetuate the matter about which (the contention is):'—contention should not be prolonged. Although 'he may suffer the small (injury) of being spoken against,' his argument is clear.

2. 'He is unequal to the contention; he retires and keeps concealed, stealthily withdrawing from it:'—for him from his lower place to contend with (the stronger one) above, would be to (invite) calamity, as if he brought it with his hand to himself.

3. 'He confines himself to the support assigned to him of old:'—(thus) following those above him, he will have good fortune.

4. 'He returns to (the study of Heaven's) ordinances, changes (his wish to contend), and rests in being firm and correct:'—he does not fail

---

[132] VI. The symbolism here is different from that in the Text of the Thwan. We have the visible sky ascending and water or rain descending, which indicate, one hardly sees how, opposition and contention. The lesson as to the course of the superior man is a good one, but might with equal propriety be deduced from many other hexagrams.

Hsiang An-shih (Sung dynasty) says that the first part of paragraph 2 is all to be taken as the language of the duke of *Kâu*, the characters being varied; the rest is the remark of the writer of this treatise.

It is observed that the returning to (the study of Heaven's) ordinances, and changing the wish to contend, in paragraph 4, are not two things, but only one; 'the ordinances (ming) meaning what is right in principle.' The wish to contend was wrong in principle, and is now abandoned.

'The robe' takes the place of 'the leathern sash' in paragraph 6; but the sash was merely an appendage of the robe.

(in doing what is right).

5. 'He contends;—and 'with great fortune:—this is shown by his holding the due mean and being in the correct place.

6. 'He receives the robe through his contention:'—but still be is not deserving of respect.

VII.[133] (The trigram representing) the earth and in the midst of it that representing water, form Sze. The superior man, in accordance with this, nourishes and educates the people, and collects (from among them) the multitudes (of the hosts).

1. 'The host goes forth according to the rules (for) such a movement:'—if those rules be not observed, there will be evil.

2. 'He is in the midst of the host, and there will be good fortune:'—he has received the favour of Heaven. 'The king has thrice conveyed to him the orders (of) his favour:'—(the king) cherishes the myriad regions in his heart.

3. 'The host with the possibility of its having many idle leaders:'— great will be its want of success.

4. 'The host is in retreat; but there is no error:'—there has been no failure in the regular course.

5. 'The oldest son leads the host:'—its movements are directed by him in accordance with his position in the centre. 'Younger men idly occupy their positions:'—the employment of such men is improper.

6. 'The great ruler delivers his charges:'—thereby he rightly apportions merit. 'Small men should not be employed:'—they are sure to throw the states into confusion.

VIII.[134] (The trigram representing) the earth, and over it (that

---

[133] VII. 'The Great Symbolism' here is not more satisfactory than in other paragraphs of it which have already come before us. Kû Hsî says:—'As the water is not outside the earth, so soldiers are not outside the people. Therefore if (a ruler) be able to nourish the people, he can get the multitudes (of his hosts).' Is the meaning this,—that originally the people and soldiers are one body; that a portion of the people are taken out from among the mass, as occasion requires, to do the duty of soldiers; and that the nourishment and education of the people is the best way to have good soldiers ready for use on any emergency? Compare the saying of Confucius in Analects XIII, xxx.

What is said on the second line, that the general 'has received the favour of Heaven,' refers of course to the entire confidence reposed in him by the ruler or king, the subject of line 5. In this way Thien here is equal to Thien wang, so frequent in the 'Spring and Autumn,' and meaning—'King by the grace of Heaven.' But the great powers given to the general are from the king's wish through him to promote the good of all the nation.

In military operations there must be one ruling will and mind. A divided authority is sure to be a failure. But 'a retreat' is no evidence of failure in a campaign. When advance would lead to disaster, retreat is the regular course to pursue.

Other ways can be found to reward small men. They ought not to be placed in situations where the condition of others will depend on them.

[134] VIII. 'Water upon the face of the earth' is supposed to be an emblem of close union. Of the mere fact of close union this may be accepted as a fair illustration, and of its completeness. Some other symbolism might set forth better the tendency of parties to

representing) water, form Pî. The ancient kings, in accordance with this, established the various states and maintained an affectionate relation to their princes.

1. From 'the seeking union with its object' shown in the first line, (divided),there will be other advantages.

2. 'The movement towards union and attachment proceeds from the inward (mind):'—(the party concerned) does not fail in what is proper to himself.

3. 'Union is sought with such as ought not to be associated with:'—but will not injury be the result?

4. 'Union is sought (by the party intended here) with one beyond himself, and (in this case) with a worthy object:'—he is following (the ruler) above him.

5. 'The good fortune belonging to the most illustrious instance of seeking union and attachment' appears in the correct and central position (of the fifth line, undivided).

(The king's) neglecting (the animals) confronting him (and then fleeing), and (only) taking those who present themselves as it were obediently, is seen in 'his allowing the escape of those in front of him.' 'That the people of his towns do not warn one another (to prevent such escape),' shows how he, in his high eminence, has made them pursue the due course.

6. 'He seeks union and attachment without taking the first (step to such an end):'—there is no possibility of a (good) issue.

IX.[135] (The trigram representing) the sky, and that representing

---

union, and their seeking it. What is said about the ancient kings is more pertinent to the meaning of the hexagram than in many other applications in 'the Great Symbolism.' The king appears in it not only as the centre, but as the cause, of union.

'The other advantages' under line 1 refer to all the benefits that will result from sincerity and union, which are in themselves good.

It is hardly possible to make what is said under line 5, on the royal huntings, agree with the account of them given on the same line in the duke of *K*âu's text. I suspect that there is some corruption of the text. The two verbs 'neglecting' and 'taking' seem to be used, the one for the other.

[135] IX. The suitability of the symbolism here is made all to turn on the wind. 'Wind,' says *K*û, 'is simply the air, without solid substance; it can restrain, but not for long.' The wind moves in the sky for a time, and then ceases. The process of thought from the symbol to the lesson is not easily traced. Is it meant to say that virtue manifesting itself outwardly—in the carriage and speech—is, however good, but a small matter, admirable in an officer, or even a feudal lord, but that we look for more in a king, the Head of a nation?

*Kh*ăng-ʒze calls attention to the addition to the duke of Kâu's explanation in the notice on line 2, that 'it is in the central place,' adding that this explains how the subject of the line restrains himself, and does not go beyond what is due from him.

Only half of the symbolism in the Text of line 3 is taken up here. Line 1, it is said, is far from line 4, the mauvais sujet of the hexagram, and little affected by it; line 2 is nearer, but, being in the centre, suffers little; line 3 is close on it, and, not being in the wind moving above it, form Hsiâo *Khû* The superior man, in accordance with this, adorns the outward manifestation of his virtue.

1. 'He returns and pursues his own path:'—it is right that there should be good fortune.

2. 'By the attraction (of the subject of the former line) he returns (to its own course),' and is in the central place:—neither will he err in what is due from him.

3. 'Husband and wife look on each other with averted eyes:'—(the subject of line three is like a husband who) cannot maintain correctly his relations with his wife.

4. 'He is possessed of sincerity; his (ground for) apprehension is dismissed:'—(the subjects of the lines) above agree in aim with him.

5. 'He is possessed of sincerity, and draws others to unite with him:'—he does not use only his own rich resources.

6. 'The rain has fallen and (the onward progress) is stayed:'—the power (denoted in the figure) has accumulated to the full. 'If the superior man prosecute his measures, there will be evil:'—he will find himself obstructed.

X.[136] (The trigram representing) the sky above, and below it (that representing the waters of) a marsh, form Lî. The superior man, in accordance with this, discriminates between high and low, and gives settlement to the aims of the people.

1. 'He treads his accustomed path and goes forward:'—singly and

---

centre, comes under its evil influence; while line 6 gives no help.

Line 4 is weak, and in an even place, appropriate to it; and hence its subject is said to 'have sincerity.' Being the first line, moreover, of Sun, the two others take their character from it.

Line 5, being undivided, and occupying the most important place in the figure, according to the value usually attached to the lines, is said 'to be rich,' or 'to have rich resources.' With these he unites with the 'subjects' of line 4 to effect their common object.

Under line 6 we are told that the restraint is at its height, and the restrained should keep still for a time. The paragraph is metrical. The paragraphs to lines 1, 2, 3, all rhyme together. So do those to 4, 5; and now under 6, we have a couplet:—

> Lo! rain, lo! rest, the power is full!
> Good man! hold hard. Obstructions rule.'

[136] X. 'The sky above and a marsh lying below it is true,' says *Kh*ăng-ȝze, 'in nature and reason; and so should be the rules of propriety on which men tread.' This symbolism is far-fetched; and so is the application of it, if in any way drawn from it. But it is true that the members of a community or nation must keep their several places and duties in order to its being in a state of good order.

For lines 1, 2, 3, and 4, see notes on the Text.

If we might translate the conclusion of what is said on line 5, by—'in the position that is correctly appropriate to him,' the meaning would he more clear, though still the assumption which I have pointed out on the Text would underlie the statement; and as evidently as there, what is said under line 6 is but a truism.

exclusively he carries out his (long-cherished) wishes.

2. 'A quiet and solitary man, to whom, being firm and correct, there will be good fortune:'—holding the due mean, he will not allow himself to be thrown into disorder.

3. 'A one-eyed man (who thinks that he) can see:'—he is not fit to see clearly. 'A lame man (who thinks that he can) tread well:'—one cannot walk along with him. 'The ill fortune of being bitten' arises from the place not being the proper one for him. 'A (mere) bravo acting the part of a great ruler:'—this is owing to his aims being (too) violent.

4. 'He becomes full of apprehensive caution, and in the end there will be good fortune:'—his aim takes effect.

5. 'He treads resolutely; and though he be firm and correct, there is peril:'—this is due to his being in the position that is correct and appropriate to him.

6. 'There will be great good fortune,' and that in the occupancy of the topmost line:—this is great matter for congratulation.

XI.[137] (The trigrams for) heaven and earth in communication together form Thâi. The (sage) sovereign, in harmony with this, fashions and completes (his regulations) after the courses of heaven and earth, and assists the application of the adaptations furnished by them,—in order to benefit the people.

1. 'The good fortune of advance, (as suggested by the emblem of) the grass pulled up,' arises from the will (of the party intended) being set on what is external to himself.

2. 'He bears with the uncultivated, and proves himself acting in accordance with the due mean:'—for (his intelligence is) bright and (his capacity is) great.

3. 'There is no going away so that there shall not be a return' refers to this as the point where the interaction of heaven and earth takes place.

4. 'He comes fluttering (down), not relying on his own rich resources:'—both he and his neighbours are out of their real (place

---

[137] XI. It is difficult to translate the application of 'the Great Symbolism' here, so that it shall be intelligible to a reader. *Khãng-ʒze* says:—'A ruler should frame his laws; and regulations so that the people may avail themselves of the seasons of heaven, and of the advantages afforded by the earth, assisting their transforming and nourishing services, and completing their abundant and admirable benefits. Thus the breath of spring, calling forth all vegetable life, gives the law for sowing and planting; the breath of autumn, completing and solidifying all things, gives the law for ingathering and storing,' &c.

The subject of line 1 has 'his will on what is external to himself:'—he is bent on going forward.

*Kû Hsî* explains what is said on paragraph 4, that the upper lines 'are out of their real place where they are,' or, literally, 'have lost their substantiality,' by the remark that 'their proper place, as being weak lines, is below.' The editors of the imperial edition prefer another explanation, on which I need not enter.

where they are). 'They have not received warning, but (come) in the sincerity (of their hearts):'—this is what they have desired in the core of their hearts.

5. 'By such a course there is happiness, and there will be great good fortune:'—(the subject of the line) employs the virtue proper to his central position to carry his wishes into effect.

6. 'The city wall returned back into the moat' shows how the (governmental) orders have (long) been in disorder.

XII.[138] (The trigrams of) heaven and earth, not in intercommunication, form Phî. The superior man, in accordance with this, restrains (the manifestation) of) his virtue, and avoids the calamities (that threaten him). There is no opportunity of conferring on him the glory of emolument.

1. 'The good fortune through firm goodness, (suggested by) the pulling up of the grass,' arises from the will (of the parties intended) being bent on (serving) the ruler.

2. 'The great man, comporting himself as the distress and obstruction require, will have success:—'he does not allow himself to be disordered by the herd (of small men).

3. That 'his shame is folded in his breast' is owing to the inappropriateness of his position.

4. 'He acts in accordance with the ordination (of Heaven), and commits no error:'—the purpose of his mind can be carried into effect.

5. The good fortune of the great man' arises from the correctness of his position.

6. 'The distress and obstruction having reached its end, it is overthrown and removed:'—how could it be prolonged?

XIII.[139] (The trigrams for) heaven and fire form Thung Zăn. The

---

[138] XII. 'The Great Symbolism' here is sufficiently explained in the first Appendix. The application, however, is here again difficult, though we may try to find in it a particular instance of the interruption of communication,—in great merit not meeting with its reward.

The subject of the first line is one of the cluster of small men who are able to change their mind, and set their hearts to love their ruler.

The subject of the second line is a 'great man,' and occupies the place in the centre.

The subject of the third line is weak, and does not occupy his correct position;—hence the symbolism.

The fourth line is near the fifth, the ruler's place. It is a strong line in an even place; but acting according to the will of Heaven or of the ruler, its subject gets his purpose carried out.

The subject of the fifth line is the great man, the ruler in his right place. Hence he is successful, and in the last line, we see how the distress and obstruction are come to an end. It was in the order of change that they should do so.

[139] XIII. The style of 'heaven and fire form Thung Zăn' is such as to suggest the appearance of fire ascending up, blazing to the sky, and uniting with it. The application of the symbolism is again perplexing.

In line 1, the party just issuing from his gate has all the world before him, with superior man, in accordance with this), distinguishes things according to their kinds and classes.

1. '(The representative of) the union of men is just issuing from his gate:'—who will blame him?

2. '(The representative of) the union of men appears in relation with his kindred:'—that is the path to regret.

3. 'He hides his arms in the thick grass:'—because of the strength of his opponent. 'For three years he makes no demonstration:'—how can he do anything?

4. 'He is mounted on his city-wall;' but yielding to the right, 'he does not proceed to make the attack (he contemplated).' (Where it is said),'There will be good fortune,' (that shows how) he feels the strait he is in, and returns to the rule of law.

5. The first action of (the representative of) the union of men (here described) arises from his central position and straightforward character. 'The meeting secured by his great host' intimates that the opponents of it have been overcome.

6. '(The representative of) the union of men appears in the suburbs:'—his object has not yet been attained.

XIV.[140] (The trigram for) heaven and (that of) fire above it form Tâ Yû The superior man, in accordance with this, represses what is evil and gives distinction to what is good, in sympathy with the excellent Heaven-conferred (nature).

1. This first line, (undivided),of Tâ Yû shows no approach to what is injurious.

2. 'A large waggon with its load' refers to the (virtue) accumulated (in the subject of the line), so that he will suffer no loss (in the conduct

---

which to unite. Selfish thoughts disposing to union have no place in him.

In line 2, union (only) with kindred implies narrowness of mind. For line 3, see note on the Text.

In line 4, stress should be laid on 'yielding to the right.'

For line 5, see note on the Text.

The Khang-hsî editors append the following note to the last paragraph: —'Under line 1 it is said that "union in the open country indicates progress and success," while here it is only said that "with union in the suburbs there is no cause for repentance." Beyond the suburbs was the open country, and till the union reached so far, the object of the hexagram was not attained. We may truly say that Confucius was a skilful reader of the duke of *K*âu.' Of course the editors did not doubt Confucius' authorship of all the Appendixes.

[140] XIV. 'Fire above the sky' will shine far; and this is supposed to symbolise the vastness of the territory or of the wealth implied in the possession of what is great. The superior man, in governing men, especially in a time of prosperity and wealth, must set himself to develope what is good in them, and repress what is evil. And this will be in accordance with the will of Heaven, which has given to all men a nature fitted for goodness.

All the comment that is necessary on the symbolism of the several lines may be gathered from the comments on the Text.

of affairs).

3. 'A feudal prince presents his offerings to the son of Heaven:'—a small man (in such a position) does (himself) harm.

4. 'He keeps his great resources under restraint:'—his wisdom discriminates clearly (what he ought to do).

5. 'His sincerity is reciprocated by all the others:'—his sincerity serves to stir and call out what is in their minds. 'The good fortune springing from a display of proper majesty' shows how they might (otherwise) feel too easy, and make no preparation (to serve him).

6. 'The good fortune attached to the topmost line of Tâ Yû' arises from the help of Heaven.

XV.[141] (The trigram for) the earth and (that of) a mountain in the midst of it form *Kh*ien. The superior man, in accordance with this, diminishes what is excessive (in himself), and increases where there is any defect, bringing about an equality, according to the nature of the case, in his treatment (of himself and others).

1. 'The superior man who adds humility to humility' is one who nourishes his (virtue) in lowliness.

2. 'The good fortune consequent on being firm and correct, where the humility has made itself recognised, is owing to the possessor's having (the virtue) in the core of his heart.

3. 'The superior man of (acknowledged) merit, and yet humble:'— the myriads of the people will submit to him.

4. 'One, whose action would be in every way advantageous, stirs up his humility the more:'(but in doing so) he does not act contrary to

---

[141] XV. The earth is low, and in the midst of it is a high mountain; but I fail to see how this can symbolise humility. Nor does Regis' representation of it much improve the case:—'Monte' (ait glossa) 'nihil est altius in terra, quae est summe abjecta. At cum is declivis sit, imago esse potest humilis modestiae.' I find the following note on the paragraph in my copy of the 'Daily Lessons'(see Preface):—'The five yin lines above and below symbolise the earth; the one yang line in the centre is "the mountain in the midst of the earth." The many yin lines represent men's desires; the one yang line, heavenly principle. The superior man, looking at this symbolism, diminishes the multitude of human desires within him, and increases the single shoot of heavenly principle; so does he become grandly just, and can deal with all things evenly according to the nature of each. In whatever circumstances or place he is, he will do what is right.' This is certainly very ingenious, but one shrinks from accepting a view that is not based on the component trigrams.

Under line 1, 'nourishes his (virtue)' is, literally, 'pastures himself.' He is all humility. That makes him what he is.

Under line 4, 'the (proper) rule' is the rule proper for the subject of the line in his circumstances so near the place of the ruler.

Under line 5, 'the refusal to submit' makes an appeal to force necessary. Even the best and humblest ruler bears the sword, and must not bear it in vain.

*Kû* Hsî bases all that is said under line 6 on its being a weak line; so that the humble ruler is unable even at the close of the action described in the figure to accomplish all his objects, and must limit his field even in appealing to arms.

the (proper) rule.

5. 'He may advantageously use the force of arms:'—correcting, that is, those who do not submit.

6. 'His humility has made itself recognised:'—(but) all his aims have not yet been attained. He may employ the force of arms, (but only) in correcting (his own) towns and state.'

XVI.[142] (The trigrams for) the earth and thunder issuing from it with its crashing noise form Yü. The ancient kings, in accordance with this, composed their music and did honour to virtue, presenting it especially and most grandly to God, when they associated with Him (at the service) their highest ancestor and their father.

1. 'The (subject of the) first six proclaims his pleasure and satisfaction:'—there will be evil; his wishes have been satisfied to overflowing.

2. '(He sees a thing) without waiting till it has come to pass; with his firm correctness there will be good fortune:'—this is shown by the central and correct position (of the line).

3. 'He looks up (for favours), while he indulges the feeling of satisfaction; there will be occasion for repentance:'—this is intimated by the position not being the appropriate one.

4. 'From him the harmony and satisfaction come; great is the success which he obtains:'—his aims take effect on a grand scale.

5. '(The subject of) the fifth six has a chronic complaint:'—this is shown by his being mounted on the strong (line). 'He still lives on without dying:'—he is in the central position, (and its memories of the past) have not yet perished.

6. 'With darkened mind devoted to the harmony and satisfaction (of the time),' as shown in the topmost (line):—how can one in such a

---

[142] XVI. 'The Great Symbolism' here is more obscure than usual. A thunderstorm clears the air and removes the feeling of oppression, of which one is conscious before its occurrence. Is this all that is meant by making the trigrams of the earth and thunder form Yü, the hexagram of harmony and satisfaction? What is meant, moreover, by making the thunder 'issue,' as the Chinese text says, from the earth? Then as to the application of this symbolism, I can trace the author's idea but imperfectly. To say that the thunder crash suggested the use of music, as some critics do, is absurd. The use of music at sacrifices, however, as assisting the union produced by those services between God and his worshippers, and the present and past generations, agrees with the general idea of the figure. I must suppose that the writer had in mind the sacrifices instituted by the duke of *K*âu, as related in the Hsiâo King, chap. ix.

Pleasure has operated injuriously on the subject of line 1. He calls attention to himself.

Only a part of the symbolism of line 2 is referred to here. Such an omission is not uncommon;—as in lines 3 and 4 also.

With 'the memories of the past not perishing' compare Mencius, II, Section i, chap. 1. 6-13.

In line 6 the action of the hexagram is over. If one puts off changing his evil way any longer, there remains no more hope for him.

condition continue long?

XVII.[143] (The trigram for the waters of) a marsh and (that for) thunder (hidden) in the midst of it form Sui. The superior man in accordance with this, when it is getting towards dark, enters (his house) and rests.

1. 'He is changing the object of his pursuit:'—but if he follow what is correct, there will be good fortune. 'He goes beyond (his own) gate to find associates:'—he will not fail (in the method he pursues).

2. 'He cleaves to the little boy:'—he cannot be with the two at the same time.

3. 'He cleaves to the man of age and experience:'—by the decision of his will, he abandons (the youth) below.

4. 'He is followed and obtains adherents:'—according to the idea (of the hexagram), this is evil. 'He is sincere in his course:'—showing his intelligence, and leading to achievement.

5. 'He is sincere in fostering what is excellent:'—his position is correct and in the centre.

6. 'The sincerity is firmly held and clung to, as shown in the topmost line:'—(the idea of the hexagram) has reached its extreme development.

XVIII.[144] (The trigram for) a mountain, and below it that for wind, form Kû. The superior man, in accordance with this, (addresses himself to) help the people and nourish his own virtue.

1. 'He deals with the troubles caused by his father:'—he feels that he has entered into the work of his father.

2. 'He deals with the troubles caused by his mother:'—he holds to the course of the due mean.

---

[143] XVII. An explosion of thunder amidst the waters of a marsh would be succeeded by a tremulous agitation of those waters; so far there would be a following of the movement of the lower trigram by the upper. Then in the application of the symbolism we have an illustration of action following the time, that is, according to the time; which is a common use of the Chinese character Sui. Neither the symbolism, however, nor its application adds much to our understanding of the text.

Paragraph 1 consists of two lines that rhyme; and paragraphs 4 (two lines), 5, and 6 do the same. According to Kû Yen-wû, paragraphs 2 and 3 also rhyme; but this appears to me doubtful. The symbolism of these paragraphs is sufficiently explained in the notes on the Text. Some peculiarities in their style (in Chinese) are owing to the bonds of the rhyme.

[144] XVIII. 'When the wind,' says *Khăng-ȝze*, 'encounters the mountain, it is driven back, and the things about are all scattered in disorder; such is the emblem of the state denoted by Kû.'

'The nourishing of virtue' appears especially in line 6; all the other lines belong to the 'helping of the people.'

The subject of line 1 has entered into the work of his father, and brings it about that his father is looked on as blameless. The 'due mean' of line 2 is according to the caution in the Text. The Khang-hsî editors interpret the explanation of line 5 as = 'he takes up (the course of his father) with all his virtue.' I think they are wrong.

3. 'He deals with the troubles caused by his father:'—in the end there will be no error.

4. 'He views indulgently the troubles caused by his father:'—if he go forward, he will not succeed.

5. 'He deals with the troubles caused by his father, and obtains praise:'—he is responded to (by the subject of line two) with all his virtue.

6. 'He does not serve either king or feudal lord:'—but his aim may be a model (to others).

XIX.[145] (The trigram for) the waters of a marsh and that for the earth above it form Lin. The superior man, in accordance with this, has his purposes of instruction that are inexhaustible, and nourishes and supports the people without limit.

1. 'The good fortune through the firm correctness of (the subject of the first line) advancing in company (with the subject of the second)' is due to his will being set on doing what is right.

2. 'The good fortune and every possible advantage attending the advance (of the subject of the second line), in company (with the subject of the first),' arises from the fact that those (to whom the advance is made) are not yet obedient to the ordinances (of Heaven).

3. 'He (shows himself) well pleased to advance:'—his position is not that appropriate to him. 'If he become anxious, however, about his action,' his error will not be continued.

4. 'The freedom from error consequent on the advance in the highest mode' is due to the (various) appropriateness of the position.

5. 'What befits the great ruler' means the pursuing the course of the due mean.

6. 'The good fortune consequent on the advance of honesty and generosity' is due to the will (of the subject of the line) being set on the

---

[145] XIX. 'The earth descending or approaching the marsh' is, according to *Kû* Hsî, symbolical of the approach of superiors to the inferior people, and then the two predicates about the superior man are descriptive of him in that approach, the instruction being symbolised by Tui, and the supporting by Khwăn. The Khang-hsî editors, wishing to defend the explanation of lin by 'great,' in Appendix VI, which they ascribe to Confucius, say:—'Lin means "great." The earth above the waters of the marsh shows how full those waters are, rising to the level of the earth, and thus expressing the idea of greatness.' This representation is lame and impotent.

*Kû* Hsî says he does not understand what is said on line 2. The interpretation in my version is the ordinary one, but I am not satisfied with it. The Khang-hsî editors try to solve the difficulty; but I am not able to follow them.

The same editors compare the conclusion of paragraph 6 in the symbolism of hexagram 11. 'What is external' there, and 'what is internal here,' have, they say, the same reference,—the state, namely, of the whole kingdom, the expressions differing according to the different standpoints from which they are made. The view in the translation is that of *Kû* Hsî. It is difficult to hold the balance between them. The newer view, perhaps, is the preferable.

subjects of (the first two lines of) the inner (trigram).

XX.[146] (The trigram representing) the earth, and that for wind moving above it, form Kwan. The ancient kings, in accordance with this, examined the (different) regions (of the kingdom), to see the (ways of the) people, and set forth their instructions.

1. 'The looking of a lad shown by the first six, (divided); indicates the way of the inferior people.

2. 'The firm correctness of a woman, in peeping out from a door' is also a thing to be ashamed of (in a superior man).

3. 'He looks at (the course of his own life, to advance or recede (accordingly):'—he will not err in the path (to be pursued).

4. 'He contemplates the glory of the kingdom:'(thence) arises the wish to be a guest (at court).

5. 'He contemplates his own life (-course):'—he should (for this purpose) contemplate (the condition of) the people.

6. 'He contemplates his own character:'—he cannot even yet let his mind be at rest.

XXI.[147] (The trigrams representing) thunder and lightning form Shih Ho. The ancient kings, in accordance with this, framed their penalties with intelligence, and promulgated their laws.

1. 'His feet are in the stocks, and he is deprived of his toes:'—there is no walking (to do evil).

2. 'He bites through the soft flesh, and (goes on) to bite off the nose:'—(the subject of the line) is mounted on the strong (first line).

3. 'He meets with what is disagreeable and hurtful:'—his position

---

[146] XX. Wind moving above the earth has the widest sweep, and nothing escapes its influence; it penetrates everywhere. This symbolism is more appropriate to the subject in hand than that of many other hexagrams. Personal influence in a ruler effects much; but the ancient kings wished to add to that the power of published instructions, specially adapted to the character and circumstances of the people. Sun, representing the wind, is well adapted to denote this influence;—see the Analects, XII, xix.

The looking in line 1 is superficial, and does not reach far.

Line 3. 'He will not err in the path to be pursued;'—advancing or receding as is best.

Line 4. 'The glory of the kingdom' is the virtue of the sovereign and the character of his administration. With the sentiment compare Mencius, VII, i, chap. 21. 2.

[147] XXI. *Kh*ăng-ʒze says that thunder and lightning are always found together, and hence their trigrams go together to give the idea of union intended in Shih Ho. The one trigram symbolising majesty and the other brightness or intelligence, the application of the hexagram here is easier and more natural than in many other cases.

1. 'There is no walking:'—that is, the subject of the line will not dare to offend any more.

2. '"Being mounted on the strong first line" means,' says *Kh*ăng-ʒze, 'punishing a strong and vehement man, when severity is required, as is denoted by the central position of the line.'

4. 'His light has not been sufficiently displayed;' that is, there is still something for him to do:—he has to realise the difficulty of his position and be firm.

is not the proper one for him.

4. 'It will be advantageous to him to realise the difficulty of his task and be firm, in which case there will be good fortune:'—his light has not yet been sufficiently displayed.

5. 'Let him be firm and correct, realising the peril (of his position), and there will be no error:'—he will possess every quality appropriate (to his position and task).

6. 'He wears the cangue and is deprived of his ears:'—he hears, but will not understand.

XXII.[148] (The trigram representing) a mountain and that for fire under it form Pî. The superior man, in accordance with this, throws a brilliancy around his various processes of government, but does not dare (in a similar way) to decide cases of criminal litigation.

1. 'He can discard a carriage and walk on foot:'—righteousness requires that he should not ride.

2. 'He adorns his beard:'—he rouses himself to action (only) along with the (subject of the) line above.

3. 'The good fortune consequent on his ever maintaining firm correctness' is due to this,—that to the end no one will insult him.

4. 'The place occupied by the fourth six, (divided),' affords ground for doubt (as to its subject); but '(as the subject of the third pursues) not as a robber, but as intent on a matrimonial alliance,' he will in the end have no grudge against him.

5. 'The good fortune falling to the fifth six, (divided); affords occasion for joy.

6. 'The freedom from error attached to (the subject of) the topmost line, with no ornament but the (simple white),' shows how he has attained his aim.

---

[148] XXII. 'A mountain,' says *Khăng-3ze*, 'is a place where we find grass, trees, and a hundred other things. A fire burning below it throws up its light, and brings them all Out in beauty; and this gives the idea of ornament, or being ornamented. The various processes of government are small matters, and elegance and ornament help their course; but great matters of judgment demand the simple, unornamented truth.'

The subject of line 1 does not care for and does not need ornament. He will walk in the way of righteousness without it.

Paragraph 3 tells us that it is not ornament, but correct firmness, which secures the respect of others.

In the fourth place, and cut off from line 1 by 2 and 3, we might doubt how far the subject of 4 would continue loyal to the subject of it. But he does continue loyal, through the character and object of the subject of 3.

The Khang-hsî editors say:—'Line 5 occupies the place of honour, and yet prefers simplicity and exalts economy; its subject might change and transform manners and customs;—it is a small matter to say of him that he affords occasion for joy.

The subject of line 6 has more of the spirit of the hexagram than in most hexagrams. His being clothed in simple white crowns the lesson that ornament must be kept in a secondary place.

XXIII.[149] (The trigrams representing) the earth, and (above it) that for a mountain, which adheres to the earth, form Po. Superiors, in accordance with this, seek to strengthen those below them, to secure the peace and stability of their own position.

1. 'He overthrows the couch by injuring its legs:'—thus (he commences) his work of ruin with what is lowest (in the superior man).

2. 'He destroys the couch by injuring its frame:'—(the superior man) has as yet no associates.

3. That 'there will be no error on the part of this one among the overthrowers' arises from the difference between him and the others above and below.

4. 'He has overthrown the couch, and (proceeds to injure) the skin (of him who lies on it):'—calamity is very near at hand.

5. 'He obtains for them the favour that lights on the inmates of the palace:'—in the end there will be no grudge against him.

6. 'The superior man finds himself in a carriage:'—he is carried along by the people. 'The small men (by their course) overthrow their own dwellings:'—they can. never again be of use to them.

XXIV.[150] (The trigram representing) the earth and that for thunder

---

[149] XXIII.A mountain,' says Yü Fan (towards the end of the Han dynasty), 'stands out high above the earth; here it appears as lying on the earth:—plainly it has been overturned.' On the other hand, Liû Mû (early in the Sung dynasty) says:—A mountain has the earth for its foundation. If the earth be thick, the mountain preserves its height. So it is with the sovereign and people.' The application might be deduced from either view.

It is hard to tell whether 'the lowest' in paragraph 1 should be supplemented as I have done. If not, then the explanation is a mere truism.

*Khăng-3ze* is precise and decisive in supplementing the explanation of paragraph 2 as in the translation.

See on the Text of lines 3 and 4.

On paragraph 5, the Khang-hsî editors say admirably:—'The fifth line is weak, and yet occupies the most honourable place in the figure,—emblematic of a queen; and as its subject leads on the subjects of the other lines to obtain the favours given to the inmates of the palace, she, it is plain, has neither jealousy nor any other injurious temper that might incur blame for tending to overthrow the ruler.'

Paragraph 6 shows the ruler restored to the favour of the people, and the restoration of concord in the state. The small men have done their worst, and there is an end of their attempts for a time.

[150] XXIV. 'Thunder in the midst of the earth' is thunder shut up and silent, just able to make its presence felt. So is it with the first genial stirrings of life after the winter solstice; so is it with the first returning steps of the wanderer to virtue. As the spring of life has to be nursed in quietness, so also has the purpose of good. The ancient statutes here referred to must have been like the present cessation from public and private business at the time of the new year, when all the Chinese people are for a time dissolved in festivity and joy.

Canon McClatchie translates here:—'The ancient kings on this culminating day (i. e. the seventh) closed their gates,' &c. 'Culminating day' does not give us the meaning so well as 'the day of the solstice;' but where does the translator find the explanatory 'the seventh,' which he puts in parentheses? In my own 'salad' days of Chinese knowledge I fancied there might be in paragraph 1 of the Text some allusion to a primitive sabbath;

in the midst of it form Fû. The ancient kings, in accordance with this, on the day. of the (winter) solstice, shut the gates of the passes (from one state to another), so that the travelling merchants could not (then) pursue their journeys, nor the princes go on with the inspection of their states.

1. 'Returning (from an error) of no great extent' is the prelude to the cultivation of the person.

2. 'The good fortune attendant on the admirable return (of the subject of the second line)' is due to his condescension to the virtuous (subject of the line) below.

3. Notwithstanding 'the perilous position of him who has made many returns,' there will be no error through (his aiming after righteousness).

4. 'He moves right in the centre (among those represented by the other divided lines), and yet returns alone:'—his object is to pursue the (proper) path.

5. 'The noble return, giving no ground for repentance,' is due to (the subject of the line) striving to perfect himself in accordance with his central position.

6. 'The evil consequent on being all astray on the subject of returning' is because the course pursued is contrary to the proper course for a ruler.

XXV.[151] The thunder rolls all under the sky, and to (every)thing there is given (its nature), free from all insincerity. The ancient kings,

---

but there is no ground for introducing 'seven days,' or 'the seventh day,' into this paragraph of the Great Symbolism.

The virtuous subject of the first line' is in paragraph 2 called zăn, 'the benevolent' or loving.' It is the only case in all the symbolism of the Yî where we find that term used as an adjective. It is emphatic here for 'humanity,' man in his ideal.

The other paragraphs present nothing for remark beyond what has been said on the Text of the duke of *Kâu*.

[151] XXV. The composition of the hexagram is given here in a manner different from what we have met with in the account of any of the preceding figures; and as the text is not called in question, I have made the best I could in the translation of the two commencing clauses. The application of the symbolism to what the ancient kings did is also hard to comprehend.

The paragraph on line 1 is another way of saying that in the course of things real goodness may be expected to be fortunate,—'by the appointment of Heaven.'

Paragraph 2. 'The thought of getting rich had not risen in his mind:'—he did what he did, because it was right, not because of the gain it would bring him.

On paragraph 3, it is said, 'The superior man seeks simply to be free from insincerity, and leaves the questions of happiness and calamity to Heaven.'

Paragraph 5. Sickness ought not to happen to one who is perfectly sincere. If it do happen, he must refer it to some inexplicable will of Heaven. As that has afflicted, so it will cure.'

Paragraph 6. 'When a thing is over and done, submission and acquiescence are what are required, and not renewed attempts at action.'

in accordance with this, (made their regulations) in complete accordance with the seasons, thereby nourishing all things.

1. When 'he who is free from insincerity makes any movement,' he will get what he desires.

2. 'He reaps without having ploughed:'—(the thought of) riches to be got had not risen (in his mind).

3. 'The passer-by gets the ox:'—this proves a calamity to the people of the neighbourhood.

4. 'If he can remain firm and correct there will be no error:'—he firmly holds fast (his correctness).

5. 'Medicine in the case of one who is free from insincerity!'—it should not be tried (at all).

6. 'The action (in this case) of one who is free from insincerity' will occasion the calamity arising from action (when the time for it is) exhausted.

XXVI.[152] (The trigram representing) a mountain, and in the midst of it that (representing) heaven, form Tâ *Khû*. The superior man, in accordance with this, stores largely in his memory the words and deeds of former men, to subserve the accumulation of his virtue.

1. 'He is in a position of peril; it will be advantageous for him to stop his advance:'—he should not rashly expose himself to calamity.

2. '(He is as) a carriage from which the strap under it has been removed:'—being in the central position, he will incur no blame.

3. 'There will be advantage in whatever direction he may advance:'—(the subject of) the topmost line is of the same mind with him.

4. 'The great good fortune indicated by the fourth six, (divided),' shows that there is occasion for joy.

5. 'The good fortune indicated by the fifth six, (divided),' shows that there is occasion for congratulation.

6. 'In command of the firmament of heaven:'—the way is grandly open for movement.

---

[152] XXVI. I have quoted, in the Introduction, p. 35, *Kû Hsî*'s remark on the Great Symbolism here. *Khăng-ȝze* says:—'Heaven is the greatest of all things, and its being in the midst of a mountain gives us the idea of a very large accumulation. And so great is the labour of the superior man in learning, acquiring, and remembering, to accumulate his virtue.'

Paragraph 1. The 'calamity' is that of opposition from, or repression by, the subject of line 4.

Paragraph 3. When the action of the hexagram has reached line 6, its work is done. The subject of 6 will no longer exercise repression, but join with that of 3, assisting him to advance.

Paragraph 4. The subject of line 4 has indeed occasion for joy. Without the use of punishment for crimes committed, by precaution anticipating them, without any trouble he has repressed evil. The 'joy' gives place in paragraph 5 to 'congratulation,' the people being all interested in the action of the ruler.

XXVII.[153] (The trigram representing) a mountain and under it that for thunder form Î. The superior man, in accordance with this, (enjoins) watchfulness over our words, and the temperate regulation of our eating and drinking.

1. 'You look at me till your (lower) jaw hangs down:'—(the subject of the line) is thus shown unfit to be thought noble.

2. 'The evil of advance by the subject of the second line, (divided),' is owing to his leaving in his movements his proper associates.

3. 'For ten years let him not take any action:'—his course is greatly opposed (to what is right).

4. 'The good fortune attached to looking downwards for (the power to) nourish,' shows how brilliant will be the diffusion (of that power) from (the subject of the line's) superior position.

5. 'The good fortune from abiding in firmness' is due to the docility (of the subject of the line) in following (the subject of the line) above.

6. 'The good fortune, notwithstanding the peril of his position, of him from whom comes the nourishing,' affords great cause for congratulation.

XXVIII.[154] (The trigram representing) trees hidden beneath that for the waters of a marsh forms Tâ Kwo. The superior man, in accordance with this, stands up alone and has no fear, and keeps retired from the world without regret.

1. 'He places mats of the white mâo grass under things set on the ground:'—he feels his weakness and his being in the lowest place, (and

---

[153] XXVII. I do not think that the Great Symbolism here is anything but that of a thunderstorm, dispersing the oppression that bangs over nature, and followed by genial airs, and the reviving of all vegetation. But there is nothing analogous to the thunder in the application. 'Words,' it is said, 'nourish virtue; food and drink nourish the body.'

Paragraph 1. As Mencius said, 'He that nourishes the little belonging to him is a little man.'

Paragraph 2. Neither the subject of line 1, nor of line 6, is the proper associate of 2.

The other paragraphs are sufficiently illustrated in the notes on the Text.

[154] XXVIII. *Kh*ăng-ʒze says on the Great Symbolism:—'The waters of a marsh moisten and nourish the trees. When here it is said that they destroy and extinguish the trees, their action is very extraordinary.' This explanation is very far-fetched; and so is what the same scholar says on the application of it. I need not give it here, nor have I found, or myself made out, any other more easy and natural.

Paragraph 2. 'Such an association is extraordinary:'—the characters also imply, perhaps, that it is successful.

Paragraph 3. The beam being broken, any attempt to sustain it will have no effect in supporting the roof.

Paragraph 5. The shoots produced in line 2 will grow into a new and vigorous tree. The flowers here will soon decay, and the withered trunk continue the same. For what will a young man marry an old woman? There will be no children;—it can only be from some mercenary object.

uses extraordinary care).

2. 'An old husband and a young wife:'—such association is extraordinary.

3. 'The evil connected with the beam that is weak' arises from this, that no help can be given (to the condition thus represented).

4. 'The good fortune connected with the beam curving upwards' arises from this, that it does not bend towards what is below.

5. 'A decayed willow produces flowers:'—but how can this secure its long continuance? 'An old wife and a young husband:'—this also is a thing to be ashamed of.

6. 'Evil follows wading with (extraordinary) boldness (through the stream):'—but (the act) affords no ground for blame.

XXIX.[155] (The representation of) water flowing on continuously forms the repeated Khan. The superior man, in accordance with this, maintains constantly the virtue (of his heart) and (the integrity of) his conduct, and practises the business of instruction.

1. 'In the double defile, he enters a cavern within it:'—he has missed his (proper) way, and there will be evil.

2. 'He will get a little (of the deliverance) that he seeks:'—he will not yet escape from his environed position.

3. 'Whether he comes or goes, he is confronted by a defile:'—he will never (in such circumstances) achieve any success.

4. '(Nothing but) a bottle of spirits and a subsidiary basket of rice:'—(these describe) the meeting at this point of (those who are represented by) the strong and weak lines.

5. 'The water in the defile is not full (so as to flow away):'—(the virtue indicated by) the central situation is not yet (sufficiently) great.

6. 'The sixth line, divided, shows its subject missing his (proper) course:'—'there will be evil for three years.'

XXX.[156] (The trigram for) brightness, repeated, forms Lî. The great

---

[155] XXIX. The application of the Great Symbolism is here more perplexing even than usual. What is said of the superior man is good, but there is no reference in it to the subject of danger.

The subject of line 3 goes and comes, moves up and down, backwards and forwards; making no advance. This can be of no use in extricating him from the danger.

Those represented in line 4 by the strong and weak lines are the ruler and his minister.

[156] XXX. In the Great Symbolism Lî is used in the sense of brightness. There was no occasion to refer to its other meaning. 'The great man' rather confirms the interpretation of the 'double brightness' in the treatise on the Thwan as indicating the ruler.

Paragraph 2. As yellow is a 'correct' colour, so is the due mean the correct course.

Paragraph 3. 'The declining sun,' say the Khang-hsî editors, 'is an emblem of the obscuration coming over the virtue of the mind.'

Paragraph 4. 'None can bear with him' refers to the second part of the symbolism of the line, which is not given here.

man, in accordance with this, cultivates more and more his brilliant (virtue), and diffuses its brightness over the four quarters (of the land).

1. 'The reverent attention directed to his confused steps' is the way by which error is avoided.

2. 'The great good fortune (from the subject of the second line) occupying his place in yellow' is owing to his holding the course of the due mean.

3. 'A position like that of the declining sun:'—how can it continue long?

4. 'How abrupt is the manner of his coming!'—none can bear with him.

5. 'The good fortune attached to the fifth line, divided),' is due to its occupying the place of a king or a prince.

6. 'The king employs him in his punitive expeditions:'—the object is to bring the regions to a correct state.

## SECTION II.

XXXI.[157] (The trigram representing) a mountain and above it that for (the waters of) a marsh form Hsien. The superior man, in accordance with this, keeps his mind free from pre-occupation, and open to receive (the influences of) others.

1. 'He moves his great toe:'—his mind is set on what is beyond (himself).

2. Though 'there would be evil; yet, if he abide (quiet) in his place,

---

[157] XXXI. In various ways the waters of a marsh, placed high above the adjacent land, will descend to water and fertilise them. This symbolism agrees sufficiently well with the idea of influence passing between a superior and inferior party in relation with each other. There is nothing in the representation, however, to suggest particularly the relation between husband and wife; and the more I think of it, the more doubtful it becomes to me that king Wan intended by the trigrams of this figure to give the idea of man and wife. The application of the symbolism is sufficiently appropriate. The commentators see in it especially the lesson of humility—emptiness of self, or poverty of spirit—in order that the influences to which we are subjected may have free course.

Paragraph 1. What is beyond one's self is represented by line 4, a proper correlate of 1. There is the desire to influence; but it is ineffectively exhibited.

Paragraph 2. 'Compliance (with the circumstances of his condition and place)' is merely another way of 'being firm and correct.'

Paragraph 3. The language, 'What he holds in his grasp is low,' makes *Kû Hsî* and the older commentators generally understand low of lines 1 and 2, and their weak subjects. But 'following' leads the mind to the lines above, as the Khang-hsî editors point out. 'Low' is to be understood in the sense of 'mean.'

Paragraph 4. The 'being firm and correct' appears here as equivalent to the want of 'a selfish wish to influence.'

Paragraph 5. The triviality of the aim explains the ineffectiveness of the movement, but not its giving no occasion for repentance. That the mei which are moved are behind and above the region of the heart seems too mechanical and trivial an explanation.

there will be good fortune:'—through compliance (with the circumstances of his condition and place) there will be no injury.

3. 'He moves his thighs:'—he still does not (want to) rest in his place. His will is set on 'following others:'—what he holds in his grasp is low.

4. 'Firm correctness will lead to good fortune, and prevent all occasion for repentance:'—there has not yet been any harm from (a selfish wish to) influence. 'He is unsettled in his movements:'(his power to influence) is not yet either brilliant or great.

5. 'He (tries to) move the flesh along the spine above the heart:'— his aim is trivial.

6. 'He moves his jaws and tongue:'—he (only) talks with loquacious mouth.

XXXII.[158] (The trigram representing) thunder and that for wind form Hăng. The superior man, in accordance with this, stands firm, and does not change his method (of operation).

1. 'The evil attached to the deep desire for long continuance (in the subject of the first line)' arises from the deep seeking for it at the commencement (of things).

2. 'All occasion for repentance on the part of the subject of the second line, (undivided,), disappears:'—he can abide long in the due mean.

3. 'He does not continuously maintain his virtue:'—nowhere will he be borne with.

4. (Going) for long to what is not his proper place, how can he get game?

5. 'Such firm correctness in a wife will be fortunate:'—it is hers to the end of life to follow with an unchanged mind. The husband must decide what is right, and lay down the rule accordingly:—for him to follow (like) a wife is evil.

6. 'The subject of the topmost line is exciting himself to long continuance:'—far will he be from achieving merit.

XXXIII.[159] (The trigram representing) the sky and below it that for

---

[158] XXXII. How the interaction of wind and thunder symbolises the lesson of the hexagram, and especially the application in this paragraph of that symbolism, is a question I have not been able to solve.

Paragraph 1. The stress of what is said under line 1 is here made to lie on its being the first line of the figure.

Paragraph 2. Line 2 is in the centre of its trigram, and that position, here as often elsewhere, symbolises the course of its subject.

Paragraph 3. The Khang-hsî editors make the application here = 'nowhere can he bear (to remain).'

From paragraph 5 it appears that what is right will vary in different cases. The lesson of the hexagram is perseverance in what is right in each particular case.

[159] XXXIII. *K* û Hsî says:—'The sky is illimitable; a mountain is high, but has its

a mountain form Thun. The superior man, in accordance with this, keeps small men at a distance, not by showing that he hates them, but by his own. dignified gravity.

1. There is 'the perilousness of the position shown by the retiring tail:'—but if 'no movement' be made, what disaster can there be?

2. 'He holds it as; by (a thong from the hide of) a yellow ox:'—his purpose is firm.

3. 'The peril connected with the case of one retiring, though bound,' is due to the (consequent) distress and exhaustion. 'If he were (to deal as in) nourishing a servant or concubine, it would be fortunate for him:'—but a great affair cannot be dealt with in this way.

4. 'A superior man retires notwithstanding his likings; a small man cannot attain to this.'

5. 'He retires in an admirable way, and with firm correctness there will be good fortune:'—this is due to the rectitude of his purpose.

6. 'He retires in a noble way, and his doing so will be advantageous in every respect:'—he who does so has no doubts about his course.

XXXIV.[160] (The trigram representing) heaven and above it that for thunder form Tâ *K*wang. The superior man, in accordance with this, does not take a step which is not according to propriety.

1. 'He manifests his vigour in his toes:'—this will certainly lead to exhaustion.

2. 'The second line, (undivided), shows that with firm correctness there will be good fortune:'—this is due to its being in the centre, (and

---

limits; the union of these is an emblem of retiring.' I do not understand such embleming. *Kh*ăng-ȝze says:—'Below the sky is a mountain. The mountain rises up below the sky, and its height is arrested, while the sky goes up higher and higher, till they come to be apart from each other. In this we have an emblem of retiring and avoiding.' We feel somewhat as if there were a meaning in this; but, as in many other cases, both the symbolism and its application are but dimly apprehended.

The symbolism of the various lines is sufficiently explained on the Text. Paragraph 5 is but a repetition of the Text without additional explanation.

[160] XXXIV. In illustration of the symbolism of the trigrams here, *Kh*ăng-ȝze says well:—'Thunder rolling above in the sky and making all things shake is the emblem of great power.' In passing on to its application he starts with a beautiful saying of antiquity, that 'the strong man is he who overcomes himself.' That this thought was in the mind of the writer of the paragraph on the Great Symbolism I can well believe; but the analogy between the natural and the moral and spiritual worlds in passing from the phenomenon of thunder to this truth is a thing to be felt, and that can hardly be described.

Paragraph 1. 'This will lead to exhaustion;' and from that will follow distress and other evils.

The central position and the due moral mean in paragraph 2 is another instance of the felt analogy referred to above.

In paragraph 3 nothing is added to the Text; and on the symbolism nothing is said.

Paragraph 5. 'He is not in his appropriate place:' this is said simply because an odd place ought to be filled by a strong line.

its subject exemplifying the due mean).

3. 'The small man uses all his strength; in the case of the superior man it is his rule not to do so.'

4. 'The fence is opened and the horns are not entangled:'—(the subject of the line) still advances.

5. 'He loses his ram and hardly perceives it:'—he is not in his appropriate place.

6. 'He is unable either to retreat or to advance:'—this is owing to his want of care. 'If he realise the difficulty (of his position), there will be good fortune:'—his error will not be prolonged.

XXXV.[161] (The trigram representing) the earth and that for the bright (sun) coming forth above it form 3in. The superior man, according to this, gives himself to make more brilliant his bright virtue.

1. 'He appears wishing to advance, but (at the same time) being kept back:'—all-alone he pursues the correct course. 'Let him maintain a large and generous mind, and there will be no error:'—he has not yet received an official charge.

2. 'He will receive this great blessing:'—for he is in the central place and the correct position for him.

3. 'All (around) trust him:'—their (common) aim is to move upwards and act.

4. '(He advances like) a marmot. However firm and correct he may be, his position is one of peril:'—his place is not that appropriate for him.

5. 'Let him not concern himself whether he fails or succeeds:'—his movement in advance will afford ground for congratulation.

6. 'He uses his horns only to punish (the rebellious people of) his city:'—his course of procedure is not yet brilliant.

XXXVI.[162] (The trigram representing) the earth and that for the

---

[161] XXXV. The sun rising above the earth, and then travelling up to his meridian height, readily suggests the idea of advancing. On the application of this symbolism, Hû Ping-wăn (Yüan dynasty) says:—'Of strong things there is none so strong as heaven; and hence the superior man after its pattern makes himself strong; of bright things there is none so bright as the sun, and after its pattern he makes himself bright.'

If the subject of line 1 had received an official charge, then when unrecognised by his sovereign, and obstructed in his progress, his correct course would have been to cease to advance, and retire from the office in which he was not allowed to carry out his principles.

There is nothing said on line 2 to explain particularly the symbolism of 'the grandmother' in the Text.

'The course of procedure' in paragraph 6 has still an element of force in it, which is more than 'the firm correctness' that was to king Wăn the ideal character of a feudal lord, and therefore his light is not yet that of the full-orbed sun.

[162] XXXVI. The application of the Great Symbolism here is in itself sufficiently natural; but this meaning of the hexagram hardly appears in the text, till we come to the sixth line.

bright (sun) entering within it form Ming Î. The superior man, in accordance with this, conducts his management of men;—he shows his intelligence by keeping it obscured.

1. 'The superior man (is revolving his) going away:'—(in such a case) he feels it right not to eat.

2. 'The good fortune of (the subject of) the second line, divided,' is due to the proper fashion of his acting according to his circumstances.

3. With the aim represented by 'hunting in the south' a great achievement is accomplished.

4. 'He has (just) entered into the left side of the belly (of the dark land):'—he is still able to carry out the idea in his (inner) mind.

5. 'With the firm correctness of the count of Kî,' his brightness could not be (quite) extinguished.

6. 'He had at first ascended to (the top of) the sky:'—he might have enlightened the four quarters of the kingdom. 'His future shall be to go into the earth:'—he has failed to fulfil the model (of a ruler).

XXXVII.[163] (The trigram representing) fire, and that for wind coming forth from it, form Kiâ Zăn. The superior man, in accordance with this, orders his words according to (the truth of) things, and his

---

Paragraph 1. 'He thinks it right not to eat;'—he does not purposely fast; but when he has nothing to eat, he does not complain. He thinks it right that it should be so in the case.

Paragraph 2. 'The proper fashion of acting' is suggested by the weak line's being in the central place.

Paragraph 3. 'The great achievement is accomplished;' but such achievement was not what prompted to action.

Paragraph 4. 'The idea in his inner mind' is the idea of withdrawing from the position and escaping; but the meaning is obscure. See on the Text.

[163] XXXVII. The Symbolism here is certainly far-fetched. 'As wind,' it is said,' comes first from fire, so does transforming influence emanate from the family.' But the subject of the hexagram is the regulation and not the influence of the family. Then the application is good for the superior man's cultivation of himself; but this again is only connected indirectly with the regulation of the family.

The sooner preventive measures are presented to the youthful mind the better; but does not prohibition imply that a change in the good will has taken place?

In paragraph 2 'docility' is suggested by the weak line. 'The humility' comes out of Sun, the upper trigram, whose attribute is pliant flexibility.

Yü Yen (Yüan dynasty) ingeniously observes on paragraph 4 that the riches of a family are not to be sought in its wealth, but in the affection and harmony of its members. Where these prevail, the family is not likely to be poor, and whatever it has will be well preserved.

The mention 'of mutual love' is unusual in Chinese writings, and must be considered remarkable here. 'The. husband,' says Khăng-ʒze, 'loves his helpmate in the house; the wife loves him who is the pattern for the family.' But however admirable the sentiment is, it comes from the mind of the writer, and is not drawn from the Text.

Paragraph 6. It is said on this, that the majesty is not designedly assumed or put on; but the effect of the character remoulded and perfected. The words of Mencius are aptly quoted in illustration of the lesson:—'If a man himself do not walk in the (right) path, it will not be walked in (even) by his wife and children.'

conduct so that it is uniformly consistent.

1. 'He establishes restrictive regulations in his household:—(he does so), before any change has taken place in their wills.

2. 'The good fortune attached to the second six, (divided),' is due to the docility (of its subject), operating with humility.

3. When 'the members of the household are treated with stern severity,' there has been no (great) failure (in the regulation of the family). When 'wife and children are smirking and chattering,' the (proper) economy of the family has been lost.

4. 'The family is enriched, and there is great good fortune:'—this is due to the docility (belonging to the subject of the line), and its being in its correct place.

5. 'The influence of the king extends to his family:'—the intercourse between them is that of mutual love.

6. 'The good fortune connected with the display of majesty' describes (the result of) the recovery of the true character.

XXXVIII.[164] (The trigram representing) fire above, and that for (the waters of) a marsh below, form Khwei. The superior man, in accordance with this, where there is a general agreement, yet admits diversity.

1. 'He meets with bad men (and communicates with them):'—(he does so), to avoid the evil of their condemnation.

2. 'He happens to meet with his lord in a bye-passage:'—but he has not deviated (for this meeting) from the (proper) course.

3. 'We see his carriage dragged back:'—this is indicated by the inappropriateness of the position (of the line).

'There is no (good) beginning, but there will be a (good) end:'—this arises from his meeting with the strong (subject of the topmost line).

4. 'They blend their sincere desires together, and there will be no error:'—their (common) aim is carried into effect.

5. 'With his hereditary minister (he unites closely and easily) as if he were biting through a piece of skin:'—his going forward will afford ground for congratulation.

6. 'The good fortune symbolised by meeting with (genial) rain' springs from the passing away of all doubts.

XXXIX.[165] (The trigram representing) a mountain, and above it

---

[164] XXXVIII. The application here of the Symbolism is correct, but neither of them comes up to the idea of disunion which is in Khwei.

The various paragraphs seem to need no illustration beyond what may be found in the notes on the Text.

[165] XXXIX. The Symbolism is described here a little differently from the form of it in Appendix I. *Kh*ăng-3ze brings the same meaning out of it, however, in the following way:—'We have here a steep and difficult mountain, and again on the top of that there is

that for water, form *K*ien. The superior man, in accordance with this, turns round (and examines) himself, and cultivates his virtue.

1. 'Advancing will conduct to (greater) difficulties, while remaining stationary will afford ground for praise:'—the proper course is to wait.

2. 'The minister of the king struggles with difficulty on difficulty:'—in the end no blame will be attached to him.

3. 'He advances, (but only) to (greater) difficulty; he remains stationary, and returns to his former associates:'—they, (represented in) the inner (trigram), rejoice in him.

4. 'To advance will (only be to) encounter (greater) difficulties; he remains stationary, and unites (with the subject of the line above):'—that is in its proper place and has the solidity (due to it in that position).

5. 'He struggles with the greatest difficulties, while friends are coming (to help him):'—he is in the central position, and possesses the requisite virtue.

6. 'To advance will (only) increase the difficulties, while his remaining stationary will (be productive of) great (merit):'—his aim is to assist the (subject of the line) inside of him.

'It will be advantageous to meet the great man:'—by his course he follows that noble (lord of the figure).

XL.[166] (The trigram representing) thunder and that for rain, with

---

water; each of the two trigrams is an emblem of perilousness. There is peril, both above and below, in the figure; and hence it represents the difficulties of the state.' The application of the symbolism is illustrated by the words of Mencius, 'When we do not, by what we do, realise (what we desire), we must turn inwards and examine ourselves in every point.'

From the lesson in paragraph 2 we saw that the moral value of conduct is independent of failure or success. It is said, 'Though the difficulties be too great for him to overcome, the sage accepts his desire, in order to stimulate others to loyal devotedness.'

On paragraph 3, Khung Ying-tâ says:—'Of the three lines of the lower trigram only the third is yang, above the two others which are of the yin nature. They cling to it, and are represented as if rejoicing in it.

The view given of paragraph 4 is that of the Khang-hsî editors.

'The friends' in paragraph 5 are the subjects of the second line, the correlate of 5, and also of the two other lines of the lower trigram.

Sû Shih (A. D. 1036-1101) remarks on paragraph 6 that by 'the inside,' and 'the noble,' we are to understand the subject of line 5.

[166] XL. It is a common saying that thunder and rain clear the atmosphere, and a feeling of oppression is relieved. The last paragraph of Appendix I, however, leads us to understand the Symbolism of the phenomena of spring. The application seems to refer to the gentle policy of a conqueror forward to forgive the opposition of those who offer no more resistance.

The subject of line 2 is a minister or officer; and the Khang-hsî editors say that while straightforwardness, symbolised by the arrow, is the first duty of an officer, if he do not temper that quality by pursuing the due medium, which is symbolised by the yellow colour of the arrow, but proceed by main force, and that only, to remove what is evil, he these phenomena in a state of manifestation, form *K*ieh. The superior man, in accordance with this, forgives errors, and deals gently with crimes.

1. The strong (fourth) line and the weak line here are in correlation:—we judge rightly in saying that 'its subject will commit no error.'

2. 'The good fortune springing from the firm correctness of the second line, (undivided),' is due to its subject holding the due mean.

3. For 'a porter with his burden to be riding in a carriage' is a thing to be ashamed of. 'It is he himself that tempts the robbers to come:'—on whom besides can we lay the blame? (See Appendix III, i, 48.)

4. 'Remove your toes:'—the places (of this line and of the third and first) are all inappropriate to them.

5. When 'the superior man executes his function of removing (whatever is injurious to the idea of the hexagram),' small men will of themselves retire.

6. 'A prince with his bow shoots a falcon:'—thus he removes (the promoters of) rebellion.

XLI.[167] (The trigram representing) a mountain and beneath it that

---

will provoke indignation and rebellion. The 'three foxes' are not alluded to in this second paragraph.

On paragraph 4 the same editors say:—'The subject of this line is not in the central nor in an odd place; he has for his correlate the subject of line 1 and for his close associate that of line 3, both of which lines are weak in strong places. Hence it is said, that they are all in places inappropriate to them.'

What paragraph 5 says, that 'the small men retire,' means that believing in the sincerity of the ruler's determination to remove all evil men, they retire of themselves, or strive to conform to his wishes.

[167] XLI. 'The waters of a marsh are continually rising up in vapour to bedew the hill above it, and thus increase its verdure; what is taken from the marsh gives increase to the hill.' This is very far-fetched. In the application again the superior man acts only on himself, and for himself;—which has nothing to do with those of low degree giving to those above them. This application, however, agrees with what, as we have seen on the Text, was *K*hǎng-ʒze's view of the meaning of the hexagram.

The explanation appended to paragraph 1 seems to be to account for the subject of line 1 hurrying away to the help of line 4.

'His aim' is to abide where he is, and help the subject of 5 by the exhibition of 'firm correctness.'

The Khang-hsî editors observe that paragraph 3 is true indeed of three men; and not of three men only, but of many repetitions of thought or action.

The same editors say on paragraph 5 that 'the blessing from above is explained, by many, of the oracles obtained through divining with the tortoise-shell; but that looking at the text on line 2 of the next hexagram, and that Tî (spoken of there) is the lord of all spirits, the term "above" here is most naturally explained of Heaven's mind, whose acceptance cannot be gainsaid by men or spirits.'

*K*hǎng-ʒze says on paragraph 6, though I do not see the relevancy of his remarks:—'Dwelling on high, and taking nothing from those below him, but on the contrary giving more to them, the superior man accomplishes his aim on a grand scale. The aim of the superior man is simply to be increasing what others have;—that and nothing else.'

for the waters of a marsh form Sun. The superior man, in accordance with this, restrains his wrath and represses his desires.

1. 'He suspends his own affairs and hurries away (to help the subject of the fourth line):'—the (subject of that) upper (line) mingles his wishes with his.

2. 'It will be advantageous for (the subject of) the second line, (undivided), to maintain his firm correctness:'—his central position gives its character to his aim.

3. 'One man, walking,' (finds his friend):—when three are together, doubts rise among them.

4. 'He diminishes the ailment under which he labours:'—this is matter for joy.

5. 'The great good fortune attached to the fifth six, (divided),' is due to the blessing from above.

6. 'He gives increase to others without taking from what is his own:'—he obtains his wish on a grand scale.

XLII.[168] (The trigram representing) wind and that for thunder form Yî. The superior man, in accordance with this, when he sees what is good, moves towards it; and when he sees his errors, he turns from them.

1. 'If the movement be greatly fortunate, no blame will be imputed to him:'—though it is not for one in so low a position to have to do with great affairs.

2. 'Parties add to his stores:'—they come from beyond (his immediate circle) to do so.

3. 'Increase is given by means of what is evil and difficult:'—as he has in himself (the qualities called forth).

4. 'His advice to his prince is followed:'—his (only) object in it being the increase (of the general good).

---

[168] XLII. The Symbolism here is different from what we gather from the former Appendix. Sun no longer symbolises wood, but, as it more commonly does, wind. Thunder and wind, it is supposed, increase each the other; and their combination gives the idea of increase. Then the application, good in itself, must be treated very nicely, as it is by the Khang-hsî editors, in order to make out any connexion between it and the Symbolism.

Paragraph 1. 'One in a low position should not move in great affairs;'—not a son, it is said, while his father is alive; nor a minister, while his ruler governs; nor a member of an official department, while its head directs its affairs. If such a one do initiate such an affair, only great success will excuse his rashness.

Paragraph 2. Line 5 is the proper correlate of 2; and its subject will be among the contributing parties. But others 'beyond' will be won to take part with him.

Paragraph 3. There is a soul of good even in men who seem only evil; and adversity may quicken it.

Paragraph 6. As in line 2 the attractive power of benevolence is shown, so in line 6 we have the repulsive power of selfishness exhibited. Mark the 'from beyond' in both paragraphs.

5. '(The ruler) with sincere heart seeks to benefit (all below):'—there need be no question (about the result). '(All below) with sincere heart acknowledge (his goodness):'—he gets what he desires on a great scale.

6. 'To his increase none will contribute:'—this expresses but half the result. 'Many will seek to assail him:'—they will come from beyond (his immediate circle) to do so.

XLIII.[169] (The trigram representing) heaven and that for the waters of a marsh mounting above it form Kwâi. The superior man, in accordance with this, bestows emolument on those below him, and dislikes allowing his gifts to accumulate (undispensed).

1. 'Without (being able to) succeed, he goes forward:'—this is an error.

2. 'Though hostile measures be taken against him, he need not be anxious:'—he pursues the course of the due mean.

3. 'The superior man looks bent on cutting off the culprit:'—there will in the end be no error.

4. 'He walks slowly and with difficulty:'—he is not in the place appropriate to him.

'He hears these words, but does not believe them:'—he hears, but does not understand.

5. 'If his action be in harmony with his central position, there will be no error:'—but his standing in the due mean is not yet clearly displayed.

6. 'There is the misery of having none on whom to call:'—the end will be that he cannot continue any longer.

XLIV.[170] (The trigram representing) wind and that for the sky

---

[169] XLIII. We can only understand the mounting of the waters of a marsh up into the sky of the phenomenon of evaporation; and certainly the waters so formed into clouds will be condensed, and come down again as rain. This may be taken as an image of dispersion, but not of displacement in the sense of the Text of the hexagram.

The first clause of the application follows naturally enough from the above interpretation of the Symbolism. *Kû Hsî* says he does not understand the second clause. Many critics adopt the view of it which appears in the translation.

Paragraph 2 does not mention the precautionary measures taken in the Text by the subject of the line, from which the conclusion would follow quite as naturally as from his central position. The Khang-hsî editors, however, say that the not having recourse lightly to force is itself the due course.

Line 3 responding, and alone of all the strong lines responding to 6, may appear at first irresolute, and not prepared for decided measures; but 1 in the end' its subject does what is required of him.

The contiguity of line 5 to the divided 6, is supposed to have some bad effect on its subject, so that while he does what his central position requires, it is not without an effort. 'If a man,' says *Khăng-ȝze*, 'cherish a single illicit desire in his mind, he has left the right way. The admonition here conveyed is deep.'

[170] XLIV. Wind, blowing all-under the sky, penetrates everywhere, and produces its natural effect; and it is a good application of this phenomenon that follows; but it has

above it form Kâu. The sovereign, in accordance with this, delivers his charges, and promulgates his announcements throughout the four quarters (of the kingdom).

1. 'Tied and fastened to a metal drag:'—(this describes the arrest of) the weak (line) in its advancing course.

2. 'He has a wallet of fish:'—it is right for him not to allow (the subject of the first line) to get to the guests.

3. 'He walks with difficulty:'—but his steps have not yet been drawn (into the course of the first line).

4. 'The evil' indicated by there being 'no fish in the wallet' is owing to (the subject of the line) keeping himself aloof from the people.

5. 'The subject of the fifth line, (undivided), keeps his brilliant qualities concealed:'—as is indicated by his central and correct position.

'(The good issue) descends (as) from Heaven:—'his aim does not neglect the ordinances (of Heaven).

6. 'He receives others on his horns:'—he is exhausted at his greatest height, and there will be cause for regret.

XLV.[171] (The trigram representing the) earth and that for the

---

nothing to do with the meaning of Kâu and the interpretation of the hexagram, as taught in the Text. The Khang-hsî editors perceive this, and deal with the Symbolism after a method of their own, on which it is unnecessary to enter.

Paragraph 1. My supplement, 'This describes the arrest of,' is a conclusion from the whole of the Text on the line. All the commentaries have it.

In the 'Daily Lecture' it is said that the lesson of paragraph 2 is that 'the subject of the line should make the repression of 1 his own exclusive work, and not allow it to pass on to the subject of any of the other lines.' That view is rather different from the one indicated in my supplement.

'His steps have not been drawn into the course of the first line:'—we have to supply, land therefore there will be no great error.'

Paragraph 4. See what is said on the Text. But that the subject of the line stands alone is owing, it is here implied, to his own impatience. If he could exercise forbearance, he would find a proper opportunity to check the advance of the subject of line 1.

The subject of line 5, while mindful of his task in the hexagram,—to repress the advance symbolised by 1,—yet keeps his wise plans concealed till the period of carrying them into execution, determined by the ordinances of Heaven, has arrived. Then comes the successful stroke of his policy as if it were directly from Heaven. The subject of line 6 really accomplishes nothing to repress the advance of the unworthy; but he keeps himself from evil communication with them. He is not to be charged with blameable error, though more and better might have been expected of him.

[171] XLV. What has this Great Symbolism to do with the idea and preservation of union? The question is answered in this way:—A marsh whose waters are high up above the earth must be kept in by banks and dykes, to keep them together, to preserve them from being dispersed. So the union of a people must be preserved by precautions against what would disturb and destroy it. Of such precautions the chief is to be prepared to resist attack from without, and to put down internal sedition.

Paragraph 3. The topmost line is the last in Tui, whose attribute is complacent satisfaction, appearing in flexibility or docility.

waters of a marsh raised above it form Ʒhui. The superior man, in accordance with this, has his weapons of war put in good repair, to be prepared against unforeseen contingencies.

1. 'In consequence disorder is brought into the sphere of his union:'—his mind and aim are thrown into confusion.

2. 'He is led forward; there will be good fortune, and freedom from error:'—(the virtue proper to) his central place has not undergone any change.

3. 'If he go forward, he will not err:'—in the subject of the topmost line there is humility and condescension.

4. 'If he be grandly fortunate, he will receive no blame:'—(this condition is necessary, because) his position is not the one proper to him.

5. 'There is the union (of all) under him in the place of dignity:'—(but) his mind and aim have not yet been brilliantly displayed.

6. 'He sighs and weeps:'—he does not yet rest in his topmost position.

XLVI.[172] (The trigram representing) wood and that for the earth with the wood growing in the midst of it form Shăng. The superior man, in accordance with this, pays careful attention to his virtue, and accumulates the small developments of it till it is high and great.

1. 'He is welcomed in his advance upwards, and there will be great good fortune:'—(the subjects of) the upper (trigram) are of the same mind with him.

2. 'The sincerity of the subject of the second line, undivided,' affords occasion for joy.

3. 'He advances upwards (as into) an empty city:'—he has no doubt or hesitation.

---

Paragraph 5. 'His mind and aim have not yet been brilliantly displayed:'—this is in explanation of the case that some may even still not have confidence in him.

Paragraph 6. The topmost position is that of the trigram; the subject of the line might bid farewell to all the work of the hexagram; but he cannot bear to do so.

[172] XLVI. See what has been said on the Great Symbolism in Appendix I. The application which is made of it here may be accepted, though it has nothing to do with the teaching of the Text about the gradual rise of a good officer to high social distinction and influence.

Paragraph x. Instead of finding in this the three lines of Khwăn and their subjects, *Kh*ăng-Ʒze makes 'the upper' denote only line 2.

Paragraph 2. The subject of line 2 in his loyal devotion to 5 will do much good and benefit many; hence we have the words, affords occasion for joy.'

Paragraph 3. 'He has no doubt or hesitation:'—but this is presuming rather on his strength.

Paragraph 4. The Khang-hsî editors say:—'Such an employment of men of worth to do service to spiritual Beings is serving them according to their mind.'

Paragraph 6. When one has reached the greatest height, he should think of retiring. Ambition otherwise may overleap itself.

4. 'The king employs him to prevent his offerings on mount *Khî*:'—such a service (of spiritual Beings) is according to (their mind).

5. 'He is firmly correct, and will therefore enjoy good fortune. He ascends the stairs (with all due ceremony):'—he grandly succeeds in his aim.

6. 'He blindly advances upwards,' and is in the highest place:—but there is decay in store for him, and he will not (preserve) his riches.

XLVII.[173] (The trigram representing) a marsh, and (below it that for a defile, which has drained the other dry so that there is) no water in it, form Khwăn. The superior man, in accordance with this, will sacrifice his life in order to carry out his purpose.

1. 'He enters a dark valley:'—so benighted is he, and without clear vision.

2. 'He is straitened amidst his wine and viands:'—(but) his position is central, and there will be ground for congratulation.

3. 'He lays hold of thorns:'—(this is suggested by the position of the line) above the strong (line).

'He enters his palace, and does not see his wife:'—this is inauspicious.

4. 'He proceeds very slowly (to help the subject of the first line):'—his aim is directed to (help) that lower (line). Although he is not in his appropriate place, he and that other will (in the end) be together.

5. 'His nose and feet are cut off:'—his aim has not yet been gained.

'He is leisurely, however, in his movements, and is satisfied:'—his position is central and (his virtue) is correct.

'It will be well for him to be (as sincere as) in sacrificing:'— so

---

[173] XLVII. The first sentence of the Great Symbolism is constructed differently from any which has presented itself in the previous 46 hexagrams. Literally translated, it would be 'a marsh with no water is Khwăn;' and this might certainly suggest to us a condition of distress. But how does this come out of the trigrams? The upper one is Tui, representing a marsh; and the lower is Khân, representing water in a defile. The collocation of the two suggests the running of the water from the marsh or lake into the stream, which will soon empty the other. Such is the view which occurred to myself; and it is the same as that given by *Kû Hsî*:—'The water descending and leaking away, the marsh above will become dry.' The application is good in itself, but the concatenation between it and the Symbolism is hardly discernible.

So stupid is the subject of line 1 that by his own act he increases his distress.

The Khang-hsî editors say that the 'ground for congratulation in paragraph 2 is the banqueting and sacrificing.' I rather think it is the measure of help, which it is intimated the subject will give in removing the straitness and distress of the time.

See the extract from the Khang-hsî editors on the symbolism of the third line of the Text.

The difficulties attending the symbolism of the Text of lines 4, 5, and 6 are not lightened by what we find in this Appendix.

shall he receive blessing.

6. 'He is straitened as if bound with creepers: (his spirit and action) are unsuitable.

'(He says), "If I move, I shall repent of it." And he does repent (of former errors), which leads to good fortune:'—so he (now) goes on.

XLVIII.[174] (The trigram representing) wood and above it that for water form 3ing. The superior man, in accordance with this, comforts the people, and. stimulates them to mutual helpfulness.

1. 'A well so muddy that men will not drink of it:'—this is indicated by the low position (of the line).

'An old well to which the birds do not come:'—it has been forsaken in the course of time.

2. 'A well from which by a hole the water escapes, and flows away to the shrimps:'—(the subject of this second line has) none co-operating with him (above).

3. 'The well has been cleared out, but is not used:'—(even) passers-by would be sorry for this.

A prayer is made 'that the king were intelligent:'—for then blessing would be received.

4. 'A well the lining of which is well laid. There will be no error:'—the well has been put in good repair.

5. 'The waters from the cold spring are (freely) drunk:'—this is indicated by the central and correct position (of the line).

6. 'The great good fortune' at the topmost place indicates the grand accomplishment (of the idea in the hexagram).

XLIX.[175] (The trigram representing the waters of) a marsh and that for fire in the midst of them form Ko. The superior man, in accordance

---

[174] XLVIII. The Great Symbolism here may well enough represent a well, it being understood that the water which is above the wood is that raised by it for irrigation and other uses. What is said, moreover, in the application is more akin to the idea of the hexagram than in most of the other cases. It is certainly one way in which the ruler should nourish the people.

Ii is said on paragraph 1:—'Those who have a mind to do something in the world, when they look at this line, and its symbolism, will learn how they ought to exert themselves.'

Rather in opposition to what I have said on the Text of line 4, the 'Daily Lecture' observes here:—'The cultivation of one's self, which is represented here, is fundamental to the government of others.'

[175] XLIX. Wise men, occupying themselves with the determination of the seasons and questions of time, have in all ages based their judgments on the observation of the heavenly bodies. We find this insisted on in the first book of the Shû, by the ancient Yâo. But how this application of the Great Symbolism really flows from it, I must confess myself unable to discover. Once, however, when I was conversing about the Yî with a high Chinese dignitary, who was a well-read scholar also so far as his own literature was concerned, he referred to this paragraph as proving that all our western science had been known to Fû-hsî and Confucius!

What is said on the several lines is sufficiently illustrated in the notes on the Text.

with this, regulates his (astronomical) calculations, and makes clear the seasons and times.

1. 'He is bound with (the skin of) a yellow ox:'—he should in his circumstances be taking action.

2. 'He makes his changes when some time has passed:'—what he does will be matter of admiration.

3. 'The change (contemplated) has been three times fully discussed:'—to what else should attention (now) be directed?

4. 'The good fortune consequent on changing (existing) ordinances' is due to the faith reposed in his aims.

5. 'The great man produces his changes as the tiger does when he changes his stripes:'—their beauty becomes more brilliant.

6. 'The superior man produces his changes as the leopard does when he changes his spots:'—their beauty becomes more elegant.

'Small men change their faces:'—they show themselves prepared to follow their ruler.

L.[176] (The trigram representing) wood and above it that for fire form Ting. The superior man, in accordance with this, keeps his every position correct, and maintains secure the appointment (of Heaven).

1. 'The caldron is overturned, and its feet turned upwards:'—but this is not (all) contrary (to what is right).

'There will be advantage in getting rid of what was bad:'—thereby (the subject of the line) will follow the more noble (subject of the fourth line).

2. 'There is the caldron with the things (to be cooked) in it:'—let (the subject of the line) be careful where he goes.

'My enemy dislikes me:'—but there will in the end be no fault (to which he can point).

3. 'There is the caldron with (the places for) its ears changed:'—(its subject) has failed in what was required of him (in his situation).

4. 'The contents designed for the ruler's use are overturned and spilt:'—how can (the subject of the line) be trusted?

---

[176] L. The Great Symbolism here has come before us in the treatise on the Thwan. Of the application of that symbolism I can only say that, as has been seen in many other hexagrams, while good enough in itself, it is far-fetched.

The same remark may be made on the explanation of the Text of the first line. I can myself do little more than guess at its meaning. The Khang-hsî editors observe that nothing is said about the case of the 'concubine' in the Text; but that it is covered by the following the more noble,' 'so condensed and complete are the words of the sage!'

The same editors find a pregnant sense in the conclusion of paragraph 2:—'There will be no fault in me to which my enemy can point, and his disposition to find fault will be diminished.'

'What was required of the caldron in the third line was that that line and line 5, instead of 6, should be correlates;' but there is little meaning in such a statement.

The subject of line 4 cannot be trusted again. He has failed in doing what was his proper work.

5. 'The caldron has yellow ears:'—the central position (of the line) is taken as (a proof of) the solid (virtue of its subject).

6. 'The rings of jade' are at the very top:—the strong and the weak meet in their due proportions.

LI.[177] (The trigram representing) thunder, being repeated, forms *Kăn*. The superior man, in accordance with this, is fearful and apprehensive, cultivates (his virtue), and examines (his faults).

1. 'When the (time of) movement comes, he will be found looking out with apprehension:'— that feeling of dread leads to happiness.

'He yet smiles and talks cheerfully:'—the issue (of his dread) is that he adopts (proper) laws (for his course).

2. 'When the movement approaches, he is in a position of peril:'—(a weak line) is mounted on a strong (one).

3. 'He is distraught amid the startling movements going on:'—(the third line) is in a position unsuitable to it.

4. 'Amid the startling movements, he sinks supinely in the mud:'—the light in him has not yet been brilliantly developed.

5. 'He goes and comes amid the startling movements, and (always) in peril:'—full of risk are his doings.

'What he has to do has to be done in his central position:'—far will he be from incurring any loss.

6. 'Amid the startling movements he is in breathless dismay:'—he has not found out (the course of) the due mean.

'Though evil (threatens), he will not fall into error:'—he is afraid of being warned by his neighbours.

LII.[178] (Two trigrams representing) a mountain, one over the other, form Kăn. The superior man, in accordance with this, does not go in his

---

[177] LI. The account of the Great Symbolism here calls for no remark. Nor does the application of it; but may it not be too late to fear, and order anew one's thoughts and actions when the retributions in providence are taking place? Commentators are haunted by the shadow of this question; but they are unable rightly to meet it.

Paragraph 1 is the same as 2 in Appendix I.

Paragraph 4. Compare paragraph 4 of hexagram 21, Appendix II.

[178] LII. According to the view of the Khang-hsî editors, the application should be translated:—'The superior man, in accordance with this, thinks anxiously how he shall not go beyond the duties of his position.' It is difficult to decide between this shade of the meaning, and the more common one which I have followed.

The toes play a great part in walking; but they are here kept at rest, and so do not lose the correct idea of Kăn.

There is no correlation between lines 2 and 3, and thence the subject of 3 will hold on its upward way without condescending to 2.

*Khăng-ȝze* finds an unsatisfactory auspice in paragraph 4. Line 4 represents a great minister who should be able to guide all to rest where they ought to be; but he can only keep himself from agitation.

Yü Păn (Ming dynasty) says on paragraph 5:—'Words should not be uttered rashly. Then, when uttered, they will be found accordant with principle. But it is only the master of the virtue belonging to the due mean who can attain to this.'

thoughts beyond the (duties of the) position in which he is.

1. 'He keeps his toes at rest:'—he does not fail in what is correct (according to the idea of the figure).

2. 'He cannot help him whom he follows:'(he whom he follows) will not retreat to listen to him.

3. 'He keeps the loins at rest:'—the danger (from his doing so) produces a glowing, heat in the heart.

4. 'He keeps the trunk of his body at rest:'—he keeps himself free (from agitation).

5. 'He keeps his cheek bones at rest:'—in harmony with his central position he acts correctly.

6. 'There is good fortune through his devotedly maintaining his restfulness:'—to the end he shows himself generous and good.

LIII.[179] (The trigram representing) a mountain and above it that for a tree form *Kien*. The superior man, in accordance with this, attains to and maintains his extraordinary virtue, and makes the manners of the people good.

1. 'The danger of a small officer (as represented in the first line)' is owing to no fault of his in the matter of what is right.

2. 'They eat and drink joyfully and at ease:'—but not without having earned their food.

3. 'A husband goes and does not return:'—he separates himself from his comrades.

'A wife is pregnant, but will not nourish her child:'—she has failed

---

[179] LIII. The Khang-hsî editors, to bring out the suitability of the Great Symbolism and its application, say:—'A tree springing up on the ground is a tree as it begins to grow. A tree on a hill is high and large. Every tree when it begins to grow, shows its branches and twigs gradually becoming long. Every morning and every evening show some difference; and when the tree is high and great, whether it be of an ordinary or extraordinary size, it has taken years to reach its dimensions. This illustrates the difference between the advance in Shăng (46) and that in *Kien*. Then the maintenance of extraordinary virtue in the application and the improvement of manners is a gradual process. The improvement of the manners, moreover, flows from the maintenance of the extraordinary virtue; which implies also a gradual operation and progress.'

Paragraph 1. The danger is the result of circumstances; the small officer has not brought it on himself.

Paragraph 2. Only the geese appear in this paragraph; but the writer is thinking of the advancing officer. I cannot but think that in the language and sentiment also there is an echo of the Shih King, 1, ix, ode 6.

The 'separation from his comrades' has respect to line 3 not finding its correlate in 6. 'The wife's failing in her proper course' has respect to the line being undivided and not in the centre.

*Kh*ăng-3ze says, on paragraph 4, that humility and right-doing will find rest and peace in all places and circumstances.

Paragraph 5. 'The natural issue cannot be prevented:'—the wife will have a child minister and ruler will meet happily.

Paragraph 6. See on the Text. But it is difficult to see the aptness of the symbolism.

in her (proper) course.

'It might be advantageous in resisting plunderers:'—by acting as here indicated men would preserve one another.

4. 'They may light on the flat branches:'—there is docility (in the line) going on to flexible penetration.

5. 'In the end the natural issue cannot be prevented. There will be good fortune:'—(the subject of the line) will get what he desires.

6. 'Their feathers can be used as ornaments. There will be good fortune:'—(the object and character of the subject of the line) cannot be disturbed.

LIV.[180] (The trigram representing the waters of) a marsh and over it that for thunder form Kwei Mei. The superior man, in accordance with this, having regard to the far-distant end, knows the mischief (that may be done at the beginning).

1. 'The younger sister is married off in a position ancillary to that of the real wife:'—it is the constant practice (for such a case).

'Lame on one leg, she is able to tramp along:'—she can render helpful service.

2. 'There will be advantage in maintaining the firm correctness of a solitary widow:'—(the subject of the line) has not changed from the constancy (proper to a wife).

3. 'The younger sister who was to be married off is in a mean position:'—this is shown by the improprieties (indicated in the line).

4. (The purpose in) 'protracting the time' is that, after waiting, the thing may be done (all the better).

5. 'The sleeves of the younger sister of (king) Tî-yî, when she was married away, were not equal to those of her (half-)sister, who accompanied her:'—such was her noble character, indicated by the central position of the line.

6. '(What is said in) the sixth line, (divided),about there being nothing in the basket' shows that the subject of it is carrying an empty basket.

LV.[181] (The trigrams representing) thunder and lightning combine

---

[180] LIV. Thunder rolling above is supposed to produce movement in the waters of the marsh below. The combination of this symbolism in Kwei Mei is recognised as an evil omen in the case which the name denotes. The application of it is not inappropriate.

Paragraph 1. 'It is the constant practice (for such a case)' seems to mean that an ancillary wife has no right to the disposition of herself, but must do what she is told. Thus it is that the mean position of the younger sister does not interfere with the service she can render.

The addition to the Text of 1 the purpose' in paragraph 4 is to show that the putting marriage off is on the part of the lady and not on the other side.

[181] LV. Lightning appears here as the natural phenomenon of which Lî is the symbol. The virtues attributed to the two trigrams are certainly required in the application of them which is subjoined; but that application has little or nothing to do with the

to form Făng. The superior man, in accordance with this, decides cases of litigation, and apportions punishments with exactness.

1. 'Though they are both of the same character, there will be no error:'—if the subject of this line seek to overpass that similarity, there will be calamity.

2. 'Let him cherish his feeling of sincere devotion, that it shall appear being put forth:'—it is by sincerity that the mind is affected.

3. 'There is an (additional) screen of a large and thick banner:'—great things should not be attempted (in such circumstances).

'He breaks his right arm:'—in the end he will not be fit to be employed.

4. 'He is surrounded by a screen large and thick:'—the position of the line is inappropriate.

'At midday he sees the constellation of the Bushel:'—there is darkness and no light.

'He meets with the subject of the line, undivided like himself. There will be good fortune:'—action may be taken.

5. 'The good fortune indicated by the fifth six, (divided),'is the congratulation (that is sure to arise).

6. 'He has made his house large:'—he soars (in his pride) to the heavens.

'He looks at his door, which is still, with no one about it:'—he (only) keeps himself withdrawn from all others.

LVI.[182] (The trigram representing) a mountain and above it that for

explanation of the hexagram supplied by the Text.

I hardly understand the conclusion of paragraph 1. My translation of it is according to the view of *Kû* Hsî, if I rightly understand that.

Paragraph 2. It is by such sincerity that the mind is affected,—that is, the mind of the ruler occupying line 5.

Line 3 has a correlate in 6, which is weak, and as it were out of the game. The light in 3 moreover is hidden. Hence the symbolism; and through the blindness of its subject his hurt, which unfits him to be employed.

The line undivided like 4 is 1; perhaps we might translate—'He meets with the subject of the parallel line.'

No one but himself has any confidence in the subject of line 6. He holds himself aloof from others, and they leave him to himself.

[182] LVI. Different attempts are made to bring the idea of a travelling stranger out of the trigrams Kăn and Lî; but none of them is satisfactory. Let Khung Ying-tâ's view serve as a specimen of them:—'A fire on a mountain lays hold of the grass, and runs with it over the whole space, not stopping anywhere long, and soon disappearing;—such is the emblem of the traveller.' The application may be derived well enough from the attributes of the trigrams; but does not fit in with the lessons of the Thwan and Hsiang.

The meanness of the subject of line 1 does not arise from the nature of his occupation; but from his mind and aim being emptied of all that is good and ennobling.

Strong and trusty servants are the most important condition for the comfort and progress of the traveller; and therefore it alone is resumed and expanded.

The subject of line 3 treats those below him with violence and arrogance, which of course alienates them from him.

fire form Lü. The superior man, in accordance with this, exerts his wisdom and caution in the use of punishments and not allowing litigations to continue.

1. 'The stranger is mean and meanly occupied:'—his aim is become of the lowest character, and calamity will ensue.

2. 'He is provided with good and trusty servants:'—he will in the end have nothing of which to complain.

3. 'The stranger burns his lodging-house:'—and he himself also suffers hurt thereby. When, as a stranger, he treats those below him (as the line indicates), the right relation between him and them is lost.

4. 'The stranger is in a resting-place:'—but he has not got his proper position.

'He has the means of livelihood, and the axe:'—but his mind is not at ease.

5. 'In the end he will obtain praise and a (high) charge:'—he has reached a high place.

6. 'Considering that the stranger is here at the very height (of distinction),' with the spirit that possesses him, it is right he (should be emblemed by a bird) burning (its nest).

'He loses his ox(-like docility) too readily and easily:'—to the end he would not listen to (the truth about the course to be pursued).

LVII.[183] (Two trigrams representing) wind, following each other, form Sun. The superior man, in accordance with this, reiterates his orders, and secures the practice of his affairs.

1. '(Now) he advances, (now) he recedes:'—his mind is perplexed.

---

'He has not got into his proper position' seems to say no more than that 4 is a strong line in an even place.

It is difficult to say what 'he has reached a high place' means. The fifth line is not in this hexagram the ruler's seat; but by his qualities and gifts the subject of it attracts the attention and regard of his friends and of his ruler.

The spirit that possesses the subject of line 6 is one of haughty arrogance, with which the humility that ought to characterise him cannot co-exist. His careless self-sufficiency has shut his mind against all lessons of wisdom.

[183] LVII. I have said on the Thwan that some commentators make the upper trigram symbolical of the ordinances of the ruler and the lower symbolical of the obedience of the people. E. g., *Khăng-3ze* says:—'Superiors, in harmony with the duty of inferiors, issue their commands; inferiors, in harmony with the wishes of their superiors, follow them. Above and below there are that harmony and deference; and this is the significance of the redoubled Sun. When governmental commands and business are in accordance with what is right, they agree with the tendencies of the minds of the people who follow them.'

Paragraph 2 seems to say that the sincerity of purpose indicated by the central position of the second line conducts its subject to the right course, despite the many considerations that might distract him.

'The will is exhausted' in paragraph 3 intimates that 'the repeated efforts' made by its subject have exhausted him. He can now only regret his failures.

What is said in paragraph 6 proceeds on a different view of the Text from that which I have followed.

It would be advantageous for him to have the firmness of a brave soldier:'—his mind would in that case be well governed.

2. 'The good fortune springing from what borders on confusion' is due to the position (of the line) in the centre.

3. 'The regret arising from the violent and repeated efforts to penetrate' shows the exhaustion of the will.

4. 'He takes game in his hunting, enough for the threefold use of it:'—he achieves merit.

5. 'The good fortune of (the subject of) the fifth line, undivided,' is owing to its correct position and its being in the centre.

6. 'The representative of penetration is beneath a couch:'—though occupying the topmost place, his powers are exhausted.

'He has lost the axe with which he executed his decisions:'—though he try to be correct, there will be evil.

LVIII.[184] (Two symbols representing) the waters of a marsh, one over the other, form Tui. The superior man, in accordance with this, (encourages) the conversation of friends and (the stimulus of) their (common) practice.

1. 'The good fortune attached to the pleasure of (inward) harmony' arises from there being nothing in the conduct (of the subject of the line) to awaken doubt.

2. 'The good fortune attached to the pleasure arising from (inward sincerity)' is due to the confidence felt in the object (of the subject of the line).

3. 'The evil predicated of one's bringing around himself whatever can give pleasure' is shown by the inappropriateness of the place (of the line).

4. 'The joy in connexion with (the subject of) the fourth line, (undivided): is due to the happiness (which he will produce).

---

[184] LVIII. The application of the Great Symbolism here will recall to many readers the Hebrew maxims in Proverbs xxvii. 17, 19. The sentiment of it, however, does not readily fit in to the teaching of the hexagram as set forth in the Text.

There is nothing in the conduct of the subject of line 1 to awaken suspicion. He has as yet taken no action; but it was not necessary to say anything like this about the subject of line 2, his central position being an assurance that he would never do anything of a doubtful character.

Line 3 should be strong, and the desire of pleasure which is the idea of the hexagram leads its weak subject to the course which is so emphatically condemned.

Paragraph 5 is incomplete. Does the correctness and appropriateness of the position of the subject of the line afford any explanation of his trusting the subject of the weak line above, who would only injure him? It ought to keep him on the contrary from doing so. The commentators have seen this, and say that the paragraph is intended by way of caution.

The action of the hexagram should culminate and end in line 5. But the subject of it has not made brilliant attainment in the firmness and correctness by which the love of pleasure should be controlled.

5. 'He trusts in one who would injure him:'—his place is that which is correct and appropriate.

6. 'The topmost line, (divided), shows the pleasure (of its subject) in leading and attracting others:'—his (virtue) is not yet brilliant.

LIX.[185] (The trigram representing) water and that for wind moving above the water form Hwân. The ancient kings, in accordance with this, presented offerings to God and established the ancestral temple.

1. 'The good fortune attached to the first six, divided),'is due to the natural course (pursued by its subject).

2. 'Amidst the prevailing dispersion, he hurries to his contrivance (for security):'—he gets what he desires.

3. 'He has no regard to his own person:'—his aim is directed to what is external to himself.

4. 'He scatters the (different) parties (in the state), and there is great good fortune:'—brilliant and great (are his virtue and service).

5. 'The accumulations of the royal (granaries) are dispersed, and there is no error:'—this is due to the correctness of the position.

6. 'His bloody wounds are gone:'—he is far removed from the danger of injury.

LX.[186] (The trigram representing) a lake, and above it that for water, form *K*ieh. The superior man, in accordance with this, constructs his (methods of) numbering and measurement, and discusses (points of) virtue and conduct.

1. 'He does not quit the courtyard outside his door:'—he knows

---

[185] LIX. The 'in accordance with this' must be equivalent to—'to remedy the state of things thus symbolised.' What follows certainly amounts to this, that the ancient kings considered the services of religion, sincerely and earnestly attended to, as calculated to counteract the tendency to mutual alienation and selfishness in the minds of men. How they operated to have this beneficial effect we are not told. Nor is it easy to account, for the extension of what is said in the Text about the establishment of the ancestral temple to the presentation also of offerings to God. Probably the writer had the same idea in his mind as in the Great Symbolism of hexagram 16, q. v.

'The natural course' pursued by the subject of line 1 is, probably, that required by the time.

'What the subject of line 2 desired' would be his success in counteracting the prevailing tendency to disunion.

The view given of paragraph 5 is that propounded by *K*û Hsî.

For paragraph 6 see the note on line 6 under the Text.

[186] LX. Various explanations of the Great Symbolism have been attempted. E. g., *K*hăng-ȝze says:—'The water which a lake or marsh will contain is limited to a certain quantity. If the water flowing in exceed that, it overflows. This gives us the idea of *K*ieh.' What is found on the application of it is to my mind equally unsatisfactory.

The subject of line 1 knows when he might have free course and when he is obstructed, and acts accordingly. He is regulated by a consideration of the time.

The subject of line 1 ought not to act, and he is still. The subject of line 2 ought to act, and he also is still. The error and the effect of it are great.

The subject of line 3 shows by his lamentation how he blames himself.

The other three paragraphs are sufficiently explained in what is said on the Text.

when he has free course and when he is obstructed.

2. 'He does not quit the courtyard inside his gate. There will be evil:'—he loses the time (for action) to an extreme degree.

3. In 'the lamentation for not observing the (proper) regulations,' who should there be to blame?

4. 'The progress and success of the quiet and natural (attention) to all regulations' is due to the deference which accepts the ways of (the ruler) above.

5. 'The good fortune arising from the regulations enacted sweetly and acceptably' is due to (the line) occupying the place (of authority) and being in the centre.

6. 'The regulations are severe and difficult. Even with firm correctness there will be evil:'—the course (indicated by the hexagram) is come to an end.

LXI.[187] (The trigram representing the waters of) a marsh and that for wind above it form *K*ung Fû. The superior man, in accordance with this, deliberates about cases of litigation and delays (the infliction of) death.

1. 'The first line, (undivided), shows its subject resting (in himself). There will be good fortune:'—no change has yet come over his purpose.

2. 'Her young ones respond to her:'—from the (common) wish of the inmost heart.

3. 'Now he beats his drum, and now he leaves off:'—the position (of the line) is the appropriate one for it.

4. 'A horse the fellow of which disappears:'—he breaks from his (former) companions, and mounts upwards.

5. 'He is perfectly sincere, and links others to him in closest union:'—the place (of the line) is the correct and appropriate one.

6. 'Chanticleer (tries to) mount to heaven:'—but how can (such an effort) continue long?

---

[187] LXI. Dissatisfied with previous attempts to explain the Great Symbolism, the Khang-hsî editors say:—'The wind penetrates things. The grass and trees of the level ground are shaken and tossed by it; the rocky valleys and caverns in their sides have it blowing round about them; and it acts also on the depths of the collected waters, the cold of which disappears and the ice is melted before it. This is what makes it the emblem of that perfect sincerity which penetrates everywhere. The litigations of the people are like the deep and dark places of the earth. The kings examine with discrimination into all secret matters connected with them.. even those which are here mentioned, till there is nothing that is not penetrated by their perfect sincerity.' But all this is greatly strained. The symbolism of the eight trigrams gets pretty well played out in the course of the 64 hexagrams.
1. 'No change has come over the purpose:'—the sincerity, that is, perfect in itself and of itself, continues.
2. One bond of loving regard unites the mother bird and her young; so answers the heart of man to man.

LXII.[188] (The trigram representing) a hill and that for thunder above it form Hsiâo Kwo. The superior man, in accordance with this, in his conduct exceeds in humility, in mourning exceeds in sorrow, and in his expenditure exceeds in economy.

1. 'There is a bird flying (and ascending) till the result is evil:'— nothing can be done to avoid this issue.

2. 'He does not attempt to reach his ruler:'—a minister should not overpass the distance (between his ruler and himself).

3. 'Some in consequence find opportunity to assail and injure him. There will be evil:'—how great will it be!

4. 'He meets the exigency (of his situation), without exceeding (the proper course):'—(he does so), the position being inappropriate (for a strong line).

'If he go forward, there will be peril, and he must be cautious:'— the result would be that his course would not be long pursued.

5. 'There are dense clouds, but no rain:'—(the line) is in too high a place.

6. 'He does not meet the exigency (of his situation), and exceeds (his proper course):'—(the position indicates) the habit of domineering.

LXIII.[189] (The trigram representing) fire and that for water above it form *Kî* 3î. The superior man, in accordance with this, thinks of evil (that may come), and beforehand guards against it.

1. 'He drags back his wheel:'—as we may rightly judge, there will be no mistake.

2. 'In seven days she will find it:'—for the course pursued is that indicated by the central position (of the line).

3. 'He was three years in subduing it:'—enough to make him

---

[188] LXII. The Khang-hsî editors endeavour to show the appropriateness of the Great Symbolism in this way:—'When thunder issues from the earth, the sound of it comes with a rush and is loud; but when it reaches the top of a hill it has begun to die away and is small.' There is nothing in the Chinese about the hills being high; and readers will only smile at the attempted explanation. The application of the symbolism, or rather of the idea of the hexagram, is good, and in entire accordance with what I have stated that idea to be.

Nothing can be done to avoid the issue mentioned in paragraph 1, for the subject of the line brings it on himself.

Paragraph 2 deals only with the symbolism in the conclusion of what is stated under line 2. The writer takes the view which I have given on the Text.

For paragraphs 3 and 4 see the notes on the Text.

In line 5 the yin line is too high. If the line were yang, the auspice would be different.

[189] LXIII. Water and fire coming together as here, fire under the water, each element occupies its proper place, and their interaction will be beneficial. Such is the common explanation of the Great Symbolism; but the connexion between it and the application of it, which also is good in itself, is by no means clear.

The notes on the different lines present nothing that has not been dealt with in the notes on the Text.

weary.

4. 'He is on his guard all the day:'—he is in doubt about something.

5. 'The slaughtering of an ox by the neighbour in the east is not equal to (the small sacrifice of) the neighbour in the west:'—because the time (in the latter case is more important and fit).

'His sincerity receives the blessing:'—good fortune comes on a great scale.

6. 'His head is immersed; the position is perilous:'—how could such a state continue long?

LXIV.[190] (The trigram representing) water and that for fire above it form Wei 3î. The superior man, in accordance with this, carefully discriminates among (the qualities of) things, and the (different) positions they (naturally) occupy.

1. 'His tail gets immersed:'—this is the very height of ignorance.

2. 'The second line, (undivided), shows good fortune arising from being firm and correct:'—it is in the central place, and the action of its subject thereby becomes correct.

3. '(The state of things is) not yet remedied. Advancing will lead to evil:'—the place (of the line) is not that appropriate for it.

4. (By firm correctness there is good fortune, and cause for repentance disappears:'—the aim (of the subject of the line) is carried into effect.

5. '(We see) the brightness of a superior man:—'the diffusion of that brightness tends to good fortune.

6. 'He drinks and gets his head immersed:'—he does not know how to submit to the (proper) regulations.

---

[190] LXIV. In this last hexagram we have water below and fire above, so that the two cannot act on each other, and the Symbolism may represent the unregulated condition of general affairs, the different classes of society not harmonising nor acting together. The application follows naturally.

*Kû Hsî* and others suspect an error in the text of paragraph 1; yet a tolerable meaning comes from it as it stands.

The Khang-hsî editors observe on paragraph 2 that an undivided line in the second place, and a divided line in the fifth place, are both incorrect, and yet it is often said of them that with firm correctness in their subjects there will be good fortune;—such is the virtue of the central position. This principle is at last clearly enunciated in this paragraph.

*Khăng-3ze* says:—'The subject of line 4 has the ability which the time requires, and possesses also a firm solidity. He can carry out therefore his purpose. There will be good fortune, and all cause for repentance will disappear. The smiting of the demon region was the highest example of firm correctness.'

Both the symbols in paragraph 6 indicate a want of caution, and an unwillingness to submit one's impulses to the regulation of reason and prudence.

## APPENDIX III. THE GREAT APPENDIX.

### SECTION I.

Chapter I.[191] 1. Heaven is lofty and honourable; earth is low. (Their symbols), *Kh*ien and Khwăn, (with their respective meanings), were determined (in accordance with this).

Things low and high appear displayed in a similar relation. The (upper and lower trigrams, and the relative position of individual lines, as) noble and mean, had their places assigned accordingly.

Movement and rest are the regular qualities (of their respective subjects). Hence comes the definite distinction (of the several lines) as the strong and the weak.

(Affairs) are arranged together according to their tendencies, and things are divided according to their classes. Hence were produced (the interpretations in the Yî, concerning) what is good [or lucky] and evil [or unlucky].

In the heavens there are the (different) figures there completed, and on the earth there are the (different) bodies there formed. (Corresponding to them) were the changes and transformations exhibited (in the Yî).

2. After this fashion a strong and a weak line were manipulated together (till there were the eight trigrams), and those eight trigrams

---

[191] Chapter I is an attempt to show the correspondency between the phenomena of external nature ever changing, and the figures of the Yî King ever varying. The first four paragraphs, it is said, show, from the phenomena of production and transformation in external nature, the principles on which the figures of the Yî were made. The fifth and sixth paragraphs show, particularly, how the attributes represented by the figures *Kh*ien and Khwăn are to be found in (the operations of) heaven and earth. The last two paragraphs show both those attributes embodied or realised in man. The realisation takes place, indeed, fully only in the sage or the ideal man, who thus becomes the pattern for all men.

In paragraph 3 we have five of the six derivative trigrams;—the six children,' according to the nomenclature of the Wăn arrangement. 'Thunder' stands for *k*ăn (☳), 'lightning' for lî (☲), 'wind' for sun (☴), and 'rain' for khan (☵). 'The sun,' however, is also an emblem of lî, and 'the moon' one of kăn (☶), generally said to represent 'mountains,' while tui (☱) representing 'collections of water,' has no place in the enumeration. *K*û Hsî says that in paragraph 3 we have the natural changes seen in the phenomena of the sky, while in 4 we have such changes as find body and figure on the earth.

Paragraphs 5 and 6 have both been misunderstood from neglect of the peculiar meaning of the character *k*ih (知), and from taking it in its common acceptation of 'knowing.' Both commentaries and dictionaries point out that it is here used in the sense of 'directing,' 'presiding over.' In paragraph 7, however, it resumes its ordinary significancy.

were added, each to itself and to all the others, (till the sixty-four hexagrams were formed).

3. We have the exciting forces of thunder and lightning; the fertilising influences of wind and rain; and the revolutions of the sun and moon, which give rise to cold and warmth.

4. The attributes expressed by *Kh*ien constitute the male; those expressed by Khwăn constitute the female.

5. *Kh*ien (symbolises Heaven, which) directs the great beginnings of things; Khwăn (symbolises Earth, which) gives to them their completion.

6. It is by the ease with which it proceeds that *Kh*ien directs (as it does), and by its unhesitating response that Khwăn exhibits such ability.

7. (He who attains to this) ease (of Heaven) will be easily understood, and (he who attains to this) freedom from laborious effort (of the Earth) will be easily followed. He who is easily understood will have adherents, and he who is easily followed will achieve success. He who has adherents can continue long, and he who achieves success can become great. To be able to continue long shows the virtue of the wise and able man; to be able to become great is the heritage he will acquire.

8. With the attainment of such ease and such freedom from laborious effort, the mastery is got of all principles under the sky. With the attainment of that mastery, (the sage) makes good his position in the middle (between heaven and earth).

Chapter II.[192] 9. The sages set forth the diagrams, inspected the emblems contained in them, and appended their explanations;—in this way the good fortune and bad (indicated by them) were made clear.

10. The strong and the weak (lines) displace each other, and

---

[192] Chapter II, paragraphs 9-14, is divided into two parts. The former contains paragraphs 9-12, and tells us how the sages, king Wăn and the duke of *K*âu, proceeded in making the Yî, so that the good fortune and bad of men's courses should be indicated by it in harmony with right and wrong, and the processes of nature. Paragraphs 13, 14 form the second part, and speak of the study of the Yî by the superior man, desirous of doing what is right and increasing his knowledge, and the advantages flowing from it.

I can follow to some extent the first two statements of paragraph 12, so far as the ideas of the writer are concerned, though asserting any correspondence between the changes of the lines of the diagrams, and the operations of external nature, as in the succession of day and night, is merely an amusement of the fancy. I all but fail, however, to grasp the idea in the last statement. In the trigram, the first line represents earth; the second, man; and the third, heaven; in the hexagram, the first and second lines are assigned to earth; the third and fourth, to man; and the fifth and sixth, to heaven. These are the three Powers, and each Power has 'a Grand Extreme,' where its nature and operation are seen in their highest ideal. This is to some extent conceivable; but when I try to follow our author, and find an analogy between the course of these extremes and the movements in the places of the diagrams, I have no clue by which to trace my way. For the concluding sentence of paragraph 14 see the duke of *K*âu on the last line of hexagram 14.

produce the changes and transformations (in the figures).

11. Therefore the good fortune and evil (mentioned in the explanations) are the indications of the right and wrong (in men's conduct of affairs), and the repentance and regret (similarly mentioned) are the indications of their sorrow and anxiety.

12. The changes and transformations (of the lines) are the emblems of the advance and retrogression (of the vital force in nature). Thus what we call the strong and the weak (lines) become the emblems of day and night. The movements which take place in the six places (of the hexagram) show the course of the three extremes (i. e. of the three Powers in their perfect operation).

13. Therefore what the superior man rests in, in whatever position he is placed, is the order shown in the Yî; and the study which gives him the greatest pleasure is that of the explanations of the several lines.

14. Therefore the superior man, when living quietly, contemplates the emblems and studies the explanations of them; when initiating any movement, he contemplates the changes (that are made in divining), and studies the prognostications from them. Thus 'is help extended to him from Heaven; there will be good fortune, and advantage in every movement.'

Chapter III.[193] 15. The Thwan speak of the emblematic figures (of the complete diagrams). The Yâo speak of the changes (taking place: in the several lines).

16. The expressions about good fortune or bad are used with reference to (the figures and lines, as) being right or wrong (according to the conditions of time and place); those about repentance or regret refer to small faults (in the satisfying those conditions); when it is said 'there will be no error,' or 'no blame,' there is reference to (the subject) repairing an error by what is good.

17. Therefore the distinction of (the upper and lower trigrams and of the individual lines) as noble or mean is decided by the (relative) position (of the lines); the regulations of small and great are found in

---

[193] Chapter III, paragraphs 15-19, gives additional information about the constituent parts of the Yî, that is, the Text of the classic as we have it from king Wăn and his son. The imperial editors say that it expands the meaning of the fourth paragraph, the third of chapter 2. It does do so, but this account hardly covers all its contents.

To understand the names 'small and great,' as used of the diagrams in paragraphs 17 and 19, it should be noted that hexagrams to which the divided or yin line gives their character are termed 'small,' and those where the undivided or yang line rules are called 'great.' Kâu (44,      ), Thun (33,      ), and Phei (12,      ) are instances of the former class; Fû (24,      ), Lin (19,      ) and Thâi (11,      ), of the other.

It is observed by 3hâi Khing (early in the Ming dynasty) that the terms 'diagrams' and 'explanations' must be understood not only of the whole figures but also as embracing the several lines.

the diagrams, and the discriminations of good and bad fortune appear in the (subjoined) explanations.

18. Anxiety against (having occasion for) repentance or regret should be felt at the: boundary line (between good and evil). The stirring up the thought of (securing that there shall be) no blame arises from (the feeling of) repentance.

19. Thus of the diagrams some are small, and some are great; and of the explanations some are startling, and some are unexciting. Every one of those explanations has reference to the tendencies (indicated by the symbols).

Chapter IV.[194] 20. The Yî was made on a principle of accordance

---

[194] Chapter IV, paragraphs 20-23, is intended still more to exalt the Yî, and seems to say that the sage by means of it can make an exhaustive study of all principles and of human nature, till he attains to the knowledge of the ordinances of Heaven. Such is the account of the chapter given by *Kû* Hsî; but the second character in paragraph 21 must be understood in the signification which it has in all the sixty-four sentences which explain the emblematic structure of the hexagrams, as = 'in accordance with' and not 'by means of.' The imperial editors append to their statement of *Kû*'s account, that it must be borne in mind that the sages had not to wait till the Yî was made to conduct their exhaustive study. They had done that before, and the Yî may be considered as a talk on the results, drawn out in its own peculiar style. It holds the mirror up to nature; but its authors knew nature before they made it.

In paragraph 21, 'the brilliant phenomena of the heavens' are the various shining bodies of the sky, with their rising and setting; 'the definite arrangements of the earth' are the different situations of its parts according to the points of the compass, and its surface as diversified by mountain and valley; and by the study of these the causes of day and night are known as being the expansion and contraction of the elementary ether. The same thing produces the facts of birth or life and death.

ʒing, which I have translated 'essence,' denotes the more subtle and pure part of matter, and belongs to the grosser form of the elementary ether; *khî*, or 'spirit,' is the breath, still material, but purer than the ʒing, and belongs to the finer, and more active form of the ether. Here *khî* is 'the breath of life.' In the hwun or 'soul (animus),' the *khî* predominates, and the ʒing in the pho or animal soul. At death the hwun wanders away, ascending, and the pho descends and is changed into a ghostly shade. So did the ancient Chinese grope their way from material things to the concept and representation of what was immaterial.

For my 'characteristics of the anima and animus,' Dr. Medhurst rendered 'the circumstances and conditions of the Kwei Shǎns' (Theology of the Chinese, pp. 10-12); but he observes that 'the Kwei Shǎns in the passage are evidently the expanding and contracting principles of human life.' The kwei shǎns are brought about by the dissolution of the human frame, and consist of the expanding and ascending shǎn, which rambles about in space, and of the contracted and shrivelled kwei, which reverts to earth and nonentity. It is difficult to express one's self clearly on a subject treated so briefly and enigmatically in the text.

We must understand that the subject of the predicates in this and the next two paragraphs is 'the sage,' who has endeavoured to give a transcript of his views and doings in the Yî. The character, which I have translated by 'spirit-like' in paragraph 23, is different from *khî* in paragraph 21. It is shǎn, a character of the phonetic class, while its primary material signification has not been satisfactorily ascertained. 'The Chinese,' says P'. Regis (vol. ii. p. 445), 'use it in naming the soul, true angels, and the genii of idolaters; and the Christian Chinese use it when they speak of God, of the Holy Spirit, of with heaven and earth, and shows us therefore, without rent or confusion, the course (of things) in heaven and earth.

21. (The sage), in accordance with (the Yî), looking up, contemplates the brilliant phenomena of the heavens, and, looking down, examines the definite arrangements of the earth;—thus he knows the causes of darkness (or, what is obscure) and light (or, what is bright). He traces things to their beginning, and follows them to their end;—thus he knows what can be said about death and life. (He perceives how the union of) essence and breath form things, and the (disappearance or) wandering away of the soul produces the change (of their constitution);—thus he knows the characteristics of the anima and animus.

22. There is a similarity between him and heaven and earth, and hence there is no contrariety in him to them. His knowledge embraces all things, and his course is (intended to be) helpful to all under the sky;—and hence he falls into no error. He acts according to the exigency of circumstances without being carried away by their current; he rejoices in Heaven and knows its ordinations;—and hence he has no anxieties. He rests in his own (present) position, and cherishes (the spirit of) generous benevolence;—and hence he can love (without reserve).

23. (Through the Yî), he comprehends as in a mould or enclosure the transformations of heaven and earth without any error; by an ever-varying adaptation he completes (the nature of) all things without exception; he penetrates to a knowledge of the course of day and night (and all other connected phenomena);—it is thus that his operation is spirit-like, unconditioned by place, while the changes which he produces are not restricted to any form.

Chapter V.[195] 24. The successive movement of the inactive and

---

angels, and of the soul of man. For what else could they do?'

[195] Chapter V, paragraphs 24-32, Still shows us the Yî fashioned so as to give a picture of the phenomena of the external universe; but the writer dwells more on the latter, and the different paragraphs give an interesting view of his ideas on the subject. He supposes a constant change from rest to movement and from movement to rest, through which all things are formed, now still, now in motion, now expanding, now contracting. It is customary to speak of two forms of an original ether as the two elementary principles, but they are really one and the same ether, in a twofold condition, with a twofold action. By their successive movement the phenomena of existence are produced,—what I have called 'the course (of things)' in paragraph 24. It is attempted, however, by many native scholars and by some sinologists, to give to tâo, the last character in that paragraph, the meaning of 'reason,' that which intelligently guides and directs the movements of the two elements. But this view is not in harmony with the scope of the chapter, nor can the characters be fairly construed so as to justify such an interpretation.

The imperial editors say that the germ of the Mencian doctrine about the goodness of human nature is in paragraph 25; but it says more widely, that 'every creature is good,' active operations constitutes what is called the course (of things).

25. That which ensues as the result (of their movement) is goodness; that which shows it in its completeness is the natures (of men and things).

26. The benevolent see it and call it benevolence. The wise see it and call it wisdom. The common people, acting daily according to it, yet have no knowledge of it. Thus it is that the course (of things), as seen by the superior man, is seen by few.

27. It is manifested in the benevolence (of its operations), and (then again) it conceals and stores up its resources. It gives their stimulus to all things, without having the same anxieties that possess the sage. Complete is its abundant virtue and the greatness of its stores!

28. Its rich possessions is what is intended by 'the greatness of its stores;' the daily renovation which it produces is what is meant by 'the abundance of its virtue.'

29. Production and reproduction is what is called (the process of) change.

30. The formation of the semblances (shadowy forms of things) is what we attribute to *Kh*ien; the giving to them their specific forms is what we attribute to Khwăn.

31. The exhaustive use of the numbers (that turn up in manipulating the stalks), and (thereby) knowing (the character of) coming events, is what we call prognosticating; the comprehension of the changes (indicated leads us to) what we call the business (to be

---

according to its ideal as from the plastic yin and yang. But few, the next paragraph tells us, can understand the measure of this goodness.

'The benevolent operations' in the course of things in paragraph 27 are illustrated from the phenomena of growth and beauty in spring and summer; and the cessation of these in autumn and winter may be called 'a concealing and storing them up.'

Paragraph 29 seems to state the origin of the name Yî as applied to the book, the Yî King.

In paragraph 30 the names *Kh*ien and Khwăn take the place of yin and yang, as used in paragraphs 24 and 32, In Khien, the symbol of heaven, every one of its three lines is undivided; it is the concentration of the yang faculty; so Khwăn, the symbol of the earth, is the concentration of the yin. The critics themselves call attention to the equivalence of the symbolic names here given to yin and yang. The connexion of the two is necessary to the production of any one substantial thing. The yang originates a shadowy outline which the yin fills up with a definite substance. So actually in nature Heaven (*Kh*ien) and Earth (Khwăn) operate together in the production of all material things and beings.

The 'numbers,' mentioned in paragraph 31, are not all or any numbers generally, but 7, 8, 9, 6, those assigned to the four 'emblematic figures,' that grow out of the undivided and divided lines, and by means of which the hexagrams are made up in divination. The 'future or coming events' which are prognosticated are not particular events, which the diviner has not already forecast, but the character of events or courses of actions already contemplated, as good or evil, lucky or unlucky, in their issue.

The best commentary on paragraph 32 is supplied by paragraphs 8-10 of Appendix VI. The 'Spirit' is that of 'God;' and this settles the meaning of tâo in paragraph 24, as being the course of nature, in which, according to the author, 'God worketh all in all.'

done).

32. That which is unfathomable in (the movement of) the inactive and active operations is (the presence of a) spiritual (power).

Chapter VI.[196] 33. Yes, wide is the Yî and great! If we speak of it in its farthest reaching, no limit can be set to it; if we speak of it with reference to what is near at hand, (its lessons are) still and correct; if we speak of it in connexion with all between heaven and earth, it embraces all.

34. There is *Kh*ien. In its (individual) stillness it is self-absorbed; when exerting its motive power it goes straight forward; and thus it is that its productive action is on a grand scale. There is Khwăn. In its (individual) stillness, it is self-collected and capacious; when exerting its motive power, it develops its resources, and thus its productive action is on a wide scale.

35. In its breadth and greatness, (the Yî) corresponds to heaven and earth; in its ever-recurring changes, it corresponds to the four seasons; in its mention of the bright or active, and the dark or inactive operation, it corresponds to the sun and moon; and the excellence seen in the ease and ready response (of its various operations) corresponds to the perfect operations (presented to us in the phenomena of nature).

Chapter VII.[197] 36. The Master said:—'Is not the Yî a perfect

---

[196] Chapter VI, paragraphs 33-35, goes on further to celebrate the Yî as holding up the mirror to nature in all its operations and in its widest extent. The grandiloquent language, however, amounts only to this, that, when we have made ourselves acquainted with the phenomena of nature, we can, with a heated fancy, see some analogy to them in the changes of the diagrams and lines of the Yî book.

*Kh*ien and Khwăn must be taken as the same names are understood in paragraph 3o above.

'The Yî,' with which paragraph 33 begins, must be understood also at the commencement of paragraph 35. The character which I have translated by 'corresponds' throughout this last chapter, should not, it is observed, have stress laid upon it. *K*û Hsî says that it is simply equal to the 'there is a similarity' of paragraph 22. 'The bright or active element' and 'the dark or inactive' are in the original, 'the yang and the yin.' The correspondence predicated between them and the sun and moon, the brightness and warmth of the one, and the paleness and coldness of the other, shows us how those names arose, and that it is foreign to the original concept of them to call them 'the male and female principles:'—with the last clause compare paragraphs 6-8.

[197] Chapter VII, paragraphs 36, 37, is understood to set forth how the sages embodied the teachings of the Yî in their character and conduct. But when it is said that 'it was by the Yî that they exalted their virtue and enlarged their sphere of occupation,' the meaning can only he that what they did in these directions was in harmony with the principles which they endeavoured to set forth in the symbols of the Yî.

'Their rules of conduct were solid,' in paragraph 36, is, literally, 'their rules were low.' To the height of heaven reached by the wisdom of the sages, the author opposes the low-lying earth, between which and their substantial practices and virtues he discovered some analogy.

It will be seen that the chapter commences with 'The Master said.' *K*û Hsî observes that 'as the Ten Appendixes were all made by the Master, these words are out of place, book?' It was by the Yî that the sages exalted their virtue, and enlarged their sphere of occupation. Their wisdom was high, and their rules of conduct were solid. That loftiness was after the pattern of heaven; that solidity, after the pattern of earth.

37. Heaven and earth having their positions as assigned to them, the changes (of nature) take place between them. The nature (of man) having been completed, and being continually preserved, it is the gate of all good courses and righteousness.

Chapter VIII.[198] 38. The sage was able to survey all the complex phenomena under the sky. He then considered in his mind how they could be figured, and (by means of the diagrams) represented their material forms and their character. Hence these (diagrams) are denominated Semblances (or emblematic figures, the Hsiang).

39. A (later) sage was able to survey the motive influences working all under the sky. He contemplated them in. their common action and special nature, in order to bring out the standard and proper tendency of each. He then appended his explanation (to each line of the diagrams), to determine the good or evil indicated by it. Hence those (lines with their explanations) are denominated Imitations (the Yâo).

40. (The diagrams) speak of the most complex phenomena under

---

and that he conjectures that wherever they occur here and elsewhere, they were added after the sage's time.' Their occurrence very seriously affects the question of the authorship of the Appendixes, which I have discussed in the Introduction, pages 28-30.

[198] Chapter VIII, paragraphs 38-48. In the first two paragraphs here we have an account of the formation of the diagrams, and of the explanation of the whole hexagrams and of the individual lines. 'The sage' in paragraph 38 is intended presumably of Fû-hsî; but we cannot say, from it, whether the writer thought of him as having formed only the eight trigrams, or all the sixty-four hexagrams. In the diagrams, however, we have semblances, or representations, of the phenomena of nature, even the most complex, and hard to be disentangled. Paragraph 39 goes on to speak of the explanation more especially of the individual lines, by the duke of Kâu, as symbolical of good luck or evil, as they turned up in the processes of divination.

Paragraph 40 declares the usableness (so to speak) of the diagrams and the explanations of them; and 41 shows us how a learner or consulter of the Yî would actually proceed in using it.

In paragraphs 42-48 we have the words of Confucius on seven lines in so many hexagrams, or rather his amplification of the words of the duke of Kâu's explanations of their symbolism. The lines are 2 of hexagram 61; 5 of 13; 1 of 28; 3 of 15; 6 of 1; 1 of 60; and 3 of 40. What Confucius says is not without interest, but does not make the principles on which the Yî was made any clearer to us. It shows how his object was to turn the symbolism that he found to a moral or ethical account; and no doubt he could have varied the symbolism, if he had been inclined to do so.

I have spoken in the preceding chapter of the difficulty which the phrase 'The Master said' presents to our accepting the Appendix as from the hand of Confucius himself. But his words in paragraph 43 are in rhyme. He did not speak so. If he rhymed his explanation of the symbolism of the line that is the groundwork of that paragraph, why did he not rhyme his explanations of the other lines? To answer these questions categorically is beyond our power. The facts that suggest them increase the difficulty in ascribing this and the other additions to the Yî to the later sage.

the sky, and yet there is nothing in them that need awaken dislike; the explanations of the lines speak of the subtlest movements under the sky, and yet there is nothing in them to produce confusion.

41. (A learner) will consider what is said (under the diagrams), and then speak; he will deliberate on what is said (in the explanations of the lines), and then move. By such consideration and deliberations he will be able to make all the changes which he undertakes successful.

42. 'Here hid, retired, cries out the crane;
    Her young's responsive cry sounds there.
    Of spirits good I drain this cup;
    With thee a cup I'll freely share.'

The Master said:—'The superior man occupies his apartment and sends forth his words. If they be good, they will be responded to at a distance of more than a thousand lî;—how much more will they be so in the nearer circle! He occupies his apartment and sends forth his words. If they be evil, they will awaken opposition at a distance of more than a thousand lî;—how much more will they do so in the nearer circle! Words issue from one's person, and proceed to affect the people. Actions proceed from what is near, and their effects are seen at a distance. Words and actions are the hinge and spring of the superior man. The movement of that hinge and spring determines glory or disgrace. His words and actions move heaven and earth;—may he be careless in regard to them?'

43'. '(The representative of) the union of men first cries out and weeps, and afterwards laughs.' The Master said, on this,—

    'The ways of good men (different seem).
    This in a public office toils;
    That in his home the time beguiles.
    One man his lips with silence seals;
    Another all his mind reveals.
    But when two men are one in heart,
    Not iron bolts keep them apart;
    The words they in their union use,
    Fragrance like orchid plants diffuse.'

44. 'The first six, (divided), shows its subject placing mats of the white grass beneath what he sets on the ground.' The Master said:—'To place the things on the ground might be considered sufficient; but when he places beneath them mats of the white grass, what occasion for blame can there be? Such a course shows the height of carefulness. The white grass is a trivial thing, but, through the use made of it, it may become important. He who goes forward using such careful art will not fall into any error.'

45. 'A superior man toiling laboriously and yet humble! He will

bring things to an end, and with good fortune.' The Master said on this:—'He toils with success, but does not boast of it; he achieves merit, but takes no virtue to himself from it;—this is the height of generous goodness, and speaks of the man who with (great) merit yet places himself below others. He wishes his virtue to be more and more complete, and in his intercourse with others to be more and more respectful;—he who is so humble, carrying his respectfulness to the utmost, will be able to preserve himself in his position.'

46. 'The dragon (is seen) beyond his proper haunts; there will be occasion for repentance.' The Master said on this:—'He is noble, but is not in his correct place; he is on high, but there are no people to acknowledge him; there is a man of virtue and ability below, but he will not assist him. Hence whatever movement he may make will give occasion for repentance.'

47. 'He does not quit the courtyard before his door;—there will be no occasion for blame.' The Master said on this:—'When disorder arises, it will be found that (ill-advised) speech was the steppingstone to it. If a ruler do not keep secret (his deliberations with his minister), he will lose that minister. If a minister do not keep secret (his deliberations with his ruler), he will lose his life. If (important) matters in the germ be not kept secret, that will be injurious to their accomplishment. Therefore the superior man is careful to maintain secrecy, and does not allow himself to speak.'

48. The Master said:—'The makers of the Yî may be said to have known (the philosophy of) robbery. The Yî says, "He is a burden-bearer, and yet rides in a carriage, thereby exciting robbers to attack him." Burden-bearing is the business of a small man. A carriage is the vehicle of a gentleman. When a small man rides in the vehicle of a gentle man, robbers will think of taking it from him. (When one is) insolent to those above him, and oppressive to those below, robbers will wish to attack him. Careless laying up of things excites to robbery, (as a woman's) adorning of herself excites to lust. What the Yî says about the burden-bearer's riding in a carriage, and exciting robbers to attack him, (shows how) robbery is called out.'

Chapter IX.[199] 49. To heaven belongs (the number) 1; to earth, 2;

---

[199] Chapter IX, paragraphs 49-58, is of a different character from any of the preceding, and treats, unsatisfactorily, of the use of numbers in connexion with the figure of the Yî and the practice of divination.

In the Thang edition of the Yî, published in the seventh century, paragraph 49 is the first of the eleventh chapter according to the arrangement now followed. *Khăng-3ze* restored it to its present place, which it occupied, as has been proved, during the Han dynasty, and to which it properly belongs. It and the next paragraph should be taken together, and are distinct from what follows, though the Thang edition is further confused in placing 51 before 50.

In 49 and 50 'heaven' and 'earth' are used as we have seen Khien and Khwăn are in paragraphs 3o and 34. Odd numbers belong to the strong or undivided line, which is symbolical of the active operation in nature, and the even numbers to the weak or divided line, symbolical of its inaction. The phraseology of the paragraphs, however, can only be understood by a reference to 'the river map,' which has been given in the Introduction, page 19.

The map, as it appeared on the back of 'the dragon-horse,' consisted of so many circles, and so many dark circular markings, the former, it was assumed, being of the yang character, and the latter of the yin. Fû-hsî for the circle substituted the strong or undivided line (———), and for the dark markings the weak or divided (— —). It will be seen that the yang symbols are the 1, 3, 5, 7 and 9 circles, and the yin are the 2, 4, 6, 8 and 10 circular markings, which is the pictorial delineation of paragraph 49. The only thing to be said upon it is that the arrangement of the five circles and ten circular markings is peculiar, and evidently, devised 'for a purpose.' So far, however, as we know, no figure of the map was attempted till after the beginning of our twelfth century.

The same figure is supposed to illustrate what is said in paragraph 50: 'The numbers of the two series correspond to each other in their fixed positions.' 1 and 2, and 3 and 4 certainly front each other, and perhaps 5 and 6; but 7 and 8, and 9 and 10 do not do so in the same way. It is said also that 'each has another that may be considered its mate.' So it is with 1 and 6, 2 and 7, 3 and 8, 4 and 9, but hardly with 5 and 10. Further, 1 + 3 + 5 + 7 + 9 = 25; 2 + 4 + 6 + 8 + 10 = 30; and 25 + 30=55; all of which points are stated.

The last statement in the paragraph, however, derives no illustration, so far as I can see, from the figure. How can the numbers effect the things that are predicated of them? There is a jargon indeed about the formation of the five elements, but in order to make it appear not reasonable, but capable of being related, writers call in 1 the Lo writing' to the aid of 1 the Ho map;' and 'the five elements' is a division of the constituents of material things, which is foreign to the Yî.

Paragraph 51 is intended to describe the process of divination in manipulating the stalks, but the description is confused by introducing into it the four seasons and the subject of intercalation, so as to be very difficult to understand.

In the middle of the Ho map are the five circles symbolical of heaven and the ten dark terrestrial markings (five above and five below the others). These multiplied together give fifty, which form 'the great expansion.' But 50 divining stalks or slips, when divided, give either two odd numbers or two even; and therefore one was put on one side. The remaining 49, however divided, were sure to give two parcels of stalks, one containing an even number of stalks, and the other an odd, and so might be said fancifully to represent the undivided or strong, and the divided or weak line. It is needless to go minutely into the other steps of the process. Then comes in the counting the stalks by four, because there are four seasons in the year, and those that remain represent the intercalary days. But how could such a process be of any value to determine the days necessary to be intercalated in any particular year? The paragraph shows, however, that, when it was written, the rule was to intercalate two months in five years. But it does not say how many days would remain to be carried on to the sixth year after the second intercalation.

Paragraph 52. The actual number of the undivided and divided lines in the hexagrams is the same, 192 of each. But the representative number of an undivided line is 9, and of a divided line 6. Now 9 x 4 (the number of the emblematic figures) x 6 (the lines of each hexagram)=216; and 6 x 4 x 6=144. The sum of these products is 360, which was assumed, for the purpose of working the intercalation, as the standard length of the year. But this was derived from observation, and other considerations;—it did not come out of the Yî.

Paragraphs 53-56. The number in 53 arises thus:—192 (the number of each series of lines in the sixty-four hexagrams) x 36 (obtained as above) =6912, and 192 x 24 = 4608, the sum of which = 11,520. This is said to be 'the number of all things,' the to heaven, 3; to earth, 4; to heaven, 5; to earth, 6; to heaven, 7; to earth, 8; to heaven, 9; to earth, 10.

50. The numbers belonging to heaven are five, and those belonging to earth are (also) five. The numbers of these two series correspond to each other (in their fixed positions), and each one has another that may be considered its mate. The heavenly numbers amount to 25, and the earthly to 30. The numbers of heaven and earth together amount to 55. It is by these that the changes and transformations are effected, and the spirit-like agencies kept in movement.

51. The numbers of the Great Expansion, (multiplied together), make 50, of which (only) 49 are used (in divination). (The stalks representing these) are divided into two heaps to represent the two (emblematic lines, or heaven and earth). One is then taken (from the heap on the right), and placed (between the little finger of the left hand and the next), that there may thus be symbolised the three (powers of heaven, earth, and man). (The heaps on both sides) are manipulated by fours to represent the four seasons; and then the remainders are returned, and placed (between) the two middle fingers of the left hand, to represent the intercalary month. In five years there are two intercalations, and therefore there are two operations; and afterwards the whole process is repeated.

52. The numbers (required) for *Kh*ien (or the undivided line) amount to 216; those for Khwăn (or the divided line), to 144. Together they are 36o, corresponding to the days of the year.

53. The number produced by the lines in the two parts (of the Yî) amount to 11,520, corresponding to the number of all things.

54. Therefore by means of the four operations is the Yî completed. It takes 18 changes to form a hexagram.

55. (The formation of) the eight trigrams constitutes the small completion (of the Yî).

56. If we led on the diagrams and expanded them, if we prolonged each by the addition of the proper lines, then all events possible under

---

meaning of which I do not know. The 'four operations' are those described in paragraph 31. They were thrice repeated in divination to determine each new line, and of course it took eighteen of them to form a hexagram. The diagrams might be extended ad infinitum, both in the number of lines and of figures, by the natural process of their formation as shown in the Introduction, page 18, without the aid of the divining stalks; and no sufficient reason can be given why the makers of the figures stopped at sixty-four.

It is difficult to believe the first statement in paragraph 57 and to understand the second. What is it 'to Shăn or spiritualise virtuous actions?' The concluding statement approximates to impiety.

We may grant what is affirmed in paragraph 58, but does the Yî really give us any knowledge of the processes of change and transformation in nature? What wiser are we after all the affirmations about numbers? 'Change' = changings, understood actively:— the work of Heaven; 'transformations' = evolution:—the finish given by earth to the changing caused by Heaven.

the sky might have their representation.

57. (The diagrams) make manifest (by their appended explanations), the ways (of good and ill fortune), and show virtuous actions in their spiritual relations. In this way, by consulting them, we may receive an answer (to our doubts), and we may also by means of them assist the spiritual (power in its agency in nature and providence).

58. The Master said:—'He who knows the method of change and transformation may be said to know what is done by that spiritual (power).'

Chapter X.[200] 59. In the Yî there are four things characteristic of the way of the sages. We should set the highest value on its explanations to guide us in speaking; on its changes for (the initiation of) our movements; on its emblematic figures for (definite action as in) the construction of implements; and on its prognostications for our practice of divination.

60. Therefore, when a superior man is about to take action of a more private or of a public character, he asks (the Yî), making his inquiry in words. It receives his order, and the answer comes as the echo's response. Be the subject remote or near, mysterious or deep, he forthwith knows of what kind will be the coming result. (If the Yî) were not the most exquisite thing under heaven, would it be concerned in such an operation as this?

---

[200] Chapter X, paragraphs 59-65, enlarges on the service rendered to men by the Yî, owing to the way in which it was made by the sages to express their views and carry into effect their wishes.

Paragraph 59 mentions the four things in which its usefulness appears. 'The emblematic figures' are the four hsiang, which are produced by the manipulation of the undivided and divided lines, and whose representative numbers are 9, 8, 7, 6. 'Divination' appears in the paragraph as pû-shih, which means 'divination by the tortoise-shell and by the stalks.' But the tortoise-shell had nothing to do with the use of the Yî. Before the composition of these Appendixes the two terms must have been combined to express the practice of divination, without reference to its mode.

Paragraph 60 speaks of the explanations and prognostications of the Yî. The 'exquisiteness' ascribed to it would be due to the sages who had devised it, and appended their explanations to it; but the whole thing has no existence save in cloud-land.

Paragraph 61 speaks of the operations with the stalks till the various changes in the results issued in the determination of the emblematic figures, and then in the fixing of the individual lines and entire hexagrams. Even Kû Hsî admits that the references to the different processes are now hardly intelligible.

Paragraph 62. How could the writer speak of the Yî without thought or action as being most 'spirit-like?' If it did what he asserts, those who contrived it might be so described? They would have been beings whose operation was indeed like that of spirits, inscrutable, 'unfathomable' (paragraph 32), even like that of the Spirit of God (VI, 10).

Paragraphs 63 and 64 ought not to be taken as saying that the sages did the things described for themselves by the Yî. They knew them of themselves, and made the Yî that others might come by it to do the same. So the writer imagined. No words could indicate more clearly than those of paragraph 65 that the paragraphs between it and 59 did not come from Confucius, but from the compiler of the Great Appendix, whoever he was.

61. (The stalks) are manipulated by threes and fives to determine (one) change; they are laid on opposite sides, and placed one up, one down, to make sure of their numbers; and the (three necessary) changes are gone through with in this way, till they form the figures pertaining to heaven or to earth. Their numbers are exactly determined, and the emblems of (all things) under the sky are fixed. (If the Yî) were not the thing most capable of change of all things under heaven, how could it effect such a result as this?

62. In (all these operations forming) the Yî, there is no thought and no action. It is still and without movement; but, when acted on, it penetrates forthwith to all phenomena and events under the sky. If it were not the most spirit-like thing under the sky, how could it be found doing this?

63. The (operations forming the) Yî are the method by which the sages searched out exhaustively what was deep, and investigated the minutest springs (of things).

64. 'Those operations searched out what was deep:'—therefore they could penetrate to the views of all under the sky. 'They made apparent the minutest springs of (things):'—therefore they could bring to a completion all undertakings under the sky. 'Their action was spirit-like:'—therefore they could make speed without hurry, and reached their destination without travelling.

65. This is the import of what the Master said, that 'In the Yî there are four things indicating the way of the sages.'

Chapter XI.[201] 66. The Master said:—'What is it that the Yî does?

---

[201] Chapter XI, paragraphs 66-74, treats of divination, and the scheme of it supplied in the Yî. That scheme must be referred first to Heaven, which produced the spirit-like things,—the divining-plant and the tortoise; and next to the sages, who knew the mind of Heaven, and made the plant and shell subservient to the purpose for which they were intended.

Paragraph 66 answers the question of what the Yî does; and if there were truth or reason in it, the book and its use would be most important. I have closed the quotation of "the Master's" words at the end of the paragraph; but really- we do not know if they extend so far, or farther.

Paragraphs 67 and 68 glorify the sages and their work. The virtues of the divining-plant all belonged to them, and it was thus that they were able to organise the scheme of divination. The production of 'the spirit-like things' is, in paragraph 73, ascribed to Heaven;' the characters about them in these paragraphs mean no more than is expressed in the translation.

Paragraph 69 shows how the antinomy of the yin and yang pervades all nature, and how the sages turned it, as existing preeminently in the divining-plant, to account.

Paragraph 70. Evidently the author had in view here the genesis of the diagrams of the Yî, the number of figures increasing in a geometrical progression with the ratio of 2, while the lines of the figures form an arithmetical progression with the common difference of 1. This is quite plain after 'the two elementary forms ( ▬▬▬ and ▬ ▬ )' have been made. They give birth to 'the four emblematic symbols,' each of two lines ( ▬▬▬, ▬▬ ▬, ▬ ▬▬, ▬ ▬ ▬ ▬, known, in this order, as the Grand or

The Yî opens up (the knowledge of the issues of) things, accomplishes the undertakings (of men), and embraces under it (the way of) all things under the sky. This and nothing more is what the Yî does. Thereby the sages, through (divination by) it, would give their proper course to the aims of all under the sky, would give stability to their undertakings, and determine their doubts.'

67. Therefore the virtue of the stalks is versatile and spirit-like; that of the diagrams is exact and wise; and the meaning given by the six lines is changeful to give (the proper information to men). The sages having, by their possession of these (three virtues), cleansed their minds, retired and laid them up in the secrecy (of their own

---

old Yang, the young Yin, the young Yang, and the Grand or old Yin). By the addition to each of these symbols first of the yang line, and then of the yin, there arise the eight trigrams, each of three lines and the process of formation might be continued indefinitely.

But how was the first step taken in the formation of the two elementary lines? Here, it is said, they were produced by the Thâi Kî, or the Grand Terminus. This is represented in *K*û Hsî's 'Youth's Introduction to the Study of the Yî,' by a circle; but he tells us that that representation of it was first made by *K*âu-ʒze (A.D. 1017-1073, called also *K*âu Tun-î, *K*âu Mâu-shû, and, most of all, *K*âu Lien-*kh*î), and that his readers must be careful not to suppose that Fû-hsî had such a figure in his mind's eye. I fail myself to understand how there can be generated from a circle the undivided and the broken line. Given those two lines, and the formation of the sixty-four hexagrams proceeds regularly according to the method above described. We must start from them, whether we can account or not for the rise of the idea of them in the mind of Fû-hsî.

Leaving the subject of the figure of the Thâi *K*î, the name gives us hardly any clue to its meaning. *K*î is used for the extreme term of anything, as the ridge-pole of a house, or the pinnacle of a pagoda. The comment on the first sentence in the paragraph by Wang Pî (A.D. 226-249) is:—'Existence must begin in nonexistence, and therefore the Grand Terminus produced the two elementary Forms. Thâi *K*î is the denomination of what has no denomination. As it cannot be named, the text takes the extreme point of anything that exists as an analogous term for the Thâi *K*î.' Expanding Wang's comment, Khung Ying-tâ says:—'Thâi *K*î means the original subtle matter, that formed the one chaotic mass before heaven and earth were divided;' and then he refers to certain passages in Lâo-ʒze's Tâo Teh King, and identifies the Thâi *K*î with his Tâo. This would seem to give to Thâi *K*î a material meaning. The later philosophers of the Sung school, however, insist on its being immaterial, now calling it lî, the principle of order in nature, now tâo, the defined course of things, now Tî, the Supreme Power or God, now shin, the spiritual working of God. According to *Kh*ăng-ʒze, all these names are to be referred to that of 'Heaven,' of which they express so many different concepts.

Paragraph 71 speaks of divination in practice, and paragraph 72 celebrates the service done by that through the plant and shell, as equal to, and indeed the complement of, all the other services rendered by heaven and earth, the seasons, the sun and moon, the sages, and the greatest potentates. Surely, it is all very extravagant.

The last two paragraphs resume the theme of the making of the Yî by the sages, and their teaching the practice of divination. Of the Ho map and the Lo writing, I have spoken in the introduction, pages 18-21. But if we accept the statement that the Lo writing had anything to do with the making of the Yî, we must except Fû-hsî from the sages to whom we are indebted for it. It was to the Great Yü, more than a thousand years later than Fû-hsî, that the Lo disclosed its writing; and Yü is never said to have had anything to do with the Yî. Nor is either of these things mentioned in Section ii, paragraph 11, where the work of Fû-hsî is described more in detail.

consciousness). But their sympathies were with the people in regard both to their good fortune and evil. By their spirit-like ability they knew (the character of) coming events, and their wisdom had stored up (all experiences of) the past. Who could be able to accomplish all this? (Only our) ancient sages, quick in apprehension and clear in discernment, of far-reaching intelligence, and all-embracing knowledge, and with a majesty, going spirit-like to its objects;—it was only they who could do so.

68. Therefore (those sages), fully understanding the way of Heaven, and having clearly ascertained the experience of the people, instituted (the employment of) these spirit-like things, as a provision for the use of the people. The sages went about the employment of them (moreover) by purifying their hearts and with reverent caution, thereby giving (more) spirituality and intelligence to their virtue.

69. Thus, a door shut may be pronounced (analogous to) Khwăn (or the inactive condition), and the opening of the door (analogous to) *Kh*ien (or the active condition). The opening succeeding the being shut may be pronounced (analogous to what we call) a change; and the passing from one of these states to the other may be called the constant course (of things).

The (first) appearance of anything (as a bud) is what we call a semblance; when it has received its complete form, we call it a definite thing.

(The divining-plant having been produced, the sages) set it apart and laid down the method of its employment,—what we call the laws (of divination). The advantage arising from it in external and internal matters, so that the people all use it, stamps it with a character which we call spirit-like.

7o. Therefore in (the system of) the Yî there is the Grand Terminus, which produced the two elementary Forms. Those two Forms produced the Four emblematic Symbols, which again produced the eight Trigrams.

71. The eight trigrams served to determine the good and evil (issues of events), and from this determination was produced the (successful prosecution of the) great business (of life).

72. Therefore of all things that furnish models and visible figures there are none greater than heaven and earth; of things that change and extend an influence (on others) there are none greater than the four seasons; of things suspended (in the sky) with their figures displayed clear and bright, there are none greater than the sun and moon; of the honoured and exalted there are none greater than he who is the rich and noble (one); in preparing things for practical use, and inventing and making instruments for the benefit of all under the sky, there are none greater than the sages; to explore what is complex, search out what is hidden, to hook up what lies deep, and reach to what is distant, thereby

determining (the issues) for good or ill of all events under the sky, and making all men under heaven full of strenuous endeavours, there are no (agencies) greater than those of the stalks and the tortoise-shell.

73. Therefore Heaven produced the spirit-like things, and the sages took advantage of them. (The operations of) heaven and earth are marked by (so many) changes and transformations; and the sages imitated them (by means of the Yî). Heaven hangs out its (brilliant) figures from which are seen good fortune and bad, and the sages made their emblematic interpretations accordingly. The Ho gave forth the map, and the Lo the writing, of (both of) which the sages took advantage.

74. In the (scheme of the) Yî there are the four symbolic figures by which they inform men (in divining of the lines making up the diagrams); the explanations appended to them convey the significance (of the diagrams and lines); and the determination (of the divination) as fortunate or the reverse, to settle the doubts (of men).

Chapter XII.[202] 75. It is said in the Yî, 'Help is given to him from

---

[202] Chapter XII, paragraphs 75-81, endeavours to show how we have in the Yî a representation of the changing phenomena of nature, and such a representation as words or speech could not convey.

Paragraph 75 has a good meaning, taken by itself; but it has no apparent connexion with the rest of the chapter. Kû Hsî thought it was misplaced in its present position, and should be at the end of chapter 8. Compare paragraph 14.

The first two statements of paragraph 76 are general, but made here specially to exalt the Yî, as teaching more clearly and fully than written characters could have done. The Khang-hsî editors decide that I the emblematic figures' here are the eight trigrams of Fû-hsî,—against the view of Kû Hsî, which restricts them to signify the undivided and divided lines. The repetition of the words, 'The Master said,' is probably the error of an early transcriber.

Paragraphs 77 and 78 refer to the phenomena of nature and the course of human affairs, as suggesting and controlling the formation of the system of the Yî. The formation of that becomes the subject in paragraph 79. Khien and Khwăn are used, as we have already seen them more than once, for the active and inactive conditions in nature, indicated by the divided and undivided lines. It is difficult to translate what is said in paragraph 78, about Tâo and Khî;—what I have called, 'an ideal method' and 'a definite' thing. P. Regis translates the text by—'Quod non est inter figurata aut corporea sed supereminet est rationale, est ratio, Tâo; quod (est) inter figurata subjacetque certae figurae est sensibile, est instrumentum! But tâo cannot here signify ratio or reason; for tâo and khî are names for the same thing under different conditions; first as a possibility, and next as an actuality. Such is the natural interpretation of the text, and so all the great scholars of the Sung dynasty construed it, as may be seen in the 'Collected Comments' of the imperial edition. So far they were correct, however many of them might stumble and fall in confounding this 'ideal method' with God.

What follows in the paragraph has no connexion with these two statements. P. Regis, who divides his translation into two paragraphs, says:—'Satis patet utramque textus hujus partem. non cohaerere. Quod ergo illas divisimus, id fecimus majoris perspicuitatis causa, non ratione ordinis qui certe nullus est, ut in re potius assuta quam connexa.'

Paragraph 79 is a repetition of paragraphs 38, 39, 'to introduce,' says Kû Hsî, 'the

Heaven. There will be good fortune; advantage in every respect.' The Master said:—'Yû (祐) is the symbol of assisting. He whom Heaven assists is observant (of what is right); he whom men assist is sincere. The individual here indicated treads the path of sincerity and desires to be observant (of what is right), and studies to exalt the worthy. Hence "Help is given to him from Heaven. There will be good fortune, advantage in every respect."'

76. The Master said:—'The written characters are not the full exponent of speech, and speech is not the full expression of ideas;—is it impossible then to discover the ideas of the sages?' The Master said:—'The sages made their emblematic symbols to set forth fully their ideas; appointed (all) the diagrams to show fully the truth and falsehood (of things); appended their explanations to give the full expression of their words; and changed (the various lines) and made general the method of doing so, to exhibit fully what was advantageous. They (thus) stimulated (the people) as by drums and dances, thereby completely developing the spirit-like (character of the Yî).'

77. May we not say that *Kh*ien and Khwăn [= the yang and yin, or the undivided and divided lines] are the secret and substance of the Yî? *Kh*ien and Khwăn being established in their several places, the system of changes was thereby constituted. If *Kh*ien and Khwăn were taken away, there would be no means of seeing that system; and if that system were not seen, *Kh*ien and Khwăn would almost cease to act.

78. Hence that which is antecedent to the material form exists, we say, as an ideal method, and that which is subsequent to the material form exists, we say, as a definite thing.

Transformation and shaping is what we call change; carrying this out and operating with it is what we call generalising the method; taking the result and setting it forth for all the people under heaven is, we say, (securing the success of) the business of life.

79. Hence, to speak of the emblematic figures:—(The sage) was able to survey all the complex phenomena under the sky. He then considered in his mind how they could be figured, and (by means of the diagrams) represented their material forms and their character. Hence those (diagrams) are denominated Semblances. A (later) sage was able to survey the motive influences working all under the sky. He contemplated them in their common action and special nature, in order to bring out the standard and proper tendency of each. He then

---

two paragraphs' that follow.

The editors of the imperial edition find in 80, 81, an amplification mainly of 76, showing how what is said there of the natural phenomena is exhibited in the Yî. The concluding sentence is a declaration (hardly necessary) about the sage makers, to the effect that they were as distinguished for virtuous conduct as for wisdom,—'the proper men' to stand between Heaven and the mass of men as they did.

appended his explanation (to each line), to determine the good or evil indicated by it. Hence those (lines with their explanations) are denominated Imitations (the Yâo).

80. The most thorough mastery of all the complex phenomena under the sky is obtained from the diagrams. The greatest stimulus to movement in adaptation to all affairs under the sky is obtained from the explanations.

81. The transformations and shaping that take place are obtained from the changes (of the lines); the carrying this out and operating with it is obtained from the general method (that has been established). The seeing their spirit-like intimations and understanding them depended on their being the proper men; and the completing (the study of) them by silent meditation, and securing the faith of others without the use of words, depended on their virtuous conduct.

### SECTION II.

Chapter I.[203] 1. The eight trigrams having been completed in their proper order, there were in each the (three) emblematic lines. They were then multiplied by a process of addition till the (six) component

---

[203] Chapter I, paragraphs 1-10, is an amplification, according to Khung Ying-tâ and the editors of the imperial edition of the present dynasty, of the second chapter of Section i. The latter say that as all the chapters of Section i from the third onwards serve to elucidate chapter 2, so it is with this chapter and all that follow in this Section. The formation of the diagrams, and of their several lines, their indication of good fortune and bad, and the analogy between the processes of nature and the operations of divination, and other kindred subjects, are all touched on.

The order of the eight trigrams in paragraph 1, is *kh*ien, tui, lî, *k*ăn, sun, khan, kăn, khwăn. The three lines of each are emblematic,—the first of heaven, the second of man, the third of earth. This is the most likely explanation of hsiang, 'the emblems' or 'similitudes' here. Why the maker—'sages'—stopt at sixty-four figures, of six lines each, is a question that cannot be answered.

Paragraph 2. Of course it was a great delusion to suppose that the changes of lines consequent on divination could be so connected with the movements of life as to justify the characterising them as good or evil, or afford any guidance in the ordering of conduct.

Paragraph 4. Who can tell 'the requirements of the time' amid the complexity of the phenomena of nature or the ever-varying events of human experience and history? The wiser men are, the more correct will be their judgments in such matters; but is there any reason for trusting to divination about them?

Paragraphs 5, 6. It is difficult to say what is 'the exact rule' intended here; unless it be that the factors in every movement shall act according to their proper nature. The Khang-hsî editors say:—'We see the good sometimes meeting with misfortune, and the bad with good fortune; but such is not the general rule.' 'The lessons that heaven and earth give forth' are those concerning the method of their operation as stated in paragraph 7, and more fully in 6, 7, 8 of Section i.

What is said in paragraph 10 is striking and important, and in harmony with the general strain of Confucian teaching;—as in the Great Learning, chapter 10, and many other places; but I fail to see its appropriateness in its present place in the Yî.

lines appeared.

2. The strong line and the weak push themselves each into the place of the other, and hence the changes (of the diagrams) take place. The appended explanations attach to every form of them its character (of good or ill), and hence the movements (suggested by divination) are determined accordingly.

3. Good fortune and ill, occasion for repentance or regret, all arise from these movements.

4. The strong and the weak (lines) have their fixed and proper places (in the diagrams); their changes, however varied, are according to the requirements of the time (when they take place).

5. Good fortune and ill are continually prevailing each against the other by an exact rule.

6. By the same rule, heaven and earth, in their course, continually give forth (their lessons); the sun and moon continually emit their light; all the movements under the sky are constantly subject to this one and the same rule.

7. *Kh*ien, (the symbol of heaven, and) conveying the idea of strength, shows to men its easy (and natural) action. *Kh*wăn, (the symbol of earth, and) conveying the idea of docility, shows to men its compendious (receptivity and operation).

8. The Yâo (or lines) are imitative representations of this. The Hsiang, or emblematic figures, are pictorial representations of the same.

9. The movements of the lines and figures take place (at the hand of the operator), and are unseen; the good fortune or ill is seen openly and is beyond. The work to be done appears by the changes; the sympathies of the sages are seen in their explanations.

10. The great attribute of heaven and earth is the giving and maintaining life. What is most precious for the sage is to get the (highest) place—(in which he can be the human representative of heaven and earth). What will guard this position for him? Men. How shall he collect a large population round him? By the power of his wealth. The right administration of that wealth, correct instructions to the people, and prohibitions against wrong-doing;—these constitute his righteousness.

Chapter II.[204] 11. Anciently, when Pâo-hsî had come to the rule of

---

[204] Chapter II, paragraphs 11-23, treats of the progress. of civilisation in China, and how the great men of antiquity who led the way in the various steps of that progress were guided by the Yî. Only five of these are mentioned;—the first, Fû-hsî, the beginning of whose reign, according to the least unlikely of the chronological accounts, must be placed in the 34th century B. C., while Shun's reign ended in B. C. 2203. The time embraced in this chapter therefore is about twelve centuries and a half. But the writer gives his own opinion that the various discoveries and inventions mentioned were suggested to their

all under heaven, looking up, he contemplated the brilliant forms exhibited in the sky, and looking down he surveyed the patterns shown on the earth. He contemplated the ornamental appearances of birds and beasts and the (different) suitabilities of the soil. Near at hand, in his own person, he found things for consideration, and the same at a distance, in things in general. On this he devised the eight trigrams, to show fully the attributes of the spirit-like and intelligent (operations working secretly), and to classify the qualities of the myriads of things.

12. He invented the making of nets of various kinds by knitting strings, both for hunting and fishing. The idea of this was taken, probably, from Lî (the third trigram, and thirtieth hexagram).

13. On the death of Pâo-hsî, there arose Shǎn-nǎng (in his place). He fashioned wood to form the share, and bent wood to make the

---

authors by certain hexagrams of the Yî. The most commonly received view, however, is that Fû-hsî had only the eight trigrams, and that the multiplication of them to the 64 hexagrams was the work of king Wǎn, fully a thousand years later than Shun. This is the view of the editors of the imperial Yî. If it be contended that Fû-hsî himself multiplied his trigrams, and gave their names to the resulting hexagrams, how could he have wrapped tip in them the intimations of discoveries which were not made till many centuries after his death? The statements in the chapter cannot be received as historical. It came from another hand, and not from Confucius himself. The writer or compiler gives the legends current about the various inventions of his time. The making of the trigrams is placed first of all to do honour to the Yî. The account of it is different from that given in paragraph 73 of the former Section, and we hear nothing of the Ho map or Lo writing.

Paragraph 11. Pâo-hsî here and in 13 is the same as Fû-hsî. As Pâo is written here, there is no meaning in it; but another character Phâo ( 庖 ) is more common, and Phâo-hsî would mean the inventor of the kitchen and cookery. This was the first step towards civilisation, and was appropriately followed by the hunting and fishing—both by means of nets—in paragraph 12.

Paragraphs 13, 14 celebrate the work of Shǎn-nǎng, 'the marvellous or spirit-like husbandman.' There was no metal about the primitive plough. The market for the exchange of commodities, without the use of coin, was an important advance.

The invention of the robes, or of dress, mentioned in paragraph 15, would seem to show that previously men had been in a very rude state. The passage indicates, however, the courtesies and proprieties of social life, in which dress plays an important part, and which now began to be organised.

The infant navigation in paragraph 16 was as little indebted to the use of metal as the agriculture of 13.

Paragraphs 17 and 18 show that in those primitive times there were already the practices of rapine and war. 'The double gates' were those of the city wall, and of the enclosed suburb. The clapper may still be heard all over China. Bows and arrows, however, came rather later, as in 20.

I suppose 'the sages' in paragraphs 21, 22, 23 refer generally to the great names mentioned in the previous chapters; nor can we define the distinction in the writer or compiler's mind between 'antiquity' and 'the highest antiquity.' Compare what is said on the rise of the coffin in 22 with Mencius' remarks on the same subject in Book III, ii, 5. 4. He would hardly have expressed himself as he did, if he had been familiar with this text. The invention of written characters is generally ascribed to Fû-hsî. Paragraph 23 does not say so, but the inventor is said to have been a sage of a subsequent age to the time of 'high antiquity.' That 'high antiquity' must stretch back very far.

plough-handle. The advantages of ploughing and weeding were then taught to all under heaven. The idea of this was taken, probably, from Yî (the forty-second hexagram).

14. He caused markets to be held at midday, thus bringing together all the people, and assembling in one place all their wares. They made their exchanges and retired, every one having got what he wanted. The idea of this was taken, probably, from Shih Ho (the twenty-first hexagram).

15. After the death of Shăn-năng, there arose Hwang Tî, Yâo, and Shun. They carried through the (necessarily occurring) changes, so that the people did (what was required of them) without being wearied; yea, they exerted such a spirit-like transformation, that the people felt constrained to approve their (ordinances) as right. When a series of changes has run all its course, another change ensues. When it obtains free course, it will continue long. Hence it was that 'these (sovereigns) were helped by Heaven; they had good fortune, and their every movement was advantageous.' Hwang Tî, Yâo, and Shun (simply) wore their upper and lower garments (as patterns to the people), and good order was secured all under heaven. The idea of all this was taken, probably, from *K*hien and Khwăn (the first and eighth trigrams, or the first and second hexagrams).

16. They hollowed out trees to form canoes; they cut others long and thin to make oars. Thus arose the benefit of canoes and oars for the help of those who had no means of intercourse with others. They could now reach the most distant parts, and all under heaven were benefited. The idea of this was taken., probably, from Hwân (the fifty-ninth hexagram).

17. They used oxen (in carts) and yoked horses (to chariots), thus providing for the carriage of what was heavy, and for distant journeys,—thereby benefiting all under the sky. The idea of this was taken, probably, from Sui (the seventeenth hexagram).

18. They made the (defence of the) double gates, and (the warning of) the clapper, as a preparation against the approach of marauding visitors. The idea of this was taken, probably, from Yü (the sixteenth hexagram).

19. They cut wood and fashioned it into pestles; they dug in the ground and formed mortar's. Thus the myriads of the people received the benefit arising from the use of the pestle and mortar. The idea of this was taken, probably, from Hsiâo Kwo (the sixty-second hexagram).

20. They bent wood by means of string so as to form bows, and sharpened wood so as to make arrows. This gave the benefit of bows and arrows, and served to produce everywhere a feeling of awe. The idea of this was taken, probably, from Khwei (the thirty-eighth hexagram).

21. In the highest antiquity they made their homes (in winter) in caves, and (in summer) dwelt in the open country. In subsequent ages, for these the sages substituted houses, with the ridge-beam above and the projecting roof below, as a provision against wind and rain. The idea of this was taken, probably, from Tâ *K*wang (the thirty-fourth hexagram).

22. When the ancients buried their dead, they covered the body thickly with pieces of wood, having laid it in the open country. They raised no mound over it, nor planted trees around; nor had they any fixed period for mourning. In subsequent ages the sages substituted for these practices the inner and outer coffins. The idea of this was taken, probably, from Tâ Kwo (the twenty-eighth hexagram).

23. In the highest antiquity, government was carried on successfully by the use of knotted cords (to preserve the memory of things). In subsequent ages the sages substituted for these written characters and bonds. By means of these (the doings of) all the officers could be regulated, and (the affairs of) all the people accurately examined. The idea of this was taken, probably, from Kwâi (the forty-third hexagram).

Chapter III.[205] 24. Therefore what we call the Yî is (a collection of) emblematic lines. They are styled emblematic as being resemblances.

25. What we call the Thwan (or king Wăn's explanations) are based on the significance (of each hexagram as a whole).

26. We call the lines (of the figures) Yâo from their being according to the movements taking place all under the sky.

27. In this way (we see) the rise of good fortune and evil, and the

---

[205] Chapter III, paragraphs 24-27, treats of the Yî as made up of figurative diagrams, which again are composed of lines ever changing, in accordance with the phenomena of nature and human experience, while to the resulting figures their moral character and providential issues are appended by the sages. It may be regarded as an epitome of chapter 2 in Section i.

Paragraph 24. It is observed by the editors of the imperial edition that a chapter should not begin with a 'therefore;' and they are inclined to agree with many critics who would enter this as the last paragraph of the preceding chapter. In that case it would be a summing-up of the concluding sentences of the different paragraphs, the truth and genuineness of which are deservedly suspected. The characters for 'therefore,' however, are very loosely used in these Appendixes.—The lines, as they were intended by Fû-hsî, were emblematic; and they are still more so, as interpreted by the duke of Kâu. Meanings are drawn from the figures that resemble or illustrate principles in the subjects to which they are applied.

Paragraph 25. The character rendered 'the significance' means materials, and is illustrated by reference to all the different materials out of which a house is composed. So there are half-a-dozen things about the diagrams, their lineal structure, emblematic intention, their attributes, &c., out of which their interpretation is fashioned.

Paragraph 26. E.g. an undivided line may appear in an odd place, which is right, or in an even place, which is wrong; and the case is the opposite with the divided lines. But what has this to do with the right or wrong of the events divined about?

manifestation of repentance and regret.

Chapter IV.[206] 28. In the Yang trigrams (or those of the undivided line) there are more of the Yin lines, and in the Yin trigrams (or those of the divided line) there are more of the Yang lines.

29. What is the cause of this? It is because the Yang lines are odd (or made by one stroke), and the Yin lines are even (or. made by two strokes).

30. What (method of) virtuous conduct is thus intimated? In the Yang trigrams we have one ruler, and two subjects,—suggesting the way of the superior man. In the Yin trigrams we have two rulers, and one subject,—suggesting the way of the small man.

Chapter V.[207] 31. It is said in the Yî, 'Full of anxious thoughts you

---

[206] Chapter IV, paragraphs 28-30. Of the distinction of the trigrams into Yang and Yin.

The trigrams that contain only one undivided line—*kăn* (☵), khan (☵), and kăn (☶)—are called Yang. The undivided line is called 'the lord' in them. It is just the opposite with the Yin trigrams, in which there are two undivided lines, and one divided,—sun (☴), lî (☲), and tui (☱). These together constitute the 'six children,' or 'three sons' and 'three daughters' in the later arrangement of the trigrams, ascribed to king Wăn.

Paragraph 29. Each part of the divided line counts as one hence a yang trigram counts as $1 + 2 + 2 = 5$ strokes, four of which are yin, while a yin trigram counts as $2 + 1 + 1 = 4$, only two of which are yang. But this is mere trifling.

In explanation of paragraph 30 it is said that 'we have in the yang trigrams two (or more) subjects serving one ruler, and in the yin one subject serving two rulers, and two rulers striving together for the allegiance of one Subject.' This is ingenious, but fanciful; as indeed this distinction of the trigrams into a yang class and a yin is a mere play of fancy.

[207] Chapter V, paragraphs 31-44, gives the words of the duke of *K*âu on eleven different lines in the Text of the Yî, along with remarks of Confucius in farther illustration of them. But they seem also to be intended to bring forth more fully the meaning of certain previous utterances about the structure and scope of the Yî.

Paragraphs 31-34 start from the fourth line of the 31st hexagram, which would seem merely to require a steady and unvarying purpose in any one, in order to the full development of his influence. The editors of the imperial edition, however, make the whole a sequel of paragraph 5. But granted that there is no 'anxious scheming' in the processes of the natural world or in the phenomena of insect life, there is really no analogy to their proceedings in the course of the man who makes himself master of 'the nature and reasons of things,' as described in 33 and 34. Nor are 'the nature and reasons of things' to be found in the Yî, as the writer believed they were. Such as it is, it requires immense thought to understand it, and when we have laid hold of it, there is nothing substantial in our grasp. The 'virtue' predicated of such attainment is not so much moral excellence, as apprehension and the power and ability to invent, and to affect others.

Paragraph 35. See on the third line of Khwăn, the 47th hexagram. If we were to translate the explanations of the line after Confucius, we should put the first two statements hypothetically; but the four that compose it seem to run on in the same way. They are all, I apprehend, hypothetical.

Paragraph 36. See on the last line of *K*ieh, the 40th hexagram.

Paragraph 37. See on the first line of Shih Ho, the 21st hexagram. The 'self-correction in what is small' implies of course that the small man has been 'awed.' What go and come; (only) friends will follow you and think with you.' The Master said:—'In all (the processes taking place) under heaven, what is there of thinking? what is there of anxious scheming? They all come to the same (successful) issue, though by different paths; there is one result, though there might be a hundred anxious schemes. What is there of thinking? what is there of anxious scheming?'

32. The sun goes and the moon comes; the moon goes and the sun comes;—the sun and moon thus take the place each of the other, and their shining is the result. The cold goes and the heat comes; the heat goes and the cold comes;—it is by this mutual succession of the cold and heat that the year is completed. That which goes becomes less and less, and that which comes waxes more and more;—it is by the influence on each other of this contraction and expansion that the advantages (of the different conditions) are produced.

33. When the looper coils itself up, it thereby straightens itself again; when worms and snakes go into the state of hybernation, they thereby keep themselves alive. (So), when we minutely investigate the nature and reasons (of things), till we have entered into the inscrutable and spirit-like in them, we attain to the largest practical application of them; when that application becomes the quickest and readiest, and all personal restfulness is secured, our virtue is thereby exalted.

34. Going on beyond this, we reach a point which it is hardly possible to know. We have thoroughly comprehended the inscrutable and spirit-like, and know the processes of transformation;—this is the

---

is said about him here is true; but we hardly expect it in this place.

Paragraph 38 should probably begin, like those before and after it, with 'The Master said.' The characters quoted from the Yî are again from the text of Shih Ho, on the last line.

Paragraph 39. See on the fifth line of Phî, the 12th hexagram.

Paragraph 40 gives Confucius' views on the fourth line of Ting, the 50th hexagram.

In paragraph 41 we are conducted to the 16th 'hexagram,—the second line of it. The being 'firm as a rock' is understood to symbolise the state of 'rest,' the quiet self-possession out of which successful movement and action is understood to spring.

In paragraph 42, 'the son of the Yen family' is Yen Hui, the favourite disciple of Confucius. The passage quoted from the Yî is that on the first line of Fû, the 24th hexagram.

To paragraph 43, as to paragraph 38, I would prefix the characters for 'The Master said.' 'Male and female' is to be taken generally, and not confined to the individuals of the human pair. One Chinese writer says that in the transformations ascribed to heaven and earth, birds, fishes, animals, and plants are included, but from the 'transformation in its living types' plants are excluded, because in their generation there is nothing analogous to the emission and reception of seed. Other Chinese writers, however, are well enough acquainted with the sexual system of plants. It would seem to me that Confucius, if the paragraph were really his, intended only plants or the vegetable world in his reference to the operation of heaven and earth, and had all living tribes in view in his mention of male and female. The passage of the Yî referred to is on the third line of Sun, the 41st hexagram. The application of it is far-fetched.

Paragraph 44. See on the fifth line of Yî, the 42nd hexagram.

fulness of virtue.

35. It is said in the Yî, '(The third line shows its subject) distressed before a rock, and trying to lay hold of thorns; entering into his palace and not seeing his wife:—there will be evil.' The Master said:—'If one be distressed by what need not distress him, his name is sure to be disgraced; if he lay hold on what he should not touch, his life is sure to be imperilled. In disgrace and danger, his death will (soon) come;—is it possible for him in such circumstances to see his wife?'

36. It is said in the Yî, 'The duke with (his bow) shoots at the falcon on the top of the high wall; he hits it:—his every movement will be advantageous.' The Master said:—'The falcon is a bird (of prey); the bow and arrow is a weapon (of war); the shooter is a man. The superior man keeps his weapon concealed about his person, and waits for the proper time to move;—doing this, how should his movement be other than successful? There is nothing to fetter or embarrass his movement; and hence, when he comes forth, he succeeds in his object. The language speaks of movement when the instrument necessary to it is ready and perfect.'

37. The Master said:—'The small man is not ashamed of what is not benevolent, nor does he fear to do what is not righteous. Without the prospect of gain he does not stimulate himself to what is good, nor does he correct himself without being moved. Self-correction, however, in what is small will make him careful in what would be of greater consequence;—and this is the happiness of the small man. It is said in the Yî, "His feet are in the stocks, and he is disabled in his toes:—there will be no (further) occasion for blame."'

38. If acts of goodness be not accumulated, they are not sufficient to give its finish to one's name; if acts of evil be not accumulated, they are not sufficient to destroy one's life. The small man thinks that small acts of goodness are of no benefit, and does not do them; and that small deeds of evil do no harm, and does not abstain from them. Hence his wickedness becomes great till it cannot be covered, and his guilt becomes great till it cannot be pardoned. This is what the Yî says, 'He wears the cangue and his ears are destroyed:—there will be evil.'

39. The Master said:—'He who keeps danger in mind is he who will rest safe in his seat; he who keeps ruin in mind is he who will preserve his interests secure; he who sets the danger of disorder before him is he who will maintain the state of order. Therefore the superior man, when resting in safety, does not forget that danger may come; when in a state of security, he does not forget the possibility of ruin; and when all is in a state of order, he does not forget that disorder may come. Thus his person is kept safe, and his states and all their clans can be preserved. This is according to what the Yî says, "(Let him say), 'Shall I perish? shall I perish?' (so shall this state be firm, as if) bound to a clump of bushy mulberry trees."'

40. The Master said:—'Virtue small and office high; wisdom small and plans great; strength small and burden heavy:—where such conditions exist, it is seldom that they do not end (in evil). As is said in the Yî, "The tripod's feet are overthrown, and the ruler's food is overturned. The body of him (who is thus indicated) is wet (with shame): there will be evil."'

41. The Master said:—'Does not he who knows the springs of things possess spirit-like wisdom? The superior man, in his intercourse with the high, uses no flattery, and, in his intercourse with the low, no coarse freedom:—does not this show that he knows the springs of things? Those springs are the slight beginnings of movement, and the earliest indications of good fortune (or ill). The superior man sees them, and acts accordingly without waiting for (the delay of) a single day. As is said in the Yî, "He is firm as a rock, (and acts) without the delay of a single day. With firm goodness there will be good fortune." Firm as a rock, how should he have to wait a single day to ensure his knowing (those springs and his course)? The superior man knows the minute and the manifested; he knows what is weak, and what is strong:—he is a model to ten thousand.'

42. The Master said:—'I may venture to say that the son of the Yen family had nearly attained (the standard of perfection). If anything that he did was not good, he was sure to become conscious of that; and when he knew it, he did not do the thing again. As is said in the Yî, "(The first line shows its subject) returning from an error that has not led him far away. There is no occasion for repentance. There will be great good."'

43. There is an intermingling of the genial influences of heaven and earth, and transformation in its various forms abundantly proceeds. There is an intercommunication of seed between male and female, and transformation in its living types proceeds. What is said in the Yî, 'Three individuals are walking together and one is made to disappear; there is (but) one man walking, and he gets his mate,' tells us of the effort (in nature) at oneness (of operation).

44. The Master said:—'The superior man (in a high place) composes himself before he (tries to) move others; makes his mind restful and easy before he speaks; settles (the principles of) his intercourse with others before he seeks anything from them. The superior man cultivates these three things, and so is complete. If he try to move others while he is himself in unrest, the people will not (act) with him; if he speak while he is himself in a state of apprehension, the people will not respond to him; if without (certain principles of) intercommunication, he issue his requests, the people will not grant them. When there are none to accord with him, those who (work to) injure him will make their appearance. As is said in the Yî, "(We see one) to whose advantage none will contribute, while some will seek to

assail him. He observes no regular rule in the ordering of his heart:—there will be evil."'

Chapter VI.[208] 45. The Master said:—'(The trigrams) *Kh*ien and Khwăn may be regarded as the gate of the Yî.' *Kh*ien represents what is of the yang nature (bright and active); Khwăn what is of the yin nature (shaded and inactive). These two unite according to their qualities, and there comes the embodiment of the result by the strong and weak (lines). In this way we have the phenomena of heaven and earth visibly exhibited, and can comprehend the operation of the spiritual intelligence.

46. The appellations and names (of the diagrams and lines) are various, but do not go beyond (what is to be ascribed to the operation of these two conditions). When we examine the nature and style (of the appended explanations), they seem to express the ideas of a decaying age.

47. The Yî exhibits the past, and (teaches us to) discriminate (the issues of) the future; it makes manifest what is minute, and brings to light what is obscure. (Then king Wăn) opened (its symbols), and distinguished things in accordance with its names, so that all his words

---

[208] The principal object, it is said, of chapter VI, paragraphs 45-48, is to set forth the views of king Wăn and his son in the explanations which they appended to the diagrams and lines; and in doing this the writer begins in 45, with Fû-hsî's starting, in the formation of his eight trigrams, from the devising of the whole and divided lines, to represent the two primitive forms in nature. The two 'pure' trigrams formed of these lines, unmixed, give rise to all the others, or rather the lines of which they are formed do so; and are thus compared to a gate by which the various diagrams enter to complete the system that is intended to represent the changing phenomena of nature and experience. The next sentence in the above version of paragraph 45 appears in Canon McClatchie's translation of the Yî, as follows:—'*Kh*ien is the membrum virile, and Khwăn is the pudendum muliebre (the sakti of *Kh*ien).' It is, hardly possible, on reading such a version, to suppress the exclamation proh pudor! Can a single passage be adduced in support of it from among all the Chinese critics in the line of centuries? I believe not. The ideas which it expresses are gratuitously and wantonly thrust into this text of the Yî. '*Kh*ien' and 'Khwăn' are not spoken of thus. If the latter half of the paragraph be unintelligible, this interpretation of the former would make the whole disgusting.

In paragraph 46 the writer passes from the work of Fû-hsî to that of king Wăn and his son, and the composition of the written Yî is referred to 'a decaying age,'—the age, namely, of the tyrant Eau. Then king Wan and the duke of *K*âu, it is said, deploring the degeneracy of their times and the enormities of the government, indicated, by their treatment of the ancient symbols, their sense of right and wrong, and the methods by which the prevailing evils might be rectified.

Paragraphs 47 and 48 follow and expand the meaning of 45. The editors of the imperial edition say that the former sentence of 47 is the sequel of 45, and the latter of 46, bringing us finally to the explanations and decisions of king Wăn, as the most important portion of the Yî. *K*û Hsî, moreover, observes that throughout the chapter, as well as in the chapters that follow, there must be many characters wanting in the text, while there are many also that are doubtful. This is specially the case with 48. Where the order of the characters has been disarranged merely, correction is easy; but where characters are evidently missing, attempts to fill the lacunae are merely guess-work.

were correct and his explanations decisive;—(the book) was now complete.

48. The appellations and names (of the diagrams and lines) are but small matters, but the classes of things comprehended under them are large. Their scope reaches far, and the explanations attached to them are elegant. The words are indirect, but to the point; the matters seem plainly set forth, but there is a secret principle in them. Their object is, in cases that are doubtful, to help the people in their conduct, and to make plain the recompenses of good and evil.

Chapter VII.[209] 49. Was it not in the middle period of antiquity that the Yî began to flourish? Was not he who made it familiar with anxiety and calamity?

50. Therefore (the 10th diagram), Lî, shows us the foundation of virtue; (the 15th), Hsien, its handle; (the 24th), Fû, its root; (the 32nd), Hăng, its solidity; (the 41st), Sun, its cultivation; (the 42nd), Yî, its abundance; (the 47th), Khwăn, its exercise of discrimination; (the 48th), Ӡing, its field and (the 57th), Sun, its regulation.

51. In Lî we have the perfection of harmony; in Hsien, we have the giving honour to others, and the distinction thence arising; in Fû we have what is small (at first), but there is in it a (nice) discrimination of (the qualities of) things; in Ming we have a mixed experience, but without any weariness; in Sun we have difficulty in the beginning and ease in the end; in Yî we have abundance of growth without any contrivance; in Khwăn we have the pressure of extreme difficulty, ending in a free course,; in Ӡing we have abiding in one's place and at the same time removal (to meet the movement of others); and in Sun we have the weighing of things (and action accordingly), but secretly and unobserved.

52. (The use of) Lî appears in the harmony of the conduct; of Hsien, in the regulation of ceremonies; of Fû, in self-knowledge; of Hăng, in uniformity of virtue; of Sun, in keeping what is harmful at a distance; of Yî, in the promotion of what is advantageous; of Khwăn, in

---

[209] Chapter VII, paragraphs 49-52, is occupied with nine hexagrams, as specially indicating how the superior man, or the ruler, should deal with a time of trouble and solicitude, specially by the cultivation of his own virtue. Not, we are told, that the same thing might not be learned from other diagrams, but these nine specially occurred to the writer, or, as many think, to Confucius.

Paragraph 49 is important as agreeing in its testimony with 46. The Yî was made in middle-antiquity; that is, in the end of the Shang dynasty, and the rise of the Kâu; and the maker or makers had personal and public reasons for anxiety about the signs of the times.

Paragraph 50 shows the particular phase of virtue in each of the nine hexagrams that are mentioned; 51, the marvellous characteristics of each phase; and 52, its use. The 'therefore' with which paragraph 50 commences shows the process of thought by which the writer passed from the anxiety that possessed the mind of the author of the Yî to the use to be derived, in such circumstances, from the study of Lî and the other hexagrams.

the diminution of resentments; of 3ing, in the discrimination of what is righteous; and of Sun, in the doing of what is appropriate to time and to circumstances.

Chapter VIII.[210] 53. The Yî is a book which should not be let slip from the mind. Its method (of teaching) is marked by the frequent changing (of its lines). They change and move without staying (in one place), flowing about into any one of the six places of the hexagram. They ascend and descend, ever inconstant. The strong and the weak lines change places, so that an invariable and compendious rule cannot be derived from them;—it must vary as their changes indicate.

54. The goings forth and comings in (of the lines) are according to rule and measure. (People) learn from them in external and internal affairs to stand in awe.

55. (The book), moreover, makes plain the nature of anxieties and calamities, and the causes of them. Though (its students) have neither master nor guardian, it is as if their parents drew near to them.

56. Beginning with taking note of its explanations, we reason out the principles to which they point. We thus find out that it does supply a constant and standard rule. But if there be not the Proper men (to carry this out), the course cannot be pursued without them.

Chapter IX.[211] 57. The Yî is a book in which the form (of each

---

[210] Chapter VIII, paragraphs 53-56, describes the method of studying the Yî as consisting very much in watching the changes that take place in the lines, and reflecting on the appended explanations; while, after all, much must depend on there being 'the proper men,' to carry its lessons into practice. There seems to be a contradiction between the statements in paragraphs 53 and 56 about the book supplying, and not supplying, a standard rule; but the meaning, probably, is that while it does not give a rule generally applicable, it gives rules for particular cases.

Kû Hsî says he does not understand 54, and thinks some characters must have been lost. 'The six places of the hexagram' in 53 are, literally, 'the six empties.' The places are so called, because it is only a temporary possession of them, which is held by the fugitive lines, whether whole or divided.

[211] Chapter IX, paragraphs 56-62, speaks of the hexagrams as made up of the different lines, and various things to be attended to in those lines to determine their meaning.

Paragraph 57. The time or order in which the lines enter determines of course the place and number of each in the figure. Their 'substance' is their form, as whole or divided, being yang or yin.

Paragraph 58 belongs to the first and sixth lines. We are hardly prepared for the statement that 'the maker or makers' had so much difficulty in determining the meaning of the first line. Of course when they had fixed that and completed the figure, explaining all the lines, it was easy for the student to follow their exposition, as paragraph 59 says.

Paragraph 60 seems to say that the work of the duke of Kâu on each line was but an indicating in detail of the processes of his father's mind in explaining the whole figure.

The last two paragraphs mention several points important to be attended to in studying, more especially, the duke of Kâu on the several lines. Three different views of the concluding statement,—'are they occupied,' &c.,—are given in the imperial edition. 'It belongs,' says Wû Kăng, 'to the fifth line;' 'to the third line,' says Hû Ping-wăn (also diagram) is determined by the lines from the first to the last, which must be carefully observed. The six lines are mixed together, according to the time (when they enter the figure) and their substance (as whole and divided).

58. There is difficulty in knowing (the significance of) the first line, while to know that of the topmost line is easy;—they form the beginning and the end (of the diagram). The explanation of the first line tasks the calculating (of the makers), but in the end they had (but) to complete this.

59. As to the variously-disposed intermediate lines with their diverse formations, for determining their qualities, and discriminating the right and wrong in them, we should be unprovided but for the explanations of them.

60. Yea, moreover, if we wish to know what is likely to be preserved and what to perish, what will be lucky and what will be unlucky, this may easily be known (from the explanations of the different lines). But if the wise will look at the explanations of the entire diagrams, their thoughts will embrace more than half of this knowledge.

61. The second and fourth lines are of the same quality (as being in even places), but their positions (with respect to the fifth line) are different, and their value is not the same; but the second is the object of much commendation, and the fourth the subject of many apprehensions,—from its nearness (to that line). But for a line in a place of weakness it is not good to be far (from the occupant of the place of strength), and what its subject should desire in such a case is (merely) to be without blame. The advantage (here) is in (the second line) being in the central place.

62. The third and fifth lines are of the same quality, (as being in odd places), but their positions are different; and the (occupant of) the third meets with many misfortunes, while the occupant of the fifth achieves much merit:—this arises from one being in the noble position and the other in the mean. Are they occupied by the symbol of weakness? There will be peril. By that of strength? There will be victory.

Chapter X.[212] 63. The Yî is a book of wide comprehension and

of the Yüan dynasty); while Hân Hsing-kwo (of the Thang dynasty) held that it belonged to both. The Khang-hsî editors say that 'by discriminating and combining these views, we get to the meaning of the text.' I am unable to do so.

[212] Chapter X, paragraphs 63, 64, speaks of the great comprehensiveness of the Yî, its figures and explanations being applicable to the three Powers—heaven, earth, and man.

With paragraph 63, compare paragraph 4, Appendix VI. In the trigram the upper line represents heaven, the middle line man, and the lowest earth. This paragraph and that other are the nearest approach I know to an attempt to account for the doubling of the great scope, embracing everything. There are in it the way of heaven, the way of man, and the way of earth. It then takes (the lines representing) those three Powers, and doubles them till they amount to six. What these six lines show is simply this,—the way of the three Powers.

64. This way is marked by changes and movements, and hence we have the imitative lines. Those lines are of different grades (in the trigrams), and hence we designate them from their component elements. These are mixed together, and elegant forms arise. When such forms are not in their appropriate places, the ideas of good fortune and bad are thus produced.

Chapter XI.[213] 65. Was it not in the last age of Yin, when the virtue of Kâu had reached its highest point, and during the troubles between king Wăn and (the tyrant) Kâu, that the (study of the Yî) began to flourish? On this account the explanations (in the book) express (a feeling of) anxious apprehension, (and teach) how peril may be turned into security, and easy carelessness is sure to meet with overthrow. The

number of lines, and stopping with the hexagram; but the doing so was entirely arbitrary. Kû Hsî says:—'The upper two characters belong to heaven, the middle two to man, and the lower two to earth.' No words could be more express; and yet Canon McClatchie says (p. 174):—'The two upper strokes represent Heaven, or Thâi-yî, the husband; the two middle strokes, Earth, his wife; and the two lower strokes, Man, their son; all being animated by the same Divine Reason (tâo) or Supreme God (Chih Shăn).' This note shows how one error, or misunderstanding of the Chinese original, draws other errors with it. The character tâo in the paragraph has not at all the sense of reason, human or divine, but its primary and ordinary signification of the path or course. As Lû Ʒî (Han dynasty) says:—'In the way of heaven there are the changes of day and night, sun and moon; in that of earth, those of hardness and softness, dryness and moisture; in that of man, those of action and rest, of movement and stillness, of good fortune and bad, of good and evil.'

'The imitative lines' in the translation of 64, is simply 'the Yâo' in the Chinese text, which I have rendered according to the account of them in paragraph 8, et al. Their different grades are their position as high or low in the figures (paragraph 1, Section i), and their 'component elements,' literally 'their substance, or thing-nature,' is their structure as being yang or yin, according to the use of wuh in paragraphs 57, 59, et al. A yang line in an even place, or a yin line in an odd, is not in its appropriate place, and gives an indication of what is bad.

[213] Chapter XI, paragraph 65. P. Regis observes on this chapter:—'I do not hesitate to say that there is found nowhere in the whole Yî a passage which affords more light for the explanation of the book.' Paragraph 49 told us that 'the study of the Yî flourished in the middle period of antiquity, and that the author of it was familiar with anxiety and troubles.' That information becomes here more particular. The Yî, existing when this Appendix was written, was made in the closing period of the Yin dynasty, and the making of it was somehow connected with the attempts of the tyrant Kâu against king Wăn. We are not told expressly that the book was written, in part at least, by king Wăn; but the tradition to that effect derives a certain amount of support from what is said here. The general object of the author is also stated clearly enough,—to inculcate a cautious and reverent administration of affairs, never forgetful of the uncertainties of life and fortune.

method in which these things come about is very comprehensive, and must be acknowledged in every sphere of things. If at the beginning there be a cautious apprehension as to the end, there will probably be no error or cause for blame. This is what is called the way of the Yî.

Chapter XII.[214] 66. (The hexagram) Khien represents the strongest of all under the sky. Through this quality its operations are always manifested with ease, for it knows where there would be peril and embarrassment. (The hexagram) Khwăn represents the most docile of all under the sky. Through this quality its operations are always manifested with the promptest decision, for it knows where there would be obstruction.

67. (The sages, who are thus represented, and who made the Yî,) were able to rejoice in heart (in the absolute truth of things), and were able (also) to weigh carefully all matters that could occasion anxiety;

---

[214] Chapter XII, paragraphs 66-72, is generally divided into three sections;—the first, embracing 66-68, and treating of the sages, the makers of the Yî, as themselves independent of it, knowing all that it enables us to know, and able to accomplish all that it enables us to accomplish; the second, embracing 69-71, and telling how the sages formed the Yî, and made all men, by means of it, partakers of their now unlimited knowledge and power; the third, comprised in paragraph 72, and saying, if it be genuine and in its proper place, that the ordinary speech of men is as mysterious and indicative of what is in them, as the explanations of the Yî are, when we consider who were its authors.

'The sages,' who are the subject of 65-68, are not mentioned in the text; but 67 makes it plain that the subject must be some personal being or beings. Neither Khien nor Khwăn can 'rejoice in heart, and weigh carefully matters occasioning anxiety.' The commentators generally interpolate 'the sages;' even Ying-tâ of the Thang dynasty, who doer, not introduce the sages in his exposition, yet makes the subject to be 'the disposer and nourisher of all things.' He gets to his view by an unnatural interpretation of two characters in 67, which are now thrown out of the text by all critics as not genuine. That 'the sages' is really the subject in the mind of the writer appears from the express mention of them in 69, when also 'heaven and earth' take the place of *Kh*ien and Khwăn. It is absurd, not to say blasphemous, to assume that the sages who made the Yî had the knowledge and ability here ascribed to them; but the theory of the Yî as containing a scheme for the discovery of the future necessitated the ascribing such attributes to them. Compare with the whole Section, and especially with paragraph 68, what is said in 'the Doctrine of the Mean,' chapter 24.

The first Section shows how the sages were themselves independent of the Yî, and had no need of it; the second goes on to tell how they devised and constructed it, to make all men equal to themselves in a knowledge of phenomena and human events, and of their indications of, and issues in, the future. Summing up its lessons, the editors of the imperial edition say, 'There is no passage in the Appendix more full and clear than this on the five points in regard to the lines which the student of the Yî has to attend to. Those points are:—their time, position, quality, mutual nearness, and responsive relation. It is by a consideration of the two latter points, moreover, that he must form his judgment on their appropriateness or inappropriateness in the three others.'

Paragraph 72 has really no connexion with the rest of the chapter. I have stated above how the critics attempt to make out such a connexion; but I agree myself with P. Regis, who appends to his version of the paragraph this note:—'Quae sententiae quidem sapiunt doctrinam Confucianam, at non ordinem, utpote cum praecedentibus minime cohaerentes, sed omnino ab iis abscissae avulsaeque.'

(thus) they fixed the good and bad fortune (of all things) under the sky, and could accomplish the things requiring strenuous efforts.

68. Therefore amid the changes and transformations (taking place in heaven and earth), and the words and deeds of men, events that are to be fortunate have their happy omens. (The sages) knew the definite principles underlying the prognostications of the former class, and the future of those of the latter, (now to be) ascertained by divination.

69. The places of heaven and earth (in the diagrams) having been determined, the sages were able (by means of the Yî) to carry out and complete their ability. (In this way even) the common people were able to share with them in (deciding about) the counsels of men and the counsels of spiritual beings.

70. The eight trigrams communicate their information by their emblematic figures. The explanations appended to the lines and the completed figures tell how the contemplation of them affected (the makers). The strong and the weak lines appear mixed in them, and (thus) the good and the evil (which they indicate) can be seen.

71. The changes and movements (which take place in the manipulation of the stalks and the formation of the diagrams) speak as from the standpoint of what is advantageous. The (intimations of) good and evil vary according to the place and nature (of the lines). Thus they may indicate a mutual influence (in any two of them) of love or hatred, and good or evil is the result; or that mutual influence may be affected by the nearness of the lines to, or their distance from, each other, and then repentance or regret is the result; or the influence may be that of truth or of hypocrisy, and then the result is what is advantageous, or what is injurious. In all these relations of the (lines in the) Yî, if two are near and do not blend harmoniously, there may be (all these results),— evil, or what is injurious, or occasion for repentance and regret.

72. The language of him who is meditating a revolt (from the right) betrays his inward shame; that of him whose inward heart doubts about it diverges to other topics. The words of a good man are few; those of a coarse man are many. The words of one who slanders what is good are unsubstantial; those of him who is losing what he ought to keep are crooked.

## APPENDIX IV.

Supplementary to the Thwan and Yâo on the first and second Hexagrams, and showing how they may be interpreted of man's nature and doings[215]

## SECTION I. *KH*IEN.

Chapter I.[216] 1. What is called (under Khien) 'the great and originating' is (in man) the first and chief quality of goodness; what is called 'the penetrating' is the assemblage of excellences; what is called 'the advantageous' is the harmony of all that is right; and what is called 'the correct and firm' is the faculty of action.

2. The superior man, embodying benevolence, is fit to preside over men; presenting the assemblage of excellences, he is fit to show in himself the union of all propriety; benefiting (all) creatures, he is fit to exhibit the harmony of all that is right; correct and firm, he is fit to manage (all) affairs.

3. The fact that the superior man practises these four virtues justifies the application to him of the words—'*Kh*ien represents what is

---

[215] The title of this Appendix is in Chinese the Wăn Yen *K*wan, 'The Record of Wăn Yen;' and according to the analogy of the titles of the three Appendixes that follow, Wăn should perform the part of a verb and Yen that of a substantive. So the characters are usually taken, and to Wăn is given the meaning of 'Explaining (Shih);' and to Yen that of 'Words or Sentences,' meaning the Thwan of king Wăn, and the Yâo of the duke of *K*âu on the first two hexagrams. The document treats of these, and of no others. 'It shows the amount and depth of meaning in them,' says *K*û Hsî, 'and the other hexagrams may be treated after the analog supplied here.' Confucius, it is said by others, died before he was able to carry out the plan which he had formed. But, as I have shown in the Introduction (pp. 28-30), it is more than doubtful whether we have in this Appendix anything at all directly from the sage.

[216] Chapter I, paragraphs 1-3, shows how the attributes of *Kh*ien, as explained by king Wăn, are to be understood of the constituent principles of human nature. What is remarkable is, that we find paragraphs 1, 2, with very little variation, in one of the narratives of the 3o Kwan, as having been spoken by a marchioness-dowager of Lû in B.C. several years before Confucius was born One so familiar as *K*û Hsî was with all the classical literature of his country could not be ignorant of this. His solution of the questions arising from it is, that anciently there was this explanation of the characters of king Wăn; that it was employed by Shû *K*iang (of Lû), and that Confucius also availed himself of it; while the chronicler used, as he does below, the phraseology of 'The Master said,' to distinguish the real words of Confucius from such ancient sayings. But who was this chronicler? No one can tell. The legitimate conclusion from *K*û's criticism is this, that so much of this Appendix as is preceded by 'The Master said' is from Confucius;— so much and no more.

The ascription in paragraph 3 of 'the four virtues' to the superior-or normal man, man in his best estate, and yet inferior to 'the sagely man,' is Confucian,—after the style of the teaching of the Master in the Analects.

great and originating, penetrating, advantageous, correct and firm.'

Chapter II.[217] 4. What is the meaning of the words under the first line, (undivided), 'The dragon lies hid (in the deep);—it is not the time for active doing?' The Master said:—There he is, with the powers of the dragon, and yet lying hid. The influence of the world would make no change in him; he would do nothing (merely) to secure his fame. He can live, withdrawn from the world, without regret; he can experience disapproval without trouble of mind. Rejoicing (in opportunity), he carries his principles into action; sorrowing (for want of opportunity), he keeps with them in retirement. Yes, he is not to be torn from his root (in himself).' This is 'the dragon lying hid.'

5. What is the meaning of the words under the second line, 'The dragon shows himself and is in the field;—it will be advantageous to see the great man?' The Master said:—'There he is, with the dragon's powers, and occupying exactly the central place. He is sincere (even) in

---

[217] In chapter II, paragraphs 4-9, Confucius is introduced, explaining, with considerable amplification, what is said by the duke of *K*âu under the several lines of the hexagram. 'The dragon' becomes the symbol of 'the superior man;' and of the great man,' or the sage upon the throne. The language approaches at times to the magniloquence of Mencius, while in paragraph 8 the voice hardly seems to be that of the sage at all.

With paragraph 5, compare chapters 8 and 14 of' the Doctrine of the Mean,' agreeing much in language and sentiment with what we have here. The line, a strong or undivided line, and therefore yang, is said to be 'exactly in the central place;' but the line is in the second, an even place, that proper to a yin line; and in other passages this might be explained in an unfavourable way. The Chinese character *k*ăng has the meaning given to it, now of 'exact,' and now of 'correct,' the latter being always favourably interpreted.

Paragraph 8. The fifth is almost always the place of honour and authority in the hexagram, and therefore 'the great man' here continues to be the great man, 'the sage.' The argument is that as things of the same kind respond to and seek one another, so is it with the sage and ordinary man. They are of the same kind, though far apart; and when a sage appears, all other men look to him with admiration and hope. The continuity of the illustrations, however, is broken by the introduction of the dragon and clouds, and the tiger and wind. Are these of the same kind? *K*û Hsî says he does not think that the real dragon and real tiger are intended; but he does not tell us how he understood the terms. 3âi *Kh*ing (early in the Ming dynasty) says:—'The dragon feels the influence of the clouds surcharged with rain, and rises from the deep, and when the tiger feels the approach of the cold winds he roars. Thus when the dragon rises, the clouds are sure to collect; and when the tiger screams, the winds follow,' but all this does not help us to appreciate any better the words of the text. And the concluding illustration is nearly as foreign to our way of conceiving things. By 'things that draw their origin from heaven' all animals—moving creatures—are intended; and by those that draw their origin from the earth are intended all plants,—things that stand and do not move. The former turn their heads to the sky, and the latter their roots to the earth. So we read in *K*û Hsî; but I continue to wonder that Confucius selected such illustrations and spoke in such a style.

Paragraph 9. As I have said above, the place of honour and authority in the hexagram belongs to the fifth line, and no other plays so unimportant a part as the sixth; and hence it is represented here as having 'no place' at all. Before he whom it represents is called to act, the battle has been won or lost. Movement from him will only accelerate and intensify the result.

his ordinary words, and earnest in his ordinary conduct. Guarding against depravity, he preserves his sincerity. His goodness is recognised in the world, but he does not boast of it. His virtue is extensively displayed, and transformation ensues. The language of the Yî, "The dragon shows himself and is in the field;—it will be advantageous to see the great man." refers to a ruler's virtue.'

6. What is the meaning of the words under the third line,' The superior man is active and vigilant all the day, and in the evening (still) careful and apprehensive;—the position is dangerous, but there will be no mistake?' The Master said:—'The superior man advances in virtue, and cultivates all the sphere of his duty. His leal-heartedness and good faith are the way by which he advances in virtue. His attention to his words and establishing his sincerity are the way by which he occupies in his sphere. He knows the utmost point to be reached, and reaches it, thus showing himself in accord with the first springs (of things); he knows the end to be rested in, and rests in it, thus preserving his righteousness in accordance with that end. Therefore he occupies a high position without pride, and a low position without anxiety. Thus it is that, being active and vigilant, and careful (also) and apprehensive as the time requires, though his position be perilous, he will make no mistake.'

7. What is the meaning of the words under the fourth line, 'He is as if he were leaping up, (but still) is in the deep;—there will be no mistake?' The Master said:—'He finds no permanent place either above or below, but he does not commit the error (of advancing). He may advance or recede;—there is no permanent place for him: but he does not leave his fellows. The superior man, advancing in virtue and cultivating the sphere of his duty, yet wishes (to advance only) at the (proper) time, and therefore there is no mistake.'

8, What is the meaning of the words under the fifth line, 'The dragon is on the wing in the sky;—it will be advantageous to see the great man?' The Master said:—'Notes of the same key respond to one another; creatures of the same nature seek one another; water flows towards the place that is (low and) damp; fire rises up towards what is dry; clouds follow the dragon, and winds follow the tiger:(so) the sage makes his appearance, and all men look to him. Things that draw their origin from heaven move towards what is above; things that draw their origin from the earth cleave to what is below:—so does everything follow its kind.'

9. What is the meaning of the words under the topmost line, 'The dragon exceeds the proper limits;—there will be occasion for repentance?' The Master said:—'The position is noble, but it is not that of office; (its occupant) dwells on high, but he has no people (to rule); and the men of talent and virtue in the positions below will give him no aid;—should he move in such a case, there will be occasion for

repentance.'

Chapter III.[218] 10. 'The dragon lies hid;—it is not the time for active doing:'—the position is (too) low.

11. 'The dragon shows himself and is in the field:'—the time (requires him still) to be unemployed.

12. 'All the day active and vigilant:'—(he now) does his (proper) business.

13. 'He is as if he were leaping up, (but still) is in the deep:'—he is making trial of himself.

14. 'The dragon is on the wing in the sky:'—(the subject of the line) is on high and ruling.

15. 'The dragon exceeds the proper limit, and there will be occasion for repentance:'—when things have been carried to extremity, calamity ensues.

16. Undivided lines appear in all these representations of the great and originating power denoted by Khien:—(what follows in the Yâo tells us how) all under the sky there will be good order.

Chapter IV.[219] 17. 'The dragon lies hid in the deep;—it is not the time for active doing:'—the energy denoted by the undivided line is laid up and hid away as in the deep.

18. 'The dragon appears in the field:'—all under heaven (begins to be) adorned and brightened.

19. 'All the day active and vigilant:'—continually, as the time passes and requires, does he act.

---

[218] Chapter III, paragraphs 10-16, goes over again the Yâo of the duke of Kâu with very brief explanations, grounded chiefly on the consideration of the place or position occupied by the several lines, and the time of their introduction into the action of the hexagram.

Paragraph 16. See the note on the Text of Khien, corresponding to this line, page 223, and also that on paragraph 7 of the symbolism of the figures and lines, Section i, page 81. There is the same difficulty in understanding the first part of the short paragraph; the conclusion of it must be a consequence of the language of the Yâo, though it is not repeated here.

[219] Chapter IV, paragraphs 7-23, goes over the same ground for a third time, treating the various paragraphs chiefly from the standpoint of time.

Paragraph 17 tells us that time and circumstances are essential, as well as inward power, to successful development and demonstration. In paragraph 18, the words of the Yâo about meeting with the great man are not quoted, but they prompted the latter half of it.

Paragraph 19. Compare the language on paragraph 6, towards the end.

Paragraph 20. The subject passes here from the lower trigram and enters into the upper. We are told not to lay stress on 'the method of Khien.' In paragraph 21 we have the sage upon the throne. Time and opportunity are both in progress in 19; here in 22, they are both passed, have reached their extremity or end.

Paragraph 23:—see on paragraph 16. 'The model of heaven,' says Wû Khăng, 'is the due blending of the strong and active with the weak and passive, the regulation of movement in accordance with the highest reason, so that there shall be neither excess nor deficiency.'

20. 'He is as if he were leaping up, (but still) is in the deep:'—a change is taking place in the method indicated by (this) Khien diagram.

21. 'The dragon is on the wing in the sky this shows that his place is based on his heavenly virtue.

22. 'The dragon exceeds the (proper) limit;—there will be occasion for repentance:'—the time is come to an end, and so also is his opportunity.

23. Undivided lines appear in all these representations of the great and originating power denoted by *Kh*ien:—and (from what follows in the Yâo) we see the model (of action) afforded by heaven.

Chapter V.[220] 24. The 'greatness' and 'originating' represented by *Kh*ien refer to it as (the symbol of) what gives their beginning (to all things), and (also) secures their growth and development.

25. 'The advantageousness and the correctness and firmness' refer to its nature and feelings (as seen in all the resulting things).

26. *Kh*ien, (thus) originating, is able with its admirable benefits to benefit all under the sky. We are not told how its benefits are conferred; but how great is (its operation)!

27. How great is (what is emblemed by) *Kh*ien!—strong, vigorous, undeflected, correct, and (in all these qualities) pure, unmixed, exquisite!

28. The six lines, as explained (by the duke of *K*âu), bring forth and display (its meaning), and everything about it is (thus) indirectly exhibited.

29. (The great man) at the proper time drives with these six dragons through the sky. The clouds move, and the rain is distributed;

---

[220] Chapter V, paragraphs 24-29. The author here, leaving the treatise on the symbolism of the Yâo, turns to that on the Thwan, or expositions of king Wǎn, and amplifies it, not quoting from it, however, so fully and exactly, as he has done in the previous chapters from the Yâo.

Paragraphs 24 and 25 are based on the statement of the significance of the Thwan under *Kh*ien, and not on the treatise on the symbolism. The originating power cannot be separated from that of penetration and development. The latter issues from the former as the summer follows on the spring, according to an illustration of *K*û Hsî. 'The advantageousness' and 'firm correctness,' he compares also to the autumn and winter, saying that the *Kh*ien power in its essence, as it is in itself, is best described by these two latter characteristics, while the two former describe it in its operation. It is thus that he tries to give his readers an idea of what he understood by 'nature and feelings' in 25. But this chapter treats of the *Kh*ien power in nature rather than in humanity. Confining our view to the power so operating, we cannot say that the description of it in 26 and 27 is magniloquent or hyperbolical.

Paragraph 28 returns to the explanations of the lines of the hexagram by the duke of *K*âu, which exhibit the power in different positions and relations, bringing out all its significance; and then 29 confines us to the fifth line, in which we have its ideal. The spheres of nature and of men seem to be in the view of the author, and therefore I introduce 'the great man,' as the subject, after the example of the best critics. Like the clouds and the rain to the thirsty earth, so is the rule of the sage to expectant humanity.

all under heaven enjoys repose.

Chapter VI.[221] 30. In the superior man his conduct is (the fruit of) his perfected virtue, which might be seen therefore in his daily course; but the force of that phrase, 'lying hid,' requires him to keep retired, and not yet show himself, nor proceed to the full development of his

---

[221] Chapter VI, paragraphs 30-36., The author leaving the Thwan, turns again to the treatise on the symbolism of the Yâo, his main object being to show how reasonable are the decisions and lessons of the duke of *Kâu*.

The subject of paragraph 30 has the virtue; but his position in the lowest place shows that his time is not yet come.

In paragraph 31 we have the superior man developing, by means of the processes described, into 'the great man,' with the attributes of a ruler, the appearance of whom is a blessing to men.

The twofold symbol of strength in paragraph 32 is the yang or undivided line in the third place (odd) proper to it. There will be no mistake, because the subject of the line, in the exercise of his caution, will abstain from any forward movement.

According to paragraph 63 of last Appendix, Section ii, both the third and fourth lines in the hexagram. belong to man, and are intermediate between those of heaven and those of earth. Khung Ying-tâ, to get over the difficulty in what is said on the fourth line, says that, as a matter of fact and locally, man is nearer earth than heaven, and is aptly represented therefore by the third line and not by the fourth;—I prefer to point out the inconsistency, and leave it. The subject of this fourth line will move very cautiously, and so escape blame.

The eulogium of 'the great man' in paragraph 34 cannot fail to recall to the classical scholar the thirty-first and other chapters of 'the Doctrine of the Mean,' where the sage is described as 'The Equal of Heaven.' In one sentence here he is spoken of as sometimes taking precedence of Heaven, which then does not act in opposition to him! I do not know of any statement about the sage, coming without doubt from Confucius, that is so extravagant as this. It is difficult—in fact impossible—to say from the Yî itself, what we are to understand by the kwei shǎn, which I have translated here by the spirit-like operations (of Providence).' The compound denomination does not often occur in the book. In Appendix III, Section i, 21, kwei is the anima and shǎn the animus; and in paragraph 50, I have translated the terms by 'the contracting and expanding operations.' In Appendix I, page 101 and page 119, the name is used as in the present text. That second instance and this paragraph were evidently constructed, the one on the model of the other. I think it likely that the breath or air, *khî*, became the name with the earliest Chinese for their first concept of spirit; then the breath inspired or inhaled was called kwei, and became the name for the grosser part of the spirit, returning to the earth; and shin, the breath exhaled or expired, the name for the subtler and intellectual spirit, ascending to a state of activity and enjoyment. The explanations of the terms in the *R* Yâ and other dictionaries seem to justify this view. The combination kwei shin is sometimes best translated by 'spiritual beings.' The school of the Sung philosophy understand by it—the contracting and expanding of the primary matter, or that matter conceived of in two forms or with two opposite qualities. *Khǎng-ȝze* says here: that I Heaven and earth are another name for tâo, and kwei shǎn another name for "the vestiges of making and transformation;" and that the sage being in harmony with the tâo or practical reason of the universe, how can men or the kwei shǎn be contrary to him?' Whatever be thought of the Sung speculations and theories, I think that a translator ought to give an indication of the primary meaning of the name kwei shǎn.

Paragraphs 35 and 36 suggest the description of Confucius by Mencius, V, ii, 1, 5, as the one among the sages who was most governed by the consideration of time, doing continually what the circumstances of the time required.

course. While this is the case, the superior man (knows that) it is not the time for active doing.

31. The superior man learns and accumulates the results of his learning; puts questions, and discriminates among those results; dwells magnanimously and unambitiously in what he has attained to; and carries it into practice with benevolence. What the Yî says, 'The dragon appears in the field:—it will be advantageous to meet with the great man,' has reference to the virtuous qualities of a ruler (as thus described).

32. In the third line, there is a twofold symbol of) strength, but (the position) is not central. (Its occupant) is not in heaven above, nor is he in the field beneath. Therefore there must be active vigilance and cautious apprehension as the time requires; and. though (the position be) perilous, there will be no mistake.

33. In the fourth line, there is (the symbol of) strength, but (the position) is not central. (Its occupant) is not in heaven above, nor is he in the field beneath, nor is he in the place of man intermediate. Hence he is in perplexity; and being so, he has doubts about what should be his movements, and so will give no occasion for blame.

34. The great man is he who is in harmony, in his attributes, with heaven and earth; in his brightness, with the sun and moon; in his orderly procedure, with the four sea-sons; and in his relation to what is fortunate and what is calamitous, in harmony with the spirit-like operations (of Providence). He may precede Heaven, and Heaven will not act in opposition to him; he may follow Heaven, but will act (only) as Heaven at the time would do. If Heaven will not act in opposition to him, how much less will men! how much less will the spirit-like operation (of Providence)!

35. The force of that phrase—'exceeding the proper limits'— indicates the knowing to advance but not to retire; to maintain but not to let perish to get but not to lose.

36. He only is the sage who knows to advance and to retire, to maintain and to let perish; and that without ever acting incorrectly. Yes, he only is the sage!

## SECTION II. KHWĂN.[222]

Chapter I. 1. (What is indicated by) Khwăn is most gentle and weak, but, when put in motion, is hard and strong; it is most still, but is able to give every definite form.

2. 'By following, it obtains its (proper) lord,' and pursues its regular (course).

3. It contains all things in itself, and its transforming (power) is glorious.

4. Yes, what docility marks the way of Khwăn! It receives the influences of heaven, and acts at the proper time.

Chapter II. 5. The family that accumulates goodness is sure to have superabundant happiness, and the family that accumulates evil is sure to have superabundant misery. The murder of a ruler by his minister, or of his father by a son, is not the result of the events of one morning or one evening. The causes of it have gradually accumulated,—through the absence of early discrimination. The words of the Yî, 'He treads on the hoar-frost; the strong ice will come (by and by),' show the natural (issue and growth of things).

6. 'Straight' indicates the correctness (of the internal principle), and 'square,' the righteousness (of the external act). The superior man, (thus represented), by his self-reverence maintains the inward (correctness), and in righteousness adjusts his external acts. His reverence and righteousness being (thus) established, his virtues are not solitary instances or of a single class. 'Straight, square, and great, working his operations, without repeated efforts, in every respect advantageous:'—this shows how (such a one) has no doubts as to what he does.

7. Although (the subject of) this divided line has excellent qualities, he (does not display them, but) keeps them under restraint. 'If he engage with them in the service of the king, and be successful, he will not claim that success for himself:'—this is the way of the earth, of a wife, of a minister. The way of the earth is-'not to claim the merit of achievement,' but on behalf (of heaven) to bring things to their proper issue.

8. Through the changes and transformations produced by heaven and earth, plants and trees grow luxuriantly. If (the reciprocal influence of) heaven and earth were shut up and restrained, we should have (a

---

[222] The hexagram Khwăn is dealt with in Section ii, and much wore briefly than *Kh*ien in Section i. Much less distinct, moreover, is the attempt in it to show how the attributes of the hexagram are to be understood of the principles of human nature. The most important portion of the Section, perhaps, is paragraph 5, the first of chapter II, and I have spoken of it in the Introduction, page 42.

state that might suggest to us) the case of men of virtue and ability lying in obscurity. The words of the Yî, 'A sack tied up:—there will be no ground for blame or for praise,' are in reality a lesson of caution.

9. The superior man (emblemed here) by the yellow' and correct (colour), is possessed of comprehension and discrimination. He occupies the correct position (of supremacy), but (that emblem) is on (the lower part of) his person. His excellence is in the centre (of his being), but it diffuses a complacency over his four limbs, and is manifested in his (conduct of) affairs:—this is the perfection of excellence.

10. (The subject of) the yin (or divided line) thinking himself equal to the (subject of the) yang, or undivided line, there is sure to be 'a contest.' As if indignant at there being no acknowledgment of the (superiority of the subject of the) yang line, (the text) uses the term 'dragons.' But still the (subject of neither line) can leave his class, and hence we have 'the blood' mentioned. The mention of that as being (both) 'azure and yellow' indicates the mixture of heaven and earth. Heaven's (colour) is azure and earth's is yellow.

## APPENDIX V.

### Treatise of Remarks on the Trigrams.

Chapter I.[223] 1. Anciently, when the sages made the Yî, in order to give mysterious assistance to the spiritual Intelligences, they produced (the rules for the use of) the divining plant.

2. The number 3 was assigned to heaven, 2 to earth, and from these came the (other) numbers.

3. They contemplated the changes in the divided and undivided lines (by the process of manipulating the stalks), and formed the trigrams; from the movements that took place in the strong and weak lines, they produced (their teaching about) the separate lines. There ensued a harmonious conformity to the course (of duty) and to virtue, with a discrimination of what was right (in each particular case). They (thus) made an exhaustive discrimination of what was right, and effected the complete development of (every) nature, till they arrived

---

[223] Chapter I, paragraphs 1-3, treats of the rise of the scheme of the Yî from the wonderful qualities of the divining plant, the use of certain numbers, and the formation of the lineal figures.

P. Regis translates paragraph 1 by—'The ancient (sages), the most excellent men, were the authors of the Yî-king, in making which they were assisted by an intelligent spirit, who for their help produced the plant called Shih.'

But the text will not admit of this version, nor have I found the view given in it in any Chinese writer. It is difficult to make up one's mind whether to translate—'the sage,' or 'the sages.' Khung Yin-tâ contends that the writer had Fû-hsî and him alone in his mind. To me it seems otherwise. Fû-hsî, if we accept the testimony of universal Chinese consent, made the eight trigrams; but he did not make the Yî, which, by the same consent, was the production of king Wăn and his son.

The text would seem to say that the sages 'produced' the plant, but this is so extravagant that the view indicated in my supplementary clause appears in all the best commentators. So understood, the Yî may be said to 'give mysterious assistance to the spiritual Intelligences,' or, if we take that name as singular (according to the analogy of chapter 6), to the Divine Being in affording a revelation of His will, as in paragraph 3. We may well say that it is a pity the revelation should be so enigmatical; but the author, it must be remembered, is writing from his own standpoint. Wăn and his son, as I have endeavoured to show in the Introduction, merely wished to convey, under the style and veil of divination, their moral and political lessons.

On paragraph 2 it is said that heaven is round; and as the circumference of a circle is three times its diameter, hence 3 is the number of heaven. Again, earth is square, and as the circumference of a square is four times its length or breadth, or it consists of two pairs of equal sides, hence 2 is the number of earth.

The concluding statement about I the other numbers' is understood of the manipulation of the divining stalks, as in Appendix III, i, 51. That manipulation, thrice repeated, might leave three stalks each time, and 3 x 3 = 9; or 2, being in the same way in all = 6; or twice 3 and once 2 = 8; or twice 2 and once 3 = 7. These are the numbers of the 4 binary symbols, employed in forming the new figures; ═══, the old yang, = 9; ══ ══, the young yin, = 8; ══ ═══, the young yang, = 7; and ══ ══, the old yin, = 6.

(in the Yî) at what was appointed for it (by Heaven).

Chapter II.[224] 4. Anciently, when the sages made the Yî, it was with the design that (its figures) should be in conformity with the principles underlying the natures (of men and things), and the ordinances (for them) appointed (by Heaven). With this view they exhibited (in them) the way of heaven, calling (the lines) yin and yang; the way of earth, calling (them) the weak (or soft) and the strong (or hard); and the way of men, under the names of benevolence and righteousness. Each (trigram) embraced (those) three Powers; and, being repeated, its full form consisted of six lines. A distinction was made of (the places assigned) to the yin and yang lines, which were variously occupied, now by the strong and now by the weak forms, and thus the figure (of each hexagram) was completed.

Chapter III.[225] 5. (The symbols of) heaven and earth received their determinate positions; (those for) mountains and collections of water interchanged their influences; (those for) thunder and wind excited each other the more; and (those for) water and fire did each other no harm. (Then) among these eight symbols there was a mutual communication.

6. The numbering of the past is a natural process.; the knowledge of the coming is anticipation. Therefore in the Yî we have (both) anticipation (and the natural process).

Chapter IV.[226] 7. Thunder serves to put things in motion; wind to scatter (the genial seeds of) them; rain to moisten them; the sun to warm them; (what is symbolised by) Kăn, to arrest (and keep them in their places); (by) Tui, to give them joyful course; (by) *Kh*ien, to rule

---

[224] Chapter II. The top line in each trigram thus belongs to the category of heaven; the bottom line to that of earth; and the middle line to that of man. The odd places should be occupied, 1 correctly,' by the undivided lines; and the even by the divided. The trigram being increased to the hexagram, lines 5 and 6 were assigned to heaven; 1 and 2 to earth; and 3 and 4 to man. 5 is the yang characteristic of heaven, and 6 the yin; so 1 and 2 in regard to earth; while 3 represents the benevolence of man, and 4 his righteousness. But all this is merely the play of fancy, and confuses the mind of the student.

[225] Chapter III, paragraphs 5 and 6, is understood, though not very clearly, by referring to the circular arrangement of the trigrams according to Fû-hsî, as shown in Figure 2, of Plate III. Paragraph 5 refers to the correlation of *Kh*ien and Khwăn, Kăn and Tui, *K*ăn and Sun, Khân and Lî. Paragraph 6 is less easy of apprehension. Starting in the same figure from Khien and numbering on the left we come to *K*ăn by a natural process. Then we turn back, and numbering on the right, from Sun, we come by a backward process to Khwăn. The same process is illustrated on a large scale by the circular arrangement of the 64 hexagrams in Plate I. But what the scope of the paragraph is I cannot tell, and am tempted to say of it, as P. Regis does, 'Haec observatio prorsus inanis est.'

[226] In chapter IV we have the same circular arrangement of the trigrams, though they are named in a different order; the last first and the first last. The first four are mentioned by their elemental names; the last four by the names of their lineal figures. No special significance is attached to this. If it ever had any, it has been lost.

them; and by Khwăn, to store them up.

Chapter V.[227] 8. God comes forth in *Kăn* (to His producing work); He brings (His processes) into full and equal action in Sun; they are manifested to one another in Lî; the greatest service is done for Him in Khwăn; He rejoices in Tui; He struggles in *Kh*ien; He is comforted and enters into rest in Khân; and He completes (the work of the year) in Kăn.

9. All things are made to issue forth in *Kăn*, which is placed at the east. (The processes of production) are brought into full and equal action in Sun, which is placed at the south-east. The being brought into full and equal action refers to the purity and equal arrangement of all things. Lî gives the idea of brightness. All things are now made manifest to one another. It is the trigram of the south. The sages turn their faces to the south when they give audience to all under the sky, administering government towards the region of brightness:—the idea in this procedure was taken from this. Khwăn denotes the earth, (and is placed at the south-west). All things receive from it their fullest nourishment, and hence it is said, 'The greatest service is done for Him in Khwăn.' Tui corresponds (to the west) and to the autumn,—the season in which all things rejoice. Hence it is said, 'He rejoices in Tui.' He struggles in *Kh*ien, which is the trigram of the north-west. The idea is that there the inactive and active conditions beat against each other. Khan denotes water. It is the trigram of the exact north,—the trigram of comfort and rest, what all things are tending to. Hence it is said, 'He is comforted and enters into rest in Khan. Kăn is the trigram of the north-east. In it all things bring to a full end the issues of the past (year), and prepare the commencement of the next. Hence it is said, 'He completes (the work of the year) in Kăn.'

Chapter VI.[228] 10. When we speak of Spirit we mean the subtle

---

[227] Chapter V, paragraphs 8 and 9, sets forth the operations of nature in the various seasons, as being really the operations of God, who is named Tî, 'the Lord and Ruler of Heaven.' Those operations are represented in the progress by the seasons of the year, as denoted by the trigrams, according to the arrangement of them by king Wăn, as shown also in Plate III, Figure 2.

'The greatest service is done for Tî in Khwăn;' Yang Wan-lî (of our twelfth century, but earlier than *K*û Hsî) says:—'Khwăn is a minister or servant. Tî is his ruler, All that a ruler has to do with his minister is to require his service.' 'On the struggles in *Kh*ien' he says:—'*Kh*ien is the trigram of the north-west, when the yin influence is growing strong and the yang diminishing.'

The 'purity' predicated in paragraph 9 of things in Sun, was explained by *K*ăng Khang-*kh*ăng (our second century) as equivalent to 'newness,' referring to the brightness of all things in the light of spring and summer. On 'all things receive from the earth their fullest nourishment' the same Yang, quoted above, says:—'The earth performs the part of a mother, All things are its children. What a mother has to do for her children is simply to nourish them.'

[228] Chapter VI is the sequel of the preceding. There ought to have been some

(presence and operation of God) with all things. For putting all things in motion there is nothing more vehement than thunder; for scattering them there is nothing more effective than wind; for drying them up there is nothing more parching than fire; for giving them pleasure and satisfaction there is nothing more grateful than a lake or marsh; for moistening them there is nothing more enriching than water; for bringing them to an end and making them begin again there is nothing more fully adapted than Kăn. Thus water and fire contribute together to the one object; thunder and wind do not act contrary to each other; mountains and collections of water interchange their influences. It is in this way, that they are able to change and transform, and to give completion to all things.

Chapter VII.[229] 11. *Kh*ien is (the symbol of) strength; Khwăn, of

---

mention of Shăn or, Spirit' in chapter 5. It is the first character in this chapter, and the two characters that follow show that it is here resumed for the purpose of being explained. As it does not occur in chapter 5, we must suppose that the author of it here brings forward and explains the idea of it that was in his mind. Many of the commentators recognise this,—e. g. Liang Yin, as quoted in the Introduction, p. 32.

Two other peculiarities in the style of the chapter are pointed out and explained (after a fashion) by 3hui *K*ing (earlier, probably, than the Sung dynasty):—'The action of six of the trigrams is described, but no mention is made of *Kh*ien or Khwăn. But heaven and earth do nothing, and yet do everything; hence they are able to perfect the spirit-like subtilty of the action of thunder, wind, and the other things. (Moreover), we have the trigram Kân mentioned, the only one mentioned by its name, instead of our reading "mountains." The reason is, that the putting in motion, the scattering, the parching, and the moistening, are all the palpable effects of thunder, wind, fire, and water. But what is ascribed to Kăn, the ending and the recommencing all things, is not so evident of mountains. On this account the name of the trigram is given, while the things in nature represented by the trigrams are given in those other cases. The style suitable in each case is employed.'

[229] Chapter VII mentions the attributes, called also the 'virtues,' of the different trigrams. It is not easy to account for the qualities—'their nature and feelings'—ascribed to them. Khung Ying-tâ says:—'*Kh*ien is represented by heaven, which revolves without ceasing, and so it is the symbol of strength; Khwăn by the earth, which receives docilely the action of heaven, and so it is the symbol of docility; *K*ân by thunder, which excites and moves all things, and so it is the symbol of what produces movement; Sun by Wind, which enters everywhere, and so it is the symbol of penetration; Khân by water, found in a place perilous and precipitous, and the name is explained accordingly; Lî by fire, and fire is sure to lay hold of things, and so it is the symbol of being attached to; Kân by a mountain, the mass of which is still and arrests progress, and so it is the symbol of stoppage or arrest; and Tui by a lake or marsh, which moistens all things, and so it is the symbol of satisfaction.'

The Khang-hsî editors consider this explanation of the qualities of the trigrams to be unsatisfactory, and certainly it has all the appearance of an e x post facto account. They prefer the views of the philosopher Shâo (of our eleventh century), which is based on the arrangement of the undivided and divided lines in the figures. This to me is more unsatisfactory than the other. The editors say, moreover, that Shâo's account of the three yang trigrams, *K*ăn, Khan, and Kăn is correct, and that of the three yin, Sun, Lî, and Tui incorrect; but this would be based on king Wăn's arrangement, which does not appear to have place here.

docility; *K*ăn, of stimulus to movement; Sun, of penetration; Khan, of what is precipitous and perilous; Lî, of what is bright and what is catching; Kăn, of stoppage or arrest; and Tui, of pleasure and satisfaction.

Chapter VIII.[230] 12. *Kh*ien (suggests the idea of) a horse; Khwăn, that of an ox; *K*ăn, that of the dragon; Sun, that of a fowl; Khan, that of a pig; Lî, that of a pheasant; Kăn, that of a dog; and Tui, that of a sheep.

Chapter IX.[231] 13. *Kh*ien suggests the idea of the head; Khwăn, that of the belly; *K*ăn, that of the feet Sun, that of the thighs; Khan, that of the cars Lî, that of the eyes; Kăn, that of the hands and Tui, that of the mouth.

Chapter X.[232] 14. *Kh*ien is (the symbol of) heaven, and hence has the appellation of father. Khwăn is (the symbol of) earth, and hence has the appellation of mother, *K*ăn shows a first application (of Khwăn to *Kh*ien), resulting in getting (the first of) its male (or undivided lines), and hence is called 'the oldest son.' Sun shows a first application (of *Kh*ien to Khwăn), resulting in getting (the first of) its female (or divided lines), and hence is called 'the oldest daughter.' Khan shows a second application (of Khwăn to *Kh*ien), resulting in getting (the second of) its male (or undivided lines), and hence is called 'the second son.' Lî shows a second application (of *Kh*ien to Khwăn), resulting in getting the second of its female (or divided lines), and hence is called 'the second daughter.' Kăn shows a third application (of Khwăn to *Kh*ien), resulting in getting (the third of) its male (or undivided lines), and hence is called 'the youngest son.' Tui shows a third application (of *Kh*ien to Khwăn), resulting in getting (the third of) its female (or divided lines), and hence is called 'the youngest daughter.'

Chapter XI.[233] 15. *Kh*ien suggests the idea of heaven; of a circle; of a ruler; of a father; of jade; of metal; of cold; of ice; of deep red; of a

---

[230] Chapter VIII. In the Great Appendix, p. 190, it is said that Fû-hsî, in making his trigrams, was guided by 'the consideration of things apart from his own person.' Of such things we have a specimen here. The creatures are assigned, in their classes, to the different trigrams, symbolising the ideas in the last chapter. We must not make any difference of sex in translating their names.

[231] Chapter IX. Fû-hsî found also 'things near at hand, in his own person,' while making the trigrams. We have here a specimen of such things.

[232] Chapter X has been discussed in the Introduction, pp. 43 and 44. Let it simply be added here, that the account which it does give of the formation of the six subsidiary trigrams is inconsistent with their gradual rise from the mutual imposition of the undivided and divided lines.

[233] Chapter XI may be made to comprehend all the paragraphs from the 15th to the end, and shows how universally the ideas underlying the Yî are diffused through the world of nature. The quality of the several trigrams will be found with more or less of truth, and with less or more of fancy, in the objects mentioned in connexion with them. More needs not to be said on the chapter than has been done in the Introduction, pp. 46 and 47.

good horse; of an old horse; of a thin horse; of a piebald horse; and of the fruit of trees.

16. Khwăn suggests the idea of the earth; of a mother; of cloth; of a caldron; of parsimony; of a turning lathe; of a young heifer; of a large waggon; of what is variegated; of a multitude; and of a handle and support. Among, soils it denotes what is black.

17. *K*ăn suggests the idea of thunder; of the dragon; of (the union of) the azure and the yellow; of development; of a great highway; of the eldest son; of decision and vehemence; of bright young bamboos; of sedges and rushes; among horses, of the good neigher; of one whose white hind-leg appears, of the prancer, and of one with a white star in his forehead. Among the productions of husbandry it suggests the idea of what returns to life from its disappearance (beneath the surface), of what in the end becomes the strongest, and of what is the most luxuriant.

18. Sun suggests the idea of wood; of wind; of the oldest daughter; of a plumb-line; of a carpenter's square; of being white; of being long; of being lofty; of advancing and receding; of want of decision; and of strong scents. It suggests in the human body, the idea of deficiency of hair; of a wide forehead; of a large development of the white of the eye. (Among tendencies), it suggests the close pursuit of gain, even to making three hundred per cent in the market. In the end it may become the trigram of decision.

19. Khan suggests the idea of water; of channels and ditches (for draining and irrigation); of being hidden and lying concealed; of being now straight, and now crooked; of a bow, and of a wheel. As referred to man, it suggests the idea of an increase of anxiety; of distress of mind; of pain in the ears;—it is the trigram of the blood; it suggests the idea of what is red. As referred to horses, it suggests the idea of the horse with an elegant spine; of one with a high spirit; of one with a drooping head; of one with a thin hoof; and of one with a shambling step. As referred to carriages, it suggests one that encounters many risks. It suggests what goes right through; the moon; a thief. Referred to trees, it suggests that which is strong, and firm-hearted.

20. Lî suggests the emblem of fire; of the sun; of lightning; of the second daughter; of buff-coat and helmet; of spear and sword. Referred to men, it suggests the large belly. It is the trigram of dryness. It suggests the emblem of a turtle; of a crab; of a spiral univalve; of the mussel; and of the tortoise. Referred to trees, it suggests one which is hollow and rotten above.

21. Kăn suggests the emblem of a mountain; of a by-path; of a small rock; of a gateway; of the fruits of trees and creeping plants; of a porter or a eunuch; of the (ring) finger; of the dog; of the rat; of birds with powerful bills; among trees, of those which are strong, with many joints.

22. Tui suggests the emblem of a low-lying collection of water; of the youngest daughter; of a sorceress; of the mouth and tongue; of the decay and putting down (of things in harvest); of the removal (of fruits) hanging (from the stems or branches); among soils, of what is strong and salt; of a concubine; and of a sheep.

## APPENDIX VI.

### The Orderly Sequence of the Hexagrams[234]

### SECTION I.

1-3. When there were heaven and earth, then afterwards all things were produced. What fills up (the space) between heaven and earth are (those) all things. Hence (*Kh*ien and Khwăn) are followed by *K*un[235]. *K*un denotes filling up.

3-6. *K*un is descriptive of things on their first production. When so produced, they are sure to be in an undeveloped condition. Hence *K*un is followed by Măng. Măng is descriptive of what is undeveloped,—the young of creatures and things. These in that state require to be nourished. Hence Măng is followed by Hsü. Hsü is descriptive of the way in which meat and drink (come to be supplied)[236]. Over meat and drink there are sure to be contentions[236]. Hence Hsü is followed by

---

[234] The few sentences on this Appendix in the Introduction, pp. 47, 48, are sufficient. It shows the importance of the meaning of the name in an attempt to explain the lineal figures, and prepares us to expect on each one a brief enigmatical essay, which, it has been seen, is the nature of the Text. But the writer, whoever he was, is by no means careful always to follow that Text in the significance of the characters, as will appear in the few instances to which attention is called in the following notices. The treatise is too slight to require, or to justify, an exhibition of all its inaccuracies.

[235] But *K*un does not denote filling up. It is the symbol of being in a state of distress and difficulty. The writer is thinking of the result of the interaction of heaven and earth as being to fill all between them with the various forms of living beings; and to represent that he gives the result of Kun, and not its meaning. He makes a blunder which might have been easily avoided, for he adds immediately that the character is descriptive of things on their first production.

[236] It is difficult to follow the writer here. Hsü in the Text is the symbol of the idea of waiting. Does he mean that a provision of food and drink can only be made gradually? There is nothing in the character Hsü to awaken in the mind the idea of nourishment, Then the genesis of contention which is given is strange. The writer probably had in his mind the lines of the Shih, II, i, ode 5. 3:—

'The loss of kindly feeling oft
  From slightest things shall grow.
Where all the fare is dry and spare,
  Resentments fierce may glow.'

But what is allowable, good even, in poetry, is out of place in this treatise.

Sung.

6-8. Sung is sure to cause the rising up of the multitudes[237]; and hence it is followed by Sze. Sze has the signification of multitudes[237], and between multitudes there must be some bond of union. Hence it is followed by Pî, which denotes being attached to.

8-11. (Multitudes in) union must be subjected to some restraint. Hence Pî is followed by Hsiâo Khû. When things axe subjected to restraint, there come to be rites of ceremony, and hence Hsiâo Khû is followed by Lî[238]. The treading (on what is proper) leads to Thâi, which issues in a state of freedom and repose, and hence Lî is followed by Thâi.

11-16. Thâi denotes things having free course. They cannot have that for ever, and hence it is followed by Phî (denoting being shut up and restricted). Things cannot for ever be shut up, and hence Phî is followed by Thung Ȝân. To him who cultivates union with men, things must come to belong, and hence Thung Ȝân is followed by Tâ Yû. Those who, have what is great should not allow in themselves the feeling of being full, and hence Tâ Yû is followed by Khien. When great possessions are associated with humility, there is sure to be pleasure and satisfaction; and hence Khien is followed by Yü.

16-19. Where such complacency is awakened, (he who causes it) is sure to have followers[239]. They who follow another are sure to have services (to perform), and hence Sui is followed by Kû[240]. Kû means (the performance of) services. He who performs such services may afterwards become great, and hence Kû is followed by Lin. Lin means great.

19-23. What is great draws forth contemplation, and hence Lin is followed by Kwân. He who attracts contemplation will then bring about the union of others with himself, and hence Kwân is followed by Shih Ho. Shih Ho means union. But things should not be united in a reckless or irregular way, and hence Shih Ho is followed by Pî. Pî denotes

---

[237] Contention on a great scale will put all the population of a state in excitement and motion, and military measures of repression will be necessary. But the idea of the multitudes in Sze would seem to be simply that of number, and not that of a numerous host. In a feudal kingdom, however, all the able-bodied people might be required to join the army.

[238] Lî, the name of the 10th hexagram, is the symbol for a shoe, and the act of treading or walking. It seems here to be derived from the homophonous lî, the symbol of acts of ceremony. The identity of sound or name must be considered as accidental. A measured step would be one of the first ways in which the inward sense of propriety would manifest itself.

[239] By the subject of Tâ Yû and Khien we must understand the possessor of the kingdom—the great man who in his greatness is yet distinguished by humility. He attracts followers.

[240] For the true meaning of Kû and Lin, the names of hexagrams 18, 19, see what is said in the notes on the Text of them.

adorning. When ornamentation has been carried to the utmost, its progress comes to an end; and hence Pî is followed by Po. Po denotes decay and overthrow.

23-26. Things cannot be done away for ever. When decadence and overthrow have completed their work at one end, reintegration commences at the other; and hence Po is followed by Fû. When the return (thus indicated) has taken place, we have not any rash disorder, and Fû. is followed by Wû Wang. Given the freedom from disorder and insincerity (which this name denotes), there may be the accumulation (of virtue), and Wû Wang is followed by Tâ *Khû*.

26-30. Such accumulation having taken place, there will follow the nourishment of it; and hence Tâ *Khû* is followed by Î. Î denotes nourishing. Without nourishment there could be no movement, and hence Î is followed by Tâ Kwo. Things cannot for ever be in a state of extraordinary (progress); and hence Tâ Kwo is followed by Khân. Khân denotes falling into peril. When one falls into peril, he is sure to attach himself to some person or thing; and hence Khân is followed by Lî. Lî denotes being attached, or adhering, to.

## SECTION II.

31, 32. Heaven and earth existing, all (material) things then got their existence. All (material) things having existence, afterwards there came male and female. From the existence of male and female there came afterwards husband and wife. From husband and wife there came father and son. From father and son there came ruler and minister. From ruler and minister there came high and low. When (the distinction of) high and low had existence, afterwards came the arrangements of propriety and righteousness.

The rule for the relation of husband and wife is that it should be long-enduring. Hence Hsien is followed by Hăng. Hăng denotes long enduring[241].

32-37. Things cannot long abide in the same place; and hence Hăng is followed by Thun. Thun denotes withdrawing. Things cannot be for ever withdrawn; and hence Thun is succeeded by Tâ *K*wang. Things cannot remain forever (simply) in the state of vigour; and hence Tâ *K*wang is succeeded by Ʒin. Ʒin denotes advancing. (But) advancing is sure to lead to being wounded; and hence Ʒin is succeeded by Ming Î. Î denotes being wounded. He who is wounded abroad will return to his home; and hence Ming Î is followed by Kiâ Ʒăn.

37-40. When the right administration of the family is at an end,

---

[241] The same reference should be made to the notes on the Text of Hsien and many of the other hexagrams that follow.

misunderstanding and division will ensue; and hence Kiâ Zăn is
followed by Khwei. Khwei denotes misunderstanding and division; and
such a state is sure to give rise to difficulties and complications. Khwei
therefore is followed by *K*ien. *K*ien denotes difficulties; but things
cannot remain for ever in such a state. *K*ien therefore is followed by
*K*ieh, which denotes relaxation and ease.

40-44. In a state of relaxation and ease there are sure to be losses;
and hence *K*ieh is followed by Sun. But when Sun (or diminution) is
going on without end, increase is sure to come. Sun therefore is
followed by Yî. When increase goes on without end, there is sure to
come a dispersing of it, and hence Yî is followed by Kwâi. Kwâi
denotes dispersion. But dispersion must be succeeded by a meeting
(again). Hence Kwâi is followed by Kâu, which denotes such meeting.

44-48. When things meet together, a collection is then formed.
Hence Kâu is followed by Ʒhui, which name denotes, being collected.
When (good men) are collected and mount to the highest places, there
results what we call an upward advance; and hence Ʒhui is followed by
Shăng. When such advance continues without stopping, there is sure to
come distress; and hence Shăng is followed by Khwăn. When distress
is felt in the height (that has been gained), there is sure to be a return to
the ground beneath; and hence Khwăn is followed by Ʒing.

48, 49. What happens under Ʒing requires to be changed, and
hence it is followed by Ko (denoting change).

49-55. For changing the substance of things there is nothing equal
to the caldron; and hence Kö is followed by Ting. For presiding over
(that and all other) vessels, no one is equal to the eldest son, and hence
Ting is followed by *K*ăn. *K*ăn conveys the idea of putting in motion.
But things cannot be kept in motion forever. The motion is stopped;
and hence *K*ăn is followed by Kăn, which gives the idea of arresting or
stopping. Things cannot be kept for ever in a state of repression, and
hence Kăn is followed by *K*ien, which gives the idea of (gradually)
advancing. With advance there must be a certain point that is arrived at,
and hence Kien is succeeded by Kwei Mei. When things thus find the
proper point to which to come, they are sure to become great. Hence
Kwei Mei is succeeded by Făng, which conveys the idea of being great.

55-57. He whose greatness reaches the utmost possibility, is sure to
lose his dwelling; and hence Făng is succeeded by Lü (denoting
travellers or strangers). We have in it the idea of strangers who have no
place to receive them, and hence Lü is followed by Sûn, which gives
the idea of (penetrating and) entering.

57-59. One enters (on the pursuit of his object), and afterwards has
pleasure in it; hence Sûn is followed by Tui. Tui denotes pleasure and
satisfaction. This pleasure and satisfaction (begins) afterwards to be
dissipated, and hence Tui is followed by Hwan, which denotes
separation and division.

59-62. A state of division cannot continue for ever, and therefore Hwan is followed by 3ieh. 3ieh (or the system of regulations) having been established, men believe in it, and hence it is followed by *K*ung Fû. When men have the belief which *K*ung Fû implies, they are sure to carry it into practice; and hence it is succeeded by Hsiâo Kwo.

62-64. He that surpasses others is sure to remedy (evils that exist), and therefore Hsiâo Kwo is succeeded by *K*î 3î. But the succession of events cannot come to an end, and therefore *K*î 3î is succeeded by Wei 3î, with which (the hexagrams) come to a close.

## APPENDIX VII.

Treatise on the Hexagrams taken promiscuously, according to the opposition or diversity of their meaning.

This last of the Appendixes is touched on very briefly in the concluding paragraph of the Introduction, p. 60. It is stated there to be in rhyme, and I have endeavoured to give a similar form to the following version of it. The rhymes and length of the lines in the original, however, are very irregular, and I found it impossible to reproduce that irregularity in English.

    1, 2. Strength in *Kh*ien, weakness in Khwăn we find.

    8, 7. Pî shows us joy, and Sze the anxious mind.

19, 20. Lin gives, Kwân seeks;—such are the several themes
        Their different figures were to teach designed.

      3. *K*un manifests itself, yet keeps its place;

      4. 'Mid darkness still, to light Măng sets its face.

51, 52. *K*ăn starts; Kăn stops. In Sun and Yî are seen

41, 42. How fulness and decay their course begin.

    26. Tâ *Kh*û keeps still, and waits the proper time.

    25. Wû Wang sets forth how evil springs from crime.

45, 46. Good men in 3hui collect; in Shang they rise:

15, 16. *Kh*ien itself, Yü others doth despise.

21, 22. Shih Ho takes eating for its theme; and Pî
        Takes what is plain, from ornament quite free.

58, 57. Tui shows its scope, but Sun's we do not see.

17, 18. Sui quits the old; Kû makes a new decree.

    23. We see in Po its subject worn away;

    24. And Fû shows its recovering from decay.

    35. Above in 3in the sun shines clear and bright;

    36. But in Ming Î 'tis hidden from the sight.

48, 47. Progress in 3ing in Khwăn encounters blight.

    31. Effect quick answering cause in Hsien appears;

    32. While Hăng denotes continuance for years.

59, 60. Hwân scatters; but 3ieh its code of rules uprears.

40. Relief and ease with *K*ieh are sure to come;
41. Hard toil and danger have in *K*ien their home.
38. Khwei looks on others as beyond its care;
37. Kiâ *Z*ăn all includes within its sphere.

12, 11. While Phî and Thâi their different scopes prefer,
34, 33. Tâ *K*wang stops here as right; withdraws Thun there.

14. Tâ Yû adhering multitudes can show;
13. Thung *Z*ăn reflects their warm affection's glow.

50, 51. Ting takes what's new; the old is left by Ko.
61, 62. Sincere is *K*ung Fû; but exceeds, Hsiâo Kwo.
55, 56. Făng tells of trouble; Lü can boast few friends.
30, 29. Fire mounts in Lî; water in Khân descends.

9. Hsiâo *Kh*û with few 'gainst many foes contends.
10. Movement in Lî, unresting, never ends.
5. Hsü shows its subject making no advance:
6. In Sung we seek in vain a friendly glance;
28. And Tâ Kwo's overthrown with sad mischance.
44. Kâu shows a meeting, where the many strong
    Are met by one that's weak, yet struggles long.
53. In *K*ien we see a bride who will delay
    To move until the bridegroom takes his way.
27. Body and mind are nourished right in Î;
63. All things are well established in Kî Ȝî.
54. Kwei Mei reveals how ends the virgin life;
64. Wei Ȝî how fails the youth (to get a wife).
43. The strong disperse the weak; Kwâi teaches so.
    Prospers the good man's way; to grief all small men go.

# HEXAGRAM ENDNOTES.

[i] The Text under each hexagram consists of one paragraph by king Wăn, explaining the figure as a whole, and of six (in the case of hexagrams 1 and 2, of seven) paragraphs by the duke of *K*âu, explaining the individual lines. The explanatory notices introduced above to this effect will not be repeated. A double space will be used to mark off the portion of king Wăn from that of his son.

Each hexagram consists of two of the trigrams of Fû-hsî, the lower being called 'the inner,' and the one above 'the outer.' The lines, however, are numbered from one to six, commencing with the lowest. To denote the number of it and of the sixth line, the terms for commencing' and 'topmost' are used. The intermediate lines are simply 'second,' 'third,' &c. As the lines must be either whole or divided, technically called strong and weak, yang and yin, this distinction is indicated by the application to them of the numbers nine and six. All whole lines are nine, all divided lines, six.

Two explanations have been proposed of this application of these numbers. The *Kh*ien trigram, it is said, contains 3 strokes (▬▬▬), and the *Kh*wăn 6 (▬ ▬). But the yang contains the yin in itself, and its representative number will be 3 + 6 = 9, while the yin, not containing the yang, will only have its own number or 6. This explanation, entirely arbitrary, is new deservedly abandoned. The other is based on the use of the 'four Hsiang,' or emblematic figures (▬▬▬ the great or old yang, ▬▬▬ the young yang, ▬ ▬ the old yin, and ▬▬▬ the young yin). To these are assigned (by what process is unimportant for our present purpose) the numbers 9, 8, 7, 6. They were 'the old yang,' represented by 9, and 'the old yin,' represented by 6, that, in the manipulation of the stalks to form new diagrams, determined the changes of figure; and so 9 and 6 came to be used as the names of a yang line and a yin line respectively. This explanation is now universally acquiesced in. The nomenclature of first nine, nine two, &c., or first six, six two, &c., however, is merely a jargon; and I have preferred to use, instead of it, in the translation, in order to describe the lines, the names 'undivided' and 'divided.'

I. Does king Wăn ascribe four attributes here to *Kh*ien, or only two? According to Appendix IV, always by Chinese writers assigned to Confucius, he assigns four, corresponding to the principles of benevolence, righteousness, propriety, and knowledge in man's nature. *K*û Hsî held that he assigned only two, and that we should translate, 'greatly penetrating,' and 'requires to be correct and firm,' two responses in divination. Up and down throughout the Text of the 64 hexagrams, we often find the characters thus coupled together. Both interpretations are possible. I have followed what is accepted as the view of Confucius. It would take pages to give a tithe of what has been written in justification of it, and to reconcile it with the other.

'The dragon' is the symbol employed by the duke of *K*âu to represent 'the superior man' and especially 'the great man,' exhibiting the virtues or attributes characteristic of heaven. The creature's. proper home is in the water, but it can disport itself on the land, and also fly and soar aloft. It has been from the earliest time the emblem with the Chinese of the highest dignity and wisdom, of sovereignty and sagehood, the combination of which constitutes 'the great man.' One emblem runs through the lines of many of the hexagrams as here.

But the dragon appears in the sixth line as going beyond the proper limits. The ruling-sage has gone through all the sphere in which he is called on to display his attributes; it is time for him to relax. The line should not be always pulled tight; the bow should not be always kept drawn. The unchanging use of force will give occasion for repentance. The moral meaning found in the line is that 'the high shall be abased.'

The meaning given to the supernumerary paragraph is the opposite of that of paragraph 6. The 'host of dragons without their heads' would give us the next hexagram, or Khwăn, made up of six divided lines. Force would have given place to submission, and haughtiness to humility; and the result would be good fortune. Such at least is the interpretation of the paragraph given in a narrative of the 3o-Kwan under B. C. 513. For further explanation of the duke of Kâu's meaning, see Appendixes II and IV.

ⁱⁱ The same attributes are here ascribed to Khwăn, as in the former hexagram to Khien;—but with a difference. The figure, made up of six divided lines, expresses the ideal of subordination and docility. The superior man, represented by it, must not take the initiative; and by following he will find his lord,—the subject, that is of Khien. Again, the correctness and firmness is defined to be that of 'a mare,' 'docile and strong,' but a creature for the service of man. That it is not the sex of the animal which the writer has chiefly in mind is plain from the immediate mention of the superior man, and his lord.

That superior man will seek to bring his friends along with himself to serve his ruler. But according to the arrangement of the trigrams by king Wăn, the place of Khwăn is in the south-west, while the opposite quarter is occupied by the yang trigram Kăn, as in Figure 2, Plate III. All that this portion of the Thwan says is an instruction to the subject of the hexagram to seek for others of the same principles and tendencies with himself to serve their common lord. But in quietness and firmness will be his strength.

The symbolism of the lines is various. Paragraph 2 presents to us the earth itself, according to the Chinese conception of it, as a great cube. To keep his excellence under restraint, as in paragraph 3, is the part of a minister or officer, seeking not his own glory, but that of his ruler. Paragraph 4 shows its subject exercising a still greater restraint on himself than in paragraph 3. There is an interpretation of the symbolism of paragraph 5 in a narrative of the 3o Kwan, under the 12th year of duke Khâo, B.C. 530. 'Yellow' is one of the five 'correct' colours, and the colour of the earth. 'The lower garment' is a symbol of humility. The fifth line is the seat of honour. If its occupant possess the qualities indicated, he will be greatly fortunate.

See the note on the sixth line of hexagram 1. What is there said to be 'beyond the proper limits' takes place here 'in the wild.' The humble subject of the divided line is transformed into a dragon, and fights with the true dragon, the subject of the undivided line. They fight and bleed, and their blood is of the colour proper to heaven or the sky, and the colour proper to the earth. Paragraph 7 supposes that the hexagram Khwăn should become changed into Khien—the result of which would be good.

ⁱⁱⁱ The character called Kun is pictorial, and was intended to show us how a plant struggles with difficulty out of the earth, rising gradually above the surface. This difficulty, marking the first stages in the growth of a plant, is used to symbolise the struggles that mark the rise of a state out of a condition of disorder, consequent on a great revolution. The same thing is denoted by the combination of the trigrams that form the figure;—as will be seen in the notes on it under Appendix II.

I have introduced within parentheses, in the translation, the words 'in the case which the hexagram presupposes.' It is necessary to introduce them. King Wăn and his son wrote, as they did in every hexagram, with reference to a particular state of affairs which they had in mind. This was the unspoken text which controlled and directed all their writing; and the student must try to get hold of this, if he would make his way with comfort and success through the Yî. Wăn saw the social and political world around him in great disorder, hard to be remedied. But he had faith in himself and the destinies of his House. Let there be prudence and caution, with unswerving adherence to the right; let the government of the different states be entrusted to good and able men:—then all would be well.

The first line is undivided, showing the strength of its subject. He will be capable of action, and his place in the trigram of mobility will the more dispose him to it. But above him is the trigram of peril; and the lowest line of that, to which especially he must look for response and co-operation, is divided and weak. Hence arise the ideas of difficulty in advancing, the necessity of caution, and the advantage of his being clothed with authority.

To the subject of the second line, divided, advance is still more difficult. He is weak in himself; he is pressed by the subject of the strong line below him. But happily that subject, though strong, is correct; and above in the fifth line, in the place of authority, is the strong one, union with whom and the service of whom should be the objects pursued. All these circumstances suggested to the duke of *K*âu the idea of a young lady, sought in marriage by a strong wooer, when marriage was unsuitable, rejecting him, and finally, after ten years, marrying a more suitable, the only suitable, match for her.

The third line is divided, not central, and the number of its place is appropriate to the occupancy of a strong line. All these things should affect the symbolism of the line. But the outcome of the whole hexagram being good, the superior man sees the immediate danger and avoids it.

The subject of the fourth line, the first of the upper trigram, has recourse to the strong suitor of line 1, the first of the lower trigram; and with his help is able to cope with the difficulties of the position, and go forward.

The subject of the fifth line is in the place of authority, and should show himself a ruler, dispensing benefits on a great scale. But he is in the very centre of the trigram denoting perilousness, and line 2, which responds to 5, is weak. Hence arises the symbolism, and great things should not be attempted.

The sixth line is weak; the third responding to it is also weak it is at the extremity of peril; the game is up. What can remain for its subject in such a case but terror and abject weeping?

[iv] As *K*un shows us plants struggling from beneath the surface, Măng suggests to us the small and. undeveloped appearance which they then present; and hence it came to be the symbol of youthful inexperience and ignorance. The object of the hexagram is to show how such a condition should be dealt with by the parent and ruler, whose authority and duty are represented by the second and sixth, the two undivided lines. All between the first and last sentences of the Thwan must be taken as an oracular response received by the party divining on the subject of enlightening the youthful ignorant. This accounts for its being more than usually enigmatical, and for its being partly rhythmical. See Appendix I, in loc.

The subject of the first line, weak, and at the bottom of the figure, is in the grossest ignorance. Let him be punished. If punishment avail to loosen the shackles and manacles from the mind, well; if not, and punishment be persevered with, the effect will be had.

On the subject of the second line, strong, and in the central place, devolves the task of enlightening the ignorant; and we have him discharging it with forbearance and humility. In proof of his generosity, it is said that 'he receives,' or learns from, even weak and ignorant women. He appears also as 'a son' taking the place of his father.

The third line is weak, and occupies an odd place belonging properly to an undivided line; nor is its place in the centre. All these things give the subject of it so bad a character.

The fourth line is far from both the second and sixth, and can get no help from its correlate,—the first line, weak as itself. What good can be done with or by the subject of it?

The fifth line is in the place of honour, and has for its correlate the strong line in the second place. Being weak in itself, it is taken as the symbol of a simple lad, willing to be taught.

The topmost line is strong, and in the highest place. It is natural, but unwise, in him to use violence in carrying on his educational measures. A better course is suggested to him.

[v] Hsü means waiting. Strength confronted by peril might be expected to advance boldly and at once to struggle with it; but it takes the wiser plan of waiting till success is sure. This is the lesson of the hexagram. That 'sincerity is declared in it' is proved from the fifth line in the position of honour and authority, central, itself undivided and in an odd place. In such a case, nothing but firm correctness is necessary to great success.

'Going through a great stream,' an expression frequent in the Yî, may mean undertaking hazardous enterprises, or encountering great difficulties, without any special reference; but more natural is it to understand by the great stream' the Yellow river, which the lords of *K*âu must cross in a revolutionary movement against the dynasty of Yin and its tyrant. The passage of it by king Wû, the son of Wăn in B. C. 1122, was certainly one of the greatest deeds in the history of China. It was preceded also by long waiting,' till the time of assured success came.

'The border' under line 1 means the frontier territory of the state. There seems no necessity for such a symbolism. 'The sand' and 'the mud' are appropriate with reference to the watery defile; but it is different with 'the border.' The subject of the line appears at work in his distant fields, not thinking of anything but his daily work; and he is advised to abide in that state and mind.

'The sand' of paragraph 2 suggests a nearer approach to the defile, but its subject is still self-restrained and waiting. I do not see what suggests the idea of his suffering from 'the strife of tongues.'

In paragraph 3 the subject is on the brink of the stream. His advance to that position has provoked resistance, which may result in his injury.

Line 4 has passed from the inner to the upper trigram, and entered on the scene of danger and strife;—'into the place of blood.' Its subject is 'weak and in the correct place for him;' he therefore retreats and escapes from the cavern, where he was engaged with his enemy.

Line 5 is strong and central, and in its correct place, being that of honour. All good qualities therefore belong to the subject of it, who has triumphed, and with firmness will triumph still more.

Line 6 is weak, and has entered deeply into the defile and its caverns. What will become of its subject? His correlate is the strong line 3 below, which comes with its two companions to his help. If they are respectfully received, that help will prove effectual. P. Regis tries to find out a reference in these 'three guests' to three princes who distinguished themselves by taking part with *K*âu in its struggle with Yin or Shang; see vol. i, pp. 279-282. I dare not be so confident of any historical reference.

[vi] We have strength in the upper trigram, as if to regulate and control the lower, and peril in that lower as if looking out for an opportunity to assail the upper; or, as it may be represented, we have one's self in a state of peril matched against strength from without. All this is supposed to give the idea of contention or strife. But the undivided line in the centre of Khân is emblematic of sincerity, and gives a character to the whole figure. An individual, so represented, will be very wary, and have good fortune; but strife is bad, and if persevered in even by such a one, the effect will be evil. The fifth line, undivided, in an odd place, and central, serves as a representative of 'the great man,' whose agency is sure to be good; but the topmost line being also strong, and with its two companions, riding as it were, on the trigram of peril, its action is likely to be too rash for a great enterprise. See the treatise on the Thwan, in loc.

The subject of line 1 is weak and at the bottom of the figure. He may suffer a little in the nascent strife, but will let it drop; and the effect will be good.

Line 2 represents one who is strong, and has the rule of the lower trigram;—he has the mind for strife, and might be expected to engage in it. But his strength is weakened by, being in an even place, and he is no match for his correlate in line 5, and therefore retreats. A town or city with only three hundred families is said to be very small. That the subject of the line should retire to so insignificant a place is further proof of his humility.

Line 3 is weak and in an odd place. Its subject therefore is not equal to strive, but withdraws from the arena. Even if forced into it, he will keep himself in the background;—and be safe. 'He keeps in the old place assigned for his support' is, literally, 'He eats his old virtue;' meaning that he lives in and on the appanage assigned to him for his services.

Line 4 is strong, and not in the centre; so that we are to conceive of its subject as having a mind to strive. But immediately above it is line 5, the symbol of the ruler, and with him it is hopeless to strive; immediately below is 3, weak, and out of its proper place, incapable of maintaining a contention. Its proper correlate is the lowest line, weak, and out of its proper place, from whom little help can come. Hence its subject takes the course indicated, which leads to good fortune.

Line 5 has every circumstance in favour of its subject.

Line 6 is strong and able to contend successfully; but is there to be no end of striving? Persistence in it is sure to end in defeat and disgrace. The contender here might receive a reward from the king for his success; but if he received it thrice in a morning, thrice it would be taken from him again. As to the nature of the reward here given, see on the Lî Kî, X, ii, 32.

P. Regis explains several of the expressions in the Text, both in the Thwan and the Hsiang, from the history of king Wăn and his son king Wû. Possibly his own circumstances may have suggested to Wăn some of the Thwan; and his course in avoiding a direct collision with the tyrant Shâu, and Wû's subsequent exploits may have been in the mind of the duke of Kâu. Some of the sentiments, however, cannot be historically explained. They are general protests against all contention and strife.

ᵛⁱⁱ The conduct of military expeditions in a feudal kingdom, and we may say, generally, is denoted by the hexagram Sze. Referring to Appendixes I and II for an explanation of the way in which the combination of lines in it is made out to suggest the idea of an army, and that idea being assumed, it is easy to see how the undivided line in the second place should be interpreted of the general, who is responded to by the divided line in the fifth and royal place. Thus entire trust is reposed in him. He is strong and correct, and his enterprises will be successful. He is denominated kang zăn, 'an old, experienced man.'

'The rules,' it is said, 'are twofold;—first, that the war be for a righteous end; and second, that the manner of conducting it, especially at the outset, be right.' But how this and the warning in the conclusion should both follow from the divided line being in the first place, has not been sufficiently explained.

How line 2 comes to be the symbol of the general in command of the army has been shown above on the Thwan. The orders of the king thrice conveyed to him are to be understood of his appointment to the command, and not of any rewards conferred on him as a tribute to his merit. Nor is stress to be laid on the 'thrice.' 'It does not mean that the appointment came to him three times; but that it was to him exclusively, and with the entire confidence of the king.'

The symbolism of line 3 is very perplexing. P. Regis translates it:—'Milites videntur deponere sarcinas in curribus. Male.' Canon McClatchie has:—'Third-six represents soldiers as it were lying dead in their baggage carts, and is unlucky.' To the same effect was my own translation of the paragraph, nearly thirty years ago. But the third line, divided, cannot be forced to have such an indication. The meaning I have now given is more legitimate, taken character by character, and more in harmony with the scope of the hexagram, The subject of line 2 is the one proper leader of the host. But line 3 is divided and weak, and occupies the place of a strong line, as if its subject had perversely jumped over two, and perched himself above it to take the command. This interpretation also suits better in the 5th paragraph.

Line 4 is weak and not central; and therefore 'to retreat' is natural for its subject. But its place is even, and proper for a divided line; and the retreat will be right in the circumstances.

In line 5 we seem to have an intimation of the important truth that only defensive war, or war waged by the rightful authority to put down rebellion and lawlessness, is right. 'The birds in the fields' symbolise parties attacking for plunder. The fifth line symbolises the chief authority,—the king, who is weak, or humble, and in the centre, and cedes the use of all his power to the general symbolised by line 2. The subject of 2 is 'the oldest son.' Those of three and four are supposed to be 'the younger brother and son,' that is, the younger men, who would cause evil if admitted to share the command.

The lesson on the topmost line is true and important, but the critics seem unable to deduce it from the nature of the line, as divided and in the sixth place.

ᵛⁱⁱⁱ The idea of union between the different members and classes of a state, and how it can be secured, is the subject of the hexagram Pî. The whole line occupying the fifth place, or that of authority, in the hexagram, represents the ruler to whom the subjects of all the other lines offer a ready submission. According to the general rules for the symbolism of the lines, the second line is the correlate of the fifth; but all the other lines are here made subject to that fifth;—which is also a law of the Yî, according to the 'Daily Lecture.' To me it has the suspicious look of being made for the occasion. The harmony of union, therefore, is to be secured by the sovereign authority of one; but he is warned to see to it that his virtue be what will beseem his place, and subjects are warned not to delay to submit to him.

Where does the 'sincerity' predicated of the subject of line 1 come from? The 'earthenware vessel' is supposed to indicate its plain, unadorned character; but there is nothing in the position and nature of the line, beyond the general idea in the figure, to Suggest the attribute.

Line 2 is the proper correlate of 5. Its position in the centre of the inner or lower trigram agrees with the movement of its subject as proceeding from the inward mind.

Line 3 is weak, not in the centre, nor in its correct place. The lines above and below it are both weak. All these things are supposed to account for what is said on it.

'The one beyond himself' in line 4 is the ruler or king, who is the subject of 5, and with whom union ought to be sought. The divided line, moreover, is in a place proper to it. If its subject be firm and correct, there will be good fortune.

The subject of line 5 is the king, who must be the centre of union. The ancient kings had their great hunting expeditions in the different seasons; and that of each season had its peculiar rules. But what is stated here was common to all. When the beating was completed, and the shooting was ready to commence, one side of the enclosure into which the game had been driven was left open and unguarded;—a proof of the royal benevolence, which did not want to make an end of all the game. So well known and understood is this benevolence of the model king of the hexagram, that all his people try to give it effect. Thus the union contemplated is shown to be characterised by mutual confidence and appreciation in virtue and benevolence.

A weak line being in the 6th place, which is appropriate to it, its subject is supposed to be trying to promote union among and with the subjects of the lines below. It is too late. The time is past. Hence it is symbolised as 'without a head,' that is, as not having taken the first step, from which its action should begin, and go on to the end.

ⁱˣ The name Hsiâo *Khû* is interpreted as meaning 'small restraint.' The idea of 'restraint' having once been determined on as that to be conveyed by the figure, it is easily made out that the restraint must be small, for its representative is the divided line in the fourth place; and the check given by that to all the undivided lines cannot be great. Even if we suppose, as many critics do, that all the virtue of that upper trigram Sun is concentrated in its first line, the attribute ascribed to Sun is that of docile flexibility, which cannot long be successful against the strength emblemed by the lower trigram *Kh*ien. The restraint therefore is small, and in the end there will be 'progress and success.'

The second sentence of the Thwan contains indications of the place, time, and personality of the writer which it seems possible to ascertain. The fief of *K*âu was the western portion of the kingdom of Yin or Shang, the China of the twelfth century B. C., the era of king Wăn. Rain coming and moistening the ground is the cause of the beauty and luxuriance of the vegetable world, and the emblem of the blessings flowing from good training and good government. Here therefore in the west, the hereditary territory of the house of *K*âu, are blessings which might enrich the whole kingdom; but they are somehow restrained. The dense clouds do not empty their stores.

P. Regis says:—'To declare openly that no rain fell from the heavens long covered with dense clouds over the great tract of country, which stretched from the western border to the court and on to the eastern sea, was nothing else but leaving it to all thoughtful minds to draw the conclusion that the family of Wan was as worthy of the supreme seat as that of Shâu, the tyrant, however ancient, was unworthy of it (vol. i, p. 356).' The intimation is not put in the Text, however, so clearly as by P. Regis.

Line 1 is undivided, the first line of *Kh*ien, occupying its proper place. Its subject, therefore, notwithstanding the check of line 4, resumes his movement, and will act according to his strong nature, and go forward.

Line 2 is also strong, and though an even place is not appropriate to it, that place being central, its subject will make common cause with the subject of line 1; and there will be good fortune.

Line 3, though strong, and in a proper place, yet not being in the centre, is supposed to be less able to resist the restraint of line 4; and hence it has the ill omens that are given.

The subject of line 4, one weak line against all the strong lines of the hexagram, might well expect wounds, and feel apprehension in trying to restrain the others; but it is in its proper place; it is the first line also of Sun, whose attribute is docile flexibility. The strong lines are moved to sympathy and help, and 'there is no mistake.'

Line 5 occupies the central place of Sun, and converts, by the sincerity, of its subject, 4 and 6 into its neighbours, who suffer themselves to be used by it, and effect their common object.

In line 6, the idea of the hexagram has run its course. The harmony of nature is restored. The rain falls, and the onward march of the strong lines should now stop. But weakness that has achieved such a result, if it plume itself on it, will be in a position of peril; and like the full moon, which must henceforth wane. Let the superior man, when he has attained his end, remain in quiet.

ˣ The character giving its name to the hexagram plays an important part also in the symbolism; and this may be the reason why it does not, as the name, occupy the first place in the Thwan. Looking at the figure, we see it is made up of the trigrams Tui, representing a marsh, and *Kh*ien, representing the sky. Tui is a yin trigram, and its top line is divided. Below *Kh*ien, the great symbol of strength, it may readily suggest the idea of treading on a tiger's tail, which was an old way of expressing what was hazardous (Shû V, XXV, 2). But what suggests the statement that 'the tiger does not bite the treader?' The attribute of Tui is pleased satisfaction. of course such an attribute could not be predicated of one who was in the fangs of a tiger. The coming scatheless out of such danger further suggests the idea of 'progress and success' in the course which king Wăn had in his mind. And according to Appendix VI, that course was 'propriety,' the observance of all the rules of courtesy. On these, as so many stepping-stones, one may tread safely amid scenes of disorder and peril.

Line 1 is an undivided line in an odd place; giving us the ideas of activity, firmness, and correctness. One so characterised will act rightly.

Line 2 occupies the middle place of the trigram, which is supposed to symbolise a path cut straight and level along the hill-side, or over difficult ground. Line, is not a proper correlate, and hence the idea of the subject of 2 being 'a quiet and solitary man.'

Line 3 is neither central nor in an even place, which would be proper to it. But with the strength of will which the occupant of an odd place should possess, he goes forward with the evil results so variously emblemed. The editors of the imperial edition, in illustration of the closing sentence, refer to Analects VII, x.

Line 4 is in contiguity with 5, whose subject is in the place of authority; but he occupies the place proper to a weak or divided line, and hence he bethinks himself, and goes softly.

Beneath the symbolism under line 5, lies the principle that the most excellent thing in 'propriety' is humility. And the subject of the line, which is strong and central, will not be lacking in this, but bear in mind that the higher he is exalted, the greater may be his fall.

What is said on line 6 is good, but is only a truism. The whole course has been shown; if every step has been right and appropriate, the issue will be very good.

[xi] The language of the Thwan has reference to the form of Thâi, with the three strong lines of *Kh*ien below, and the three weak lines of Khwăn above. The former are 'the great,' active and vigorous; the latter are 'the small,' inactive and submissive. But where have the former 'come' from, and whither are the latter gone?' In many editions of the Yî beneath the hexagram of Thâi here, there appears that of Kwei Mei, the 54th in order ▦ , which becomes Thâi, if the third and fourth lines exchange places. But in the notes on the Thwan, in the first Appendix, on hexagram 6, I have spoken of the doctrine of 'changing figures,' and intimated my disbelief of it. The different hexagrams arose necessarily by the continued manipulation of the undivided and divided lines, and placing them each over itself and over the other. When king Wăn wrote these Thwan, he was taking the 64 hexagrams, as they were ready to his hand, and not forming one from another by any process of divination. The 'gone' and 'come' are merely equivalent to 'below' and 'above,' in the lower trigram or in the upper.

A course in which the motive forces are represented by the three strong, and the opposing by the three weak lines, must be progressive and successful. Thâi is called the hexagram of the first month of the year, the first month of the natural spring, when for six months, through the fostering sun and genial skies, the processes of growth will be going on.

The symbolism of paragraph 1 is suggested by the three strong lines of *Kh*ien all together, and all possessed by the same instinct to advance. The movement of the first will be supported by that of the others, and be fortunate.

The second line is strong, but in an even place. This is supposed to temper the strength of its subject; which is expressed by the first of his characteristics. But the even place is the central; and it is responded to by a proper correlate in the fifth line above. Hence come all the symbolism of the paragraph and the auspice of good fortune implied in it.

Beneath the symbolism in paragraph 3 there lies the persuasion of the constant change that is taking place in nature and in human affairs. As night succeeds to day, and winter to summer, so calamity may be expected to follow prosperity, and decay the flourishing of a state. The third is the last of the lines of *Kh*ien, by whose strength and activity the happy state of Thâi has been produced. Another aspect of things may be looked for; but by firmness and correctness the good estate of the present may be long continued.

According to the treatise on the Thwan, the subjects of the fourth and other upper lines are not 'the small returning' as opponents of the strong lines below, as is generally supposed; but as the correlates of those lines, of one heart and mind with them to maintain the state of Thâi, and giving them, humbly but readily, all the help in their power.

Tî-yî, the last sovereign but one of the Yin dynasty, reigned from B. C. 1191 to 1155; but what was the history of him and his sister here referred to we do not know. P. Regis assumes that he gave his sister in marriage to the lord of *K*âu, known in subsequent time as king Wăn, and that she was the famous Thaî-sze;—contrary to all the evidence I have been able to find on the subject. According to *Kh*ăng-3ze, Tî-yî was the first to enact a law that daughters of the royal house, in marrying princes of the states, should be in subjection to them, as if they were not superior to them in rank. Here line 5, while occupying the place of dignity and authority in the hexagram, is yet a weak line in the place of a strong and its subject, accordingly, humbly condescends to his one, strong and proper correlate in line 2.

The course denoted by Thâi has been run; and will be followed by one of a different and unhappy character. The earth dug from the moat had been built up to form a protecting wall; but it is now again fallen into the ditch. War will only aggravate the evil;

and however the ruler may address good proclamations to himself and the people of his capital, the coming evil cannot be altogether averted.

xii The form of Phî, it will be seen, is exactly the opposite of that of Thâi. Much of what has been said on the interpretation of that will apply to this, or at least assist the student in making out the meaning of its symbolism. Phî is the hexagram of the seventh month. Genial influences have done their work, the processes of growth are at an end. Henceforth increasing decay must be looked for.

Naturally we should expect the advance of the subject of the first of the three weak lines to lead to evil; but if he set himself to be firm and correct, he will bring about a different issue.

Patience and obedience are proper for the small man in all circumstances. If the great man in difficulty yet cherish these attributes, he will soon have a happy issue out of the distress.

The third line is weak. Its place is odd, and therefore for it incorrect. Its subject would vent his evil purpose, but has not strength to do so. He is left therefore to the shame which he ought to feel without a word of warning. Does the ming of the fourth line mean 'the ordination of Heaven,' as Kû Hsî thinks; or the orders of the ruler, as Khăng-3ze says? Whichever interpretation be taken (and some critics unite the two), the action of the subject of the line, whose strength is tempered by the even position, will be good and correct, and issue in success and happiness.

The strong line in the fifth, (its correct), place, brings the distress and obstruction to a close. Yet its subject—the ruler in the hexagram-is warned to continue to be cautious in two lines of rhyme:—

> 'And let him say, "I die! I die I"
> So to a bushy clump his fortune he shall tie.'

There is an end of the condition of distress. It was necessary, that condition should give place to its opposite; and the strong line in the topmost place fitly represents the consequent joy.

xiii Thung Zăn describes a condition of nature and of the state opposite to that of Phî. There was distress and obstruction; here is union. But the union must be based entirely on public considerations, without taint of selfishness.

The strong line in the fifth, its correct, place, occupies the most important position, and has for its correlate the weak second line, also in its correct place. The one divided line is naturally sought after by all the strong lines. The upper trigram is that of heaven, which is above; the lower is that of fire, whose tendency is to mount upwards. All these things are in harmony with the idea of union. But the union must be free from all selfish motives, and this is indicated by its being in the remote districts of the country, where people are unsophisticated, and free from the depraving effects incident to large societies. A union from such motives will cope with the greatest difficulties; and yet a word of caution is added.

Line 1 emblems the first attempts at union. It is strong, but in the lowest place; and it has no proper correlate above. There is, however, no intermixture of selfishness in it.

Lines 2 and 5 are proper correlates, which fact suggests in this hexagram the idea of their union being limited and partial, and such as may afford ground for blame.

Line 3 is strong, and in an odd place; but it has not a proper correlate in 6. This makes its subject more anxious to unite with 2; but 2 is devoted to its proper correlate in 5, of whose strength 3 is afraid, and takes the measures described. His abstaining so long, however, from any active attempt, will save him from misfortune.

Line 4 is strong, but in an even place, which weakens its subject, He also would fain make an attempt on 2; but he is afraid, and does not carry his purpose into effect.

Line 5 is strong, in an odd, and the central place; and would fain unite with 2, which indeed is the proper correlate of its subject. But 3 and 4 are powerful foes that oppose the union, Their opposition makes him weep; but he collects his forces, defeats them, and effects his purpose.

The union reaches to all within the suburbs, and is riot yet universal; but still there is no cause for repentance.

[xiv] Tâ Yû means 'Great Havings;' denoting in a kingdom a state of prosperity and abundance, and in a, family or individual, a state of opulence. The danger threatening such a condition arises from the pride which it is likely to engender. But everything here is against that issue. Apart from the symbolism of the trigrams, we have the place of honour occupied by a weak line, so that its subject will be humble; and all the other lines, strong as they are, will act in obedient sympathy. There will be great progress and success.

Line 2, though strong, is at the lowest part of the figure, and has no correlate above. No external influences have as yet acted injuriously on its subject. Let him do as directed, and no hurtful influence will ever affect him.

The strong line 2 has its proper correlate in line 5, the ruler of the figure, and will use its strength in subordination to his humility. Hence the symbolism.

Line 3 is strong, and in the right (an odd) place. The topmost line of the lower trigram is the proper place for a feudal lord. The subject of this will humbly serve the condescending ruler in line 5. A small man, having the place without the virtue, would give himself airs.

Line 4 is strong, but the strength is tempered by the position, which is that of a weak line. Hence he will do no injury to the mild ruler, to whom he is so near.

Line 5 symbolises the ruler. Mild sincerity is good in him, and affects his ministers and others. But a ruler must not be without an awe-inspiring majesty.

Even the topmost line takes its character from 5. The strength of its subject is still tempered, and Heaven gives its approval.

[xv] An essay on humility rightly follows that on abundant possessions. The third line, which is a whole line amid five others divided, occupying the topmost place in the lower trigram, is held by the Khang-hsî editors and many others to be 'the lord of the hexagram,' the representative of humility, strong, but abasing itself. There is nothing here in the text to make us enter farther on the symbolism of the figure. Humility is the way to permanent success.

A weak line, at the lowest place of the figure, is the fitting symbol of the superior man adding humility to humility.

Line 2 is weak, central, and in its proper place, representing a humility that has 'crowed;' that is, has proclaimed itself.

Line 3 is strong, and occupies an odd (its proper) place. It is 'the lord of the hexagram,' to whom all represented by the lines above and below turn.

Line 4 is weak and in its proper position. Its subject is sure to be successful and prosperous, but being so near the fifth line, he should still use the greatest precaution.

All men love and honour humility, in itself and without the adjuncts which usually command obedience and respect. Hence his neighbours follow the ruler in the fifth line, though he may not be very rich or powerful. His humility need not keep him from asserting the right, even by force of arms.

The subject of the sixth line, which is weak, is outside the game, so to speak, that has been played out. He will use force, but only within his own sphere and to assert what is right. He will not be aggressive.

[xvi] The Yü hexagram denoted to king Wăn a condition of harmony and happy contentment throughout the kingdom, when the people rejoiced in and readily obeyed their sovereign. At such a time his appointments and any military undertakings would be hailed and supported. The fourth line, undivided, is the lord of the figure, and being close to the fifth or place of dignity, is to be looked on as the minister or chief officer of the ruler. The ruler gives to him his confidence; and all represented by the other lines yield their obedience.

Line 1 is weak, and has for its correlate the strong 4. Its subject may well enjoy the happiness of the time. But he cannot contain himself, and proclaims, or boasts of, his satisfaction;—which is evil.

Line 2, though weak, is in its correct position, the centre, moreover, of the lower trigram. Quietly and firmly its subject is able to abide in his place, and exercise a far-seeing discrimination. All is indicative of good fortune.

Line 3 is weak, and in an odd place. Immediately below line 4, its subject keeps looking up to the lord of the figure, and depends on him, thinking of doing nothing, but how to enjoy himself. The consequence will be as described, unless he speedily change.

The strong subject of line 4 is the agent to whom the happy condition is owing; and it is only necessary to caution him to maintain his confidence in himself and his purpose, and his adherents and success will continue.

Line 5 is in the ruler's place; but it is weak, and he is in danger of being carried away by the lust of pleasure. Moreover, proximity to the powerful minister represented by 4 is a source of danger. Hence he is represented as suffering from a chronic complaint, but nevertheless he does not die. See Appendix II on the line.

Line 6, at the very top or end of the hexagram, is weak, and its subject is all but lost. Still even for him there is a chance of safety, if he will but change.

xvii Sui symbolises the idea of following. It is said to follow Yü, the symbol of harmony and satisfaction. Where there are these conditions men are sure to follow; nor will they follow those in whom they have no complacency. The hexagram includes the cases where one follows others, and where others follow him; and the auspice of great progress and success is due to this flexibility and applicability of it. But in both cases the following must be guided by a reference to what is proper and correct. See the notes on the Thwan and the Great Symbolism.

Line 1 is strong, and lord of the lower trigram. The weak lines ought to follow it; but here it is below them, in the lowest place of the figure. This gives rise to the representation of one changing his pursuit. Still through the native vigour indicated by the line being strong, and in its correct place, its subject will be fortunate. Going beyond his gate to find associates indicates his public spirit, and superiority to selfish considerations.

Line 2 is weak. Its proper correlate is the strong 5; but it prefers to cleave to the line below, instead of waiting to follow 5. Hence the symbolism of the text, the bad omen of which needs not to be mentioned.

Line 3 is also weak, but it follows the strong line above it and leaves line 1, reversing the course of 2;—with a different issue. It is weak, however, and 4 is not its proper correlate; hence the conclusion of the paragraph is equivalent to a caution.

Line 4 is strong, and in the place of a great minister next the ruler in 5. But his having adherents may be injurious to the supreme and sole authority of that ruler, and only a sincere loyalty will save him from. error and misfortune.

Line 5 is strong, and in its correct place, with 2 as its proper correlate; thus producing the auspicious symbolism.

The issue of the hexagram is seen in line 6; which represents the ideal of following, directed by the most sincere adherence to what is right. This influence not only extends to men, but also to spiritual beings. 'The western hill' is mount *Khî*, at the foot of which was the original settlement of the house of *K*âu, in B. C. 1325. The use of the name 'king' here brings us down from Wăn into the time of king Wû at least.

xviii In the 6th Appendix it is said, They who follow another are sure to have services (to perform), and hence Sui is followed by Kû.' But Kû means the having painful or troublesome services to do. It denotes here a state in which things are going to ruin, as if through poison or venomous worms; and the figure is supposed to describe the arrest of the decay and the restoration to soundness and vigour, so as to justify its auspice of great progress and success. To realise such a result, however, great efforts will be required, as in crossing the great stream; and a careful consideration of the events that have brought on the state of decay, and the measures to be taken to remedy it is also necessary. See

Appendix I on the 'three days.'

The subject of line 1, and of all the other lines, excepting perhaps 6, appears as a son. Yet the line itself is of the yin nature, and the trigram in which it plays the principal part is also yin. Line 2 is strong, and of the yang nature, with the yin line 5 as its proper correlate. In line 2, 5 appears as the mother; but its subject there is again a son, and the upper trigram altogether is yang. I am unable to account for these things. As is said in the note of Regis on line 2:—'Haec matris filiique denominatio ad has lineas mere translatitia est, et, ut ait commentarius vulgaris, ad explicationem sententiarum eas pro matre et filio supponere dicendum est. Nec ratio reddetur si quis in utroque hoc nomine mysterium quaerat. Cur enim aliis in figuris lineae nunc regem, nunc vasallum, jam imperii administrum, mox summum armorum praefectum referre dicantur? Accommodantur scilicet lineae ad verba sententiae et verba sententiae ad sensum, queniadmodum faciendum de methodis libri Shih King docet Mencius, V, i, ode 4.2.'

We must leave this difficulty. Line 1 is weak, and its correlate 4 is also weak. What can its subject do to remedy the state of decay? But the line is the first of the figure, and the decay is not yet great. By giving heed to the cautions in the Text, he will accomplish what is promised.

The ruler in line 5 is represented by a weak line, while 2 is strong. Thus the symbolism takes the form of a son dealing with the prevailing decay induced somehow by his mother. But a son must be very gentle in all his intercourse with his mother, and especially so, when constrained by a sense of duty to oppose her course. I do not think there is anything more or better to be said here. The historical interpretation adopted by Regis and his friends, that the father here is king Wăn, the mother Thâi-sze, and the son king Wû, cannot be maintained. I have searched, but in vain, for the slightest Chinese sanction of it, and it would give to Kû the meaning of misfortunes endured, instead of troubles caused.

Line 3 is strong, and not central, so that its subject might well go to excess in his efforts. But this tendency is counteracted by the line's place in the trigram Sun, often denoting lowly submission.

Line 4 is weak, and in an even place, which intensifies that weakness. Hence comes the caution against going forward.

The weak line 5, as has been said, is the seat of the ruler; but its proper correlate is the strong 2, the strong siding champion minister, to whom the work of the hexagram is delegated.

Line 6 is strong, and has no proper correlate below. Hence it suggests the idea of one outside the sphere of action, and taking no part in public affairs, but occupied with the culture of himself.

[xix] In Appendix VI Lin is explained as meaning 'great.' The writer, having misunderstood the meaning of the previous Kû, subjoins—'He who performs such services may become "great."' But Lin denotes the approach of authority,—to inspect, to comfort, or to rule. When we look at the figure, we see two strong undivided lines advancing on the four weak lines above them, and thence follows the assurance that their action will be powerful and successful. That action must be governed by rectitude, however, and by caution grounded on the changing character of all conditions and events. The meaning of the concluding sentence is given in Appendix I as simply being—that, 'the advancing power will decay in no long time.' Lû *Kăn-khî* (Ming dynasty) says:— 'The sun (or the day) is the symbol of what is Yang; and the moon is the symbol of what is Yin. Eight is the number of the second of the four emblematic figures (the smaller Yin), and seven is the number of the third of them (the smaller Yang). Hence to indicate the period of the coming of what is Yin, we use the phrase, "the eighth month;" and to indicate the period of the coming of what is Yang, we use the phrase, "the seventh day."' The Khang-hsî editors say that this is the best explanation of the language of the Text that can be given:—"The Yang numbers culminate in 9, the influence then receding and producing the 8 of the smaller Yin. The Yin numbers culminate in 6, and the next

advance produces the 7 of the smaller Yang; so that 7 and 8 are the numbers indicating the first birth of what is Yin and what is Yang.' 'If we go to seek,' they add, 'any other explanation of the phraseology of the Text, and such expressions as "3 days," "3 years," "10 years," &c., we make them unintelligible.' Lin is the hexagram of the twelfth month.

Line 1 is a strong line in its proper place. The danger is that its subject may be more strong than prudent, hence the caution in requiring firm correctness.

Line 2, as strong, should be in an odd place; but this is more than counterbalanced by the central position, and its correlate in line 5.

Line 3 is weak, and neither central, nor in its correct position. Hence its action will not be advantageous; but being at the top of the trigram Tui, which means being pleased, its subject is represented as 'well pleased to advance.' Anxious reflection will save him from error.

Line 4, though weak, is in its proper place, and has for its correlate the strong 1. Hence its advance is 'in the highest style.'

Line 5 is the position of the ruler. It is weak, but being central, and having for its correlate the strong and central 2, we have in it a symbol of authority distrustful of itself, and employing fit agents;—characteristic of the wise ruler.

Line 6 is the last of the trigram Khwăn, the height therefore of docility. Line 2 is not its correlate, but it belongs to the Yin to seek for the Yang; and it is so emphatically in this case. Hence the characteristic and issue as assigned.

[xx] The Chinese character Kwân, from which this hexagram is named, is used in it in two senses. In the Thwan, the first paragraph of the treatise on the Thwan, and the paragraph on the Great Symbolism, it denotes showing, manifesting; in all other places it denotes contemplating, looking at. The subject of the hexagram is the sovereign and his subjects, how he manifests himself to them, and how they contemplate him. The two upper, undivided, lines belong to the sovereign; the four weak lines below them are his subjects,—ministers and others who look up at him. Kwân is the hexagram of the eighth month.

In the Thwan king Wăn symbolises the sovereign by a worshipper when he is most solemn in his religious service, at the commencement of it, full of sincerity and with a dignified carriage.

Line 1 is weak, and in the lowest place, improper also for it;—the symbol of a thoughtless lad, who cannot see far, and takes only superficial views.

Line 2 is also weak, but in its proper place, showing a woman, living retired, and only able to peep as from her door at the subject of the fifth line. But ignorance and retirement are proper in a woman.

Line 3, at the top of the lower trigram Khwăn, and weak, must belong to a subject of the utmost docility, and will wish to act only according to the exigency of time and circumstances.

Line 4, in the place proper to its weakness, is yet in immediate proximity to 5, representing the sovereign. Its subject is moved accordingly, and stirred to ambition.

Line 5 is strong, and in the place of the ruler. He is a superior man, but this does not relieve him from the duty of self-contemplation or examination.

There is a slight difference in the 6th paragraph from the 5th, which can hardly be expressed in a translation. By making a change in the punctuation, however, the different significance may be brought out. Line 6 is strong, and should be considered out of the work of the hexagram, but its subject is still possessed by the spirit of its idea, and is led to self-examination.

[xxi] Shih Ho means literally 'Union by gnawing.' We see in the figure two strong lines in the first and last places, while all the others, with the exception of the fourth, are divided. This suggests the idea of the jaws and the mouth between them kept open by something in it. Let that be gnawed through and the mouth will close and the jaws come together. So in the body politic. Remove the obstacles to union, and high and low will come together with a good understanding. And how are those obstacles to be removed?

By force, emblemed by the gnawing; that is, by legal constraints. And these are sure to be successful. The auspice of the figure is favourable. There will be success.

Lines 1 and 6 are much out of the game or action described in the figure. Hence they are held to represent parties receiving punishment, while the other lines represent parties inflicting it. The punishment in line 1 is that of the stocks, administered for a small offence, and before crime has made much way. But if the 'depriving' of the toes is not merely keeping them in restraint, but cutting them off, as the Chinese character suggests, the punishment appears to a western reader too severe.

Line 2 is weak, appropriately therefore in an even place, and it is central besides. The action therefore of its subject should be effective; and this is shown by the 'biting through the soft flesh,' an easy thing. Immediately below, however, is a strong offender represented by the strong line, and before he will submit it is necessary to 'bite off his nose;' for punishment is the rule it must be continued and increased till the end is secured.

Line 3 is weak, and in an even place. The action of its subject will be ineffective; and is emblemed by the hard task of gnawing through dried flesh, and encountering, besides, what is distasteful and injurious in it. But again comes in the consideration that here punishment is the rule, and the auspice is not all bad.

Of old, in a civil case, both parties, before they were heard, brought to the court an arrow (or a bundle of arrows), in testimony of their rectitude, after which they were heard; in a criminal case, they in the same way deposited each thirty pounds of gold, or some other metal. See the Official Book of *K*au, 27. 14, 15. The subject of the fourth line's getting those pledges indicates his exercising his judicial functions; and what he gnaws through indicates their difficulty. Moreover, though the line is strong, it is in an even place; and hence comes the lesson of caution.

The fifth line represents 'the lord of judgment.' As it is a weak line, he will be disposed to leniency; and his judgments will be correct. This is declared by his finding the 'yellow metal;' for yellow is one of the five 'correct' colours. The position is in the centre and that of rule; but the line being weak, a caution is given, as under the previous line.

The action of the figure has passed, and still we have, in the subject of line 6, one persisting in wrong, a strong criminal, wearing the cangue, and deaf to counsel. Of course the auspice is evil.

[xxii] The character Pî is the symbol of what is ornamental and of the act of adorning. As there is ornament in nature, so should there be in society; but its place is secondary to that of what is substantial. This is the view of king Wăn in his Thwan. The symbolism of the separate lines is sometimes fantastic.

Line 1 is strong, and in an odd place. It is at the very bottom of the hexagram, and is the first line of Lî, the trigram. for fire or light, and suggesting what is elegant and bright. Its subject has nothing to do but to attend to himself. Thus he cultivates—adorns— himself in his humble position; but if need be, righteousness requiring it, he can give up every luxury and indulgence.

Line 2 is weak and in its proper place, but with no proper correlate above. The strong line 3 is similarly situated. These two lines therefore keep together, and are as the beard and the chin. Line 1 follows 2. What is substantial commands and rules what is merely ornamental.

Line 3 is strong, and between two weak lines, which adorn it, and bestow their favours on it. But this happy condition is from the accident of place. The subject of the line must be always correct and firm to ensure its continuance.

Line 4 has its proper correlate in 1, from whose strength it should receive ornament, but 2 and the strong 3 intervene and keep them apart, so that the ornament is only white, and of no bright colour. Line 4, however, is faithful to 1, and earnest for their union. And finally line 3 appears in a good character, and not with the purpose to injure, so that the union of 1 and 4 takes place. All this is intended to indicate how ornament recognises the superiority of solidity. Compare the symbolism of the second line of Kun (3), and that of the topmost line of Khwei (38).

Line .5 is in the place of honour, and has no proper correlate in 2. It therefore associates with the strong 6, which is symbolised by the heights and gardens round a city, and serving both to protect and to beautify it. Thus the subject of the line receives adorning from without, and does not of itself try to manifest it. Moreover, in his weakness, his offerings of ceremony are poor and mean. But, as Confucius said, 'In ceremonies it is better to be sparing than extravagant.' Hence that stinginess does not prevent a good auspice.

Line 6 is at the top of the hexagram. Ornament has had its course, and here there is a return to pure, 'white,' simplicity. Substantiality is better than ornament.

[xxiii] Po is the symbol of falling or of causing to fall, and may be applied, both in the natural and political world, to the process of decay, or that of overthrow. The figure consists of five divided lines, and one undivided, which last thus becomes the prominent and principal line in the figure. Decay or overthrow has begun at the bottom of it, and crept up to the top. The hexagram is that of the ninth month, when the beauty and glory of summer have disappeared, and the year is ready to fall into the arms of sterile winter. In the political world, small men have gradually displaced good men and great, till but one remains; and the lesson for him is to wait. The power operating against him is too strong; but the fashion of political life passes away. If he wait, a change for the better will shortly appear.

The lesser symbolism is chiefly that of a bed or couch with its occupant. The idea of the hexagram requires this occupant to be overthrown, or at least that an attempt be made to overthrow him. Accordingly the attempt in line 1 is made by commencing with the legs of the couch. The symbolism goes on to explain itself. The object of the evil worker is the overthrow of all firm correctness of course there will be evil.

Line 2 is to the same effect as 1; only the foe has advanced from the legs to the frame of the couch.

Line 3 also represents an overthrower; but it differs from the others in being the correlate of 6. The subject of it will take part with him. His association is with the subject of 6, and not, as in the other weak lines, with one of its own kind.

From line 4 the danger is imminent. The couch has been overthrown. The person of the occupant is at the mercy of the destroyers.

With line 5 the symbolism changes. The subject of 5 is 'lord of all the other weak lines,' and their subjects are at his disposal. He and they are represented as fishes, following one another as if strung together. All fishes come under the category of yin. Then the symbolism changes again. The subject of 5, representing and controlling all the yin lines, is loyal to the subject of the yang sixth line. He is the rightful sovereign in his palace, and 5 leads all the others there to enjoy the sovereign's favours.

We have still different symbolism under line 6. Its strong subject, notwithstanding the attempts against him, survives, and acquires fresh vigour. The people again cherish their sovereign, and the plotters have wrought to their own overthrow.

[xxiv] Fû symbolises the idea of returning, coming back or over again. The last hexagram showed us inferior prevailing over superior men, all that is good in nature and society yielding before what is bad. But change is the law of nature and society. When decay has reached its climax, recovery will begin to take place. In Po we had one strong topmost line, and five weak lines below it; here we have one strong line, and five weak lines above it. To illustrate the subject from what we see in nature,—Po is the hexagram of the ninth month, in which the triumph of cold and decay in the year is nearly complete.

It is complete in the tenth month, whose hexagram is Khwăn ䷁ ䷁; then follows our hexagram Fû, belonging to the eleventh month, in which was the winter solstice when the sun turned back in his course, and moved with a constant regular progress towards the summer solstice. In harmony with these changes of nature are the changes in the political and social state of a nation. There is nothing in the Yî to suggest the hope of a perfect society or kingdom that cannot be moved.

The strong bottom line is the first of *K*ăn, the trigram of movement, and the upper trigram is Khwăn, denoting docility and capacity. The strong returning line will meet with no distressing obstacle, and the weak lines will change before it into strong, and be as friends. The bright quality will be developed brighter and brighter from day to day, and month to month.

The sentence, 'In seven days comes his return,' occasions some perplexity. If the reader will refer to hexagrams 44, 33, 12, 20, 23, and 2, he will see that during the months denoted by those figures, the 5th, 6th, 7th, 8th, 9th, and 10th, the yin lines have gradually been prevailing over the yang, until in Khwăn (2) they have extruded them entirely from the lineal figure. Then comes our Fû, as a seventh figure, in which the yang line begins to reassert itself, and from which it goes on to extrude the yin lines in their turn. Explained therefore of the months of the year, we have to take a day for a month. And something analogous—we cannot say exactly what—must have place in society and the state.

The concluding auspice or oracle to him who finds this Fû by divination is what we might expect.

The subject of line 1 is of course the undivided line, meaning here, says *K*hăng-ȝze, 'the way of the superior man.' There must have been some deviation from that, or 'returning' could not be spoken of.

Line 2 is in its proper place, and central; but it is weak. This is more than compensated for, however, by its adherence to line 1, the fifth line not being a proper correlate. Hence the return of its subject is called excellent or admirable.

Line 3 is weak, and in the uneven place of a strong line. It is the top line, moreover, of the trigram whose attribute is movement. Hence the symbolism; but any evil issue may be prevented by a realisation of danger and by caution.

Line 4 has its proper correlate in i; different from all the other weak lines; and its course is different accordingly.

Line 5 is in the central place of honour, and the middle line of Khwăn, denoting docility. Hence its auspice.

Line 6 is weak; and being at the top of the hexagram, when its action of returning is all concluded, action on the part of its subject will lead to evils such as are mentioned. 'Ten years' seems to be a round number, signifying a long time, as in hexagram 3. 2.

[xxv] Wang is the symbol of being reckless, and often of being insincere; Wû Wang is descriptive of a state of entire freedom from such a condition; its subject is one who is entirely simple and sincere. The quality is characteristic of the action of Heaven, and of the highest style of humanity. In this hexagram we have an essay on this noble attribute. An absolute rectitude is essential to it. The nearer one comes to the ideal of the quality, the more powerful will be his influence, the greater his success. But let him see to it that he never swerve from being correct.

The first line is strong; at the commencement of the inner trigram denoting movement, the action of its subject will very much characterise all the action set forth, and will itself be fortunate.

Line 2 is weak, central, and in its correct place. The quality may be predicated of it in its highest degree. There is an entire freedom in its subject from selfish or mercenary motive. He is good simply for goodness' sake. And things are so constituted that his action will be successful.

But calamity may also sometimes befal the best, and where there is this freedom from insincerity; and line 3 being weak, and in the place of an even line, lays its subject open to this misfortune. 'The people of the neighbourhood' are of course entirely innocent.

Line 4 is the lowest in the trigram of strength, and 1 is not a proper correlate, nor is the fourth the place for a strong line. Hence the paragraph must be understood as a caution.

Line 5 is strong, in the central place of honour, and has its proper correlate in 2. Hence its subject must possess the quality of the hexagram in perfection. And yet he shall he sick or in distress. But he need not be anxious. Without his efforts a way of escape for him will be opened.

Line 6 is at the top of the hexagram, and comes into the field when the action has run its course. He should be still, and not initiate any fresh movement.

xxvi *Khû* has two meanings. It is the symbol of restraint, and of accumulation. What is repressed and restrained accumulates its strength and increases its volume. Both these meanings are found in the treatise on the Thwan; the exposition of the Great Symbolism has for its subject the accumulation of virtue. The different lines are occupied with the repression or restraint of movement. The first three lines receive that repression, the upper three exercise it. The accumulation to which all tends is that of virtue; and hence the name of Tâ *Khû*, 'the Great Accumulation.'

What the Thwan teaches, is that he who goes about to accumulate his virtue must be firm and correct, and may then, engaging in the public service, enjoy the king's grace, and undertake the most difficult enterprises.

Line 1 is subject to the repression of 4, which will be increased if he try to advance. It is better for him to halt.

Line 2 is liable to the repression of 5, and stops its advance of itself, its subject having the wisdom to do so through its position in the central place. The strap below, when attached to the axle, made the carriage stop; he himself acts that part.

Line 3 is the last of *Kh*ien, and responds to the sixth line, the last of Kăn, above. But as they are both strong, the latter does not exert its repressive force. They advance rapidly together; but the position is perilous for 3. By firmness and caution, however, its subject will escape the peril, and the issue will be good.

The young bull in line 4 has not yet got horns. The attaching to their rudiments the piece of wood to prevent him from goring is an instance of extraordinary precaution; and precaution is always good.

A boar is a powerful and dangerous animal. Let him be castrated, and though his tusks remain, he cares little to use them. Here line 5 represents the ruler in the hexagram, whose work is to repress the advance of evil. A conflict with the subject of the strong second line in its advance would be perilous; but 5, taking early precaution, reduces it to the condition of the castrated pig. Not only is there no evil, but there is good fortune.

The work of repression is over, and the strong subject of line 6 has now the amplest scope to carry out the idea of the hexagram in the accumulation of virtue.

xxvii Î is the symbol of the upper jaw, and gives name to the hexagram; but the whole figure suggests the appearance of the mouth. There are the two undivided lines at the bottom and top, and the four divided lines between them. The first line is the first in the trigram *Kă*n, denoting movement; and the sixth is the third in Kăn, denoting what is solid. The former is the lower jaw, part of the mobile chin; and the other the more fixed upper jaw. The open lines are the cavity of the mouth. As the name of the hexagram, Î denotes nourishing,—one's body or mind, one's self or others. The nourishment in both the matter and method will differ according to the object of it; and every one must determine what to employ and do in every case by exercising his own thoughts, only one thing being premised,—that in both respects the nourishing must be correct, and in harmony with what is right. The auspice of the whole hexagram is good.

The first line is strong, and in its proper place; its subject might suffice for the nourishing of himself, like a tortoise, which is supposed to live on air, without more solid nourishment. But he is drawn out of himself by desire for the weak 4, his proper correlate, at whom he looks till his jaw hangs down, or, as we say, his mouth waters. Hence the auspice is bad. The symbolism takes the form of an expostulation addressed, we must suppose, by the fourth line to the first.

The weak 2, insufficient for itself, seeks nourishment first from the strong line below, which is not proper, and then from the strong 6, not its proper correlate, and too far removed. In either case the thing is evil.

Line 3 is weak, in an odd place; and as it occupies the last place in the trigram of movement, all that quality culminates in its subject. Hence he considers himself sufficient for himself, without any help from without, and the issue is bad.

With line 4 we pass into the upper trigram. It is next to the ruler's place in 5 moreover, and bent on nourishing and training all below. Its proper correlate is the strong 1; and though weak in himself, its subject looks with intense desire to the subject of that for help; and there is no error.

The subject of line 5 is not equal to the requirements of his position; but with a firm reliance on the strong 6, there will be good fortune. Let him not, however, engage in the most difficult undertakings.

The topmost line is strong, and 5 relies on its subject; but being penetrated with the idea of the hexagram, he feels himself in the position of master or tutor to all under heaven. The task is hard and the responsibility great; but realising these things, he will prove himself equal to them.

xxviii Very extraordinary times require very extraordinary gifts in the conduct of affairs in them. This is the text on which king Wǎn and his son discourse after their fashion in this hexagram. What goes, in their view, to constitute anything extraordinary is its greatness and difficulty. There need not be about it what is not right.

Looking at the figure we see two weak lines at the top and bottom, and four strong lines between them, giving us the idea of a great beam unable to sustain its own weight. But the second and fifth lines are both strong and in the centre; and from this and the attributes of the component trigrams a good auspice is obtained.

Line 1 being weak, and at the bottom of the figure, and of the trigram Sun, which denotes flexibility and humility, its subject is distinguished by his carefulness, as in the matter mentioned; and there is a good auspice.

Line 2 has no proper correlate above. Hence he inclines to the weak 1 below him; and we have the symbolism of the line. An old husband with a young wife will yet have children; the action of the subject of 2 will be successful.

Line 3 is strong, and in an odd place. Its subject is confident in his own strength, but his correlate in 6 is weak. Alone, he is unequal to the extraordinary strain on him, and has for his symbol the weak beam.

Line 4 is near 5, the ruler's place. On its subject devolves the duty of meeting the extraordinary exigency of the time; but he is strong; and, the line being in an even place, his strength is tempered. He will be equal to his task. Should he look out for the help of the subject of 1, that would affect him with another element of weakness; and his action would give cause for regret.

Line 5 is strong and central. Its subject should be equal to achieve extraordinary merit. But he has no proper correlate below, and as 2 inclined to 1, so does this to 6. But here the willow only produces flowers, not shoots;—its decay will soon reappear. An old wife will have no children. If the subject of the line is not to be condemned as that of 3, his action does not deserve praise.

The subject of 6 pursues his daring course, with a view to satisfy the extraordinary exigency of the time, and benefit all under the sky. He is unequal to the task, and sinks beneath it; but his motive modifies the judgment on his conduct.

xxix The trigram Khan, which is doubled to form this hexagram, is the lineal symbol of water. Its meaning, as a character, is 'a pit,' 'a perilous cavity, or defile;' and here and elsewhere in the Yî it leads the reader to think of a dangerous defile, with water flowing through it. It becomes symbolic of danger, and what the authors of the Text had in mind was to show how danger should be encountered, its effect on the mind, and how to get out of it.

The trigram exhibits a strong central line, between two divided lines. The central represented to king Wǎn the sincere honesty and goodness of the subject of the hexagram, whose mind was sharpened and made penetrating by contact with danger, and who acted in a manner worthy of his character. It is implied, though the Thwan does not say it, that he would get out of the danger,

Line 1 is weak, at the bottom of the figure, and has no correlate above, no helper, that is, beyond itself. All these things render the case of its subject hopeless. He will by his efforts only involve himself more deeply in danger.

Line 2 is strong, and in the centre. Its subject is unable, indeed, to escape altogether from the danger, but he does not involve himself more deeply in it like the subject of 1, and obtains some ease.

Line 3 is weak, and occupies the place of a strong line. Its subject is in an evil case.

Line 4 is weak, and will get no help from its correlate in 1. Its subject is not one who can avert the danger threatening himself and others. But his position is close to that of the ruler in 5, whose intimacy he cultivates with an unostentatious sincerity, symbolled by the appointments of the simple feast, and whose intelligence he cautiously enlightens. In consequence, there will be no error.

The subject of line 5 is on the eve of extrication and deliverance. The waters of the defile will ere long have free vent and disappear, and the ground will be levelled and made smooth. The line is strong, in a proper place, and in the place of honour.

The case of the subject of line 6 is hopeless. When danger has reached its highest point, there he is, represented by a weak line, and with no proper correlate below. The 'thicket of thorns' is taken as a metaphor for a prison; but if the expression has a history, I have been unable to find it.

xxx Lî is the name of the trigram representing fire and light, and the sun as the source of both of these. Its virtue or attribute is brightness, and by a natural metaphor intelligence. But Lî has also the meaning of inhering in, or adhering to, being attached to. Both these significations occur in connexion with the hexagram, and make it difficult to determine what was the subject of it in the minds of the authors. If we take the whole figure as expressing the subject, we have, as in the treatise on the Thwan, 'a double brightness,' a phrase which is understood to denominate the ruler. If we take the two central lines as indicating the subject, we have weakness, dwelling with strength above and below. In either case there are required from the subject a strict adherence to what is correct, and a docile humility. On the second member of the Thwan Khăng-3ze says:— 'The nature of the ox is docile, and that of the cow is much more so. The subject of the hexagram adhering closely to what is correct, he must be able to act in obedience to it, as docile as a cow, and then there will be good fortune.'

Line 1 is strong, and at the bottom of the trigram for fire, the nature of which is to ascend. Its subject therefore will move upwards, and is in danger of doing so coarsely and vehemently. But the lowest line has hardly entered into the action of the figure, and this consideration operates to make him reverently careful of his movements; and there is no error.

Line 2 is weak, and occupies the centre. Yellow is one of the five correct colours, and here symbolises the correct course to which the subject of the line adheres.

Line 3 is at the top of the lower trigram, whose light may be considered exhausted, and suggests the symbol of the declining sun. The subject of the line should accept the position, and resign himself to the ordinary amusements which are mentioned, but he groans and mourns instead. His strength interferes with the lowly contentment which he should cherish.

The. strength of line 4, and its being in an even place, make its subject appear in this unseemly manner, disastrous to himself.

Line 5 is in the place of honour, and central. But it is weak; as is its correlate. Its position between the strong 4 and 6 fills its subject with anxiety and apprehension, that express themselves as is described. But such demonstrations are a proof of his inward adherence to right and his humility. There will be good fortune.

Line 6, strong and at the top of the figure, has the intelligence denoted by its trigrams in the highest degree, and his own proper vigour. Through these his achievements are great, but his generous consideration is equally conspicuous, and he falls into no error.

[xxxi] With the 31st hexagram commences the Second Section of the Text. It is difficult to say why any division of the hexagrams should be made here, for the student tries in vain to discover any continuity in the thoughts of the author that is now broken. The First Section does not contain a class of subjects different from those which we find in the Second. That the division was made, however, at a very early time, appears from the sixth Appendix on the Sequence of the Hexagrams, where the writer sets forth an analogy between the first and second figures, representing heaven and earth, as the originators of all things, and this figure and the next, representing (each of them) husband and wife, as the originators of all the social relations. This, however, is far from carrying conviction to my mind. The division of the Text of the Yî into two sections is a fact of which I am unable to give a satisfactory account.

Hsien, as explained in the treatise on the Thwan, has here the meaning of mutual influence, and the duke of *K*âu, on the various lines, always uses Kan for it in the sense of 'moving' or 'influencing to movement or action.' This is to my mind the subject of the hexagram considered as an essay,—'Influence; the different ways of bringing it to bear, and their issues.'

The Chinese character called hsien is 咸, the graphic symbol for 'all, together, jointly.' Kan, the symbol for 'influencing,' has hsien in it as its phonetic constituent (though the changes in pronunciation make it hard for an English reader to appreciate this), with the addition of hsin, the symbol for the heart.' Thus 感 kan, 'to affect or influence,' = 咸 + 心; and it may have been that while the name or word was used with the significance of 'influencing,' the 心 was purposely dropt from it, to indicate the most important element in the thing,—the absence of all purpose or motive. I venture to think that this would have been a device worthy of a diviner.

With regard to the idea of husband and wife being in the teaching of the hexagram, it is derived from the more recent symbolism of the eight trigrams ascribed to king Wăn, and exhibited on p. 32 and plate III. The more ancient usage of them is given in the paragraph on the Great Symbolism of Appendix II. The figure consists of Kăn (☵) 'the youngest son,' and over it Tui (☱), 'the youngest daughter.' These are in 'happy union.' No influence, it is said, is so powerful and constant as that between husband and wife; and where these are young, it is especially active. Hence it is that Hsien is made up of Kăn and Tui. All this is to me very doubtful. I can dimly apprehend why the whole line (———) was assumed as the symbol of strength and authority, and the broken line as that of weakness and submission. Beyond this I cannot follow Fû-hsî in his formation of the trigrams; and still less can I assent to the more recent symbolism of them ascribed to king Wăn.

Coming now to the figure, and its lines, the subject is that of mutual influence; and the author teaches that that influence, correct in itself, and for correct ends, is sure to be effective. He gives an instance,—the case of a man marrying a young lady, the regulations for which have been laid down in China from the earliest times with great strictness and particularity. Such influence will be effective and fortunate.

Line 1 is weak, and at the bottom of the hexagram. Though 4 be a proper correlate, yet the influence indicated by it must be ineffective. However much a man's great toes may be moved, that will not enable him to walk.

The calves cannot move of themselves. They follow the moving of the feet. The moving of them indicates too much anxiety to move. Line 2, moreover, is weak. But it is also the central line, and if its subject abide quiet, till he is acted on from above, there will be good fortune.

Neither can the thighs move of themselves. The attempt to move them is inauspicious. Its subject, however, the line being strong, and in an odd place, will wish to move, and follows the subject of 4, which is understood to be the seat of the mind. He exercises his influence therefore with a mind and purpose, which is not good.

Line 4 is strong, but in an even place. It is the seat of the mind. Its subject therefore is warned to be firm and correct in order to a good issue. If he be wavering and uncertain, his influence will not extend beyond the circle of his friends.

The symbolism of line 5 refers to a part of the body behind the heart, and is supposed therefore to indicate an influence, ineffective indeed, but free from selfish motive, and not needing to be repented of.

Line 6 is weak, and in an even place. It is the topmost line also of the trigram of satisfaction. Its influence by means of speech will only be that of loquacity and flattery, the evil of which needs not to be pointed out.

[xxxii] The subject of this hexagram may be given as perseverance in well doing, or in continuously acting out the law of one's being. The sixth Appendix makes it a sequel of the previous figure. As that treats, it is said, of the relation between husband and wife, so this treats of the continuous observance of their respective duties. Hsien, we saw, is made up of Kăn, the symbol of the youngest son, and Tui, the symbol of the youngest daughter, attraction and influence between the sexes being strongest in youth. Hăng consists of Sun, 'the oldest daughter,' and Kăn, the oldest son. The couple are more staid. The wife occupies the lower place; and the relation between them is marked by her submission. This is sound doctrine, especially from a Chinese point of view; but I doubt whether such application of his teaching was in the mind of king Wăn. Given two parties, an inferior and superior in correlation. If both be continuously observant of what is correct, the inferior being as submissive, and the superior firm, good fortune and progress may be predicated of their course.

Line 1 has a proper correlate in 4; but between them are two strong lines; and it is itself weak. These two conditions are against its subject receiving much help from the subject of 4. He should be quiet, and not forward for action.

Line 2 is strong, but in the place of a weak line. Its position, however, being central, and its subject holding fast to the due mean, the unfavourable condition of an even place is more than counteracted.

Line 3 is strong, and in its proper place; but being beyond the centre of the trigram, its subject is too strong, and coming under the attraction of his correlate in 6, he is supposed to be ready to abandon his place and virtue. He may try to be firm and correct, but circumstances are adverse to him.

Line 4 is strong in the place of a weak line, and suggests the symbolism of the duke of Kâu.

The weak 5th line responds to the strong 2nd, and may be supposed to represent a wife conscious of her weakness, and docilely submissive; which is good. A husband, however, and a man generally, has to assert himself, and lay down the rule of what is right.

In line 6 the principle of perseverance has run its course; the motive power of Kăn is exhausted. The line itself is weak. The violent efforts of its subject can only lead to evil.

[xxxiii] Thun is the hexagram of the sixth month; the yin influence is represented by two weak lines, and has made good its footing in the year. The figure thus suggested to king Wăn the growth of small and unprincipled men in the state, before whose advance superior men were obliged to retire. This is the theme of his essay,—how, I when small men multiply and increase in power, the necessity of the time requires superior men to withdraw before them.' Yet the auspice of Thun is not all bad. By firm correctness the threatened evil may be arrested to a small extent.

'A retiring tail' seems to suggest the idea of the subject of the lines hurrying away, which would only aggravate the evil and danger of the time.

'His purpose' in line 2 is the purpose to withdraw. The weak 2 responds correctly to the strong 5, and both are central. The purpose therefore is symbolled as in the text. The 'yellow' colour of the ox is introduced because of its being 'correct,' and of a piece with the central place of the line.

Line 3 has no proper correlate in 6 and its subject allows himself to be entangled and impeded by the subjects of 1 and 2. He is too familiar with them, and they presume, and fetter his movements;—compare Analects, 17. 25. He should keep them at a distance.

Line 4 has a correlate in 1, and is free to exercise the decision belonging to its subject. The line is the first in *Khi*en, symbolic of strength.

In the Shû IV, v, Section 2. 9, the worthy Î Yin is made to say, 'The minister will not for favour or gain continue in an office whose work is done;' and the Khang-hsî editors refer to his words as an illustration of what is said on line 5. It has its correlate in 2, and its subject carries out the purpose to retire 'in an admirable way.'

Line 6 is strong, and with no correlate to detain it in 3. Its subject vigorously and happily carries out the idea of the hexagram.

[xxxiv] The strong lines predominate in Tâ *K*wang. It suggested to king Wăn a state or condition of things in which there was abundance of strength and vigour. Was strength alone enough for the conduct of affairs? No. He saw also in the figure that which suggested to him that strength should be held in subordination to the idea of right, and exerted only in harmony with it.

This is the lesson of the hexagram, as sententiously expressed in the Thwan.

Line 1 is strong, in its correct place, and also the first line in *Khi*en, the hexagram of strength, and the first line in Tâ Kwang. The idea of the figure might seem to be concentrated in it; and hence we have it symbolised by 'strength in the toes,' or 'advancing.' But such a measure is too bold to be undertaken by one in the lowest place, and moreover there is no proper correlate in 4. Hence comes the evil auspice.

Line 2 is strong, but the strength is tempered by its being in an even place, instead of being excited by it, as might be feared. Then the place is that in the centre. With firm correctness there will be good fortune.

Line 3 is strong, and in its proper place. It is at the top moreover of *Khi*en. A small man so symbolled will use his strength to the utmost; but not so the superior man. For him the position is beyond the safe middle, and he will be cautious; and not injure himself, like the ram, by exerting his strength.

Line 4 is still strong, but in the place of a weak line; and this gives occasion to the cautions with which the symbolism commences. The subject of the line going forward thus cautiously, his strength will produce good effects, such as are described.

Line 5 is weak, and occupies a central place. Its subject will cease therefore to exert his strength; but this hexagram does not forbid the employment of strength, but would only control and direct it. All that is said about him is that he will give no occasion for repentance.

Line 6 being at the top of *K*ăn, the symbol of movement, and at the top of Tâ *K*wang, its subject may be expected to be active in exerting his strength; and through his weakness, the result would be as described. But he becomes conscious of his weakness, reflects and rests, and good fortune results, as he desists from the prosecution of his unwise efforts.

[xxxv] The Thwan of this hexagram expresses its subject more fully and plainly than that of any of the previous thirty-four. It is about a feudal prince whose services to the country have made him acceptable to his king. The king's favour has been shown to him by gifts and personal attentions such as form the theme of more than one ode in the Shih; see especially III, iii, 7. The symbolism of the lines dimly indicates the qualities of such a prince. 3in means to advance.' Hexagrams 46 and 53 agree with this in being called by names that indicate progress and advance. The advance in 3in is like that of the sun, 'the shining light, shining more and more to the perfect day.'

Line 1 is weak, and in the lowest place, and its correlate in 4 is neither central nor in its correct position. This indicates the small and obstructed beginnings of his subject. But by his firm correctness he pursues the way to good fortune; and though the king does not yet believe in him, he the more pursues his noble course.

Line 2 is weak, and its correlate in 5 is also weak. Its subject therefore has still to mourn in obscurity. But his position is central and correct, and he holds on his way, till success comes ere long. The symbolism says he receives it 'from his grandmother;' and readers will be startled by the extraordinary statement, as I was when I first read it. Literally the Text says 'the king's mother,' as P. Regis rendered it,—'Istam magnam felicitatem a matre regis recipit.' He also tries to give the name a historical reference;—to Thâi-*K*iang, the grandmother of king Wăn; Thâi-Zăn, his mother; or to Thâi-sze, his wife, and the mother of king Wû and the duke of *K*âu, all famous in Chinese history, and celebrated in the Shih. But 'king's father' and 'king's mother' are well-known Chinese appellations for 'grandfather' and 'grandmother.' This is the view given on the passage, by *K*hăng-ӡze, *K*û Hsî, and the Khang-hsî editors, the latter of whom, indeed, account for the use of the name, instead of 'deceased mother,' which we find in hexagram 62, by the regulations observed in the ancestral temple. These authorities, moreover, all agree in saying that the name points us to line 5, the correlate of 2, and 'the lord of the hexagram.' Now the subject of line 5 is the sovereign, who at length acknowledges the worth of the feudal lord, and gives him the great blessing. The 'New Digest of Comments on the Yî (1686),' in its paraphrase of the line, has, 'He receives at last this great blessing from the mild and compliant ruler.' I am not sure that 'motherly king' would not be the best and fairest translation of the phrase.

Canon McClatchie has a very astonishing note on the name, which he renders 'Imperial Mother' (p. 164):—'That is, the wife of Imperial Heaven (Juno), who occupies the "throne of the diagram," viz. the fifth stroke, which is soft and therefore feminine. She is the Great Ancestress of the human race. See Imp. Ed. vol. iv, Sect. v, p. 25, Com.' Why such additions to the written word?

Line 3 is weak, and in an odd place; but the subjects of 1 and 2 are possessed by the same desire to advance as the subject of this. A common trust and aim possess them; and hence the not unfavourable auspice.

Line 4 is strong, but it is in an even place, nor is it central. It suggests the idea of a marmot (? or rat), stealthily advancing. Nothing could be more opposed to the ideal of the feudal lord in the hexagram.

In line 5 that lord and his intelligent sovereign meet happily. He holds on his right course, indifferent as to results, but things are so ordered that he is, and will continue to be, crowned with success.

Line 6 is strong, and suggests the idea of its subject to the last continuing his advance, and that not only with firm correctness, but with strong force. The 'horns' are an emblem of threatening strength, and though he uses them only in his own state, and against the rebellious there, that such a prince should have any occasion to use force is matter for regret.

[xxxvi] In this hexagram we have the representation of a good and intelligent minister or officer going forward in the service of his country, notwithstanding the occupancy of the throne by a weak and unsympathising sovereign. Hence comes its name of Ming Î, or 'Intelligence Wounded,' that is, injured and repressed. The treatment of the subject shows how such an officer will conduct himself, and maintain his purpose. The symbolism of the figure is treated of in the same way in the first and second Appendixes. Appendix VI merely says that the advance set forth in 35 is sure to meet with wounding, and hence ӡin is followed by Ming Î.

Line 1 is strong, and in its right place;—its subject should be going forward. But the general signification of the hexagram supposes him to be wounded. The wound, however, being received at the very commencement of its action, is but slight. And hence conies the emblem of a bird hurt so as to be obliged to droop its wings. The subject then appears directly as 'the superior man.' He sees it to be his course to desist from the struggle for a time, and is so rapt in the thought that he can fast for three days and not think of it. When he does withdraw, opposition follows him; but it is implied that he holds on to his own good purpose.

Line 2 is weak, but also in its right place, and central; giving us the idea of an officer, obedient to duty and the right. His wound in the left thigh may impede his movements, but does not disable him. He finds means to save himself, and maintains his good purpose.

Line 3, strong and in a strong place, is the topmost line of the lower. trigram. It responds also to line 6, in which the idea of the sovereign, emblemed by the upper trigram, is concentrated. The lower trigram is the emblem of light or brightness, the idea of which again is expressed by the south, to which we turn when we look at the sun in its meridian height. Hence the subject of the line becomes a hunter pursuing his game, and successfully. The good officer will be successful in his struggle; but let him not be over eager to put all things right at once.

Line 4 is weak, but in its right place. *Kû* Hsî says he does not understand the symbolism, as given in the Text. The translation indicates the view of it commonly accepted. The subject of the line evidently escapes from his position of danger with little damage.

Line 5 should be the place of the ruler or sovereign in the hexagram; but 6 is assigned as that place in Ming Î. The officer occupying 5, the centre of the upper trigram, and near to the sovereign, has his ideal in the count of *Kî*, whose action appears in the Shû, III, pp. 123, 127, 128. He is a historical personage.

Line 6 sets forth the fate of the ruler, who opposes himself to the officer who would do him good and intelligent service. Instead of becoming as the sun, enlightening all from the height of the sky, he is as the sun hidden below the earth. I can well believe that the writer had the last king of Shang in his mind.

[xxxvii] *Kiâ Zăn*, the name of the hexagram, simply means 'a household,' or 'the members of a family.' The subject of the essay based on the figure, however, is the regulation of the family, effected mainly by the co-operation of husband and wife in their several spheres, and only needing to become universal to secure the good order of the kingdom. The important place occupied by the wife in the family is seen in the short sentence of the Thwan. That she be firm and correct, and do her part well, is the first thing necessary to its regulation.

Line 1 is strong, and in a strong place. It suggests the necessity of strict rule in governing the family. Regulations must be established, and their observance strictly insisted on.

Line 2 is weak, and in the proper place for it,—the centre, moreover, of the lower trigram. It fitly represents the wife, and what is said on it tells us of her special sphere and duty; and that she should be unassuming in regard to all beyond her sphere; always being firm and correct. See the Shih, III, 350.

Line 3 is strong, and in an odd place. If the place were central, the strength would be tempered; but the subject of the line, in the topmost place of the trigram, may be expected to exceed in severity. But severity is not a bad thing in regulating a family;—it is better than laxity and indulgence.

Line 4 is weak, and in its proper place. The wife is again suggested to us, and we are told, that notwithstanding her being confined to the internal affairs of the household, she can do much to enrich the family.

The subject of the strong fifth line appears as the king. This may be the husband spoken of as also a king; or the real king whose merit is revealed first in his family, as often in the Shih, where king Wăn is the theme. The central place here tempers the display of the strength and power.

Line 6 is also strong, and being in an even place, the subject of it might degenerate into stern severity, but he is supposed to be sincere, complete in his personal character and self-culture, and hence his action will only lead to good fortune.

xxxviii *Kh*wei denotes a social state in which division and mutual alienation prevail, and the hexagram teaches how in small matters this condition may be healed, and the way prepared for the cure of the whole system. The writer or writers of Appendixes I and II point out the indication in the figure of division and disunion according to their views. In Appendix VI those things appear as a necessary sequel to the regulation of the family; while it is impossible to discover any allusion to the family in the Text.

Line 1 is strong, and in an odd place. A successful course might be auspiced for its subject; but the correlate in line 4 is also strong; and therefore disappointment and repentance are likely to ensue. In the condition, however, indicated by Khwei, where people have a common virtue, they will help one another. Through the good services of 4, the other will not have to repent. His condition may be emblemed by a traveller's loss of his horses, which return to him of themselves.

Should he meet with bad men, however, let him not shrink from them. Communication with them will be of benefit. His good may overcome their evil, and at least it will help to silence their slanderous tongues.

Line 5 is weak, and its subject is the proper correlate of the strong 2. They might meet openly; but for the separation and disunion that mark the time. A casual, as it were a stolen, interview, as in a bye-lane or passage, however will be useful, and may lead on to a better understanding.

Line 3 is weak, where it ought to be strong. Its correlate, however, in 6 is strong, and the relation between them might seem what it ought to be. But the weak 3 is between the strong lines in 2 and 4; and in a time of disunion there ensue the checking and repulsion emblemed in the Text. At the same time the subject of line 6 inflicts on that of 3 the punishments which are mentioned. It is thus bad for 3 at first, but we are told that in the end it will be well with him; and this will be due to the strength of the sixth line. The conclusion grows out of a conviction in the mind of the author that what is right and good is destined to triumph over what is wrong and bad. Disorder shall in the long run give place to order, and disunion to union.

Line 4 has no proper correlate, and might seem to be solitary. But, as we saw on line 1, in this hexagram, correlates of the same class help each other. Hence the subjects of 4 and 1, meeting together, work with good will and success.

The place of 5 is odd, but the line itself is weak, so that there might arise occasion for repentance. But the strong 2 is a proper correlate to the weak 5. Five being the sovereign's place, the subject of 2 is styled the sovereign's relative, of the same surname with him, and head of some branch of the descendants of the royal house. It is as easy for 5, so supported, to deal with the disunion of the time, as to bite through a piece of skin.

Line 6 is an even place, and yet the line is strong;—what can its subject effect? He looks at 3, which, as weak, is a proper correlate; but he looks with the evil eye of disunion. The subject of 3 appears no better than a filthy pig, nor more real than an impossible carriage-load of ghosts. He bends his bow against him, but he unbends it, discovering a friend in 3, as x did in 4, and 5 in 2. He acts and with good luck, comparable to the falling rain, which results from the happy union of the yang and yin in nature.

xxxix Kien is the symbol for incompetency in the feet and legs, involving difficulty in walking; hence it is used in this hexagram to indicate a state of the kingdom which makes the government of it an arduous task. How this task may be successfully performed, now by activity on the part of the ruler, and now by a discreet inactivity:—this is what the figure teaches, or at least gives hints about. For the development of the meaning of the symbolic character from the structure of the lineal figure, see Appendixes I and II.

The Thwan seems to require three things—attention to place, the presence of the great man, and the firm observance of correctness—in order to cope successfully with the difficulties of the situation. The first thing is enigmatically expressed, and the language should be compared with what we find in the Thwan of hexagrams 2 and 40. Referring to Figure 2, in Plate III, we find that, according to Wăn's arrangement of the trigrams, the southwest is occupied by Khwăn (⚏), and the north-east by *K*ăn (☶). The former represents the champaign country; the latter, the mountainous region. The former is easily traversed and held; the latter, with difficulty. The attention to place thus becomes transformed into a calculation of circumstances; those that promise success in an enterprise, which should be taken advantage of, and those that threaten difficulty and failure, which should be shunned.

This is the generally accepted view of this difficult passage. The Khang-hsî editors have a view of their own. I have been myself inclined to find less symbolism in it, and to take the southwest as the regions in the south and west of the kingdom, which we know from the Shih were more especially devoted to Wăn and his house, while the strength of the kings of Shang lay in the north and east.

'The idea of "the great man," Mencius's "minister of Heaven,"' is illustrated by the strong line in the fifth place, having for its correlate the weak line in 2. But favourableness of circumstances and place, and the presence of the great man do not dispense from the observance of firm correctness. Throughout these essays of the Yî this is always insisted on.

Line 1 is weak, whereas it ought to be strong as being in an odd place. If its subject advance, he will not be able to cope with the difficulties of the situation, but be overwhelmed by them. Let him wait for a more favourable time.

Line 2 is weak, but in its proper place. Its correlation with the strong 5, and consequent significance, are well set forth.

Line 3 is strong, and in a place of strength; but its correlate in 6 is weak, so that the advance of its subject would be unsupported. He waits therefore for a better time, and cherishes the subjects of the two lines below, who naturally cling to him.

Line 4 is weak, and, though in its proper place, its subject could do little of himself. He is immediately below the king or great man, however, and cultivates his loyal attachment to him, waiting for the time when he shall be required to act.

Line 5 is the king, the man great and strong. He can cope with the difficulties, and the subjects of 2 and the other lines of the lower trigram give their help.

The action of the hexagram is over; where can the weak 6 go forward to? Let him abide where he is, and serve the great man immediately below him. So shall he also be great;—in meritorious action at least.

ˣˡ *K*ieh is the symbol of loosing,—untying a knot or unravelling a complication; and as the name of this hexagram, it denotes a condition in which the obstruction and difficulty indicated by the preceding *K*ieh have been removed. The object of the author is to show, as if from the lines of the figure, how this new and better state of the kingdom is to be dealt with. See what is said on the Thwan of *K*ien for 'the advantage to be found in the south-west.' If further active operations be not necessary to complete the subjugation of the country, the sooner things fall into their old channels the better. The new masters of the kingdom should not be anxious to change all the old manners and ways. Let them do, as the duke of *K*âu actually did do with the subjugated people of Shang. If further operations be necessary, let them be carried through without delay. Nothing is said in the Thwan about the discountenancing and removal of small men,—unworthy ministers or officers; but that subject appears in more! than one of the lines.

There is a weak line, instead of a strong, in the first place; but this is compensated for by its strong correlate in 4.

*K*û Hsî says he does not understand the symbolism under line 2. The place is even, but the line itself is strong; the strength therefore is modified or tempered. And 2 is the correlate of the ruler in 5. We are to look to its subject therefore for a minister striving to realise the idea of the hexagram, and pacify the subdued kingdom. He becomes a hunter, and disposes of unworthy men, represented by 'the three foxes.' He also gets the yellow arrows, the instruments used in war or in hunting, whose colour is 'correct,' and whose form is 'straight.' His firm correctness will be good.

Line 3 is weak, when it should be strong; and occupying, as it does, the topmost place of the lower trigram, it suggests the symbolism of a porter in a carriage. People will say, 'How did he get there? The things cannot be his own.' And robbers will attack and plunder him. The subject of the line cannot protect himself, nor accomplish anything good.

What is said on the fourth line appears in the form of an address to its subject. The line is strong in an even place, and 1, its correlate, is weak in an odd place. Such a union will not be productive of good. In the symbolism 1 becomes the toe of the subject of 4. How the friend or friends, who are to come to him on the removal of this toe, are represented, I do not perceive.

Line 5 is weak in an odd place; but the place is that of the ruler, to whom it belongs to perfect the idea of the hexagram by removing all that is contrary to the peace and good order of the kingdom. It will be his duty to remove especially all the small men represented by the divided lines, which he can do with the help of his strong correlate in 2. Then even the small men will change their ways, and repair to him.

Line 6 is the highest line in the figure, but not the place of the ruler. Hence it appears as occupied by a feudal duke, who carries out the idea of the figure against small men, according to the symbolism employed.

[xli] The interpretation of this hexagram is encompassed with great difficulties. Sun is the symbol for the idea of diminishing or diminution; and what is said in Appendix I has made it to be accepted as teaching the duty of the subject to take of what is his and contribute to his ruler, or the expenses of the government under which he lives; in other words, readily and cheerfully to pay his taxes. P. Regis says, Sun seu (vectigalis causa) minuere . . . est valde utile;' and Canon McClatchie in translating Appendix I has:— 'Diminishing (by taxation for instance) .... is very lucky.' Possibly, king Wăn may have seen in the figures the subject of taxation; but the symbolism of his son takes a much wider range. My own reading of the figure and Text comes near to the view of Khăng-ȝze, that 'every diminution and repression of what we have in excess to bring it into accordance with right and reason is comprehended under Sun.'

Let there be sincerity in doing this, and it will lead to the happiest results. It will lead to great success in great things; and if the correction, or it may be a contribution towards it, appear to be very small, yet it will be accepted;—as in the most solemn religious service. This is substantially the view of the hexagram approved by the Khang-hsî editors.

Line 1 is strong, and its correlate in 4 is weak. Its subject will wish to help the subject of 4; but will not leave anything of his own undone in (loin. so. Nor will he diminish of his own for the other without due deliberation.

Line 2 is strong, and in the central place. But it is in the place of a weak line, and its subject should maintain his position without moving to help his correlate in 5. Maintaining his own firm correctness is the best way to help him.

Paragraph 3 is to my mind full of obscurity. Kû Hsî, adopting the view in Appendix I, says that the lower trigram was originally Khien, three undivided lines, like 'three men walking together,' and that the third line, taken away and made to be the topmost line, or the third, in what was originally Khwăn, three divided lines, was 'the putting away of one man;' and that then the change of place by 3 and 6, while they continued their proper correlation, was, one going away, and finding his friend. I cannot lay hold of any thread of reason in this.

Line 4 is weak, and in an even place; like an individual ailing and unable to perform his proper work. But the correlate in 1 is strong; and is made to hasten to its relief. The 'joy' of the line shows the desire of its subject to do his part in the work of the hexagram.

Line 5 is the seat of the ruler, who is here humble, and welcomes the assistance of his correlate, the subject of 2. He is a ruler whom all his subjects of ability will rejoice to serve in every possible way; and the result will be great good fortune.

Line 6 has been changed from a weak into a strong line from line 3; has received therefore the greatest increase, and will carry out the idea of the hexagram in the highest degree and style. But he can give increase to others without diminishing his own resources, and of course the benefit he will confer will be incalculable. Ministers will come to serve him; and not one from each clan merely, but many. Such is the substance of what is said on this last paragraph. I confess that I only discern the meaning darkly.

xlii Yî has the opposite meaning to Sun, and is the symbol of addition or increasing. What king Wăn had in his mind, in connexion with the hexagram, was a ruler or a government operating so as to dispense benefits to, and increase the resources of all the people. Two indications are evident in the lines;—the strong line in the ruler's seat, or the fifth line, and the weak line in the correlative place of 2. Whether there be other indications in the figure or its component trigrams will be considered in dealing with the Appendixes. The writer might well say, on general grounds, of the ruler whom he had in mind, that he would be successful in his enterprises and overcome the greatest difficulties.

Line 1 is strong, but its low position might seem to debar its subject from any great enterprise. Favoured as he is, however, according to the general idea of the hexagram, and specially responding to the proper correlate in 4, it is natural that he should make a movement; and great success will make his rashness be forgotten.

With paragraph 2 compare paragraph 5 of the preceding hexagram. Line 2 is weak, but in the centre, and is the correlate of 5. Friends give its subject the valuable gifts mentioned; 'that is,' says Kwo Yung (Sung dynasty), 'men benefit him; the oracles of the divination are in his favour,—spirits, that is, benefit him; and finally, when the king sacrifices to God, He accepts. Heaven confers benefit from above.'

Line 3 is weak, neither central, nor in its correct position. It would seem therefore that its subject should have no increase given to him. But it is the time for giving increase, and the idea of his receiving it by means of evil things is put into the line. That such things serve for reproof and correction is well known to Chinese moralists. But the paragraph goes on also to caution and admonish.

Line 4 is the place for a minister, near to that of the ruler. Its subject is weak, but his place is appropriate, and as he follows the due course, his ruler will listen to him, and he will be a support in the most critical movements. Changing the capital from place to place was frequent in the feudal times of China. That of Shang, which preceded *K*âu, was changed five times.

Line 5 is strong, in its fitting position, and central. It is the seat of the ruler, who has his proper correlate in 2. Everything good, according to the conditions of the hexagram, therefore, may be said of him;—as is done.

Line 6 is also strong; but it should be weak. Occupying the topmost place of the figure, its subject will concentrate his powers in the increase of himself, and not think of benefiting those below him; and the consequence will be as described.

xliii In Kwâi we have the hexagram of the third month, when the last remnant, cold and dark, of winter, represented by the sixth line, is about to disappear before the advance of the warm and bright days of the approaching summer. In the yin line at the top king Wăn saw the symbol of a small or bad man, a feudal prince or high minister, lending his power to maintain a corrupt government, or, it might be, a dynasty that was waxen old and ready to vanish away; and in the five undivided lines he saw the representatives of good order, or, it might be, the dynasty which was to supersede the other. This then is the subject of the hexagram,—how bad men, statesmen corrupt and yet powerful, are to be put out of the way. And he who would accomplish the task must do so by the force of his character more than by force of arms, and by producing a general sympathy on his side.

The Thwan says that he must openly denounce the criminal in the court, seek to awaken general sympathy, and at the same time go about his enterprise, conscious of its difficulty and danger. Among his own adherents, moreover, as if it were in his own city, he must make it understood how unwillingly he takes up arms. Then let him go forward, and success will attend him.

Line 1 is strong, the first line of that trigram, which expresses the idea of strength. But it is in the lowest place. The stage of the enterprise is too early, and the preparation too small to make victory certain. Its subject had better not take the field.

Line 2 is strong, and central, and its subject is possessed with the determination to do his part in the work of removal. But his eagerness is tempered by his occupancy of an even place; and he is cautious, and no attempts, however artful, to harm him will take effect.

Line 3 is strong, and its subject displays his purpose too eagerly. Being beyond the central position, moreover, gives an indication of evil. Lines 3 and 6 are also proper correlates; and, as elsewhere in the Yî, the meeting of yin and yang lines is associated with falling rain. The subject of 3, therefore, communicates with 6, in a way that annoys his associates; but nevertheless he commits no error, and, in the end, incurs no blame.

Line 4 is not in the centre, nor in an odd place, appropriate to it as undivided. Its subject therefore will not be at rest, nor able to do anything to accomplish the idea of the hexagram. He is symbolised by a culprit, who, according to the ancient and modern custom of Chinese courts, has been bastinadoed till he presents the appearance in the Text. Alone he can do nothing; if he could follow others, like a sheep led along, he might accomplish something, but he will not listen to advice.

Purslain grows in shady places, and hence we find it here in close contiguity to the topmost line, which is yin. As 5 is the ruler's seat, evil may come to him from such contiguity, and strenuous efforts must be made to prevent such an evil. The subject of the line, the ruler in the central place, will commit no error. It must be allowed that the symbolism in this line is not easily managed.

The subject of the 6th line, standing alone, may be easily disposed of.

[xliv] The single, divided, line at the top of Kwâi, the hexagram of the third month, has been displaced, and *Kh*ien has ruled over the fourth month of the year. But the innings of the divided line commence again; and here we have in Kâu the hexagram of the fifth month, when light and heat are supposed both to begin to be less.

In that divided line Wăn saw the symbol of the small or unworthy man, beginning to insinuate himself into the government of the country. His influence, if unchecked, would go on to grow, and he would displace one good man after another, and fill the vacant seats with others like-minded with himself. The object of Wăn in his Thwan, therefore, was to enjoin resistance to the encroachment of this bad man.

Kâu is defined as giving the idea of suddenly and casually encountering or meeting with. So does the divided line appear all at once in the figure. And this significance of the name rules in the interpretation of the lines, so as to set on one side the more common interpretation of them according to the correlation; showing how the meaning of the figures was put into them from the minds of Wăn and Tan in the first place. The sentiments of the Text are not learned from them; but they are forced and twisted, often fantastically, and made to appear to give those sentiments forth of themselves.

Here the first line, divided, where it ought to be the contrary, becomes the symbol of a bold, bad woman, who appears unexpectedly on the scene, and wishes to subdue or win all the five strong lines to herself. No one would contract a marriage with such a female; and every good servant of his country will try to repel the entrance into the government of every officer who can be so symbolised.

Line 1 represents the bête noire of the figure. If its subject can be kept back, the method of firm government and order will proceed. If he cannot be restrained, he will become disgusting and dangerous. It is not enough for the carriage to be stopt by the metal drag; it is also tied or bound to some steadfast object. Internal and external restraints should be opposed to the bad man.

The 'wallet of fish' under line 2 is supposed to symbolise the subject of line r. It has come into the possession of the subject of 2, by virtue of the meaning of the name Kâu, which I have pointed out. With his strength therefore he can repress the advance of 1. He becomes in fact 'the lord of the hexagram,' and all the other strong lines are merely guests; and especially is it important that he should prevent 1 from approaching them. This is a common explanation of what is said under this second line. It seems farfetched; but I can neither find nor devise anything better.

With what is said on line 3, compare the fourth paragraph of the duke's Text on the preceding hexagram. Line 3 is strong, but has gone beyond the central place; has no correlate above; and is cut off from 1 by the intervening 2. It cannot do much therefore against 1; but its aim being to repress that, there will be no great error.

Line 1 is the proper correlate of 4; but it has already met and associated with 2. The subject of 4 therefore stands alone; and evil to him may be looked for.

Line 5 is strong, and in the ruler's place. Its relation to 1 is like that of a forest tree to the spreading gourd. But let not its subject use force to destroy or repress the growth of 1; but let him restrain himself and keep his excellence concealed, and Heaven will set its seal to his virtue.

The symbolism of line 6 is difficult to understand, though the meaning of what is said is pretty clear. The Khang-hsî editors observe:—'The subject of this line is like an officer who has withdrawn from the world. He can accomplish no service for the time; but his person is removed from the workers of disorder.'

[xlv] Ʒhui denotes collecting together, or things so collected and hence this hexagram concerns the state of the kingdom when a happy union prevails between the sovereign and his ministers, between high and low; and replies in a vague way to the question how this state is to be preserved; by the influence of religion, and the great man, who is a sage upon the throne.

He, 'the king,' will repair to his ancestral temple, and meet in spirit there with the spirits of his ancestors. Whatever he does, being correct and right, will succeed. His religious services will be distinguished by their dignity and splendour. His victims will he the best that can be obtained, and other things will be in harmony with them.

Line 1 is weak, and in the place of a strong line. It has a proper correlate in 4, but is separated from him by the intervention of two weak lines. The consequence of these things is supposed to be expressed in the first part of the symbolism; but the subject of the line is possessed by the desire for union, which is the theme of the hexagram. Calling out to his correlate for help, he obtains it, and his sorrow is turned into joy.

Line 2 is in its proper place, and responds to the strong ruler in 5, who encourages and helps the advance of its subject. He possesses also the sincerity, proper to him in his central position; and though he were able to offer only the sacrifice of the spring, small compared with the fulness of the sacrifices in summer and autumn, it would be accepted.

Line 3 is weak, in the place of a strong line, and advanced from the central place. The topmost line, moreover, is no proper correlate. But its subject is possessed by the desire for union; and though 2 and 4 decline to associate with him, he presses on to 6, which is also desirous of union. That common desire brings them together, notwithstanding 3 and 6 are both divided lines; and with difficulty the subject of 3 accomplishes his object.

[But that an ordinary rule for interpreting the lineal indications may be thus overruled by extraordinary considerations shows how much of fancy there is in the symbolism or in the commentaries on it.]

Line 4 has its correlate in 1, and is near to the ruling line in 5. We may expect a good auspice for it; but its being strong in an odd place, calls for the caution which is insinuated.

Line 5 is strong, central, and in its correct position. Through its subject there may be expected the full realisation of the idea of the hexagram.

Line 6, weak, and at the extremity of the figure, is still anxious for union; but he has no proper correlate, and all below are united in 5. Its subject mourns his solitary condition; and his good feeling will preserve him from error and blame.

[xlvi] The character Shǎng is used of advancing in an upward direction, 'advancing and ascending.' And here, as the name of the hexagram, it denotes the advance of a good

officer to the highest pinnacle of distinction. The second line, in the centre of the lower trigram, is strong, but the strength is tempered by its being in an even place. As the representative of the subject of the hexagram, it shows him to be possessed of modesty and force. Then the ruler's seat, the fifth place, is occupied by a divided line, indicating that he will welcome the advance of 2. The officer therefore both has the qualities that fit him to advance, and a favourable opportunity to do so. The result of his advance will be fortunate.

It is said that after he has met with the ruler, 'the great man' in 5, 'advance to the south will be fortunate.' *Kû Hsî* and other critics say that 'advancing to the south' is equivalent simply to 'advancing forwards.' The south is the region of brightness and warmth; advance towards it will be a joyful progress. As P. Regis explains the phrase, the traveller will proceed 'via recta simillima illi qua itur ad austrates felicesque plagas.'

Line 1 is weak, where it should be strong; its subject, that is, is humble and docile. Those above him, therefore, welcome his advance. Another interpretation of the line is suggested by Appendix I; which deserves consideration. As the first line of Sun, moreover, it may be supposed to concentrate in itself its attribute of docility, and be the lord of the trigram.

See on the second line of ʒhui. Line 2 is strong, and the weak 5 is its proper correlate. We have a strong officer serving a weak ruler; he could not do so unless he were penetrated with a sincere and devoted loyalty.

Paragraph 3 describes the boldness and fearlessness of the advance of the third line. According to the Khang-hsî editors, who, I think, are right, there is a shade of condemnation in the line. Its subject is too bold.

Line 4 occupies the place of a great minister, in immediate contiguity to his ruler, who confides in him, and raises him to the highest distinction as a feudal prince. The mention of mount *Khî*, at the foot of which was the capital of the lords of *Kâu*, seems to take the paragraph out of the sphere of symbolism into that of history. 'The king' in it is the last sovereign of Shang; the feudal prince in it is Wăn.

In line 5 the advance has reached the highest point of dignity, and firm correctness is specially called for. 'Ascending the steps of a stair' may intimate, as *Kû Hsî* says, the ease of the advance; or according to others (the Khang-hsî editors among them), its ceremonious manner.

What can the subject of the hexagram want more? He has gained all his wishes, and still he is for going onwards. His advance is blind and foolish; and only the most exact correctness will save him from the consequences.

[xlvii] The character Khwăn presents us with the picture of a tree within an enclosure; 'a plant,' according to Williams, 'fading for want of room;' 'a tree,' according to Tai Tung, 'not allowed to spread its branches.' However this be, the term conveys the idea of being straitened and distressed; and this hexagram indicates a state of things in which the order and government that would conduce to the well-being of the country can hardly get the development, which, by skilful management on the part of 'the great man' and others, is finally secured for them.

Looking at the figure we see that the two central places are occupied by strong lines; but 2 is confined between 1 and 3, both of which are weak, and 5 (the ruler), as well as 4 (his minister), is covered by the weak 6; all which peculiarities are held to indicate the repression or straitening of good men by bad. For the way in which the same view is derived from the great symbolism, see Appendix II, in loc.

The concluding sentence of the Thwan is literally, 'If he speak, he will not be believed;' but the Khang-hsî editors give sufficient reasons for changing one character so as to give the meaning in the translation. 'Actions,' not words, are what are required in the case.

The symbolism of 'buttocks' is rather a favourite with the duke of *Kâu*;—'chacun à son goût.' The poor subject of line 1 sitting on a mere stump, which affords him no shelter, is indeed badly off. The line is at the bottom of the trigram indicating peril, and 4, which is its proper correlate, is so circumstanced as not to be able to render it help; hence comes the unfavourable auspice. 'Three years' is used, as often, for a long time.

The three strong lines in the figure (2, 4, and 5) are all held to represent 'superior men;' and their being straitened is not in their persons or estates, but in their principles which are denied development. Hence the subject of 2 is straitened while he fares sumptuously. His correlate in 5, though not quite proper, occupies the ruler's place, and comes to his help. That it is the ruler who comes appears from his red or vermillion knee-covers, different from the scarlet knee-covers worn by nobles, as in paragraph 5. Let 2 cultivate his sincerity and do the work of the hexagram as if he were sacrificing to spiritual beings; and then, if he keep quiet, all will be well.

For I a full explanation' of paragraph 3 Kû Hsî refers his readers to what Confucius is made to say on it in Appendix III, ii, 35. The reader, however, will probably not find much light in that passage. The Khang-hsî editors say here:—'The subjects of the three divided lines (1, 3, and 6) are all unable to deal aright with the straitened state indicated by the figure. The first is at the bottom, sitting and distressed. The second, occupies the third place, where he may either advance or retreat; and he advances and is distressed. Wounded abroad, he returns to his family, and finds none to receive him; so graphically is there set forth the distress which reckless action brings.'

Line 4 is the proper correlate of 1, but it is a strong line in an even place, and its assistance is given dilatorily. Then 1 is overridden by 2, which is represented by 'a chariot of metal.' It is difficult for the subjects of 1 and 4 to come together, and effect much; but 4 is near 5, which is also a strong line. Through a common sympathy, the subject of 5 will have a measure of success. So the symbolism of this line has been explained,—not very satisfactorily.

Line 5 is repressed by 6, and pressed on by 4. Above and below its subject is wounded. Especially is he straitened by the minister in 4, with his scarlet knee-covers. But the upper trigram is Tui, with the quality of complacent satisfaction. And this indicates, it is said, that the subject of 5 gets on notwithstanding his straits, especially by his sincerity. This explanation is not more satisfactory than the last.

Line 6 is at the top of the figure, where the distress may be supposed to reach its height. Its subject appears bound and on a perilous summit. But his extremity is also his opportunity. He is moved to think of repenting; and if he do repent, and go forward, his doing so will be fortunate.

[xlviii] 3ing, which gives its name to this hexagram, is the symbol of a well. The character originally was pictorial (井), intended to represent a portion of land, divided into nine parts, the central portion belonging to the government, and being cultivated by the joint labour of the eight families settled on the other divisions. In the centre of it, moreover, was a well, which was the joint property of all the occupants.

What is said on 3ing might be styled 'Moralisings on a well,' or Lessons to be learned from a well for the good order and government of a country.' What a well is to those in its neighbourhood, and indeed to men in general, that is government to a people. If rulers would only rightly appreciate the principles of government handed down from the good ages of the past, and faithfully apply them to the regulation of the present, they would be blessed themselves and their people with them.

In the Thwan we have the well, substantially the same through many changes of society; a sure source of dependance to men, for their refreshment and for use in their cultivation of the ground. Its form is what I have seen in the plains of northern China; what may be seen among ourselves in many places in Europe. It is deep, and the water is drawn up by a vessel let down from the top; and the value of the well depends on the water being actually raised. And so the principles of government must be actually carried out.

Line 1, being weak, and at the very bottom of the figure, suggests, or is made to suggest, the symbolism of it. Many men in authority are like such a well; corrupt, useless, unregarded.

Line 2 is strong, and might very well symbolise an active spring, ever feeding the well and, through it, the ground and its cultivators; but it is in an inappropriate place, and has no proper correlate. Its cool waters cannot be brought to the top. So important is it that the ministers of a country should be able and willing rightly to administer its government. In the account of the ancient Shun it is stated that he once saved his life by an opening in the lining of a well.

Line 3 is a strong line, in its proper place; and must represent an able minister or officer. But though the well is clear, no use is made of it. I do not find anything in the figure that can be connected with this fact. The author was wise beyond his lines. After the first sentence of the paragraph, the duke of *K*âu ceases from his function of making emblems; reflects and moralises.

Line 4 is weak, but in its proper place. Its subject is not to be condemned, but neither is he to be praised. He takes care of himself, but does nothing for others.

Line 5 is strong, and in its right place. The place is that of the ruler, and suggests the well, full of clear water, which is drawn up, and performs its useful work. Such is the good Head of government to his people.

Line 6 is in its proper place, but weak. If the general idea of the figure was different, a bad auspice might be drawn from it. But here we see in it the symbol of the water drawn up, and the top uncovered so that the use of the well is free to all. Then the mention of 'sincerity' suggests the inexhaustibleness of the elemental supply.

[xlix] The character called Ko or Keh is used here in the sense of changing. Originally used for the skin of an animal or bird, alive or dead, it received the significance of changing at a very early time. Its earliest appearance, indeed, in the first Book of the Shû, is in that sense. How the transition was made from the idea of a skin or hide to that of change is a subject that need not be entered on here. The author has before him the subject of changes occurring—called for—in the state of the country; it may be on the greatest scale. The necessity of them is recognised, and hints are given as to the spirit and manner in which they should be brought about.

For the way in which the notion of change is brought out of the trigrams of the figure, see Appendixes I and II. It is assumed in the Thwan that change is viewed by people generally with suspicion and dislike, and should not be made hastily. When made as a necessity, and its good effects appear, the issues will be great and good. A proved necessity for them beforehand; and a firm correctness in the conduct of them:—these are the conditions by which changes should be regulated.

Line 1, at the bottom of the figure, may be taken as denoting change made at too early a period. It has no proper correlate or helper, moreover, above. Hence its subject is represented as tied up, unable to take any action.

Line 2, though weak, is in its correct place. It is in the centre also of the trigram Lî, signifying brightness and intelligence, and has a proper correlate in the strong 5. Let its subject take action in the way of change.

The symbolism of paragraph 3 is twofold. The line is strong, and in the correct position, but it has passed the centre of Sun and is on its outward verge. These conditions may dispose its subject to reckless and violent changing which would be bad. But if he act cautiously and with due deliberation, he may take action, and he will be believed in.

Line 4 is strong, but in the place of a weak line. This might vitiate any action of its subject in the way of change, and give occasion for repentance. But other conditions are intimated that will have a contrary effect; and if he have further secured general confidence, he may proceed to the greatest changes, even to change the dynasty,—'with good fortune.' The conditions favourable to his action are said to be such as these:—The line has passed from the lower trigram into the upper; water and fire come in it into contact; the fourth place is that of the minister immediately below the ruler's seat. All these considerations demand action from the subject of 4 in harmony with the idea of the hexagram.

Line 5 has every quality proper to 'the lord of the hexagram,' and his action will be in every way beneficial. He is symbolled by the tiger; and the changes which he makes by the bright stripes of the tiger when he has changed his coat.

Line 6 is weak, but its subject is penetrated with the spirit of the hexagram. If its subject be a superior man, only inferior to 'the great man,' immediately below, the changes he makes will be inferior only to his. If he be a small man, he will be compliant and submissive. The lesson for him, however, is to abide firm and correct without taking any action of his own.

¹ Ting was originally a pictorial character, representing a caldron with three feet and two ears, used for cooking and preparing food for the table (the mat in old times) and the altar. The picture has disappeared from the character, but it is said that in the hexagram we have an outline from which fancy may construct the vessel. The lower line, divided, represents its feet; lines 2, 3, 4, all undivided, represent the body of it; line 5, divided, represents its two ears; and line 6, undivided, the handle by which it was carried, or suspended from a hook. Appendix VI makes Ting follow Ko in the order of the hexagrams, because there is no changer of the appearance and character of things equal to the furnace and caldron!

Ting and 3ing (48) are the only two hexagrams named from things in ordinary use with men; and they are both descriptive of the government's work of nourishing. There are three hexagrams of which that is the theme, Î (27), under which we are told in Appendix I that 'the sages nourished men of worth, by means of them to reach to the myriads of the people.' 3ing treats of the nourishment of the people generally by the government through its agricultural and other methods; Ting treats of the nourishment of men of talents and virtue; and that being understood, it is said, without more ado, that it 'intimates great progress and success.' The Text that follows, however, is more difficult to interpret than that of 3ing.

Line 1 is weak, and little or nothing can be expected from its subject. But it has a proper correlate in the strong 4; and the disastrous overthrow, causing the feet to be directed towards 4, is understood to be lucky, as accelerating the co-operation of their two lines! The overturned caldron is thereby emptied of bad stuff that had accumulated in it!! The writer uses another illustration, which comes to the same thing. A concubine is less honourable than a wife,—like the overthrown caldron. But if she have a son, while the proper wife has none, he will be his father's heir, and the mother, the concubine, will share in the honour of his position. Thus the issue of what was so unpromising is good. At least 'there is no mistake.' The above is what is found in the best commentaries on the paragraph. I give it, but am myself dissatisfied with it.

Line 2 is strong. 'The enemy' is the first line, which solicits 1. One, however, is able to resist the solicitation; and the whole paragraph gives a good auspice. The personal pronoun seems to show that the whole was, or was intended to be, understood as an oracular response in divination. This paragraph is rhymed, moreover, as are also 1, 3, and 4:—

> 'In the caldron is good fare,
>   See my foe with angry glare;
>   But touch me he does not dare.'

Line 3 is also strong, and in the proper place; and if its correlate were the divided 5, its auspice would be entirely good. But instead of 5, its correlate is the strong 6. The place of the ears at 5 has been changed. Things promise badly. The advance of 3 is stopped. The good meat in the caldron which it symbolises will not be eaten. But 3 keeping firm 5 will by and by seek its society! The yin and the yang will mingle, and their union will be followed by genial rain. The issue will he good.

Line 4 is in the place of a great minister, who is charged with the most difficult duties, which no single man can sustain. Then the strength of 4 is weakened by being in an even place, and its correlate is the weak 1 in the lowest place. Its subject is insufficient of himself for his work, and he has no sufficient help; and the result will be evil.

'Paragraph 5,' says the Daily Lecture, 'praises the ruler as condescending to the worthy with his humble virtue.' 'Yellow' has occurred repeatedly as 'a correct colour;' and here 'the yellow ears and strong rings of metal' are intended to intensify our appreciation of the occupant of 5. As the line is divided, a caution is added about being firm and correct.

Line 6 is strong, but the strength is tempered by its being in an even place. It is this which makes the handle to be of jade, which, though very hard, is supposed to have a peculiar and rich softness of its own. The auspice of the line is very good. 'The great minister,' it is said, 'the subject of 6,' performs for the ruler, the subject of 5, in helping his government and nourishing the worthy, the part which the handle does for the caldron.

[li] Kǎn among the trigrams represents thunder, and, according to Wǎn's arrangement and significance of them, 'the oldest son.' It is a phonetic character in which the significant constituent is Yü, meaning rain, and with which are formed most characters that denote atmospherical phenomena. The hexagram is formed of the trigram Kǎn redoubled, and may be taken as representing the crash or peal of thunder; but we have seen that the attribute or virtue of the trigram is 'moving, exciting power;' and thence, symbolically, the character is indicative of movement taking place in society or in the kingdom. This is the meaning of the hexagram; and the subject is the conduct to be pursued in a time of movement—such as insurrection or revolution—by the party promoting, and most interested in, the situation. It is shown how he ought to be aware of the dangers of the time, and how by precaution and the regulation of himself he may overcome them.

The indication of a successful issue given by the figure is supposed to be given by the undivided line at the bottom of the trigram. The subject of it must be superior to the subjects of the two divided lines above. It is in the idea of the hexagram that he should be moving and advancing;—and what can his movement be but successful?

The next sentence shows him sensible of the danger of the occasion, but confident and self-possessed. The concluding sentence shows him rapt in his own important affairs, like a sincere worshipper, thinking only of the service in which he is engaged. Such a symbol is said to be suggested by Wǎn's significance of Kǎn as 'the oldest son (page 32).' It is his to succeed to his father, and the hexagram, as following Ting, shows him presiding over the sacrifices that have been prepared in the caldron. This is too fanciful.

What is said on line 1 is little more than a repetition of the principal part of the Thwan. The line is undivided, and gives the auspice of good fortune.

'The position of peril' to the subject of line 2 is suggested, as Appendix II says, by its position, immediately above 1. But the rest of the symbolism is obscure, and Kû Hsî says he does not understand it. The common interpretation appears in the version. The subject of the line does what he can to get out of danger; and finally, as is signified by the central position of the line, the issue is better than could have been expected. On the specification of 'seven days,' see what is said in the treatise on the Thwan of hexagram 24. On its use here Khǎng-ȝze says:—'The places of a diagram amount to 6. The number 7 is the first of another. When the movement symbolised by Kǎn is gone by, things will be as they were before.'

Line 3 is divided, and where an undivided line should be; but if its subject move on to the fourth place, which would be right for him, the issue will not be bad.

The 4th line, however, has a bad auspice of its own. It is undivided in an even place, and it is pressed by the divided line on either side, hence its subject is represented as supinely sinking in the mud.

Line 5 is divided, in an odd place, and that in which the action of the hexagram may be supposed to be concentrated. Hence its subject is always in peril; but his central position indicates safety in the end.

Line 6 is weak, and has to abide the concluding terrors of the movement. Action on the part of its subject is sure to be evil. If, however, he were to take precautions, he might escape with only the censures of his relatives. But I do not see anything in the figure to indicate this final symbolism. The writer, probably, had a case in his mind, which it suited; but what that was we do not know.

[lii] The trigram Kăn represents a mountain. Mountains rise up grandly from the surface of the earth, and their masses rest on it in quiet and solemn majesty; and they serve also to arrest the onward progress of the traveller. Hence the attribute ascribed to Kăn is twofold; it is both active and passive-resting and arresting. The character is used in this hexagram with both of those significations. As the name of the figure, it denotes the mental characteristic of resting in what is right; especially resting, as it is expressed by Chinese critics, 'in principle,'—that which is light, on the widest scale, and in the absolute conception of the mind; and that which is right in every different position in which a man can be placed. We find this treated of in the Great Learning (Commentary, chapter 3), and in the Doctrine of the Mean, chapter 14, and other places. This is the theme of the hexagram; and the symbolism of it is all taken from different parts of the human body, as in hexagram 31, and the way in which they are dealt with. Several of the paragraphs are certainly not easy to translate and interpret.

The other parts of the body, such as the mouth, eyes, and ears, have their appetencies, which lead them to what is without themselves. The back alone has nothing to do with anything beyond itself-hardly with itself even; all that it has to do is to stand straight and strong. So should it be with, us, resting in principle, free from the intrusion of selfish though s and external objects. Amidst society, he who realises the idea of the hexagram is still alone, and does not allow himself to be distracted from the contemplation and following of principle. He is not a recluse, however, who keeps aloof from social life; but his distinction is that he maintains a supreme regard to principle, when alone, and when mingling with others.

In the symbolism the author rises from one part of the body to the other. The first line at the bottom of the figure fitly suggests 'the toes.' The lesson is that from the first men should rest in, and be anxious to do, what is right in all their affairs. The weakness of the line and its being in an odd place give occasion for the caution, with which the paragraph concludes.

Above the toes are the calves, represented by the second line, weak, but in its proper place. Above this, again, are the loins, represented by 3, strong, and in danger of being violent. Line 2 follows 3, and should help it; but is unable to do so; and there results dissatisfaction.

When the calves are kept at rest, advance is stopped, but no other harm ensues. Not so when the loins are kept at rest, and unable to bend, for the connexion between the upper and lower parts of the body is then broken. The dissatisfaction increases to an angry heat. Paragraph 3 is unusually difficult. For 'loins' P. Regis has scapulae, and for ribs renes; Canon McClatchie says:—'Third Nine is stopping at a limit, and separating what is in continued succession (i. e. the backbone); thus the mind,' &c.

Line 4 is a weak line resting in a proper place; hence it gives a good auspice. The Khang-hsî editors, however, call attention to the resting of the trunk as being inferior to the resting of the back in the Thwan.

The place of the weak fifth line is not proper for it; and this accounts for the mention of its subject 'repenting,' for which, however, there is no occasion.

The third line of the trigrams, and the sixth of the hexagram, is what makes Kăn what it is,—the symbol of a mountain. The subject of it therefore will carry out the resting required by the whole figure in the highest style.

[liii] Kien is ordinarily used in the sense of gradually; but there is connected with that the idea also of progress or advance. The element of meaning in the character is the symbol of water; and the whole of it denotes gradual advance, like the soaking in of water. Three hexagrams contain in them the idea of advance, 3in (35), Shăng (46), and

this *K*ien; but each has its peculiarity of meaning, and that of *K*ien is the gradual manner in which the advance takes place. The subject then of the hexagram is the advance of men to offices in the state, how it should take place gradually and by successive steps, as well as on certain other conditions that may be gathered from the Text. P. Regis gives this exposition of the subject, as taken by him from the symbolism, which he ascribes to Confucius:—'Viri probi, seu republica digni, in virtutis soliditate instituendi sunt a sapiente, bonisque regulis ut altis radicibus firmandi, nec alii ad rempublicam tractandam promovendi, nisi qui paulatim per varios minoresque gradus ad magnum hoc regimen periculo facto ascendere digni sint.' He then illustrates this sentiment by the words of Pliny:—'Eligetur multis experimentis eruditus, et qui futura possit ex praeteritis praevidere.'

But how does the lineal figure give the idea of a gradual advance? We shall see how it is attempted in the Great Symbolism to get this from the component trigrams. The account there is not satisfactory; and still less so is what else I have been able to find on the subject. E. g., the trigrams were originally Khwăn and *Kh*ien; but the third line of Khwăn and the first of *Kh*ien have changed places; and the trigrams now denote 'the youngest son,' and 'the eldest daughter.' If all this, which is a mere farrago, were admitted, it would not help us to the idea of an advance.

Again, the lines 2, 3, 4, 5 are all in the places proper to them as strong or weak; we ascend by them as by regular steps to the top of the hexagram; and this, it is said, gives the notion of the gradual steps of the advance. But neither does this carry conviction with it to the mind. We must leave the question. King Wăn, for reasons which we cannot discover, or without such reasons, determined that the hexagram *K*ien should denote the gradual advance of men to positions of influence and office.

The marriage of a young lady is mentioned in the Thwan as an illustration of an important event taking place with various preliminary steps, continued from its initiation to its consummation. But all must he done in an orderly and correct manner. And so must it be with the rise of a man in the service of the state.

The goose from the most ancient times played an important part in the marriage ceremonies of the Chinese; and this may have suggested the use of it in the symbolism of the different lines. Its habits as a bird of passage, and flying in processional order, admirably suited the writer's purpose. In paragraph 1 it appears for the first time in the season approaching the shore. Then comes the real subject of the line; and the facts of its being weak, and without a proper correlate, agree with, if they do not suggest, what is said about him, and the caution added.

The geese have advanced in line 2, and so has the officer, though he is not mentioned. The line is weak or humble, and central, and has a proper correlate in 5. Hence comes the good auspice.

Line 3 is strong, and has passed the central place, to the top of the lower trigram, and has not a proper correlate in 6. Its subject is likely to be violent and at the same time unsuccessful in his movements. He is like a husband who does not care for his wife, or a wife who does not care for her child. But in the case supposed, his strength in the end would be useful.

The web-footed goose is not suited for taking hold on the branches; but on flat branches it can rest. Line 4, weak, but in an even place, does not promise a good auspice for its subject; but it is the first line in the trigram of humility, and it is concluded that he will not fall into error.

Line 5 is a strong line in the ruler's seat; and yet it appears here as the symbol of a wife. Somehow its subject has been at variance with, and kept in disgrace by, calumniating enemies such as the plunderers of paragraph 3; but things come right in the end. The wife, childless for three years, becomes at last a mother; and there is good fortune.

The subject of line 6 has reached the top of the hexagram. There is no more advance for him; and he has no correlate. But he may still do some good work for the state, and verify the auspice derived from the ornamental plumes of the geese.

[liv] Mei Kwei is a common way of saying that a young lady is married, or, literally, 'is going home.' If the order of the characters be reversed, the verb kwei will be transitive, and the phrase will signify 'the marrying away of a daughter,' or 'the giving the young lady in marriage.' In the name of this hexagram, Kwei is used with this transitive force. But Mei means 'a younger sister,' and not merely a young lady or a daughter. Kwei Mei might be equivalent to our 'giving in marriage;' but we shall find that the special term has a special appropriateness. The Thwan makes the hexagram give a bad auspice concerning its subject; and for this the following reasons are given:— According to Wăn's symbolism of the trigrams, Tui, the lower trigram here, denotes the youngest daughter, and *K*ăn, the upper trigram, the oldest son. And as the action of the hexagram begins with that of the lower trigram, we have in the figure two violations of propriety. First, the marriage represented is initiated by the lady and her friends. She goes to her future home instead of the bridegroom coming to fetch her. Second, the parties are unequally matched. There ought not to be such disparity of age between them. Another reason assigned for the bad auspice is that lines 2, 3, 4, and 5 are all in places not suited to them, quite different from the corresponding lines in the preceding hexagram.

Is then such a marriage as the above, or marriage in general, the theme of the hexagram? I think not. The marriage comes in, as in the preceding essay, by way of illustration. With all the abuses belonging to it as an institution of his country, as will immediately appear, the writer acknowledged it without saying a word in deprecation or correction of those abuses; but from the case he selected he wanted to set forth some principles which should obtain in the relation between a ruler and his ministers. This view is insisted on in Wan King's 'New Collection of Comments on the Yî (A. D. 1686).'

A feudal prince was said to marry nine ladies at once. The principal of them was the bride who was to be the proper wife, and she was attended by two others, virgins from her father's harem; a cousin, and a half-sister, a daughter of her father by another mother of inferior rank. Under line 1 the younger sister of the hexagram appears in the inferior position of this half-sister. But the line is strong, indicative in a female of firm virtue. The mean condition and its duties are to be deplored, and give the auspice of lameness; but notwithstanding, the secondary wife will in a measure discharge her service. There will be good fortune. Notwithstanding apparent disadvantages, an able officer may do his ruler good service.

Line 2 is strong, and in the centre. The proper correlate is 5, which, however, is weak, and in the place of a strong line. With such a correlate, the able lady in 2 cannot do much in the discharge of her proper work. But if she think only of her husband, like the widow who will die rather than marry again, such devotion will have its effect and its reward. Though blind of one eye, she yet manages to see. And so devoted loyalty in an officer will compensate for many disadvantages.

Line 3 is weak, where it should be strong; and the attribute of pleased satisfaction belonging to Tui culminates in its subject. She turns out to be of so mean a character and such a slave of passion that no one will marry her. She returns and accepts the position of a concubine.

Line 4 is strong, where it should be weak; but in the case of a female the indication is not bad. The subject of the line, however, is in no haste. She waits, and the good time will come.

King Tî-yî has been already mentioned under the fifth line of hexagram 11, and in connexion with some regulation which he made about the marriage of daughters of the royal house. His sister here is honourably mentioned, so as to suggest that the adorning which she preferred was 'the ornament of the hidden man of the heart.' The comparison of her to 'the moon almost full' I am ready to hail as an instance where the duke of *K*âu is for once poetical. *Kh*ăng-ȝze, however, did not see poetry, but a symbol in it. 'The moon is not full,' he says, 'but only nearly full. A wife ought not to eclipse her husband!'

However, the sister of Tî-yî gets happily married, as she deserved to do, being represented by the line in the place of honour, having its proper correlate in 2.

Line 6 is weak, at the top of the hexagram, and without a proper correlate. Hence its auspice is evil. The marriage-contract is broken, according to *Kû* Hsî, and does not take effect. The parties mentioned in the paragraph appear engaged in the temple, offering or sacrificing to the spirits of their ancestors. But the woman's basket which should contain her offerings (The Shih, I, ii, ode 4) is empty, and the man attempts to perform his part in slaying the victim (The Shih, II, vi, ode 6. 5) without effect.

[lv] The character Făng is the symbol of being large and abundant, and, as the name of this hexagram, denotes a condition of abundant prosperity. In the changes of human affairs a condition of prosperity has often given place to one of an opposite character. The lesson of the hexagram is to show to rulers how they may preserve the prosperity of their state and people. The component trigrams have the attributes of intelligence and of motive force, and the second is under the direction of the first. A ruler with these attributes is not likely to fail in maintaining his crown and prosperity, and it may well be said that the figure intimates progress and development. The king is told not to be anxious, but to study how he may always be like the sun in his meridian height, cheering and enlightening all.

The explanation of the Thwan is thus natural and easy. It will be found that a change is introduced in explaining the symbolism of the lines, which it is as well to point out here. Thus far we have found that to constitute a proper correlation between two lines, one of them must be whole, and the other divided. Here two undivided lines make a correlation. The law, evidently made for the occasion, goes far to upset altogether the doctrine of correlated lines. I have been surprised that the rules about the lines stated in the Introduction, p. 19, have held good so often. There have been various deviations from them, but none so gross as that in this hexagram.

Line 1 is strong, and in an odd place. Its correlate is 4, which would in other figures be deemed unfortunate. But here even the Text calls 4 (for the reference must be to it) the mate of 1, and makes their belonging to different categories of no account. The lesson taught is that mutual helpfulness is the great instrument for the maintenance of prosperity. The subject of line 1 is encouraged to go forward.

Line 2 is divided, and in its proper place. Occupying the centre of the trigram of brightness, the intelligence of it should be concentrated in its subject; but his correlate is the weak 5, weak and in an improper place, so that he becomes the benighted ruler, and darkness is shed from him down on 2, which is strangely symbolised. The subject of 2 therefore, if he advance, will not be acceptable to his ruler, and will not be employed. The only way in which he. can be useful by developing the light that is in him is pointed out in the conclusion. The constellation of the Bushel corresponds to our Ursa Major, or perhaps part of Sagittarius.

Line 3 is strong, in its proper place. It is the last line moreover of the trigram of Brightness. All these conditions are favourable to the employment of its subject; but its correlate is the weak 6, which is at the extremity of the trigram of movement. There is no more power therefore in 6, and the subject of 3 has no one to co-operate with him. His symbolism and auspice are worse than those of 2; but his own proper goodness and capacity will save him from error. Mei is a small star in or near the Bushel.

The symbolism of line 4 is the same as that of 2, till we come to the last sentence. Then there is the strange correlation of the two strong lines in 4 and 1; and the issue is good.

The subject of line 5 is in the ruler's place, himself weak, but 'the lord' of the trigram of movement. He can do little unhelped, but if he can bring into the work and employ in his service the talents of 1, 3, and 4, and even of 2, his correlate, the results will be admirable. Nothing consolidates the prosperity of a country so much as the co-operation of the ruler and able ministers.

All the conditions of line 6 are unfavourable, and its subject is left to himself without any helpers. He is isolated for long, and undone. The issue is only evil.

[lvi] The name Lü denotes people travelling abroad, and is often translated by 'strangers.' As early as the time of king Wăn, there was a class of men who went about from one state to another, pursuing their business as pedlars or travelling merchants; but in Mencius II, i, chap. 5. 3, it is used for travellers generally, whatever it was that took them out of their own states. Confucius himself is adduced as a travelling stranger; and in this hexagram king Wăn is supposed to have addressed himself to the class of such men, and told them how they ought to comport themselves. They ought to cultivate two qualities,—those of humility and integrity (firm correctness). By means of these they would escape harm, and would make some little attainment and progress. Their rank was too low to speak of great things in connexion with them. It is interesting to find travellers, strangers in a strange land, having thus a place in the Yî.

For the manner in which the component trigrams are supposed to give the idea that is in Lü, see Appendix II. In Appendix I there is an endeavour to explain the Thwan by means of the lines and their relation to one another.

Line 1 is weak, in an odd place, and at the very bottom or commencement of the hexagram, These conditions are supposed to account for the unfavourable symbolism and auspice.

Line 2 is weak, but in its proper place. That place, moreover, is the central. Hence the traveller—and he might here very well be a travelling merchant—is represented in the symbolism as provided with everything he can require; and though the auspice is not mentioned, we must understand it as being good.

Line 3 is strong, and in an even place. But it occupies the topmost place in the lower trigram; and its strength may be expected to appear as violence. So it does in the symbolism, and extraordinary violence as well. It seems unreasonable to suppose, as in the conclusion, that one so described could be in any way correct. The Khang-hsî editors remark that the subjects of 2 and 3 are represented as having 'lodging-houses,' and not any of those of the other lines, because these are the only two lines in the places proper to them!

Line 4 is strong, but in an even place. Hence its subject has not a lodging-house;' but has found a situation where he has shelter, though he is exposed to perils. Hence he is represented as having an axe, which may be available for defence. Still he is not at peace in his mind. The Khang-hsî editors observe well that the mention of an axe makes us think of caution as a quality desirable in a traveller.

Line 5, though weak, is in the centre of the upper trigram, which has the quality of brightness and elegance. It is held to be the lord of the trigram Lî; and lines 4 and 6 are on either side in loyal duty to defend and help. Then the shooting a pheasant is supposed to be suggested; an elegant bird,—by the trigram of elegance. When an officer was travelling abroad in ancient times, his gift of introduction at any feudal court was a pheasant. The traveller here emblemed is praised by his attached friends, and exalted to a place of dignity by the ruler to whom he is acceptable. It will be seen how the idea of the fifth line being the ruler's seat is dropt here as being alien from the idea of the hexagram, so arbitrary is the interpretation of the symbolism.

Line 6 is strong, in an even place, at the extremity of Lî and of the whole hexagram. Its subject will be arrogant and violent; the opposite of what a traveller should be; and the issue will be evil. The symbolism must be allowed to be extravagant. What bird ever burned its nest? And the character for 'ox' is strangely used for 'ox-like docility.'

[lvii] With Sun as the fifth of the Fû-hsî trigrams we have become familiar. It symbolises both wind and wood; and has the attributes of flexibility (nearly allied to docility) and penetration. In this hexagram we are to think of it as representing wind with its penetrating power, finding its way into every corner and cranny.

Confucius once said (Analects 12. 19):—'The relation between superiors and inferiors is like that between the wind and the grass. The grass must bend when the wind blows upon it.' In accordance with this, the subject of the hexagram must be understood as the influence and orders of government designed to remedy what is wrong in the people. The 'Daily Lecture' says that the upper trigram denotes the orders issuing from the ruler, and the lower the obedience rendered to them by the people; but this view is hardly borne out by the Text.

But how is it that the figure represents merely 'some little attainment?' This is generally explained by taking the first line of the trigram as indicating what the subject of it can do. But over the weak first line are two strong lines, so that its subject can accomplish but little. The Khang-hsî editors, rejecting this view, contend that, the idea of the whole figure being penetration, line 1, the symbol of weakness and what is bad, will not be able to offer much resistance to the subjects of the other lines, which will enter and dispel its influence. They illustrate this from processes of nature, education, and politics; the effect they say is described as small, because the process is not to revolutionise or renew, but only to correct and improve. Such as it is, however, it requires the operation of the strong and virtuous, 'the great man.' Even all this criticism is not entirely satisfactory.

Line 1 is weak, where it should be strong. The movements of its subject are expressive of perplexity. He wants vigour and decision.

Line 2 is strong, and in the right place, and has a good auspice. Things are placed or hidden beneath a couch or bed; and the subject of the line appears as searching for them. He calls in divination to assist his judgment, and exorcists to expel for him what is bad. The work is great and difficult, so that he appears almost distracted by it; but the issue is good. For this successful explanation of the line, I am indebted to the Khang-hsî editors. The writer of the Text believed of course in divination and exorcism; which was his misfortune rather than his fault or folly.

Line 3 is in the right place for a strong line. But its position at the top of the lower trigram is supposed to indicate the restlessness, and here the vehemence, of its subject. And 6 is no proper correlate. All the striving is ineffective, and there is occasion for regret.

Line 4 is weak, as is its correlate in 1. But 4 is a proper place for a weak line, and it rests under the shadow of the strong and central 5. Hence the omens of evil are counteracted; and a good auspice is obtained. The game caught in hunting was divided into three portions:—the first for use in sacrifices; the second for the entertainment of visitors; and the third for the kitchen generally. A hunt which yielded enough for all these purposes was deemed very successful.

On line 5 *Kh*ăng-*3*ze says:—'It is the seat of honour, and the place for the lord of Sun, from whom there issue all charges and commands. It is central and correct; we must find in its subject the qualities denoted by Sun in their greatest excellence. But those qualities are docility and accordance with what is right; and the advantage of firm correctness is insisted on. With this all will be right.' With the concluding sentence compare the conclusion of the Thwan of hexagram 18.

The evil that paragraph 6 concludes with would arise from the quality of Sun being carried to excess. I have followed the Khang-hsî editors in adopting a change of one character in the received Text.

lviii The trigram Tui symbolises water as collected in a marsh or lake; and its attribute or virtus is pleasure or complacent satisfaction. It is a matter of some difficulty to determine in one's mind how this attribute came to be connected with the trigram. The Khang-hsî editors say:—'When the airs of spring begin to blow, from the collections of water on the earth the moistening vapours rise up (and descend again); so, when the breath of health is vigorous in a man's person, the hue of it is displayed in his complexion. Akin to this is the significance of the hexagram Tui representing a marsh, as denoting pleasure. Although the yin lines give it its special character they owe their power and effect to the yang; so when the qualities of mildness and harmony prevail in a man, without true-heartedness and integrity to control and direct them, they will fail to be correct, and may degenerate into what is evil. Hence it is said that it will be advantageous to be firm and correct!'

The feeling then of pleasure is the subject of this hexagram. The above quotation sufficiently explains the concluding characters of the Thwan; but where is the intimation in Tui of progress and attainments? It is supposed to be in the one weak line surmounting each trigram and supported by the two strong lines. Fancy sees in that mildness and benignity energised by a double portion of strength.

Line 1, strong in the place of strength, with no proper correlate above, is thus confined to itself. But its subject is sufficient for himself. There will be good fortune.

Line 2, by the rule of place, should be weak, but it is strong. Without any proper correlate, and contiguous to the weak 3, the subject of it might be injuriously affected, and there would be cause for repentance. But the sincerity natural in his central position counteracts all this.

The view of the third paragraph that appears in the translation is derived from the Khang-hsî editors. The evil threatened in it would be a consequence of the excessive devotion of its subject to pleasure.

'The bordering on what is injurious' in paragraph 4 has reference to the contiguity of line 4 to the weak 3. That might have an injurious effect; but the subject of 4 reflects and deliberates before he will yield to the seduction of pleasure, and there is cause for joy.

The danger to the subject of line 5 is from the weak 6 above, in whom he is represented as 'trusting.' Possibly his own strength and sincerity of mind may be perverted into instruments of evil; but possibly, they may operate beneficially.

The symbolism of paragraph 6 is akin to that of 3, though no positive auspice is expressed. The subject of line 3 attracts others round itself for the sake of pleasure; the subject of this leads them to follow himself in quest of it.

[lix] Hwân, the name of this hexagram, denotes a state of dissipation or dispersion. It is descriptive primarily of men's minds alienated from what is right and good. This alienation is sure to go on to disorder in the commonwealth; and an attempt is made to show how it should be dealt with and remedied.

The figure is made up of one of the trigrams for water and over it that for wind. Wind moving over water seems to disperse it, and awakes naturally in the beholder the idea of dissipation.

The intimation of progress and success is supposed to be given by the strong lines occupying the central places. The king goes to the ancestral temple, there to meet with the spirits of his ancestors. His filial piety moves them by the sincerity of its manifestation. Those spirits come and are present. Let filial piety—in our language, let sincere religion—rule in men's minds, and there will be no alienation in them from what is right and good or from one another. And if the state of the country demand a great or hazardous enterprise, let it be undertaken. But whatever is done, must be done with due attention to what is right, firmly and correctly.

Line 1, at the commencement of the hexagram, tells us that the evil has not yet made great progress, and that dealing with it will be easy. But the subject of the line is weak, and in an odd place. He cannot cope with the evil himself. He must have help, and he finds that in a strong horse, which description is understood to be symbolical of the subject of the strong second line.

'Line 2 is strong, but in an even place. That place is, indeed, the central, but the attribute of the lower trigram Khan is peril. These conditions indicate evil, and action will be dangerous; but the subject of 2 looks to 1 below him, and takes shelter in union with its subject. Since the commentary of *Kh*ăng-ʒze, this has been the interpretation of the line.

Line 3 is weak, and in an odd place. A regard for himself that would unfit its subject for contributing any service to the work of the hexagram might be feared; but he discards that regard, and will do nothing to be repented of. There is a change of style in the Chinese text at this point. As Wang Shăn-ʒze (Yüan dynasty) says:—'Here and henceforth the scattering is of what should be scattered, that what should not be scattered may be collected.'

Line 4, though weak, is in its correct place, and adjoins the strong 5, which is in the ruler's seat. The subject of 4, therefore, will fitly represent the minister, to whom it belongs to do a great part in remedying the evil of dispersion. And this he does. He brings dissentient partizanship to an end; and not satisfied with that, he collects multitudes of those who had been divided into a great body so that they stand out conspicuous like a hill.

Line 5 gives us the action of the ruler himself;—by his proclamations, and by his benevolence. *K*û Hsî and other critics enlarge on the symbolism of the perspiration, which they think much to the point. P. Regis avoids it, translating—'Ille, magnas leges dissipans, facit ut penetrent(ur?).' Canon McClatchie has an ingenious and original, so far as my Chinese reading goes, note upon it:—'As sweat cures fevers, so do proclamations cure rebellions.' Both of these translators miss the meaning of the other instance of the king's work.

Line 6 is occupied by a strong line, which has a proper correlate in 3; but 3 is at the top of the trigram of peril. The subject of 6 hurries away from association with the subject of it, but does so in the spirit of the hexagram, so that there is no error or blame attaching to him.

[ix] The primary application of the character *K*ieh was to denote the joints of the bamboo; it is used also for the joints of the human frame; and for the solar and other terms of the year. Whatever makes regular division may be denominated a *K*ieh; there enter into it the ideas of regulating and restraining; and the subject of this hexagram is the regulations of government enacted for the guidance and control of the people. How the constituent trigrams are supposed to suggest or indicate this meaning will be seen in Appendix II.

*K*û Hsî anticipates that symbolism in trying to account for the statement that the figure gives the promise of success and attainment; but the ground of this is generally made out by referring to the equal division of the undivided and divided lines and our having in 2 and 5, the central places, two undivided lines. An important point concerning 'regulations' is brought out in the conclusion of the Thwan,—that they must be adapted to circumstances, and not made too strict and severe.

Line 1 is strong, and in its correct place. Its subject therefore would not be wanting in power to make his way. But he is supposed to be kept in check by the strong 2, and the correlate 4 is the first line in the trigram of peril. The course of wisdom therefore is to keep still. The character here rendered door is that belonging to the inner apartments, leading from the hall into which entrance is found by the outer gate, mentioned under line 2. The courtyard outside the door and that inside the gate is one and the same. The 'Daily Lecture' says that the paragraph tells an officer not to take office rashly, but to exercise a cautious judgment in his measures.

Line 2 is strong, in the wrong place; nor has it a proper correlate. Its subject keeps still, when he ought to be up and doing. There will be evil.

Line 3 should be strong, but it is weak. It is neither central nor correct. It has no proper correlate, and it is the topmost line in the trigram of complacent satisfaction. Its subject will not receive the yoke of regulations; and he will find out his mistake, when it is too late.

Line 4 is weak, as it ought to be, and its subject has respect to the authority of the strong ruler in 5. Hence its good symbolism and auspice.

Line 5 is strong, and in its correct place. Its subject regulates himself, having no correlate; but he is lord of the hexagram, and his influence is everywhere beneficially felt.

Line 6 is weak, in its proper place. The subject of the topmost line must be supposed to possess an exaggerated desire for enacting regulations. They will be too severe, and the effect will be evil. But as Confucius (Analects 3. 3) says, that is not so great a fault as to be easy and remiss. It may be remedied, and cause for repentance will disappear.

<sup>lxi</sup> *K*ung Fû, the name of this hexagram, may be represented in English by 'Inmost Sincerity.' It denotes the highest quality of man, and gives its possessor power so that he prevails with spiritual beings, with other men, and with the lower creatures. It is the subject of the 'Doctrine of the Mean' from the 21st chapter onwards, where Remusat rendered it by 'la perfection,' 'la perfection morale,' and Intorcetta and his coadjutors by 'vera solidaque perfectio.' The lineal figure has suggested to the Chinese commentators, from the author of the first Appendix, two ideas in it which deserve to be pointed out. There are two divided lines in the centre and two undivided below them and above them. The divided lines in the centre are held to represent the heart or mind free from all pre-occupation, without any consciousness of self; and the undivided lines, on each side of it, in the centre of the constituent trigrams are held to denote the solidity of the virtue of one so free from selfishness. There is no unreality in it, not a single flaw.

The 'Daily Lecture' at the conclusion of its paraphrase of the Thwan refers to the history of the ancient Shun, and the wonderful achievements of his virtue. The authors give no instance of the affecting, of 'pigs and fishes' by sincerity, and say that these names are symbolical of men, the rudest and most unsusceptible of being acted on. The Text says that the man thus gifted with sincerity will succeed in the most difficult enterprises. Remarkable is the concluding sentence that he must be firm and correct. Here, as elsewhere throughout the Yî, there comes out the practical character which has distinguished the Chinese people and their best teaching all along the line of history.

The translation of paragraph 1 is according to the view approved by the Khang-hsî editors. The ordinary view makes the other to whom the subject of line 1 looks or might look to be the subject of 4; but they contend that, excepting in the case of 3 and 6, the force of correlation should be discarded from the study of this hexagram; for the virtue of sincerity is all centred in itself, thence derived and thereby powerful.

For paragraph 2, see Appendix III, Section i, 42. It is in rhyme, and I have there rendered it in rhyme. The 'young ones of the crane' are represented by line 1. In the third and fourth sentences we have the symbolism of two men brought together by their sympathy in virtue. The subject of the paragraph is the effect of sincerity.

The 'mate' of line 3 is 6. The principle of correlation comes in. Sincerity, not left to itself, is influenced from without, and hence come the changes and uncertainty in the state and moods of the subject of the line.

Line 4 is weak, and in its correct place. The subject of it has discarded the correlate in 1, and hastens on to the confidence of the ruler in 5, being symbolised as the moon nearly full. The other symbol of the horse whose fellow has disappeared has reference to the discarding of the subject of 1. Anciently chariots and carriages were drawn by four horses, two outsides and two insides. Lines 1 and 4 were a pair of these; but 1 disappears here from the team, and 4 goes on and joins 5.

Line 5 is strong and central, in the ruler's place. Its subject must be the sage on the throne, whose sincerity will go forth and bind all in union with himself.

Line 6 should be divided, but is undivided; and coming after 5, what can the subject of it do? His efforts will be ineffectual, and injurious to himself. He is symbolised by a cock—literally, 'the plumaged voice.' But a cock is not fitted to fly high, and in attempting to do so will only suffer hurt.

<sup>lxii</sup> The name Hsiâo Kwo is explained both by reference to the lines of the hexagram, and to the meaning of the characters. The explanation from the lines appears immediately on comparing them with those of Tâ Kwo, the 28th hexagram. There the first and sixth lines are divided, and between are four undivided lines; here the third and fourth lines are undivided, and outside each of them are two divided lines. The undivided or yang lines are great, the divided or yin lines are called small. In Hsiâo Kwo the divided or small lines predominate. But this peculiar structure of the figure could be of no interest to the student, if it were not for the meaning of the name, which is 'small excesses' or 'exceeding in what is small.' The author, accepted by us as king Wăn, had in his mind our distinction of essentials and non-essentials. Is it ever good to deviate from what is

recognised as the established course of procedure? The reply is—never in the matter of right but in what is conventional and ceremonial—in what is nonessential—the deviation may be made, and will be productive of good. The form may be given up, but not the substance. But the thing must be done very carefully,—humbly and reverently, and in small matters.

The symbolism of the bird is rather obscure. The whole of it is intended to teach humility. It is better for the bird to descend, keeping near to where it can perch and rest, than to hold on ascending into the homeless regions of the air.

Line 1 is weak, in an odd place, and possessed by the 'idea of exceeding,' which belongs to the hexagram. Its correlate is the strong 4, belonging to the trigram *Kăn*, the attribute of which is movement. There is nothing to repress the tendency of i; rather it is stimulated; and hence the symbolism.

Line 2 is weak, but in its proper place, and in the centre. Its correlate is 5, which is also a weak line. The lines 3 and 4 between them are both strong; and are supposed to represent the father and grandfather of the subject of 2; but he or she goes past them, and meets with the grandmother in 5. Again, 5 is the ruler's seat. The subject of 2 moves on to him, but not as an enemy; but humbly and loyally, as his minister according to the attributes of a weak line in the central place. It must be allowed that this view of the symbolism and its interpretation is obscure and strained.

The subject of line 3 is too confident in his own strength, and too defiant of the weak and small enemies that seek his hurt. Line 4 is also strong, but the exercise of his strength by its subject is tempered by the position in an even place. He is warned, however, to continue quiet and restrain himself.

Line 5, though in the ruler's seat, is weak, and incapable of doing anything great. Its subject is called king or duke because of the ruler's seat; and the one whom in the concluding sentence he is said to capture is supposed to be the subject of 2.

The first part of the symbolism is the same as that of the Thwan under hexagram 9, q.v. I said there that it probably gave a testimony of the merit of the house of *Kâu*, as deserving the throne rather than the kings of Shang. That was because the Thwan contained the sentiments of Wăn, while he was yet only lord of *Kâu*. But the symbolism here was the work of the duke of *Kâu*, after his brother king Wû had obtained the throne. How did the symbolism then occur to him? May we not conclude that at least the hsiang of this hexagram was written during the troubled period of his regency, after the accession of Wû's son, king *Khăng*?

The Khang-hsî editors find in the concluding symbolism an incentive to humility:— 'The duke, leaving birds on the wing, is content to use his arrows against those in a cave!'

Line 6 is weak, and is at the top of the trigram of movement. He is possessed by the idea of the hexagram in an extreme degree, and is incapable of keeping himself under restraint.

[lxiii] The character called *Kî* is used as a symbol of being past or completed. Ʒî denotes primarily crossing a stream, and has the secondary meaning of helping and completing. The two characters, combined, will express the successful accomplishment of whatever the writer has in his mind. In dealing with this lineal figure, king Wăn was thinking of the condition of the kingdom, at length at rest and quiet. The vessel of the state has been brought safely across the great and dangerous stream. The distresses of the kingdom have been relieved, and its disorders have been repressed. Does anything remain to be done still? Yes, in small things. The new government has to be consolidated. Its ruler must, without noise or clamour, go on to perfect what has been wrought, with firmness and correctness, and ever keeping in mind the instability of all human affairs. That every line of the hexagram is in its correct place, and has its proper correlate is also supposed to harmonize with the intimation of progress and success.

Line 1, the first of the hexagram, represents the time immediately after the successful achievement of the enterprise it denotes;—the time for resting and being quiet.

For a season, at least, all movement should be hushed. Hence we have the symbolism of a driver trying to stop his carriage, and a fox who has wet his tail, and will not tempt the stream again.

Line 2 is weak, and in its proper place. It also has the strong correlate 5; and might be expected to be forward to act. But it occupies its correct and central place, and suggests the symbol of a lady whose carriage has lost its screen. She will not advance further so soon after success has been achieved; but keep herself hidden and retired. Let her not try to find the screen. When it is said that she will find this 'after seven days,' the meaning seems to be simply this, that the period of *Kî 3î* will then have been exhausted, the six lines having been gone through, and a new period, when action will be proper, shall have commenced.

The strong line 3, at the top of the lower trigram, suggests for its subject one undertaking a vigorous enterprise. The writer thinks of *Kâo 3ung*, the sacrificial title of *Wû Ting*, one of the ablest sovereigns of the Shang dynasty (B. C. 1364-1324), who undertook an expedition against the barbarous hordes of the cold and bleak regions north of the Middle States. He is mentioned again under the next hexagram. He appears also in the Shû, IV, ix, and in the Shih, IV, iii, ode 5. His enterprise may have been good, and successful, but it was tedious, and the paragraph concludes with a caution.

Line 4 is weak, and has advanced into the trigram. for water. Its subject will be cautious, and prepare for evil, as in the symbolism, suggested probably by the nature of the trigram.

'The neighbour in the East' is the subject of line 5, and 'the neighbour in the West' is the subject of the correlate 2, the former quarter being yang and the latter yin. Line 5 is strong, and 2 is weak; but weakness is more likely to be patient and cautious than strength. They are compared to two men sacrificing. The one presents valuable offerings; the other very poor ones. But the second excels in sincerity, and his small offering is the more acceptable.

The topmost line is weak, and on the outmost edge of Khân, the trigram, of peril. His action is violent and perilous, like that one attempting to cross a ford, and being plunged overhead into the water.

[lxiv] Wei 3î is the reverse of *Kî 3î*. The name tells us that the successful accomplishment of whatever the writer had in his mind had not yet been realised. The vessel of the state has not been brought across the great and dangerous stream. Some have wished that the Yî might have concluded with *Kî 3î*, and the last hexagram have left us with the picture of human affairs all brought to good order. But this would not have been in harmony with the idea of the Yî, as the book of change. Again and again it has been pointed out that we find in it no idea of a perfect and abiding state. just as the seasons of the year change and pursue an ever-recurring round, so is it with the phases of society. The reign of order has been, and has terminated; and this hexagram calls us to see the struggle for its realisation recommenced. It treats of how those engaged in that struggle should conduct themselves with a view to secure the happy consummation.

How the figure sets forth the state of things by its constituent trigrams will appear in Appendix II. A similar indication is supposed to be given by the lines, not one of which is in the correct place; the strong lines being all in even places, and t he weak lines in odd. At the same time each of them has a proper correlate; and so the figure gives an intimation of some successful progress. See also Appendix I.

The symbolism of the young fox suggests a want of caution on the part of those, in the time and condition denoted by the hexagram, who try to remedy prevailing disorders. Their attempt is not successful, and they get themselves into trouble and danger. Whatever can be done must be undertaken in another way.

I suppose a fox to be intended by the symbolism of line 1, bringing that animal on from the Thwan. Some of the commentators understand it of any animal. The line is weak, at the bottom of the trigram of peril, and responds to the strong 4, which is not in its correct place. Its subject attempts to be doing, but finds cause to regret his course.

The subject of line 2, strong, and in the centre, is able to repress himself, and keep back his carriage from advancing and there is good fortune.

The Khang-hsî editors say that it is very difficult to understand what is said under line 3; and many critics suppose that a negative has dropt out, and that we should really read that 'it will not be advantageous to try and cross the great stream.'

Line 4, though strong, is in an even place; and this might vitiate the endeavours of its subject to bring about a better state of things. But he is firm and correct. He is in the fourth place moreover, and immediately above there is his ruler, represented by a weak line, humble therefore, and prepared to welcome his endeavours. Let him exert himself vigorously and long, as Kâo ȝung did in his famous expedition (see last hexagram, line 3), and he will make progress and have success. Expeditions beyond the frontiers in those days were not very remote. Intercourse was kept up between the army and the court. Rewards, distinctions, and whatever was necessary to encourage the army, were often sent to it.

Line 5 is weak, in an odd place. But its subject is the ruler, humble and supported by the subject of the strong 2; and hence the auspice is very good.

The subject of line 6, when the work of the hexagram has been done, appears disposed to remain quiet in the confidence of his own power, but enjoying himself; and thereby he will do right. If, on the contrary, he will go on to exert his powers, and play with the peril of the situation, the issue will be bad.